Lecture Notes in Computer Science   14183

Founding Editors

Gerhard Goos
Juris Hartmanis

Editorial Board Members

The series Lecture Notes in Computer Science (LNCS), including its subseries Lecture Notes in Artificial Intelligence (LNAI) and Lecture Notes in Bioinformatics (LNBI), has established itself as a medium for the publication of new developments in computer science and information technology research, teaching, and education.

LNCS enjoys close cooperation with the computer science R & D community, the series counts many renowned academics among its volume editors and paper authors, and collaborates with prestigious societies. Its mission is to serve this international community by providing an invaluable service, mainly focused on the publication of conference and workshop proceedings and postproceedings. LNCS commenced publication in 1973.

George A. Papadopoulos · Florian Rademacher ·
Jacopo Soldani

Editors

Service-Oriented and Cloud Computing

10th IFIP WG 6.12 European Conference, ESOCC 2023
Larnaca, Cyprus, October 24–25, 2023
Proceedings

 Springer

Editors
George A. Papadopoulos (iD)
University of Cyprus
Nicosia, Cyprus

Florian Rademacher (iD)
RWTH Aachen University
Aachen, Germany

Jacopo Soldani (iD)
University of Pisa
Pisa, Italy

ISSN 0302-9743   ISSN 1611-3349 (electronic)
Lecture Notes in Computer Science
ISBN 978-3-031-46234-4   ISBN 978-3-031-46235-1 (eBook)
https://doi.org/10.1007/978-3-031-46235-1

This Springer imprint is published by the registered company Springer Nature Switzerland AG
The registered company address is: Gewerbestrasse 11, 6330 Cham, Switzerland

Paper in this product is recyclable.

Preface

Service-oriented and cloud computing have made a huge impact, both on the software industry and on the research community. Today, service and cloud technologies are applied to build large-scale software landscapes and to provide single software services to end users. Services are nowadays developed and deployed independently, based on a variety of technologies, and freely composed, which is quite an important fact from a business perspective. Similarly, cloud computing aims at enabling flexibility by offering a centralized sharing of resources. The industry's need for agile and flexible software and IT systems has made cloud computing the dominating paradigm for provisioning computational resources in a scalable, on-demand fashion. Nevertheless, service developers, providers, and integrators still need to create methods, tools, and techniques to support cost-effective and secure development, as well as the use of dependable devices, platforms, services, and service-oriented applications in the cloud.

The European Conference on Service-Oriented and Cloud Computing (ESOCC) is the premier European conference on advances in the state of the art and practice of service-oriented computing and cloud computing. ESOCC's main objectives are to facilitate the exchange between researchers and practitioners in the areas of service-oriented computing and cloud computing, and to explore new trends in those areas and foster future collaborations in Europe and beyond. The tenth edition of ESOCC, ESOCC 2023, was held in Larnaca (Cyprus) during October 24–25, 2023, under the auspices of the University of Cyprus.

ESOCC 2023 was a multi-event conference that covered both an academic and industrial audience with its main research track focusing on the presentation of cutting-edge research in both the service-oriented and cloud computing areas. In conjunction, a Projects and Industry Track was held, bringing together academia and industry by showcasing the application of service-oriented and cloud computing research, especially in the form of case studies. Overall, 40 submissions were received, out of which 12 outstanding full and four short papers were accepted. Thus, the overall acceptance rate for full papers was 30%.

Each submission was peer-reviewed by three main reviewers, comprising either Program Committee (PC) members or their colleagues. The PC Chairs would like to thank all the reviewers that participated in the reviewing process. Their comments were essential for improving the quality of the received manuscripts and especially for giving constructive comments to the authors of papers that, in their current forms, were rejected from ESOCC 2023.

The attendees of ESOCC had the opportunity to follow two outstanding keynotes that were part of the conference program. The first keynote was conducted by George Pallis of the University of Cyprus. The keynote presented three novel adaptive monitoring frameworks and a fog computing emulation framework. The frameworks allow for reducing energy consumption and data volume transmitted over edge computing networks, and the experiment-based optimization of complex fog topologies.

The second keynote was conducted by Herodotos Herodotou of Cyprus University of Technology. This keynote first reviewed, among other things, the current state of the art in big data stream processing and edge-based stream processing, cloud resource management and tuning, and machine and deep learning on data streams. Next, it presented a general architecture design for an optimized, multi-cloud and edge orchestrator that enables machine and deep learning over voluminous and heterogeneous data streams on hybrid cloud and edge settings. This orchestrator also includes necessary functionalities for practical and scalable processing.

Additional events held at ESOCC 2023 included the PhD Symposium, enabling PhD students to present their work in front of real experts, as well as the Projects and Industry Track, providing researchers and practitioners with the opportunity to present the main research results that they achieved in the context of currently operating research and industrial projects. The papers of both events are also included in this proceedings volume.

The PC Chairs and the General Chair would like to gratefully thank all the people involved in making ESOCC 2023 a success. This includes both the PC members and their colleagues who assisted in the reviews, as well as the organizers of the PhD Symposium and the Projects and Industry Track. The Chairs also thank EasyConferences Ltd. for their administrative support and local organization. Finally, a special thanks to all the authors of the manuscripts submitted to ESOCC 2023, the presenters of the accepted papers who gave interesting and fascinating presentations of their work, and the active attendees of the conference who initiated interesting discussions and gave fruitful feedback to the presenters. All these people have enabled not only the successful organization and execution of ESOCC 2023 but also an active and vibrant community, which continuously contributes to research in service-oriented and cloud computing. This also encourages ESOCC to keep supporting and enlarging its community, by providing a forum in which new research outcomes can be shared and discussions on how to achieve greater impact can be held.

September 2023

George A. Papadopoulos
Florian Rademacher
Jacopo Soldani

Organization

Organizing Committee

General Chair

George A. Papadopoulos   University of Cyprus, Cyprus

Program Chairs

Florian Rademacher   RWTH Aachen University, Germany
Jacopo Soldani   University of Pisa, Italy

Projects and Industry Track Chairs

Andrea Janes   FHV Vorarlberg University of Applied Sciences,
      Austria
Valentina Lenarduzzi   University of Oulu, Finland

PhD Symposium Chairs

Stefano Forti   University of Pisa, Italy
Christian Zirpins   Karlsruhe University of Applied Sciences,
      Germany

Steering Committee

Antonio Brogi   University of Pisa, Italy
Schahram Dustdar   TU Wien, Austria
Paul Grefen   Eindhoven University of Technology,
      The Netherlands
Einar Broch Johnson   University of Oslo, Norway
Kyriakos Kritikos   ICS-FORTH, Greece
Winfried Lamersdorf   University of Hamburg, Germany
Flavio de Paoli   University of Milano-Bicocca, Italy
Ernesto Pimentel   University of Malaga, Spain
Pierluigi Plebani   Politecnico di Milano, Italy

Ulf Schreier	Hochschule Furtwangen University, Germany
Stefan Schulte	TU Wien, Austria
Massimo Villari	University of Messina, Italy
Olaf Zimmermann	Eastern Switzerland University of Applied Sciences, Switzerland
Wolf Zimmermann	Martin Luther University Halle-Wittenberg, Germany

Program Committee

Nour Ali	Brunel University London, UK
Vasilios Andrikopoulos	University of Groningen, The Netherlands
Hernán Astudillo	Federico Santa María Technical University, Chile
Luciano Baresi	Politecnico di Milano, Italy
Javier Berrocal	Universidad de Extremadura, Spain
Justus Bogner	University of Stuttgart, Germany
Uwe Breitenbücher	Reutlingen University, Germany
Antonio Brogi	University of Pisa, Italy
Tomás Cerný	Baylor University, USA
Marco Comuzzi	Ulsan National Institute of Science and Technology, South Korea
Elisabetta Di Nitto	Politecnico di Milano, Italy
Dario Di Nucci	University of Salerno, Italy
Schahram Dustdar	TU Wien, Austria
Rik Eshuis	Eindhoven University of Technology, The Netherlands
Stefano Forti	University of Pisa, Italy
Jonas Fritzsch	University of Stuttgart, Germany
Ilche Georgievski	University of Stuttgart, Germany
Saverio Giallorenzo	University of Bologna, Italy
Paul Grefen	Eindhoven University of Technology, The Netherlands
Andrea Janes	FHV Vorarlberg University of Applied Sciences, Austria
Blagovesta Kostova	Swiss Federal Institute of Technology (EPFL), Switzerland
Indika Kumara	Tilburg University, The Netherlands
Valentina Lenarduzzi	University of Oulu, Finland
Zoltan Adam Mann	University of Amsterdam, The Netherlands
Jacopo Massa	University of Pisa, Italy
Jacopo Mauro	University of Southern Denmark, Denmark

José Merseguer	University of Zaragoza, Spain
Fabrizio Montesi	University of Southern Denmark, Denmark
Phu Nguyen	SINTEF, Norway
Claus Pahl	Free University of Bozen-Bolzano, Italy
Francisco Ponce	UTFSM, Chile
George A. Papadopoulos	University of Cyprus, Cyprus
Cesare Pautasso	University of Lugano, Switzerland
Ernesto Pimentel	University of Malaga, Spain
Larisa Safina	Inria Lille – Nord Europe, France
Nuno Santos	Natixis, Portugal
Ulf Schreier	Furtwangen University, Germany
Stefan Schulte	Hamburg University of Technology, Germany
Davide Taibi	Tampere University, Finland
Rudrajit Tapadar	Microsoft, USA
Orazio Tomarchio	University of Catania, Italy
Massimo Villari	University of Messina, Italy
Philip Wizenty	Dortmund University of Applied Sciences and Arts, Germany
Robert Woitsch	BOC ProductsServices AG, Austria
Gianluigi Zavattaro	University of Bologna, Italy
Olaf Zimmermann	Eastern Switzerland University of Applied Sciences, Switzerland
Wolf Zimmermann	Martin Luther University Halle-Wittenberg, Germany
Christian Zirpins	Karlsruhe University of Applied Sciences, Germany

Additional Reviewers

Nuha Alshuqayran
Alessandro Bocci
Jose Carrasco
Rafael García-Luque
Stefan Kapferer
Angelo Marchese
Andrea Melis
Minh-Tri Nguyen
José Antonio Peregrina Pérez
Dan Plyukhin
Saulo S. de Toledo

Conference Logo

Sponsors

International Federation for Information Processing

Springer and Springer LNCS

Microservices Community

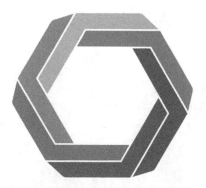

Contents

Microservices

μXL: Explainable Lead Generation with Microservices and Hypothetical
Answers 3
    Luís Cruz-Filipe, Sofia Kostopoulou, Fabrizio Montesi, and Jonas Vistrup

One Microservice per Developer: Is This the Trend in OSS? 19
    Dario Amoroso d'Aragona, Xiaozhou Li, Tomas Cerny, Andrea Janes,
    Valentina Lenarduzzi, and Davide Taibi

End-to-End Test Coverage Metrics in Microservice Systems:
An Automated Approach 35
    Amr S. Abdelfattah, Tomas Cerny, Jorge Yero Salazar, Austin Lehman,
    Joshua Hunter, Ashley Bickham, and Davide Taibi

Quality of Service

Time-Aware QoS Web Service Selection Using Collaborative Filtering:
A Literature Review 55
    Ezdehar Jawabreh and Adel Taweel

Enhanced Time-Aware Collaborative Filtering for QoS Web Service
Prediction 70
    Ezdehar Jawabreh and Adel Taweel

Comparison of Performance and Costs of CaaS and RDBaaS Services 84
    Piotr Karwaczyński, Mariusz Wasielewski, and Jan Kwiatkowski

Service Orchestration

Horizontal Scaling of Transaction-Creating Machines for Blockchains 103
    Ole Delzer, Ingo Weber, Richard Hobeck, and Stefan Schulte

Uncovering Effective Roles and Tasks for Fog Systems 119
    Maximilian Blume, Sebastian Lins, and Ali Sunyaev

Cooperative Virtual Machine Placement 136
    José G. Quenum and Samir Aknine

Edge Computing

A Multi-pronged Self-adaptive Controller for Analyzing Misconfigurations
for Kubernetes Clusters and IoT Edge Devices 153
  Areeg Samir, Abdo Al-Wosabi, Mohsin Khan, and Håvard Dagenborg

Adaptive Controller to Identify Misconfigurations and Optimize
the Performance of Kubernetes Clusters and IoT Edge Devices 170
  Areeg Samir and Håvard Dagenborg

Streamlining XR Application Deployment with a Localized Docker
Registry at the Edge 188
  Antonios Makris, Evangelos Psomakelis, Ioannis Korontanis,
  Theodoros Theodoropoulos, Antonis Protopsaltis, Maria Pateraki,
  Zbyszek Ledwoń, Christos Diou, Dimosthenis Anagnostopoulos,
  and Konstantinos Tserpes

PhD Symposium

Towards Cloud Storage Tier Optimization with Rule-Based Classification 205
  Akif Quddus Khan, Nikolay Nikolov, Mihhail Matskin, Radu Prodan,
  Christoph Bussler, Dumitru Roman, and Ahmet Soylu

Industry Projects Track

Towards a Decentralised Federated Learning Based Compute Continuum
Framework 219
  Mohamad Moussa, Philippe Glass, Nabil Abdennahder,
  Giovanna Di Marzo Serugendo, and Raphaël Couturier

Detecting Model Changes in Organisational Processes: A Cloud-Based
Approach 231
  J. Fabra, V. Gallego-Fontenla, J. C. Vidal, J. García de Quirós,
  P. Álvarez, M. Lama, A. Bugarín, and A. Ramos-Soto

Short Papers

A Taxonomy for Workload Deployment Orchestration in the Edge-Cloud
Continuum 239
  Toon Albers, Mattia Fogli, Edwin Harmsma, Elena Lazovik,
  and Harrie Bastiaansen

Intent-Based AI-Enhanced Service Orchestration for Application
Deployment and Execution in the Cloud Continuum 251
  Efthymios Chondrogiannis, Efstathios Karanastasis,
  Vassiliki Andronikou, Adrian Spătaru, Anastassios Nanos,
  Aristotelis Kretsis, and Panagiotis Kokkinos

Optimizing the Cost-Performance Ratio of FaaS Deployments 263
  Richard Patsch and Karl Michael Göschka

The Microservice Dependency Matrix 276
  Amr S. Abdelfattah and Tomas Cerny

Author Index 289

Microservices

μXL: Explainable Lead Generation with Microservices and Hypothetical Answers

Luís Cruz-Filipe[ID], Sofia Kostopoulou[ID], Fabrizio Montesi[ID], and Jonas Vistrup[(✉)][ID]

Department of Mathematics and Computer Science, University of Southern Denmark, Odense, Denmark
{lcf,fmontesi,vistrup}@imada.sdu.dk, skos@sdu.dk

Abstract. Lead generation refers to the identification of potential topics (the 'leads') of importance for journalists to report on. In this paper we present a new lead generation tool based on a microservice architecture, which includes a component of explainable AI. The lead generation tool collects and stores historical and real-time data from a web source, like Google Trends, and generates current and future leads. These leads are produced by an engine for hypothetical reasoning based on logical rules, which is a novel implementation of a recent theory. Finally, the leads are displayed on a web interface for end users, in particular journalists. This interface provides information on why a specific topic is or may become a lead, assisting journalists in deciding where to focus their attention. We carry out an empirical evaluation of the performance of our tool.

Keywords: Lead generation · Microservices · Explainable AI

1 Introduction

Background. Journalists at news media organisations can regularly come across a plethora of available information and events from various online data sources, including social media. Therefore, it is of great significance to explore automated procedures that can support journalists in dealing efficiently with such continuous streams of real-time data. This explains why AI in journalism, or automated/computational journalism, has been intensely studied in the last years.

In this article, we are interested in automated support for *lead generation.* That is, supporting journalists with useful information about what they could report on. Lead generation is connected to trend detection and prediction. Trending topic detection is a problem that has been researched extensively for the specific application domain [1,13]. In another line of research, there are several works that try to predict trending topics, news, or users' interest in advance.

Work partially supported by Villum Fonden, grants no. 29518 and 50079, and the Independent Research Fund Denmark, grant no. 0135-00219.

G. A. Papadopoulos et al. (Eds.): ESOCC 2023, LNCS 14183, pp. 3–18, 2023.
https://doi.org/10.1007/978-3-031-46235-1_1

For instance, the authors in [5] aim to predict trending keywords, the work in [18] targets forecasting article popularity, and [20] focuses on the prediction of future users' interests. Automated news generation is another field of research that received much attention by researchers. The authors in [12] present an architecture for automated journalism and in [10] they propose an automatic news generation solution by integrating audio, video, and text information. All the aforementioned works, even though they are closely related, do not tackle the challenging problem of alerting journalists about imminent leads for potential future articles. In this direction, the 'Lead Locator' tool [6] suggests locations relevant to political interest and produces 'tip sheets' for reporters.

Motivation. Our motivation for this work stems from a collaboration with media companies in Denmark,[1] which elicited a number of requirements that are not met by current solutions for lead generation. The first requirement is explainability: the system should present its reasoning for the suggestions that it brings forward, such that the journalist can apply their own intuition as to how promising a lead is. (In general, explanations can be crucial in guiding journalists towards valuable reporting decisions.) The second requirement is flexibility: the system should be designed with extensibility in mind, in particular regarding the future additions of new data sources and processors. The third requirement is reusability: the system should expose its operations through well-defined service APIs, such that it can be integrated in different contexts.

Meeting these requirements is challenging because it requires designing a loosely-coupled system that accumulates different kinds of data. Also, to the best of our knowledge, there are no reasoning tools available for deriving and explaining potentially-interesting scenarios (the leads) from online data streams.

This Work. We present μXL, a new lead generation tool that meets the aforementioned requirements thanks to two key aspects.

First, μXL is implemented as a microservice architecture. Components are clearly separated and can interact purely by formally-defined APIs. These APIs are defined in the Jolie programming language [15], whose API language is designed to be technology agnostic: Jolie APIs allow only for semi-structured data with widely-available basic values (strings, integers, etc.) and can be implemented with different technologies [14]. Most of our microservices are written in Jolie, but we leverage this flexibility to use Java in our most performance-critical component. In particular, we can use Jolie to lift a simple Java class to a microservice without requiring any additional API definitions or Java libraries.

Second, μXL includes the first implementation of the recent theory of hypothetical answers to continuous queries over data streams [4]. This allows our system to present potential leads given the facts that are currently available, and accompany them with rule-based explanations that clearly distinguishes observed facts from hypotheses about the future.

The contributions of our paper can be summarised as follows:

---

[1] https://www.mediacityodense.dk/en/.

- A microservice architecture that (i) collects historical and current data relevant for lead generation from various online data sources, and (ii) integrates artificial intelligence (AI) to generate explainable leads.
- A technology-agnostic description of the APIs and patterns used in our system, which are respectively expressed in Jolie [15] and the API patterns recently exposed in [21]. This serves three purposes. For us, Jolie and API patterns were useful guides. For the reader, it clarifies our design. And for Jolie and the collection of API patterns, it is an additional validation of their usefulness in practice. (For both Jolie and API patterns, it is the first validation in the journalistic domain that we know of.)
- The first implementation of a hypothetical answer reasoning engine – which given rules and online datastreams can produce explainable leads – and its integration in our architecture. Our engine is based on the theory originally presented in [4], so our work also serves as the first validation of its usefulness.
- A performance evaluation of our lead generation component (the reasoner).

Structure of the Paper. Section 2 presents relevant related work and background on the reasoning theory that we use. Section 3 describes our explainable AI engine. Section 4 is dedicated to the system's architecture. Section 5 provides our experimental evaluation. Finally, Sect. 6 concludes with future work.

2   Related Work

AI and Journalism. The use of AI in journalism is seeing increased focus. One of the perspectives relevant to this work is automated news generation. In this realm, the authors in [17] designed 'News robot', a system that automatically generates live events or news of the 2018 Winter Olympic Games. This system generates six news types by joining general and individualised content with a combination of text, image, and sound. In another work [10], an automatic news generation solution with semantically meaningful content was proposed by integrating audio, video, and text information in the context of broadcast news. While in [12] the authors presented an automatic news generation system that is largely language and domain independent.

Another perspective is trending topic detection, where programs try to distinguish trending topics in a wealth of news sources. In that context, the authors in [1] compared six methods used for topic detection relevant to major events on Twitter. Moreover, the work in [13] proposed a tool that detects trends in online Twitter data and synthesises a topic description. The system also offers user interactivity for selection by means of criteria-selection and topic description. While the authors in [2] designed a novel framework to collect messages related to a specific organisation by monitoring microblog content, like users and keywords, as well as their temporal sequence.

There is also a lot of research dedicated to predicting trends, mostly using machine learning techniques. For instance, the authors of [5] tackled trending topic prediction as a classification problem. They used online Twitter data to detect features that are distinguished as trending/non-trending hashtags, and developed classifiers using these features. Furthermore, the work in [18] proposed a solution that extracts keywords from an article and then predicts its popularity based on these keywords. They compared their approach to other popular ones based on the BERT model and text embeddings. A connected problem is that of predicting future user interests, which the authors of [20] explored in the context of microblogging services and unobserved topics. Specifically, they built topic profiles for users based on discrete time intervals, and then transferred user interests to the Wikipedia category structure.

The most relevant work to lead generation is the one proposed by the authors in [6]. They designed, developed, and evaluated a news discovery tool, called 'Lead Locator', which supplements the reporting of national politics by suggesting possibly noteworthy locations to write a story about. They analysed a national voter file using data mining to rank counties with respect to their possible newsworthiness to reporters. Then, they automatically produced 'tip sheets' using natural language generation. Reporters have access to these 'tip sheets' through an interactive interface, which includes information on why they should write an article based on that county. In a similar way, the authors in [19] developed 'CityBeat', a system that finds potential news events. It collects geo-tagged information in real-time from social media, finds important stories, and makes an editorial choice on whether these events are newsworthy.

Microservices and Jolie. Microservices are cohesive and independently-executable software applications that interact by message passing. Their origins and reasons for diffusion are surveyed in [7], along with open challenges and future directions.

Jolie is a service-oriented programming language that provides native linguistic constructs for the programming of microservices [15]. Its abstractions have been validated both in terms of industrial productivity [9], development of security strategies [16], and engineering: Jolie's structures resemble the architectural metamodels found in tools for Model-Driven Engineering of microservices based on Domain-Driven Design [8]. We mention a few relevant aspects. First, Jolie comes with an algebraic language for composing communication actions, which facilitates the composition of services by other services. Second, in the definition of services, Jolie's syntax separates APIs, deployment, access points (how APIs can be reached, e.g., with which protocol), and behaviours (service implementations). Some notable consequences for our work include: (i) Jolie APIs can be implemented with different technologies (we use Jolie itself for some, and Java when fine-tuning performance is important); and (ii) the different parts of our architecture can be flexibly deployed together (communication supported by shared memory), all separate (remote communication), or in a hybrid fashion (some together, some not). We use the 'all separate' option in our description, but adopters are free to change this decision.

Hypothetical Query Answering. The explainable AI component of μXL implements the theory presented in [4], which allows for producing hypothetical answers (answers that depend on the occurrence of future events). We dedicate the rest of this section to the necessary background on this theory.

The theory in [4] is based on *Temporal Datalog* [3], which is a negation-free variant of Datalog where predicates include temporal attributes. Temporal Datalog has two types of terms: *object* and *time*. An object term is either an object (constant) or an object variable. A time term is either a natural number, called a *time point* (one time point for each natural number), a *time variable*, or an expression on the form $T + k$ where T is a time variable and k is an integer.

Predicates take exactly one temporal parameter, which is always the last one. This gives all atomic formulas, hereafter called atoms, the form $P(t_1, \ldots, t_n, \tau)$, where P is a name of a predicate with $n \in \mathbb{N}$ object terms, t_1 to t_n are all object terms, and τ is a time term. Intuitively the semantics of $P(t_1, \ldots, t_n, \tau)$ is defined such that predicate P holds for terms t_1 to t_n at time τ.

Programs are sets of rules of the form $\alpha \leftarrow \alpha_1 \wedge \ldots \wedge \alpha_n$ with $\alpha, \alpha_1, \ldots, \alpha_n$ atoms. The *head* of the rule is α, and the *body* of the rule is $\alpha_1 \wedge \ldots \wedge \alpha_n$. A predicate that occurs in the head of at least one rule with non-empty body is an *intensional* predicate, otherwise it is an *extensional* predicate.

A *datastream* is a set of *dataslices*, one for each natural number. Each dataslice consists of a finite number of atoms with extensional predicates, each with the dataslice's index as their temporal parameter. A *query* is a list of atoms, and an *answer* to a query is a substitution that makes the query valid.

Given a Temporal Datalog program and a datastream, we can compute *hypothetical answers* for a given query. A hypothetical answer is a substitution σ paired with a set of atoms H (the *hypotheses*) such that σ is an answer to the query if the atoms in H appear later in the datastream. The algorithm from [4] is a modification of SLD-resolution [11] from logic programming. It maintains a list of hypothetical answers that are updated as new dataslices are produced.

To provide explainability of how hypothetical answers are deduced, they are associated to a set of atoms called evidence. These atoms are the past atoms from the datastream that have been used in deducing the answer. As new dataslices arrive, new hypothetical answers are generated; atoms in hypotheses are moved to evidence if they appear in the dataslice; and hypothetical answers whose hypothesis include atoms with the current time that do not appear are discarded.

3 HARP: Hypothetical Answer Reasoning Program

The microservice implementing the AI of this architecture is called Hypothetical Answer Reasoning Program (HARP). HARP contains an implementation of the reasoning framework of [4] to perform lead deduction from a set of rules and a datastream. This architecture allows for an arbitrary datastream and an almost arbitrary specification of rules.[2] The core functionalities of HARP are implemented in Java; the resulting microservice and APIs are in Jolie, which wraps the Java code by using Jolie's embedding feature for foreign code [15].

---

[2] Rules have to be stratified, i.e., they cannot have circular dependencies [4].

3.1   Specification of Rules

We illustrate the specification of rules by using streams of data that originate from Google Trends. The implementation requires that variables start with an uppercase letter and constants start with a lowercase letter. Time points must be natural numbers and expressions must be of the form $T + k$ or $T - k$ for a time variable T and a natural number k. (In our examples, time points represent hours and timestamps from Google Trends are rounded up to the next hour.)

Our rules cover three arguments for why a topic should be considered a lead.

1. If a topic becomes a daily trend in a region and its popularity rises over the next two hours, then it is a popularity lead. The rule is written as:

```
DailyTrend(Topic, Region, T), Popularity(Topic, Region, Pop0, T),
Popularity(Topic, Region, Pop1, T+1),
Popularity(Topic, Region, Pop2, T+2),
Less(Pop0,Pop1), Less(Pop1,Pop2) -> PopularityLead(Topic, Region, T)
```

2. If a topic is a daily trend in a region, and then becomes a daily trend in another region, then it is a global trend – but only if it continues to spread to new regions every hour for the next two hours. If a global trend remains a global trend for the next two hours, then it is a global lead. This argument is written as two rules: one rule specifying what makes a topic a global trend,

```
DailyTrend(Topic, Region0, T), DailyTrend(Topic, Region1, T+1),
DailyTrend(Topic, Region2, T+2), DailyTrend(Topic, Region3, T+3),
AllDiff(Region0,Region1,Region2,Region3) -> GlobalTrend(Topic, T+1)
```

and one rule specifying how a global trend becomes a global lead.

```
GlobalTrend(Topic, T), GlobalTrend(Topic, T+1),
GlobalTrend(Topic, T+2) -> GlobalLead(Topic, T)
```

3. The third argument uses the notion of *certain leads* – some leads are more certain than others. While our architecture does not capture probabilities, we can specify that both popularity leads and global leads are certain leads.

```
PopularityLead(Topic, Region, T) -> CertainLead(Topic, Region, T)
GlobalLead(Topic, T) -> CertainLead(Topic, Region, T)
```

If two topics are certain leads and if both topics closely relates to a third topic, then the third topic is a lead derived from other leads:[3]

```
CertainLead(Topic1, Region, T), CertainLead(Topic2, Region, T),
RelatedTopic(Topic1, Topic), RelatedTopic(Topic2, Topic)
    -> DerivedLead(Topic, Region, T)
```

---

[3] This rule captures the idea that if Peyton Manning and Tom Brady are both in the news, then it might be interesting to write an article about NFL Quarterbacks.

We differentiate between certain leads and derived leads to avoid derived leads being used to derive other derived leads. This would make a topic a lead solely because related topics twice or more removed are trending. The final rules denote that both certain leads and derived leads are leads.

```
CertainLead(Topic, Region, T) -> Lead(Topic, Region, T)
DerivedLead(Topic, Region, T) -> Lead(Topic, Region, T)
```

At each hour, the datastream contains information about topics that are daily trends in a region, `DailyTrend(Topic, Region, T)`, popularity of topics that are daily trends, `Popularity(Topic, Region, Pop, T)`, and which topics are related, `RelatedTopic(Topic1, Topic2, T)`.

3.2 User-Defined Predicates (UDPs)

Predicates such as `Less` and `AllDiff` are not practical to specify as rules, but rather algorithmically. Our implementation allows for specifying such *User-Defined Predicates* (UDP). An atom whose predicate is a UDP is called a *User-Defined Atom* (UDA). UDAs in hypotheses are evaluated by running the function defining the corresponding UDP as soon as all variables have been instantiated, after which they are processed similar to other hypotheses. Therefore, all uses of UDAs in rules must be *safe*: any variable that appears in a UDA in a rule must also appear in a non-UDA in the same rule.

UDPs are specified by implementing the Java Interface `UserDefinedPredicate`, whose local path is given in the internal initialisation of **HARP**. Therefore, adding different UDPs requires updating a configuration file within **HARP**. The interface `UserDefinedPredicate` includes four methods:

- `id()` returns the textual representation of the UDP;
- `toString(List<Term> terms)` returns the textual representation of a UDA with this UDP and arguments `terms`;
- `nArgs()` returns the number of arguments of the UDP;
- `run(List<Constant> constantList` returns **true** if the UDP holds for the list of objects (constants) arguments given, **false** otherwise.

The list arguments of both `toString` and `run` must be of length `nArgs()`.

3.3 **HARP** as a Microservice

HARP allows our implementation of [4] to interface with the rest of the architecture. It maintains an instance of the reasoning framework that can be used after rules and queries are specified. (The original framework [4] only considers a single query, but **HARP** allows for multiple queries to be evaluated simultaneously.)

When **HARP** is initialised with a set of rules and queries, it performs a preprocessing step to compute the initial hypothetical answers. Later, it periodically fetches dataslices, rounds the time point up to the nearest hour, and passes them to the reasoner to update the hypothetical answers. The time required for this step depends on the current number of hypothetical answers and the size of the dataslice. Since dataslices are produced every hour, this computation time must be shorter than this limit. This issue is discussed in more detail in Sect. 5.

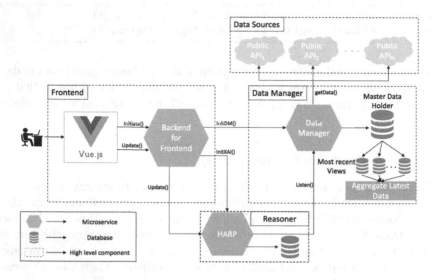

Fig. 1. Architecture overview.

4   Architecture

The overall architecture as shown in Fig. 1 consists of four basic components: **Frontend**, **Data Sources**, **Data Manager**, and **Reasoner**.

There are two operations that can be executed through the **Frontend**. The first is the initialisation of the processing pipeline. The user (an administrator) provides the input parameters of the **Data Manager** microservice and the **HARP** microservice. The **Data Manager** takes as input the necessary information for retrieve data from the specified public APIs, e.g., Google Trends. This information will be used to make requests to these APIs. This process takes place recurrently every t seconds, where t is a user-defined parameter. The data received by the **Data Manager** are stored in a database and the most recent views of data are aggregated, representing the current state of the system. At the same time, the **HARP** microservice is also initialised with the appropriate parameters provided by the user through the **Frontend**. In particular, the **HARP** microservice sends a request to the **Aggregate Latest Data** and receives as response the aggregated most recent views of data. This process takes place recurrently as well. **HARP** processes these data and returns the current answers.

The second operation retrieves the most recent answers. The user makes a request that reaches the **HARP** microservice and retrieves as a response the current answers, which are displayed to the **Frontend**.

4.1 Application of Patterns for API Design

The proposed architecture can be analysed wrt the following categories of patterns for API design, as described in [21]:

- The **Foundation Patterns**, which deal with issues like *API Accessibility* (from where APIs should be accessed) and *API Integration* (e.g., whether a client interacts directly with the API or through other means).
- The **Responsibility Patterns**, which clarify the *Endpoint Roles* (the architectural roles of API endpoints) and the responsibilities of their operations.
- The **Quality Patterns**, which deal with the compromises between providing a high-quality service and cost-effectiveness. The Quality Patterns category comprises the following patterns: *Data Transfer Parsimony, Reference Management*, and *Quality Management and Governance*.

Data Manager. The Data Manager microservice employs the *Backend Integration* pattern for API Integration: it integrates with two other backends of the same application, the Backend for Frontend and **HARP**, and multiple other public APIs, by exposing its services via a message-based remote Backend Integration API. In more detail, the Data Manager integrates with:

- The Backend for Frontend, which makes `initDM()` requests of this type to the Data Manager:

```
1  type InitDMRequest { hl: string, /* Host language */
2     tz: int, /* Timezone offset in minutes */
3     ns: int, geo: string, /* Geolocation */, t: long }
```

A JSON payload example is as follows:

```
1  { "hl": "en-us", "tz": 300, "ns": 15, "geo": "DK", "t": "100" }
```

The corresponding response is of the following format:

```
1  type InitDMResponse { ack: boolean /* Acknowledgement */ }
```

- Public APIs, like Google Trends, with messages of the following format:

```
1  type DailytrendsRequest { hl: string, /* Host language */
2     tz: int, /* Timezone offset in minutes */
3     ns: int, geo: string /* Geolocation */ }
```

An example of JSON payload is the following:

```
1  { "hl": "en-us", "tz": 300, "ns": 15, "geo": "DK" }
```

The corresponding response is a message of the following format:

```
1  type DailytrendsResponse { entry*: DailytrendsElement }
2  type DailytrendsElement { query:, string /* Trending topic */
3     traffic: string /* Approximate traffic in string format */
4     urllist*: string /* URLs of articles about trending topic */ }
```

An example of JSON payload is the following:

```
1  {[{"query":"Detroit Lions", "traffic": "10K",
2     "urllist": ["https://en.as.com/resultados/superbowl/detroit_lions",
                "https://www.football-espana.net/superbowl/detroit_lions"]},
3   {"query": "Thanksgiving parade", "traffic": "50K",
4     "urllist":
5         ["https://www.cbsnews.com/news/thanksgiving_parade_2022/"] }]}
```

- **HARP**, which sends requests to and receives responses from the Data Manager with the following formats:

```
1  type HARPRequest { datasource*: string }
2  type HARPResponse { t: long, facts*: string }
```

A JSON request example is the following:

```
1  { "t": 1669306702000, "facts": ["Popularity(detroit lions,10K,
       1669306702000)", "Popularity(thanksgiving parade,50K,
       1669306702000)", "Popularity(uruguay,5K,1669306702000)"] }
```

As far as it concerns API Accessibility, for the Data Manager we follow the *Solution-Internal API* pattern: its APIs are offered only to system-internal communication partners, such as other services in the application backend.

The Data Manager utilises two Endpoint Roles, a *Processing Resource* and an *Information Holder Resource*. The former has to do with the initDM() request of the Backend for Frontend, which triggers the Data Manager to start requesting user-specified data from the public APIs. This is a *State Transition Operation*, where a client initiates a processing action that causes the provider-side application state to change. The Information Holder Resource endpoint role concerns the responses of the public APIs, which are data that need to be stored in some persistence and the requests from the HARP, which need to get the aggregated most recent views of data. This is both a *Master Data Holder*, because it accumulates historical data, and an *Operational Data Holder*, because it supports clients that want to read the most recent views of data.

Finally, regarding the Quality Patterns, the Data Manager follows *Rate Limit*, which is dictated both by the user's Data Manager initDM() request and the possible rate limits that public APIs might have.

Backend for Frontend. Regarding API Integration, the Backend for Frontend microservice employs the *Frontend Integration* pattern and more specifically the Backend for Frontend pattern, since it integrates the frontend with the backend of our application, by exposing its services via a message-based remote Frontend Integration API. In more detail, the Backend for Frontend integrates with (i) the Data Manager, using operation initDM() as previously described; and (ii) **HARP**, using the initXAI() and update() operations. We discuss those in the description of the **HARP** component, coming next.

For API Accessibility, the Backend for Frontend follows the *Community API* pattern, since in the future it is intended to support different kinds of frontends and the integration of our system with other tools used by journalists.

The Backend for Frontend utilises two endpoints with one Endpoint Role. Both endpoints are *Processing Resources*, which has to do with the `initDM()` and `initXAI()` request to the Data Manager and HARP, respectively, and the `update()` request to the HARP. The first two are *State Transition Operations*, where a client initiates a processing action that causes the provider-side application state to change, while the latter is a *Retrieval Operation*, where information available from **HARP** gets retrieved for an end user.

. Finally, regarding the Quality Patterns, the Backend for Frontend follows *Rate Limit* which is dictated by the user's `initDM()` and `initXAI()` requests.

HARP. **HARP** employs the *Backend Integration* pattern: it exposes its message-based API to two other backend services of the same application, the Backend for Frontend and the Data Manager. In more detail, **HARP** integrates with the:

– Backend for Frontend, which makes `initXAI()` requests of the type:

```
1  type InitXAIRequest { name: string, /* Instance name */
2      t: long, /* Interval period for each call (in ms) */
3      target: string, /* Location of the data source */
4      datasources*: string /* Data sources to retrieve data */
5      rules*: string /* Rules to be initialised at HARP instance */
6      queries*: string /* Queries to be initilizated at HARP instance }
```

An example of JSON payload is shown below:

```
1  { "name": "HARP-example", "t": 3600000,
2    "target": "getDailyTrends",
3    "datasources": ["GoogleTrends_dailytrends"],
4    "rules": ["GlobalLead(Topic, T) -> CertainLead(Topic, Region, T)",
5             "CertainLead(Topic, Region, T) -> Lead(Topic, Region, T)"]
6    "queries":["Lead(Topic, dk, T)","GlobalLead(Topic,T)"] }
```

The corresponding response is of the following format:

```
1  type InitXAIResponse { ack: boolean /* Acknowledgement */}
```

The Backend for Frontend can also make `update()` requests to **HARP**:

```
1  type UpdateRequest { query: string }
```

An example of JSON payload is the following:

```
1  {"query": "Lead(Topic, Region, T)"}
```

Furthermore, **HARP** gives the following response:

```
1  type UpdateResponse { answers*: answerElement,
2    hypotheticalAnswers*: HypotheticalAnswerElement }
```

```
3  type ActualAnswerElement { answer: string, evidence*: string }
4  type HypotheticalAnswerElement {
5    answer: string, hypothesis*: string, evidence*: string }
```

An example of JSON payload is as follows:

```
1  {"answers": [
2    {"answer": "Lead(detroit lions,dk,1669299502000)",
3     "evidence": [
4        "DailyTrend(detroit lions,dk,1669299502000)",
5        "Popularity(detroit lions,dk,8K,1669299502000)",
6        "Popularity(detroit lions,dk,9k,1669303102000)",
7        "Popularity(detroit lions,dk,10K,1669306702000),"
8        "8K<9k","9k<10k"]},
9    {"answer": "Lead(thanksgiving parade,dk,1669299502000)",
10    "evidence": [
11       "DailyTrend(thanksgiving parade,dk,1669299502000)"
12       "Popularity(thanksgiving parade,35K,1669299502000)",
13       "Popularity(thanksgiving parade,47K,1669303102000)",
14       "Popularity(thanksgiving parade,50K,1669306702000)"
15       "35K<47K","47K<50K"]}],
16  "hypotheticalAnswers": [
17    {"answer": "Lead(detroit lions,dk,1669303102000)",
18     "hypothesis": ["10k<Pop2",
19        "Popularity(detroit lions,dk,Pop2,1669311402000)"],
20     "evidence": [
21        "Popularity(detroit lions,dk,9K,1669303102000)",
22        "Popularity(detroit lions,dk,10K,1669306702000)",
23        "9k<10k"]},
24    {"answer": "Lead(thanksgiving parade,dk,1669303102000)",
25     "hypothesis": ["50k<Pop2"
26        "Popularity(thanksgiving parade,dk,Pop2,1669311402000)"],
27     "evidence": ["47k<50k",
28        "DailyTrend(thanksgiving parade,dk,1669303102000)",
29        "Popularity(thanksgiving parade,dk,47K,1669303102000)",
30        "Popularity(thanksgiving parade,dk,50K,1669306702000)"]}] }
```

– Data Manager, which **HARP** makes listen() requests to of the form:

```
1  type ListenRequest { datasources*: string /* Data sources */}
```

and receives a response like the following:

```
1  type ListenResponse { t: long, facts*: string /* Facts for time t */}
```

A JSON payload example is given below:

```
1  { "t": 1669306702000, "facts": [
2    "Popularity(detroit lions,10K,1669306702000)",
3    "Popularity(thanksgiving parade,50K,1669306702000)",
4    "Popularity(uruguay,5K,1669306702000)"] }
```

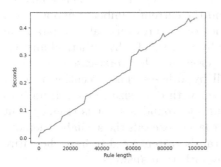 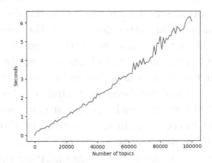

Fig. 2. Left: preprocessing time for a single rule with a body of 0 to 100 000 atoms, at intervals of 1 000, averaged over 10 runs. Right: updating time for a datastream with atoms of the form `DailyTrend(Topic, dk, t)` and `Popularity(Topic, dk, t, t)` for 0 to 100 000 different values of `Topic`, at intervals of 1 000, averaged over 10 runs.

For API Accessibility, **HARP** follows the *Solution-Internal API* pattern.

HARP uses two Endpoint Roles, a *Processing Resource* and an *Information Holder Resource*. The former concerns the response of the Data Manager, which triggers **HARP** to produce the current answers. This is actually a *State Transition Operation*, where the Data Manager's response initiates a processing action that causes the provider-side application state to change. The same applies also for the `initXAI()` request. The Information Holder Resource endpoint role concerns the `update()` requests from the Backend for Frontend, which asks for the most recent answers. In more detail, this is an *Operational Data Holder* in the sense that it supports clients that want to read the most recent calculated answers.

Finally, **HARP** follows the *Rate Limit* Quality Pattern, dictated both by the initial `initXAI()` request and the rate limits that public APIs might have.

5   Experimental Evaluation

The bottleneck of our system consists of the preprocessing and update steps in the reasoner. In this section we empirically explore the cost of these computations. Experiments were performed on a machine with an Intel i5-10400 CPU, 64GB RAM, and Windows 11. Our results are shown in Fig. 2.

The preprocessing time depends on the rules. (Determining the precise form that rules must have for the worst-case preprocessing time is a task beyond the scope of this paper.) In the simple case of a single rule, the preprocessing time increases linearly as the size of the rule's body varies from 0 to 100 000 atoms (Fig. 2, left side). The general case is known to be exponential [11].

The time for updating the set of hypothetical answers depends on two factors: the amount of data in the given dataslice and the current number of hypothetical answers. The latter depends on the relevance of the previous data. If data from the datastream matches with atoms in the hypothesis of a hypothetical answer, then more hypothetical answers might be created. The worst-case scenario is that every data matches with atoms in all hypotheses. The execution time of this update has been evaluated for this case, with data size ranging from 0 to 100 000 atoms, with execution time peaking at around 6 seconds (Fig. 2, right side). Increasing the data size to 1 000 000 or larger exceeds the available memory limits of our testing setup, due to the program's current need to have the entire dataslice in memory before updating the hypothetical answers.

Overall, this preliminary evaluation of the performance of our reasoner is satisfactory: service startup is affected only minimally (under a second), and updates can be performed reasonably often. (Note that the **Frontend** does not need to wait for updates when it asks for the current state, since the latter is cached until a new state is produced by finishing an update.) Nevertheless, we discuss potential improvements in the next section.

6   Conclusions and Future Work

We have developed μXL, the first extensible system for lead generation that integrates the integration benefits of microservices with explainable AI. Our development is motivated by concrete needs identified in a collaboration with Danish media companies. These needs oriented us towards the adoption of recent theories and tools, in particular API Patterns [21], the Jolie programming language [15], and hypothetical reasoning over data streams [4]. Thus, our work also serves as a practical validation of these methods.

In this work we have focused on the architectural and technical aspects of μXL. In the future we would like to evaluate the usefulness of μXL for journalists by: carrying out systematic comparisons against other tools based on different architectures and AI; and conducting controlled user experiments. Other future directions include extending the system to more data sources and integrating more kinds of AI in addition to **HARP**. Regarding our reasoner, extending **HARP** such that it could process dataslices in chunks could be interesting for processing large amounts of data with small amounts of RAM. Another interesting improvement is parallelising **HARP**'s update operation, such that it can scale to dataslices with sizes of billions or more. A more conceptual extension is to incorporate the possibility of having delays in the data, as described in [4]. Finally, we plan on exploring procedures that suggest interesting rules, for example based on statistical observations of journalistic behaviour.

Acknowledgements. We thank Narongrit Unwerawattana for his technical support.

References

1. Aiello, L.M., et al.: Sensing trending topics in Twitter. IEEE Trans. Multim. **15**(6), 1268–1282 (2013)
2. Chen, Y., Amiri, H., Li, Z., Chua, T.: Emerging topic detection for organizations from microblogs. In: Proceedings of SIGIR, pp. 43–52. ACM (2013)
3. Chomicki, J., Imielinski, T.: Temporal deductive databases and infinite objects. In: Proceedings of SIGMOD, pp. 61–73. ACM (1988)
4. Cruz-Filipe, L., Nunes, I., Gaspar, G.: Hypothetical answers to continuous queries over data streams. In: Proceedings of AAAI, pp. 2798–2805 (2020)
5. Das, A., Roy, M., Dutta, S., Ghosh, S., Das, A.K.: Predicting trends in the twitter social network: a machine learning approach. In: Panigrahi, B.K., Suganthan, P.N., Das, S. (eds.) SEMCCO 2014. LNCS, vol. 8947, pp. 570–581. Springer, Cham (2015). https://doi.org/10.1007/978-3-319-20294-5_49
6. Diakopoulos, N., Dong, M., Bronner, L.: Generating location-based news leads for national politics reporting. In: Proceedings of Computational + Journalism Symposium (2020)
7. Dragoni, N., et al.: Microservices: yesterday, today, and tomorrow. In: Mazzara, M., Meyer, B. (eds.) Present and Ulterior Software Engineering, pp. 195–216. Springer, Cham (2017). https://doi.org/10.1007/978-3-319-67425-4_12
8. Giallorenzo, S., Montesi, F., Peressotti, M., Rademacher, F., Sachweh, S.: Jolie and LEMMA: model-driven engineering and programming languages meet on microservices. In: Damiani, F., Dardha, O. (eds.) COORDINATION 2021. LNCS, vol. 12717, pp. 276–284. Springer, Cham (2021). https://doi.org/10.1007/978-3-030-78142-2_17
9. Guidi, C., Maschio, B.: A jolie based platform for speeding-up the digitalization of system integration processes. In: Proceedings of Microservices (2019)
10. Huang, Q., Liu, Z., Rosenberg, A.E., Gibbon, D.C., Shahraray, B.: Automated generation of news content hierarchy by integrating audio, video, and text information. In: Proceedings of ICASSP, pp. 3025–3028. IEEE Computer Society (1999)
11. Kowalski, R.A.: Predicate logic as programming language. In: Proceedings of IFIP, pp. 569–574. North-Holland (1974)
12. Leppänen, L., Munezero, M., Granroth-Wilding, M., Toivonen, H.: Data-driven news generation for automated journalism. In: Proceedings of INLG, pp. 188–197. Association for Computational Linguistics (2017)
13. Mathioudakis, M., Koudas, N.: TwitterMonitor: trend detection over the Twitter stream. In: Proceedings of SIGMOD, pp. 1155–1158. ACM (2010)
14. Montesi, F.: Process-aware web programming with jolie. Sci. Comput. Program. **130**, 69–96 (2016)
15. Montesi, F., Guidi, C., Zavattaro, G.: Service-oriented programming with Jolie. In: Bouguettaya, A., Sheng, Q., Daniel, F. (eds.) Web Services Foundations, pp. 81–107. Springer, New York (2014). https://doi.org/10.1007/978-1-4614-7518-7_4
16. Montesi, F., Weber, J.: From the decorator pattern to circuit breakers in microservices. In: Proceedings of ACM SAC, pp. 1733–1735. ACM (2018)
17. Oh, C., et al.: Understanding user perception of automated news generation system. In: Proceedings of CHI, pp. 1–13. ACM (2020)
18. Pugachev, A., Voronov, A., Makarov, I.: Prediction of news popularity via keywords extraction and trends tracking. In: van der Aalst, W.M.P., et al. (eds.) AIST 2020. CCIS, vol. 1357, pp. 37–51. Springer, Cham (2021). https://doi.org/10.1007/978-3-030-71214-3_4

19. Schwartz, R., Naaman, M., Teodoro, R.: Editorial algorithms: using social media to discover and report local news. In: Proceedings of ICWSM, pp. 407–415 (2015)
20. Zarrinkalam, F., Fani, H., Bagheri, E., Kahani, M.: Predicting users' future interests on twitter. In: Jose, J.M., et al. (eds.) ECIR 2017. LNCS, vol. 10193, pp. 464–476. Springer, Cham (2017). https://doi.org/10.1007/978-3-319-56608-5_36
21. Zimmermann, O., Stocker, M., Lübke, D., Zdun, U., Pautasso, C.: Patterns for API Design: Simplifying Integration with Loosely Coupled Message Exchanges. Addison-Wesley Signature Series (Vernon). Addison-Wesley Professional (2022)

One Microservice per Developer: Is This the Trend in OSS?

Dario Amoroso d'Aragona[1](✉), Xiaozhou Li[2](✉), Tomas Cerny[3],
Andrea Janes[4], Valentina Lenarduzzi[2], and Davide Taibi[1,2]

[1] Tampere University, Tampere, Finland
dario.amorosodaragona@tuni.fi, davide.taibi@oulu.fi
[2] University of Oulu, Oulu, Finland
xiaozhou.li@oulu.fi, valentina.lenarduzzi@oulu.fi
[3] University of Arizona, Tucson, USA
tcerny@arizona.edu
[4] Vorarlberg University of Applied Sciences, Dornbirn, Austria
andrea.janes@fhv.at

Abstract. When developing and managing microservice systems, practitioners suggest that each microservice should be owned by a particular
team. In effect, there is only one team with the responsibility to manage a given service. Consequently, one developer should belong to only
one team. This practice of "one-microservice-per-developer" is especially
prevalent in large projects with an extensive development team.

Based on the bazaar-style software development model of Open Source
Projects, in which different programmers, like vendors at a bazaar,
offer to help out developing different parts of the system, this article
investigates whether we can observe the "one-microservice-per-developer"
behavior, a strategy we assume anticipated within microservice based
Open Source Projects.

We conducted an empirical study among 38 microservice-based OS
projects. Our findings indicate that the strategy is rarely respected by
open-source developers except for projects that have dedicated DevOps
teams.

1 Introduction

Microservices are increasing their diffusion both in industry and in Open Source
Software (OSS) projects [4].

Microservices are small and autonomous services deployed independently,
with a single and clearly defined purpose [11,24]. Because of their independent deployment, each microservice can scale independently from others. Some
authors see microservices not primarily as a technological benefit but also as a
way to scale up the number of development teams: "*microservices are not necessarily required to manage huge software, but rather to manage a huge number of
people working on them* [29]". The rationale is that since microservices decou-
ple software components, less communication is necessary to develop them, and
larger teams become possible.

ⓒ IFIP International Federation for Information Processing 2023
Published by Springer Nature Switzerland AG 2023
G. A. Papadopoulos et al. (Eds.): ESOCC 2023, LNCS 14183, pp. 19–34, 2023.
https://doi.org/10.1007/978-3-031-46235-1_2

Practitioners suggest that a microservice should be *owned* and managed by a single team [1,3,4,27,29,30,36]. The supportive argument sources from "Conway's law" [9] states that *"organizations which design systems (in the broad sense) are constrained to produce designs which are copies of the communication structures of these organizations."* Following this law, it would be ineffective or detrimental to have two separate teams working on one microservice. Working on one microservice requires communication within the team, and if these communication structures are not present, the work on a joint microservice becomes hard. Therefore, it is suggested that each team is responsible for one or more business functions [1,30]. While some authors (and Conway himself [9]) clearly foresee that each team can own more than one microservice/subsystem [8,30,36], others suggest that "a team should have exactly one service unless there is a proven need to have multiple services", to not exceed the cognitive capacity of a team [30]. Particularly if business functions are large (e.g., "customer management" or "order management"), practitioners suggest that one team is fully dedicated to one microservice [27].

Therefore, following the practitioners' recommendations [8,9,27,30,36], a developer must belong only to one team, and each team must contribute only to one microservice. Consequently, we can deduct that each team member, and therefore each developer, must contribute to only one microservice. Based on these assumptions, it would be interesting to investigate the "one-microservice-per-developer" strategy to verify to which extent it is considered in practice.

The goal of this paper is to investigate to which degree it is correct to assume that in microservice OSS projects, the one-microservice-per-developer strategy is respected.

Particularly, teams developing OSS projects using a bazaar-style software development model (as described in Eric Raymond's seminal essay "The Cathedral and the Bazaar", in which different programmers, like vendors at a bazaar, offer to help out developing different parts of the system [28]), require a decoupled software architecture, which—what we assume—would manifest in a decoupled collaboration structure. Within OSS projects adopting a microservice architecture, we hypothesize, we observe that developers, during a given time window, commit only to one microservice at a time.

For these aims, we designed and conducted an empirical study among 38 microservice-based OSS projects selected from the dataset created by Baresi et al. [4]. Using code repositories of these projects and analyzing the history of commits, we calculated the average number of microservices developed by each developer determining how well is the one-microservice-per-developer strategy employed. In addition, we further investigated the potential developer profiles using Exploratory Factor Analysis (EFA) to detect the patterns of developer behaviors in the core contributor groups of these projects.

Paper Structure: Section 3 describes the empirical study design, while Sect. 4 reports the obtained results. Section 5 discusses the results, and Sect. 6 highlights the limitation of this work. Section 2 presents the related work, and Sect. 7 concludes.

2 Related Work

Developer interaction analysis has been approached from different perspectives in OSS communities. Given the large quantities of produced communication artifacts throughout the developer interaction in the development process, various automated approaches have been proposed. Common sources of input for such analysis include version control systems (performing mining source code repositories) [15, 16], mailing lists, and issue trackers [5, 26], or developer online surveys [22]. Prior to the era of microservices, Bird et al. [5] considered social network communities and system modularity. They researched code artifact changes across modules and analyzed email archives to derive social networks and assess community alignment with modularity. The conclusions and research questions of Bird et al. [5] in the scope of microservices drive new perspectives. Microservices are self-contained, and with regard to Conway's law, we can consider well-defined teams assigned to particular microservice development. In addition, the remaining challenge related to crosscutting concerns cannot be simply negated in microservices.

With regards to microservices and well-defined separation boundaries by code repositories (or at least repository modules). It can thus be assumed that code artifacts modified by developers within the same community are placed in a related repository location.

Throughout OSS software development, it can be expected that developer assignments to subsystems remain stable (i.e., given expertise alignments, subsystem assignment, etc.). Ashraf and Panichella [2] analyzed a set of OSS projects to examine developer communities from the perspective of their subsystem assignment and interaction highlighting that emerging communities change considerably across a project's lifetime and do align with each other.

The microservices perspective, as suggested by Lenarduzzi et al. [21], enables teams to work independently, reducing cross-team communication. At the same time, upon microservice integration, issues are reported across teams, as suggested by Bogner et al. [7] who report on ripple effects. There are other underlying issues behind this relevant to system evolution, such as missing system-centered perspective and lack of tools to analyze coherence across microservices, perform modification trade-off analysis, or evaluate the conformance of the as-built and as-documented architectures.

Besides interaction analysis to understand communities, other interesting research directions took place. For instance, Marco et al. [25] analyzed GitHub commit comments regarding emotions and feelings expression showing that "one-commit" developers are more active and polite when posting comments as opposed to "multi-commit" developers, that are less active in posting comments, and when commenting, they are less polite.

In a timely thesis, Shi [31] looked into establishing contributor roles within software repositories by mining architectural information. In a case study on Apache Tomcat, they used the metric to deduce these roles and validate them with particular roles listed on the project website. Such a research direction aligns with the perspective of microservices with established separation of duty.

Furthermore, the classification of experts responsible for re-engineering or management can lead to better insights into the applicability of Conway's law across microservice developers.

It is also important to take into account that enterprise companies like Red Hat manage OSS projects [33] rather than projects based on volunteer contribution. This can influence role identification, contributor duty spread across modules, and also the community network. Spinellis et al. [33] considered the detection of OSS projects that are supported by enterprises. Such projects can serve as better benchmarks for practical case studies.

With respect to inter-project dependency identification, Blincoe et al. [6] considered reference coupling. The reference coupling method often identifies technical dependencies between projects that arc untracked by developers. Understanding inter-project dependency is important for change impact analysis and coordination. In their study, they manually analyzed identified dependencies and categorized and compared them to dependencies specified by the development team. They also assessed how the ecosystem structure compares with the social behavior of project contributors and owners. As a result, of socio-technical alignment analysis within the GitHub ecosystems, they found that the project owners' social behavior aligns well with the technical dependencies within the ecosystem. Still, the project contributors' social behavior does not align with these dependencies. In microservices, this could possibly translate into system architects aware of consequences and microservice developers who operate in isolation as suggested by Lenarduzzi et al. [21] and unaware of such as inter-project dependency.

In a similar perspective, Scaliante Wiese et al. [34] researched co-change prediction. They use issues, developers' communication, and commit metadata to analyze change patterns for prediction models. They demonstrate that such models based on contextual information from software changes are accurate and can support software maintenance and evolution, warning developers when they miss relevant artifacts while performing a software change.

3   The Empirical Study

In this section, we describe our empirical study reporting the goal and research questions, context, data collection, and data analysis following the guideline defined by Wohlin et al. [35].

Our goal is to evaluate to what extent the one-microservice-per-developer strategy, recommended by practitioners [1,3,4,27,30] is respected in OSS projects. To allow verifiability and replicability, we published the raw data in the replication package[1].

Then, we formulated two Research Questions (RQs).

RQ$_1$. How well is the one-microservice-per-developer strategy respected in OSS projects following a microservice architecture?

---

[1] https://figshare.com/s/6ba4e0063ab04d03d6d6.

RQ$_2$. Which developer roles better respect the one-microservice-per-developer strategy?

With **RQ$_1$**, we investigated if developers are actually responsible, and therefore committing, only to a single microservice. In **RQ$_2$**, we aimed to understand if specific roles are respecting the aforementioned strategy differently. We expect that some roles (e.g. DevOps) can be involved in multiple microservices, while other roles (e.g. coders) are involved only in a single microservice.

3.1 The Selected Projects

We considered the manually validated dataset including 145 microservice-based projects, proposed by Baresi et al. [4]. The authors developed, validated, and released a tool to recognize the architecture (e.g., the microservices, the external services, and the databases used) in a given microservices-based project. In addition, the authors provided a list of 145 projects that have been manually validated as non-toy projects regularly using microservices, for which they also reported the list of built-in microservices in the form of relative paths and some other set-up information not used in our case. In particular, for our analysis, we leveraged the list of projects and the related list of microservices identified by a list of sub-project folders. The dataset consists of projects whose source code is accessible on GitHub[2] and is complemented with further data, including the microservice list.

In order to select a set of relevant projects for our study, we defined the following inclusion criteria:

- Project with at least 2 microservices. With this threshold, we aim to exclude non-microservices projects.
- Projects with at least 2 microservices committed in the last 12 months. To analyze projects that are still maintained.

By requiring a minimum number of microservices and activities in the last non-representative outliers for our study can be excluded. It is important to note that we did not exclude projects based on their programming languages.

As a result, we included 38 microservice-based projects with a total of 379 microservices (10 microservices per project on average).

3.2 Data Collection

To collect statistics about the development process, we browsed every project commit. We gathered the timestamp, the author's name, and the precise change locations for each commit. With the latter, a modification is connected to a microservice. We specifically created a heuristic that matches if the path of the modified file is contained in the project's list of microservices. If so, we updated the list of microservice changes in the aforementioned author's commit.

---

[2] https://github.com.

3.3 Data Analysis

To answer RQ_1, the goal is to investigate the microservice coverage by the developers on average by examining their commits on the microservices. Here, we considered only the commits involving source code files and excluded all the commits regarding documentation and setup files. We analyzed the distribution of commits over developers and microservices to understand 1) how many microservices have developers in common, and 2) how many developers work on more than one single microservice.

However, the threat, in this case, is the situation where a developer finishes work on a microservice and gets started to work on another microservice, or for some reason, he/she is just moved to another team of developers. From our point of view, this situation does not lead to a real violation of the *one-microservice-per-developer* strategy. For this reason, we have defined a metric for counting how many times a developer recommits to a microservice after starting work on another microservice; in other words, if a developer D_1 commits to microservice m_1, switches the team, and starts committing to a m_2 microservice, then the result of our metric will be 0 because the developer never goes back to the previous microservice; otherwise, if after a while the developer commits back to m_1, our metric results will give 1, because the developer goes back to the previous microservice (m_1).

To answer RQ_2, we need to understand how to identify the role of each contributor in OSS microservice projects. Different from industrial projects, within OSS projects on GitHub, contributors, are neither assigned roles by "project managers" or "product owners" nor obliged to focus on the tasks assigned to them in the corresponding areas. Therefore, we shall only be able to understand the roles based on the domains each contributor has been contributing to.

To identify the roles of the project contributors, we adopted the approach proposed by Montandon et al. [23] combined with the Exploratory Factor Analysis (EFA).

Montandon et al. [23] proposed a machine-learning-based approach based on the extensions of the committed files. They used more than 100k developers' data from GitHub together with Stack Overflow data and studied five critical roles: *Backend, Frontend, Data scientist, DevOps,* and *Mobile.* Herein, we initially adopt the same settings.

The Exploratory Factor Analysis (EFA) [13] aims to discover not only the number of factors but also what measurable variables together influence which individual factors [10]. With EFA, we can reduce the complexity of the data, and also are able to explain the observations with a smaller set of latent factors. Importantly, by doing so we can also discover the relations among the variables.

Herein, we follow these steps to conduct EFA on our commit dataset and determine the profile of each developer:

1. **Preprocessing.** Firstly, we group the obtained developer behavior data.
2. **Data Verification.** Secondly, we verify its sampling adequacy and statistical significance. For example, we can use Bartlett's Test of Sphericity [32] and Kaiser-Meyer-Olkin (KMO) Test [18] for such a purpose.

3. **Determining Factor Number.** Thirdly, we find the number of factors using parallel analysis (PA) [14]. Herein, we employ the Monte Carlo simulation technique to simulate random samples consisting of uncorrelated variables. Then, We extract the eigenvalues of the correlation matrix of the simulated data and compare the extracted eigenvalues that are ordered by magnitude to the average simulated eigenvalues. Significant factors are the ones with ob.served eigenvalues higher than the corresponding simulated eigenvalues

4. **Factor Extraction and Interpretation.** With the number of factors determined, we conduct the EFA on the dataset. To simplify the interpretation of the factor analysis result, we employ the *varimax* rotation technique [17] to maximize the variance of each factor loading.

5. **Determining Individual Developer Role Allocation.** To apply the factor-variable relation to individual contributors, we shall calculate the similarity between the developers' contributions in terms of the languages and each detected factor. By comparing the contributor's similarity to each role factor, we shall understand more intuitively which role(s) he/she leans to. Such results can be visualized in a radar chart.

For this study, as a result of the EFA, we shall have a set of factors, each of which is closely related to a set of latent variables, i.e., programming languages. To be noted, due to the fact that the original data are collected from projects of different programming languages, it is likely that contributors working on different languages lean toward similar roles. For example, contributors working on CSS and VUE can both be *Frontend* contributors. Therefore, we shall observe the loadings of the EFA and manually merge factors related to only closely-connected languages into the unified roles.

Particularly, the contributor's similarity to each role-factor can be calculated using the Kumar-Hassebrook (KH) similarity, which incorporates also the inner product of the assigned values of the variables [20]. Moreover, using the KH similarity, we can evaluate each contributor's effort level in each pre-detected role-factor, respectively.

4   Results

In this Section, we report the obtained results to answer our Research Questions (RQs).

RQ_1 How well is the one-microservice-per-developer strategy respected in OSS projects following a microservice architecture?

To answer RQ_1, we investigated the single developer, assuming that a single developer does not belong to more than one team at the same time. Figure 1 compares the number of microservices with shared developers (*MSs with Shared Dev*) with the number of microservices where all developers committed only to the same microservice (*MSs without Shared Dev*).

Unexpectedly, only 2 projects always respected the one-microservice-per-developer strategy, while the remaining projects shared among services.

Since the vast majority of the projects (Fig. 3) a developer works on more than one microservice, we continue our analysis to understand if developers are simply switching teams, or are working on more microservices at the same time.

Figure 2 shows the result of the number of times developers commit back on a microservice after moving to another one among the projects. In two projects out of 38, developers never commit back to the previous microservice. In most of the projects (53%), the median is 0, in 34% of the projects the median is between 1 and 10, and finally in the 13% of the projects is more than 10. However, analyzing the figure, we can see that the boxplots are very stretched, thus in the same project there are some developers that do not return back after changing microservice (or never change microservice) and some developers that instead, commit to the previous microservice.

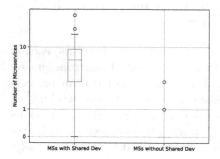

Fig. 1. # microservices with shared and not shared developers (RQ$_1$)

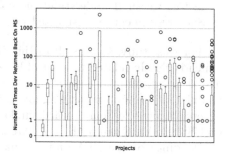

Fig. 2. Frequency that developers have committed back (RQ$_1$)

🔍 As a result, we conclude that in an OSS context, the *one-microservice-per-developer* strategy is not respected as in most cases, developers work on more than one microservice in parallel.

RQ$_2$ Which developer roles better respect the one-microservice-per-developer strategy?

To tackle RQ$_2$, we first investigated the strategies of different contributor-microservice effort allocations. Figure 4 shows the distribution of the "microservices per developer" of each of the selected projects. To be noted, the *light-example-4j*, which contains 155 different microservices, is not shown in Fig. 4. Because one outlier in this project reaches 154 microservices, showing this project in the chart will make the details of all other projects invisible. Nonetheless, this project was certainly included in the analysis process.

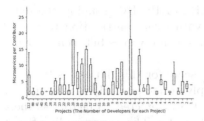

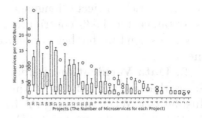

Fig. 3. MS Per Developer sorted by #Developer (RQ$_1$)

Fig. 4. MS Per developer sorted by #Microservice (RQ$_2$)

From Fig. 4, we can easily find that for all the projects, the *one-microservice-per-developer* strategy has not been respected. For the selected projects, the majority of the medians range from one to seven. For all projects, there are always some developers committing across multiple microservices.

On the contrary, many projects that contain various numbers of microservices have one individual contributor who contributes to all the microservices. We name such a strategy *One-Dev-ALL-MS*. For example, in project *geoserver-cloud*, contributor `gabriel.roldan` committed in all the 11 microservices, and in project *eShopOnContainers*, contributor `mvelosop` covers all the 17 microservices. Furthermore, many projects even have multiple contributors that cover all the microservices. We name such a strategy *Multi-Dev-All-MS*. For example, in project *loopback4-microservice-catalog*, there are eight contributors covering all 18 microservices; and in project *DeathStarBench* six contributors cover all three microservices. It is likely that such a phenomenon is irrelevant to either the microservice number or a number of contributors.

Based on this phenomenon, we can intuitively categorize the projects as follows.

- *One-Dev-ALL-MS projects*: Projects where only one individual contributor covers all microservices while all the others cover part of them (16 out of 38)
- *Multi-Dev-ALL-MS projects*: Projects with multiple contributors covering all microservices (10 out of 38)
- *Multi-Dev-SOME-MS projects*: Any projects with no contributors covering all microservices; nor do they adopt "One-microservice-per-developer" strategy (12 out of 38)
- *One-MS-per-developer projects*: Any projects with each contributor/team working only on one microservice

To further investigate the potential roles of the contributors that cover all microservices and the other common contributors, we used EFA to detect the latent factors.

1. Preprocessing. Firstly, for the preprocessing, we grouped the original dataset by the contributors. For each contributor, we synthesized his/her contribution in every language by checking the extensions of the committed files.

We crawl each project's languages using GitHub API. By grouping the data, we obtained the 1 536 contributors' dataset with their contribution to the 33 languages. And we further normalized the dataset into values between zero and one.

2. Data Verification. Herein, the KMO score for this dataset is 0.585. It shows that the sampling is adequate and applying factor analysis is useful for this dataset. When applying PA to the dataset, we detected 13 factors as there are 13 out of 33 observed eigenvalues greater than 1.0. The corresponding factor loadings are shown in the replication package (see footnote 1).

3. Determining Factor Number. Based on the result of the parallel analysis (PA), the turning point can be found easily by examining the differences between observed eigenvalues and simulated eigenvalues. Since the simulated eigenvalue becomes greater than the observed eigenvalue in the 14th factor (1.00049 and 0.90517, respectively), the first 13 factors are retained. The number of factors is therefore 13. According to Guadagnoli and Velicer [12], scores greater than 0.4 are considered stable, especially when all variables are not cross-loaded heavily.

4. Factor Extraction and Interpretation. The initially detected factors and the correlated variables are reported in the replication package (see footnote 1). Herein, we adapted Montandon et al.'s role-language relevance results [23] as the reference to analyze the interpretation of each factor. To be noted, we added several languages that are not listed in Montandon et al's study based on common knowledge and experts' opinions.

Meanwhile, we also considered the other contributors that are not related to any specific roles above as *Others*. By calculating the KH similarity between the role factors in the factor table obtained previously and the reference table [23]. Here we assigned the role with the highest similarity score to each factor.

Furthermore, we combined the factors with the same roles and obtained the final role-factor reference model.

5. Determining Individual Developer Role Allocation. By using this role-factor relevance model, we simply calculated the factor similarities of any contributor, given his/her contribution allocation in terms of the 33 languages. Furthermore, we investigated the difference in terms of the contributor roles of the project strategies mentioned above.

Figure 5 shows the average behavior patterns of the different types of contributors in terms of the technical roles. From Fig. 5, we can easily observe that the individual contributors who cover all microservices (i.e., One-Dev-ALL-MS) of the projects contribute largely as Documentation+. And they are also heavily involved in Frontend, when slightly less in Backend and DevOps roles. To be noted, they also contribute as Fullstack but are nearly non-existent in the other aspects. In addition, the One-Dev-ALL-MS also contributes as the Data Scientist role more than the others. On the other hand, for the multiple contributors that cover all the microservices (i.e., Multi-Dev-ALL-Ms), these contributors, on average, contribute less than the One-Dev-ALL-MS mentioned above. However, they contribute slightly more as Frontend than the other roles. They cover the

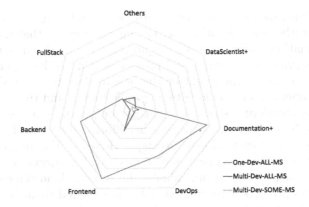

Fig. 5. Average Role-Factor Distribution of Each Strategy (RQ$_2$)

Fullstack role a little less but surprisingly at a similar level compared to One-Dev-ALL-MS. Furthermore, they contribute more in other languages that are not role-related than that from the One-Dev-ALL-MS. The Multi-Dev-ALL-MS also contributes to Backend, Documentation, and Data Scientist, but much less than the other aspects. Regarding all the Multi-Dev-SOME-MS contributors, they contribute much less in terms of all working roles than the One-Dev-ALL-Ms and Multi-Dev-ALL-Ms.

> ♀ The majority of the microservice projects have one or multiple contributors who commit to all microservices. The single contributor who covers all microservices (One-Dev-ALL-MS) contributes much more than the multiple contributors covering all microservices (Multi-Dev-ALL-MS) in all roles, except that Multi-Dev-ALL-MS contribute more in non-role-related languages. Multi-Dev-SOME-MS contribute much less in all roles.

5   Discussion

Using a large established 145-microservice project dataset [4] we selected 38 projects with a sufficient number of contributors and commits as a representative OSS sample. This project sample did not adopt the same strategy suggested for proprietary (closed-source) software projects. In the analyzed sample we identified that developers typically work on multiple microservices, and focus on various features, often in parallel. These conclusions are also confirmed by the vast majority of the projects when considering different developer roles.

One of the explanations might be the dynamics of OSS projects. In OSS projects, developers commit their time voluntarily at random, non-fixed hours and schedules, oftentimes driven by feature priority requests or error reports. In particular, none of the selected projects is directly sponsored by a company that allocates developers to the project. Therefore, developers commonly select a set of issues to be implemented (either new features or bug fixing) and work on them independently rather than adopting the specific microservice that they maintain. Another explanation might be that, despite the decentralized nature of OSS and the microservice architecture, OSS projects might not have yet assimilated this strategy. Another reason might be the lack of clear teams in OSS projects (i.e. each developer does not belong to a specific team), and therefore the "one-microservice-per-developer" strategy might not be perceived as an issue.

It must also be recognized that additional effort and overhead are related to the "one-microservice-per-developer" strategy. However, this might not be the proper fit for the OSS environment and context. OSS projects are often driven by small development teams or individuals who stand behind the entire project, occasionally OSS projects have professional teams behind them (i.e., Red Hat); however, we did not include these projects in the study.

Microservice architecture is the mainstream architecture for cloud-native systems. However, not necessarily all microservice systems are cloud-native. In a similar parallel, the decentralized development model connected with cloud-native systems might collide with the OSS development model. Perhaps the main driver for the microservice architecture in these OSS projects is scalability and the decentralized development aspect goes away with the OSS model.

As practitioners often suggest [1,3,4,27,30], if the development team is too small to be split into multiple teams, and there are multiple microservices, to respect the one-microservice-per-developer strategy, the system should rather remain monolithic. The reasons for OSS might be prioritized system scalability for the price of this strategy violation. Perhaps some projects might have decided to split their systems into multiple microservices for maintainability reasons, to increase the separation of concerns, or to better identify different business domains, independently from the team that is working on the same services.

Another explanation might be given by Mariusz, who investigated whether Conway's Law applies to OSS projects [19] and concludes that teams "organize themselves spontaneously around tasks, and since those tasks concern software modules, teams naturally follow Conway's law".

The result of this study will serve the practitioners' community to understand how OSS microservice projects are being developed. Moreover, it will help researchers to further investigate the one-microservice-per-developer strategy.

6   Threats to Validity

Construct Validity. Replying to RQ_1 we tried to understand if the *one-microservice-per-developer* strategy is adopted. But we measure how well this strategy is adopted in an OSS context by analyzing individual developer behavior and assuming that a single developer belongs to one team at a time. We recognized that this assumption could lead to some threats. We planned to expand our work in the future by adding information (such as developer communications, and issue/pull request comments) to extract teams to fine-grain our analysis.

Internal Validity. The dataset used is one of the most recent in the context of microservices and open-source projects. However, the dataset is very heterogeneous (for the number of microservices, the age of the projects, and the number of developers), and we could only analyze a subset of the projects. We want to extend the dataset to get a better picture of the real state of the art.

External Validity. The findings of this paper can be simply extended when more microservice projects are taken into account. It is reasonable that all the currently included projects shall also inevitably evolve when the proposed method should be replicated with the results updated. Especially for RQ_2, the findings can also be generalized to projects that are not specifically microservice-based if we use modules or features to functionally separate the projects instead of using microservices. In this way, such extended findings shall provide insights into the collective contributor profiles for any given OSS project scope. In addition, when the language-role relations can be further defined (e.g., new roles defined, new languages assigned to different roles, etc.), the findings can also be updated accordingly with the changes conducted in the reference table.

Reliability. Using the dataset we provided in the replication package(see footnote 1) with the same approach, the practitioners and scholars can easily obtain the same results as described above. Only when any changes are introduced in the data itself or when the interpretation of the obtained factors varies based on different expertise, the findings shall differ accordingly.

7   Conclusion

Based on the suggestion of practitioners that "a developer should have exactly one service unless there is a proven need to have multiple services" and the assumption that developers developing open source software using a bazaar-style software development model would encourage a "one microservice per developer" strategy, we learned in this study that OSS projects do not comply with this strategy. Oftentimes, we could identify projects with a greater number of microservices than project contributors, and the OSS development model with a few main contributors dominated the proprietary software strategy. Still, we must assume that the contributor dedication to OSS has a very different dynamics than fully-funded organization projects that can afford multiple developers with regular commitments to contribution. One might question if Conway's law collides with the OSS development model, and the results of this study add weight to the doubts. In this work, we showed that OSS microservice projects rarely follow the "one-microservice-per-developer" strategy.

We have demonstrated this by analyzing the OSS project source code repositories of an established microservices project dataset. We further supported this result by analyzing the different developers' roles in contributing to these projects.

As future work, we aim at further study if "one-microservice per developer" holds in OSS projects trying to observe emerging or stable developer-like collaborations between developers. To do so, we plan to analyze the commits of source code repositories of microservice projects, also parsing the actual code modifications to understand if a collaboration took place. Also, following the suggestion by Mariusz [19] projects, which states that "developers organize themselves spontaneously around tasks", we plan to study issue-tracking systems in combination with source code repositories to investigate if we are able to detect such spontaneous developers acting on single microservices. Moreover, we aim to investigate the developers' team composition to classify the developers who contribute to the same code.

Acknowledgement. This work was supported by a grant from the Academy of Finland (grant n. 349488 - MuFAno) and a grant from Business Finland ("6G-Bridge 6GSoft").

References

1. Amazon: Service per team pattern (2023). https://docs.aws.amazon.com/presc riptive-guidance/latest/modernization-decomposing-monoliths/service-per-team. html
2. Ashraf, U., Mayr-Dorn, C., Mashkoor, A., Egyed, A., Panichella, S.: Do communities in developer interaction networks align with subsystem developer teams? An empirical study of open source systems. In: International Conference on Software and System Processes, pp. 61–71 (2021)
3. Balalaie, A., Heydarnoori, A., Jamshidi, P.: Microservices architecture enables DevOps: migration to a cloud-native architecture. IEEE Softw. **33**(3), 42–52 (2016). https://doi.org/10.1109/MS.2016.64
4. Baresi, L., Quattrocchi, G., Tamburri, D.A.: Microservice Architecture Practices and Experience: a Focused Look on Docker Configuration Files (2022). https://doi.org/10.48550/ARXIV.2212.03107. https://arxiv.org/abs/2212.03107
5. Bird, C., Pattison, D., D'Souza, R., Filkov, V., Devanbu, P.: Latent social structure in open source projects. In: International Symposium on Foundations of Software Engineering, pp. 24–35 (2008)
6. Blincoe, K., Harrison, F., Kaur, N., Damian, D.: Reference coupling: an exploration of inter-project technical dependencies and their characteristics within large software ecosystems. Inf. Softw. Technol. **110**, 174–189 (2019)
7. Bogner, J., Fritzsch, J., Wagner, S., Zimmermann, A.: Industry practices and challenges for the evolvability assurance of microservices: an interview study and systematic grey literature review. Empirical Softw. Eng. **26**(5), 1–39 (2021)
8. Carneiro, C., Schmelmer, T.: Microservices From Day One: Build robust and scalable software from the start. Apress (2016)
9. Conway, M.E.: How Do Committees Invent? Datamation (1968)
10. DeCoster, J.: Overview of factor analysis (1998)
11. Fowler, M.: CodeSmell (2006). https://martinfowler.com/bliki/CodeSmell.html
12. Guadagnoli, E., Velicer, W.F.: Relation of sample size to the stability of component patterns. Psychol. Bull. **103**(2), 265 (1988)

13. Hair, J.F., Black, W.C., Babin, B.J., Anderson, R.E., Tatham, R.L., et al.: Multivariate data analysis, vol. 6 (2006)
14. Horn, J.L.: A rationale and test for the number of factors in factor analysis. Psychometrika **30**(2), 179–185 (1965)
15. Jermakovics, A., Sillitti, A., Succi, G.: Mining and visualizing developer networks from version control systems. In: International Workshop on Cooperative and Human Aspects of Software Engineering (2011)
16. Joblin, M., Mauerer, W., Apel, S., Siegmund, J., Riehle, D.: From developer networks to verified communities: a fine-grained approach. In: International Conference on Software Engineering, pp. 563–573 (2015)
17. Kaiser, H.F.: The varimax criterion for analytic rotation in factor analysis. Psychometrika **23**(3), 187–200 (1958)
18. Kaiser, H.F.: An index of factorial simplicity. Psychometrika **39**(1), 31–36 (1974)
19. Kamola, M.: How to verify Conway's law for open source projects. IEEE Access **7**, 38469–38480 (2019). https://doi.org/10.1109/ACCESS.2019.2905671
20. Kumar, B.V., Hassebrook, L.: Performance measures for correlation filters. Appl. Opt. **29**(20), 2997–3006 (1990)
21. Lenarduzzi, V., Sievi-Korte, O.: On the negative impact of team independence in microservices software development. In: XP Conference (2018)
22. Meneely, A., Williams, L.: Socio-technical developer networks: should we trust our measurements? In: International Conference on Software Engineering, pp. 281–290 (2011)
23. Montandon, J.E., Valente, M.T., Silva, L.L.: Mining the technical roles of GitHub users. Inf. Softw. Technol. **131**, 106485 (2021)
24. Newman, S.: Building Microservices, 1st edn. O'Reilly Media Inc., Springfield (2015)
25. Ortu, M., Hall, T., Marchesi, M., Tonelli, R., Bowes, D., Destefanis, G.: Mining communication patterns in software development: a github analysis. In: International Conference on Predictive Models and Data Analytics in Software Engineering, PROMISE 2018, pp. 70–79 (2018)
26. Panichella, S., Bavota, G., Penta, M.D., Canfora, G., Antoniol, G.: How developers' collaborations identified from different sources tell us about code changes. In: International Conference on Software Maintenance and Evolution, pp. 251–260 (2014)
27. Qcon2022: Dark Energy, Dark Matter and the Microservices Patterns? (2022). https://shorturl.at/etHM5
28. Raymond, E.S., O'Reilly, T.: The Cathedral and the Bazaar, 1st edn. O'Reilly & Associates Inc., Springfield (1999)
29. Reinfurt, M.: The horror of microservices in small teams - and why you shouldn't build them (2021). https://shorturl.at/bgHKR
30. Richardson, C.: A pattern language for microservices (2021). https://shorturl.at/bGS34
31. Shi, K.: Establishing contributor roles within software repositories by mining architectural information (2021). https://fse.studenttheses.ub.rug.nl/25608/1/bCS_ShiK.pdf
32. Snedecor, G.W., Cochran, W.G.: Statistical Methods, 8th edn, vol. 54, pp. 71–82. Iowa State University Press, Ames (1989)
33. Spinellis, D., Kotti, Z., Kravvaritis, K., Theodorou, G., Louridas, P.: A dataset of enterprise-driven open source software. In: International Conference on Mining Software Repositories, pp. 533–537 (2020)

34. Wiese, I.S., et al.: Using contextual information to predict co-changes. J. Syst. Softw. **128**, 220–235 (2017)
35. Wohlin, C., Runeson, P., Höst, M., Ohlsson, M.C., Regnell, B., Wesslén, A.: Experimentation in Software Engineering. Springer, Heidelberg (2012). https://doi.org/10.1007/978-3-642-29044-2
36. Wolff, E.: Microservices Primer: A Short Overview. Leanpub (2021)

End-to-End Test Coverage Metrics in Microservice Systems: An Automated Approach

Amr S. Abdelfattah[1], Tomas Cerny[2]($\boxtimes$), Jorge Yero Salazar[1],
Austin Lehman[1], Joshua Hunter[1], Ashley Bickham[1], and Davide Taibi[3]

[1] Computer Science, Baylor University, One Bear Place, Waco, TX 97141, USA
amr_elsayed1@baylor.edu
[2] Systems and Industrial Engineering, University of Arizona, Tucson, AZ, USA
tcerny@arizona.edu
[3] University of Oulu, Oulu, Finland
davide.taibi@oulu.fi

Abstract. Microservice architecture gains momentum by fueling systems with cloud-native benefits, scalability, and decentralized evolution. However, new challenges emerge for end-to-end (E2E) testing. Testers who see the decentralized system through the user interface might assume their tests are comprehensive, covering all middleware endpoints scattered across microservices. However, they do not have instruments to verify such assumptions. This paper introduces test coverage metrics for evaluating the extent of E2E test suite coverage for microservice endpoints. Next, it presents an automated approach to compute these metrics to provide feedback on the completeness of E2E test suites. Furthermore, a visual perspective is provided to highlight test coverage across the system's microservices to guide on gaps in test suites. We implement a proof-of-concept tool and perform a case study on a well-established system benchmark showing it can generate conclusive feedback on test suite coverage over system endpoints.

Keywords: microservices · end-to-end testing · API tests · test quality

1 Introduction

Microservice architecture enables practitioners to build scalable software systems broken down into a collection of loosely coupled interacting services. Each service is responsible for a specific business capability and can be developed and deployed independently of other services. This allows for faster development cycles, easier maintenance, and better scalability.

However, the end-to-end testing of microservice systems can be challenging due to the system's distributed nature hidden from testers. During E2E system validation, testers primarily interact with the system through its user interface,

© IFIP International Federation for Information Processing 2023
Published by Springer Nature Switzerland AG 2023
G. A. Papadopoulos et al. (Eds.): ESOCC 2023, LNCS 14183, pp. 35–51, 2023.
https://doi.org/10.1007/978-3-031-46235-1_3

thereby concealing the underlying logical system structure. However, microservice architecture entails more intricate details compared to traditional monolithic systems, including multiple services, inter-dependencies, and continuous evolution. Testers may lack knowledge about the specific services being involved and executed within the system. Consequently, they may encounter difficulties in testing all possible scenarios. This complexity introduces challenges in E2E testing of microservice systems, as it obscures crucial details that can influence testing completeness and efficiency.

The extent to which a particular system's microservices are involved in individual E2E tests or E2E test suites should be recognized to give testers better insights into system coverage and test-to-microservice dependencies (i.e., test evolution). E2E tests interact with the system through the user interface which mediates the interaction to microservice endpoint level. Thus, associating tests with impacted microservice endpoints they interact with would provide testers with insights into how comprehensive their test suites are when contrasted to all system endpoints.

This paper aims to establish metrics for calculating the coverage of endpoints in E2E test suites their individual tests, and microservices. Furthermore, it aims to propose a practical method and measurement approach through a case study. This work considers microservice endpoints as the points of overlap between the logical system structure and the E2E tests. It proposes an automated approach mapping individual tests to system microservices and their endpoints to guide testers in test design completeness. With the detailed knowledge of test-to-endpoint associations, testers can better understand their test suite coverage and identify unobvious gaps.

This paper makes the following contributions in the context of microservices:

- Proposal of three metrics (Microservice endpoint coverage, Test case endpoint coverage, and Complete Test suite endpoint coverage) to assess the coverage of endpoints in E2E testing.
- Metric extraction process and proof-of-concept tool imlementation.
- A practical system case study deriving and validating the coverage metrics.

This paper elaborates on related work in Sect. 2 and describes the metrics and process in Sect. 3. A case study is detailed in Sect. 4 followed by a discussion in Sect. 5 and conclusions in Sect. 6.

2   Related Work

Various studies have identified the lack of assessment techniques for microservice systems. A systematic literature review by Ghani et al. [3] concluded that most articles focused on testing approaches for microservices lacked sufficient assessment and experimentation. Jiang et al. [5] emphasized the need for improved test management in microservice systems to enhance their overall quality.

Waseem et al. [9] conducted a survey and revealed that unit and E2E testing are the most commonly used strategies in the industry. However, the complexity of microservice systems presents challenges for their monitoring and testing, and there is currently no dedicated solution to address these issues. Similarly, Giamattei et al. [4] identified the monitoring of internal APIs as a challenge in black box testing microservice systems, advocating for further research in this area.

To address these gaps, it is crucial to develop an assistant tool that improves system testing and provides appropriate test coverage assessment methods. Corradini et al. [1] conducted an empirical comparison of automated black-box test case generation approaches specifically for REST APIs. They proposed a test coverage framework that relies on the API interface description provided by the OpenAPI specification. Within their framework, they introduced a set of coverage metrics, consisting of eight metrics (five request-related and three response-related), which assess the coverage of a test suite by calculating the ratio of tested elements to the total number of elements defined in the API. However, these metrics do not align well with the unique characteristics of microservice systems. They do not take into account the specific features of microservices, such as inter-service calls and components like API gateway testing.

Giamattei et al. [4] introduced MACROHIVE, a grey-box testing approach for microservices that automatically generates and executes test suites while analyzing the interactions among inter-service calls. Instead of using the commonly used tools such as SkyWalking or Jaeger, MACROHIVE builds its own infrastructure, which incurs additional overhead by requiring the deployment of a proxy for each microservice to monitor. It also involves implementing communication protocols for sending information packets during request-response collection. MACROHIVE employs combinatorial tests and measures the status code class and dependencies coverage of internal microservices. However, compared to our proposed approach, MACROHIVE lacks static analysis of service dependencies, relying solely on runtime data. In contrast, our approach extracts information statically from the source code, providing accurate measurements along with three levels of system coverage.

Ma et al. [6] utilized static analysis techniques and proposed the Graph-based Microservice Analysis and Testing (GMAT) approach. GMAT generates Service Dependency Graphs (SDG) to analyze the dependencies between microservices in the system. This approach enhances the understanding of interactions among different parts of the microservice system, supporting testing and development processes. GMAT leverages Swagger documentation to extract the SDG, and it traces service invocation chains from centralized system logs to identify successful and failed invocations. The GMAT approach calculates the coverage of service tests by determining the percentage of passed calls among all the calls, and it visually highlights failing tests by marking the corresponding dependency as yellow on the SDG. However, GMAT is tailored to test microservices using the Pact tool and its APIs. In contrast, our approach introduces three coverage metrics that focus on different levels of microservice system parts, emphasizing endpoints as fundamental elements of microservice interaction. While our approach doesn't consider the status code of each test, combining GMAT with our proposed approach could offer further insights for evaluating microservice testing and assessment criteria.

In summary, this paper tackles the gap in assessment techniques for microservice testing. It aims to introduce test coverage metrics and develop an analytical tool that can assess microservice systems and measure their test coverage.

3   The E2E Test Coverage Metrics

This section presents our proposed metrics and provides a comprehensive overview of our automated approach, outlining its stages for extracting the data required for calculating the metrics over systems. The objective is to assess E2E testing suites in achieving coverage of endpoints within microservices-based systems.

3.1   The Proposed Metrics Calculations

E2E testing involves test suites, where each test suite contains test cases that represent a series of steps or actions defining a specific test scenario. We introduce three metrics to assess the coverage of endpoints in microservice systems: microservice endpoint coverage, test case endpoint coverage, and complete test suite coverage. These metrics are described in detail below:

- **Microservice endpoint coverage:** determines the tested endpoints within each microservice. It is obtained by dividing the number of tested endpoints from all tests by the total number of endpoints in that microservice. This metric offers insights into the comprehensiveness of coverage for individual microservices. The formula for microservice endpoint coverage is:

$$C_{\text{ms}(i)} = \frac{|E_{\text{ms}(i)}^{\text{tested}}|}{|E_{\text{ms}(i)}|} \quad ;$$

  $C_{\text{ms}(i)}$- the coverage per microservice i,

  $E_{\text{ms}(i)}^{\text{tested}}$ - the set of tested endpoints in microservice i,

  $E_{\text{ms}(i)}$ - the set of all endpoints in microservice i.

- **Test case endpoint coverage:** gives a percentage of endpoints covered by each test case. It is calculated by dividing the number of endpoints covered by each test by the total number of endpoints in the system. This provides insights into the effectiveness of individual tests in covering the system's endpoints. The formula for test case endpoint coverage is:

$$C_{\text{test}(i)} = \frac{|E_{\text{test}(i)}^{\text{tested}}|}{|\bigcup_{j}^{m\_total} E_{\text{ms}(j)}|} \quad ;$$

$C_{\text{test}(i)}$ - the coverage per test i,

$E_{\text{test}(i)}^{\text{tested}}$ - the set of tested endpoints from test i,

m_total - the total number of microservices in the system,

$\bigcup_{j}^{m\_total} E_{\text{ms}(j)}$ - the set of all endpoints in the system.

- **Complete Test suite endpoint coverage:** determines the test suite overall coverage of the system by dividing the total number of unique endpoints covered by all tests by the total number of endpoints in the system. It provides insights into the completeness of test suites in covering all endpoints within the system. The formula for complete test suite endpoint coverage is:

$$C_{\text{suite}} = \frac{|\bigcup_{i}^{t\_total} E_{\text{test}(i)}^{tested}|}{|\bigcup_{j}^{m\_total} E_{\text{ms}(j)}|} \quad ;$$

C_{suite} - the complete test suite coverage,

m_total - the total number of microservices in the system,

t_total - the total number of tests in the test suite,

$\bigcup_{i}^{t\_total} E_{\text{test}(i)}^{tested}$ - the set of all tested endpoints from all tests,

$\bigcup_{j}^{m\_total} E_{\text{ms}(j)}$ - the set of all endpoints in the system.

To provide further clarification, consider a system consisting of three microservices (MS-1, MS-2, MS-3), each with two endpoints, with a test suite composed of two tests (Test-1, Test-2), as depicted in Fig. 1. In the example, the tests interact with endpoints through the user interface, which triggers the initiation of endpoint requests passed through the API gateway component. The example demonstrates that Test-1 calls two endpoints, one from MS-1 (E1.1) and one from MS-2 (E2.1). On the other hand, Test-2 calls two endpoints from MS-2 (E2.1, E2.2), E2.2 has an inter-service call to endpoint E3.1 in MS-3.

Applying our metrics, we can calculate the microservice endpoint coverage $(C_{\text{ms}(i)})$ for each microservice. For MS-1 and MS-3, only one out of their two endpoints is tested throughout all tests, resulting in a coverage of 50% $(C_{\text{ms}(1)} = C_{\text{ms}(3)} = \frac{1}{2})$ for each. However, for MS-2, both of its endpoints are tested at least once, leading to a coverage of 100% $(C_{\text{ms}(2)} = \frac{2}{2})$.

Next, we calculate the test case endpoint coverage $(C_{\text{test}(i)})$ per each test. Test-1 covers two out of the six endpoints in the system, resulting in a coverage of approximately 33.3% ($C_{\text{test}(1)} = \frac{2}{6}$). Test-2 covers three distinct end-points, resulting in a coverage of 50% ($C_{\text{test}(2)} = \frac{3}{6}$). It is important to highlight that Test-2 contains an inter-service call to endpoint E3.1, which is considered in our approach.

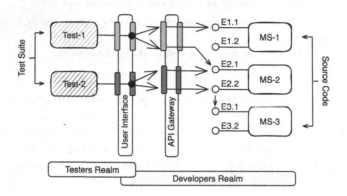

Fig. 1. Calculation Clarification Example

Finally, we can calculate the complete test suite endpoint coverage (C_{suite}) of the system. Out of the six endpoints in the system, four distinct endpoints are tested from the two tests. This results in ≈ 66.6% coverage ($C_{\text{suite}} = \frac{4}{6}$).

3.2 The Metrics Extraction Process

To automatically collect the data for calculating the test coverage metrics, we propose to employ a combination of static and dynamic analysis methods.

The static analysis phase focuses on examining the source code to extract information about the implemented endpoints in the system. The dynamic analysis phase involves inspecting system logs and traces to identify the endpoints called by the automation tests. By combining the data obtained from both analyses, the approach applies the proposed metrics to generate the E2E endpoint coverage, and then it provides two visualization approaches to depict the coverage over the system representation. This process involves the following four stages as illustrated in Fig. 2:

Stage 1. Endpoint Extraction From Source Code (Static Analysis).
Stage 2. Endpoint Extraction From Log Traces (Dynamic Analysis).
Stage 3. Coverage Calculation.
Stage 4. Coverage Visualization.

We will delve into the details of each stage to demonstrate the approach.

Stage 1: Expoint Extraction from Source Code (Static Analysis): Our approach applies a static analysis approach to the system's source code to extract the employed endpoints in each microservice ($E_{\mathrm{ms}(i)}$). Static analysis refers to the process of analyzing the syntax and structure of code without executing it in order to extract information about the system. As depicted in Fig. 3, initially, microservices can be divided and detected from the system codebase. Each microservice's codebase is then processed by the *endpoint extraction process*, which produces the endpoints corresponding to each microservice.

The identification of API endpoints typically relies on specific frameworks or libraries. For example, in the Java Spring framework, annotations such as `@RestController` and `@RequestMapping` are commonly used. This ensures consistency in metadata identification. Code analysis extracts metadata attributes about each endpoint, including the path, HTTP method, parameters, and return type. However, identification of endpoints can be performed across platforms as demonstrated by Schiewe et al. [7] or accomplished by frameworks like Swagger[1]

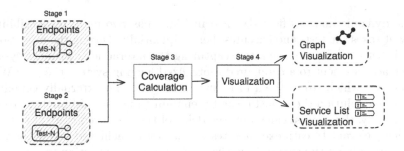

Fig. 2. The proposed approach overview

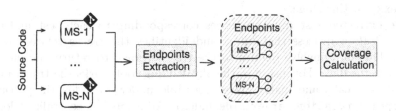

Fig. 3. Stage 1: Static analysis flow

As a result, a list of endpoints is generated and organized according to the respective microservice they belong to. This comprehensive list of endpoints becomes one of the inputs for our *coverage calculation process*, where it combines the output of the dynamic analysis flow.

---

[1] Swagger https://swagger.io.

Stage 2: Endpoint Extraction from Log Traces (Dynamic Analysis):
We utilize dynamic analysis to identify the endpoints called during the execution of each test case in test suites ($E_{test(i)}^{tested}$. It also identifies the microservices containing these tested endpoints ($E_{ms(i)}^{tested}$). The analyzed system is executed to observe its runtime behavior and transactions. This analysis involves running multiple E2E tests and capturing the traces that occur, as illustrated in Fig. 4.

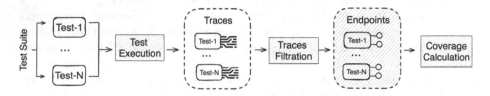

Fig. 4. Stage 2: Dynamic analysis flow

The dynamic analysis flow sketched in Fig. 4 has two main responsibilities. Firstly, it takes the tests and executes them sequentially. During the execution of the E2E tests, traces are generated, capturing the interactions with the system. These traces are sent to a configured centralized logging system (i.e., SkyWalking, Jaeger), which stores them in its own storage, or an externally configured data storage solution (i.e., Elasticsearch), enabling analysis and further processing. Secondly, the process calculates the delta of the produced traces to identify the traces relevant to each executed test. This can be achieved in various ways, such as recording a timestamp from the start of a test's execution to its completion, retrieving the traces after each test execution and calculating the difference based on the latest track record, or sending a dynamically generated trace before and after the execution of each test to mark the start and end. In our approach, we have employed the first strategy, as it avoids unnecessary processing and complexity at this stage.

The extracted test trace sequences corresponding to each test undergo a *traces filtration* process that filters and identifies the traces related to endpoints. This may involve queries to the trace storage to return specific trace indexes in the data. For instance, the SkyWalking tool marks the traces involving endpoint calls and makes them accessible under an index (in particular, sw_endpoint_relation_server_side index). Additionally, centralized logging systems encode the data records using Base64[2] when sending them to external storage like Elasticsearch. Therefore, this step may include an additional decoding process if needed to detect the endpoints. These endpoint-related trace records contain information about the source and destination endpoints involved in the call relationship.

As a result, a list of endpoints is generated and organized according to the respective test suite they belong to. This list of endpoints becomes the second

---

[2] Base64: https://developer.mozilla.org/en-US/docs/Glossary/Base64.

input for the *coverage calculation process*, where it is combined with the output of the static analysis stage.

Stage 3: Coverage Calculation: This stage combines the extracted equations from the previous two stages to calculate the three metrics of coverage $(C_{\text{ms}(i)}, C_{\text{test}(i)}, C_{\text{suite}})$.

A challenge arises when matching the extracted system endpoints from the source code with those extracted from the traces. Since traces contain invoked endpoints with arguments' values, while those identified by static analysis hold parameter types and names. A similar challenge has been accounted for when profiling systems using log analysis and matching log lines with logging statements in the source code [11]. The source code contains a log message template with parameters, and execution logs contain a message with values from the execution context, which is not a direct match (i.e., source code `log.info('calling {a} from {b}')` vs. a contextual log statement `'calling for from bar'` where both a and b are interpreted). Zhao et al. have identified all code log statements to extract templates that could be matched using regular expressions to identify and match the parameter types whose values are present in the log output.

In our approach, we employ signature matching to solve the challenge. It involves comparing the endpoint method signature with the data and parameters exchanged during REST calls communication to detect and verify the authenticity and matches of the requests. Thus, to determine which system endpoints were called by the test we consider the comparison of extracted attributes of the endpoints (such as path, request type, and parameter list) from the source code with the REST calls extracted from the test traces. This matching process helps to establish the coverage levels and determine which endpoints were effectively exercised by the tests.

Stage 4: Coverage Visualization: The approach offers two ways to visualize these coverage metrics. The first displays a list of microservices, with each microservice showing its endpoints. Covered endpoints are marked in green, while missed endpoints are marked in red, as demonstrated in Fig. 7a. The second representation utilizes the service dependency graph, where microservices are represented as nodes, and the dependencies between them are shown as edges. The nodes in the graph are color-coded based on the coverage percentage, allowing users to visually observe the coverage on the holistic system view depicting service dependencies, as exampled in Fig. 7b. These techniques help in visualizing the two metrics of $C_{\text{ms}(i)}$ and $C_{\text{test}(i)}$. Thus, these coverage calculations and visualizations provide valuable insights into the extent of test coverage achieved by automation frameworks in the context of microservices, enabling users to assess the effectiveness of their testing efforts and identify areas that require improvement.

4   Case Study

To demonstrate the completeness of our approach, we implemented a prototype and conducted a case study on an open-source system benchmark and an
E2E test suite designed for the same system. We calculated our metrics on the
testbench and compared the results with a manually calculated ground truth.

4.1   Proof of Concept Implementation

This section describes the implementation of a prototype[3] to showcase the four
phases of the proposed approach. We focused on statically analyzing Java-based
project source codes that use the Java Spring Cloud framework, an open-source
framework that is widely used for building cloud-native applications. It provides
developers with a comprehensive set of tools and libraries to build scalable and
resilient applications in the Java ecosystem.

For the endpoint extraction from source code (Stage 1), we utilized the open-
source JavaParser[4] library. It allowed us to parse Java source code files, generate
an Abstract Syntax Tree (AST) representation, and traverse it to detect spring
annotations such as @GetMapping and @PostMapping. We extracted the relevant
attributes once the endpoints were detected.

For the endpoint extraction from log traces (Stage 2), we utilized Apache
Maven, a build automation tool for Java projects, to execute our JUnit test
suites. JUnit, a widely adopted unit testing framework, offers seamless integration with various automation test frameworks, including Selenium. On the
other hand, we focused on extracting logs and traces from Elasticsearch, which
is widely adopted as a central component in the ELK[5] (Elasticsearch, Logstash,
Kibana) stack. We used the Elasticsearch Java High-Level REST Client[6], which
offers a convenient way to interact with Elasticsearch. It provided a QueryBuilder
class to construct queries for searching and filtering data, such as creating a query
to retrieve the logs that are between specific start and end timestamps.

Then, the prototype performs the coverage calculation (Stage 3). It integrates
the results of the static and dynamic processes, and applies the proposed metrics. For the coverage visualization (Stage 4), we provided the two visualization
approaches discussed earlier. We implemented a web application[7] that presents
the information in an expandable list view for easy navigation. To integrate with
the service dependency graph visualization, we utilized the Prophet library[8], an
open-source project that generates the graph from source code. Additionally, we

---

[3] Prototype: https://github.com/cloudhubs/test-coverage-backend.
[4] JavaParser: https://github.com/javaparser/javaparser.
[5] ELK: https://aws.amazon.com/what-is/elk-stack.
[6] Elasticsearch Java Client: https://www.elastic.co/guide/en/elasticsearch/client/
java-rest/current/java-rest-high.html.
[7] Coverage Visualizer: https://github.com/cloudhubs/test-coverage-frontend.
[8] Prophet: https://github.com/cloudhubs/graal-prophet-utils.

utilized the visualizer library[9], which offers a tailored 3D microservices visualization for service dependency graphs.

4.2 Benchmark and Test Suites

To ensure unbiased testing of our application, we utilized an open-source testbench consisting of the TrainTicket system and associated test suites.

TrainTicket [2] is a microservice-based train ticket booking system that is built using the Java Spring framework. It uses the standard annotations for defining the endpoints and uses the *RestTemplate* Java client to initiate requests to endpoints. This benchmark consists of 41 Java-based microservices and makes use of Apache SkyWalking[10] as its application performance monitoring system.

In order to run the TrainTicket system and execute tests on it, certain configuration fixes were necessary. To address this, a fork[11] of the TrainTicket repository was created, specifically from the 1.0.0 release. This fork incorporated the necessary fixes and a deployment script. TrainTicket integrates with Elasticsearch, allowing our prototype to utilize SkyWalking for forwarding system logs to Elasticsearch for additional processing and analysis.

For the test suites, we utilized an open-source test benchmark[12] published in [8]. This benchmark aims to test the same version of the TrainTicket system. It contains 11 E2E test cases using the Selenium framework.

4.3 Ground Truth

To validate the completeness of our approach, we performed a manual analysis to construct the ground truth for the test benches. The complete results of the ground truth are published in an open accessed dataset[13]. This involved manual extraction of the data related to the first two stages in our proposed process in Sect. 3.2, as follows: endpoint extraction from source code and endpoint extraction from log traces.

For Stage 1, we validated the endpoints extracted during the static analysis by manually inspecting the source code of the microservices' controller classes. This allowed us to identify and extract information such as the endpoint's path, request type, parameter list, and return type. This process extracted 262 defined endpoints in the TrainTicket testbench codebase.

For Stage 2, we validated the endpoints extracted during the dynamic analysis by examining the Selenium test suites. Since the Selenium tests do not explicitly reference endpoints but rather perform UI-based actions, we manually analyzed the logs generated by the tests, which were stored in Elasticsearch. These logs contained encoded information about the source and destination endpoints,

---

[9] 3D Visualizer: https://github.com/cloudhubs/graal_mvp.
[10] SkyWalking: https://skywalking.apache.org/docs.
[11] TrainTicket: https://github.com/cloudhubs/train-ticket/tree/v1.0.1.
[12] Test benchmark: https://github.com/cloudhubs/microservice-tests.
[13] Dataset: https://zenodo.org/record/8055457.

which we decoded and filtered to extract the list of endpoints called during the tests. It produced 171 unique endpoints from the logs.

4.4   Case Study Results

We began the execution by running the deployment script to set up the TrainTicket system on a local instance. Subsequently, our prototype executed the test cases from the provided test benchmark, generated the list of called endpoints and calculated the test coverage according to the described metrics.

The results of the experiment execution revealed a total of 171 unique endpoints extracted from a set of 953 log records generated during the execution of the test cases, out of which 119 endpoints are actual endpoints within the system, 52 endpoints that are related to API-gateway calls. The complete data analysis phases with their results are published in a dataset (see footnote 13). This dataset contains the complete calculations of $C_{ms(i)}$, $C_{test(i)}$ metrics.

In terms of evaluating the completeness of our prototype, this case study confirmed that we captured all the endpoints declared in the ground truth. The prototype successfully captured all 262 implemented endpoints in the system, demonstrating the completeness of Stage 1 outcome. For Stage 2 completeness, the prototype extracted all 171 endpoints. Out of the total 171 endpoint calls, our prototype identified 52 distinct calls associated with the API gateway, which are not considered actual endpoints in the system.

Through the complete data extraction, we calculate the complete test suite coverage to be approximately 45.42% ($C_{suite} = \frac{119}{262} \approx 45.42\%$). The summary statistics for the metrics calculations are provided in Table 1.

The calculation of $C_{test(i)}$ shows that the maximum coverage achieved by a test case in the study is approximately 15.27%. This was observed in the Booking test case, which made 53 calls to 40 unique endpoints in the system. On the other hand, the minimum coverage is approximately 1.14%, which occurred in the Login test case that only called three endpoints. The analysis shows that the average test case endpoint coverage is approximately 7.29%, while the most common coverage among the test cases is approximately 7.25%. This coverage was observed in the following five test cases: AdminConfigList, ContactList, PriceList, AdminStationList, and AdminTrainList. Figure 5 illustrates the endpoint coverage achieved by the 11 test cases, along with the average coverage for better measurement.

Table 1. Summary Statistics of Coverage Metrics

Metric	Coverage (%)			
C_{suite}	45.42			
	Minimum	Average	Maximum	Mode
$C_{ms(i)}$	0	44.5	100	25
$C_{test(i)}$	1.14	7.29	15.27	7.25

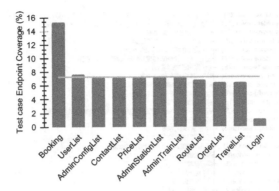

Fig. 5. Test case Endpoint Coverage in the Benchmark Test cases ($C_{\text{test}(i)}$)

The calculation of $C_{\text{ms}(i)}$ reveals that the maximum coverage is 100%, observed in the `ts-verification-code-service` which has two endpoints covered by the test cases. On the other hand, the minimum coverage is 0%, indicating that the test suite completely missed testing any endpoints in the following four microservices: *ts-wait-order-service, ts-preserve-other-service, ts-notification-service,* and *ts-food-delivery-service.* The average microservice endpoint coverage is approximately 44.5%, while the mode statistics show that 25% is the most common coverage, observed in the following four microservices: *ts-travel2-service, ts-payment-service, ts-route-plan-service,* and *ts-order-other-service.* The complete calculations for each microservice are illustrated in Fig. 6.

The metrics calculations are visualized using two visualization approaches, as shown in Fig. 7a and Fig. 7b. One with per service view and the other providing the holistic service dependency overview in the context of endpoint coverage. For example, the `ts-config-service` microservice has an approximate coverage of 83.33%, missing only one out of six endpoints. This information is also represented in yellow color in the 3D graph visualization, where the color of each node corresponds to the coverage percentage of the respective microservice.

5 Discussion

Our approach has shown promising results in mitigating E2E test degradation and contributing to the continuous reliability and quality assurance of decentralized microservice systems. While further comprehensive data analysis is ongoing, initial findings indicate a positive impact. It determines the log traces connecting tests with endpoints from the current system and a current test suite by automated means. Such traces can help testers manage change propagation as it directly indicates a co-change dependency between specific microservices or endpoints and particular tests. Furthermore, integrating it with CI/CD pipelines would make it an ideal tool to ensure coverage across system evolution changes. On the other hand, it is crucial to consider the context in which the approach

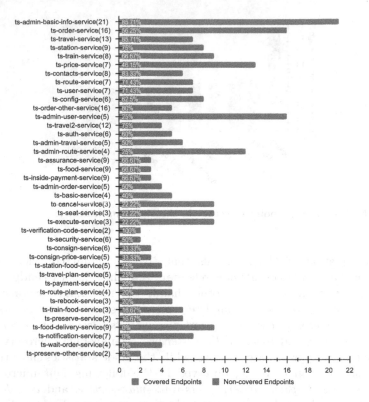

Fig. 6. Microservice Endpoint Coverage in the Benchmark System ($C_{ms(i)}$) *The numbers in parentheses indicate the total number of endpoints in each ms.*

is applied, as the user interface may not interact with all middleware endpoints. This can be reflected in the provided metrics, indicating that the E2E test might not achieve 100% coverage. At the same time, it raises the question of whether the remaining endpoints represent the smell known as *Nobody Home* where the wiring is missing from the user interface, or possibly the endpoints are outdated or dead code.

It is worth noting that microservices often implement `isAlive` endpoints for health checks. While some libraries, like Hystrix, can automatically generate these endpoints, some systems implement them manually. As an example, Train-Ticket implemented 39 endpoints that were not utilized in the user interface, rendering them meaningless. Nevertheless, validating these endpoints can guarantee that the system is correctly initialized.

5.1 Threats to Validity

In this section, we address the potential validity threats to our approach. We adopt Wohlin's taxonomy [10], which encompasses construction, external, internal, and conclusion threats to validity, as a framework for our analysis.

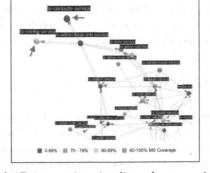

(a) Microservice endpoint list

(b) 3D interactive visualizer shows service dependencies (cropped view)

Fig. 7. Microservices endpoint coverage visualization (full pictures (see footnote 7))

A potential **construction validity threat** arises from the dependency on static analysis for endpoint extraction and dynamic analysis of centralized traces generated by E2E tests. It includes missing or non-standard source code and a lack of support for centralized traces, which can hinder our approach.

Our prototype is currently implemented for specific programming languages and frameworks. However, it is important to note that the methodology itself is not limited to these specifications. It can be adapted and applied to other languages and frameworks, mitigating construction threats related to dependencies. Moreover, asynchronous messaging poses a potential risk to test execution by causing ghost endpoint call trace events. To mitigate this threat, potential approaches include disabling asynchronous services or conducting repeated test executions to minimize the impact.

Internal validity threats arise from potential mismatches between the extracted endpoint signatures from the source code and the traces. Although overloads are infrequent, inaccurate matching may occur due to trace values not aligning precisely with the defined types in the code. For example, if a trace contains an integer in the URL, it may match with an integer parameter type even if the corresponding endpoint has a string parameter type. Moreover, Multiple authors collaborated to ensure accurate data and calculations. They independently verified and cross-validated the results, rotating across validation processes to minimize learning effects.

To address **external validity threats**, our case study utilized a widely recognized open-source benchmark to evaluate its endpoints coverage using our proposed approach. Still, it is important to acknowledge that the results and conclusions drawn from this specific benchmark may not fully represent the entire range of microservices systems that adhere to different standards and practices.

One potential **conclusion validity threat** is that our tool was tested on an open-source project rather than an industry project. However, we aimed to address this by selecting an open-source project that employed widely-used frameworks in the industry. Furthermore, to ensure the reliability and consistency of our results, we performed the case study in multiple environments and confirmed that the outcomes remained consistent.

6 Conclusion

Despite the broad adoption of microservices for software solutions, there are open challenges practitioners face with E2E testing. While testers might assume complete test coverage, verification mechanisms on the actual state of test completeness within the system are missing. We sought to define metrics and establish an approach to calculate the E2E test suites coverage of microservice system endpoints. Our approach determines the connection between individual tests and microservice endpoints, which are the system entry points for user interfaces used by E2E testers. We performed a case study on an established system benchmark and a test suite aiming for full coverage, revealing that the achieved coverage fell significantly short of being comprehensive.

In future work, we will explore system and test suite evolution, evaluating how our approach guides co-coupling between system changes and tests to ensure quality assurance and reduce test suite degradation. We also plan to expand our metrics to encompass different test paths within the endpoints.

Acknowledgements. This material is supported by the National Science Foundation under Grant No. 2245287 and Grant No. 349488 (MuFAno) from the Academy of Finland.

References

1. Corradini, D., Zampieri, A., Pasqua, M., Ceccato, M.: Empirical comparison of black-box test case generation tools for restful APIs. In: 2021 IEEE 21st International Working Conference on Source Code Analysis and Manipulation (SCAM), pp. 226–236 (2021). https://doi.org/10.1109/SCAM52516.2021.00035
2. FudanSELab: Home. https://github.com/FudanSELab/train-ticket/wiki
3. Ghani, I., Wan-Kadir, W.M., Mustafa, A., Imran Babir, M.: Microservice testing approaches: a systematic literature review. Int. J. Integr. Eng. 11(8), 65–80 (2019). https://publisher.uthm.edu.my/ojs/index.php/ijie/article/view/3856
4. Giamattei, L., Guerriero, A., Pietrantuono, R., Russo, S.: Automated grey-box testing of microservice architectures. In: 2022 IEEE 22nd International Conference on Software Quality, Reliability and Security (QRS), pp. 640–650 (2022)
5. Jiang, P., Shen, Y., Dai, Y.: Efficient software test management system based on microservice architecture. In: 2022 IEEE 10th Joint International Information Technology and Artificial Intelligence Conference, vol. 10, pp. 2339–2343 (2022)
6. Ma, S.P., Fan, C.Y., Chuang, Y., Lee, W.T., Lee, S.J., Hsueh, N.L.: Using service dependency graph to analyze and test microservices. In: 2018 IEEE 42nd Annual Computer Software and Applications Conference, vol. 2, pp. 81–86 (2018)

7. Schiewe, M., Curtis, J., Bushong, V., Cerny, T.: Advancing static code analysis with language-agnostic component identification. IEEE Access **10**, 30743–30761 (2022). https://doi.org/10.1109/ACCESS.2022.3160485
8. Smith, S., et al.: Benchmarks for end-to-end microservices testing (2023)
9. Waseem, M., Liang, P., Shahin, M., Di Salle, A., Márquez, G.: Design, monitoring, and testing of microservices systems: the practitioners' perspective. J. Syst. Softw. **182**, 111061 (2021)
10. Wohlin, C., Runeson, P., Hst, M., Ohlsson, M.C., Regnell, B., Wessln, A.: Experimentation in Software Engineering. Springer, Heidelberg (2012). https://doi.org/10.1007/978-3-642-29044-2
11. Zhao, X., et al.: lprof: a non-intrusive request flow profiler for distributed systems. In: 11th {USENIX} Symposium on Operating Systems Design and Implementation, pp. 629–644 (2014)

Quality of Service

Time-Aware QoS Web Service Selection Using Collaborative Filtering: A Literature Review

Ezdehar Jawabreh[1,2]([✉]) [iD] and Adel Taweel[1] [iD]

[1] Department of Computer Science, Birzeit University, Birzeit, Palestine
{eajawabreh,ataweel}@birzeit.edu
[2] Palestine Polytechnic University, Hebron, Palestine
ezdehar@ppu.edu

Abstract. The large increase in the number of available Web services makes the selection of suitable services a big challenge. Several methods have been developed to predict the Quality of Service (QoS) values in order to solve the service selection problem. However, these methods face many limitations that hinder their prediction accuracy. A particular issue is the dynamic nature of the service environment, which causes variations in QoS values (due to network load, hardware problems, etc.). To overcome, QoS selection methods have utilized contextual information, of the surrounding environments, such as service invocation time and/or user and service locations. Amongst these methods are Collaborative Filtering(CF). In the last few years, several CF methods have augmented service invocation time in their prediction process, forming, what is popularly known as, time-aware CF methods. However, current research lacks a dedicated and comprehensive literature review on time-aware CF prediction methods. To this end, this paper analysed the literature and reviewed forty (40) most prominent studies in this field. It provides a thematic categorization of these studies and an insightful analysis detailing their objectives, benefits, and limitations. It identifies the main research gaps and possible research directions for future work. The literature review provides a state-of-the-art update for researchers pursuing research in service oriented computing.

Keywords: Web service · QoS · Time-aware · Prediction · Collaborative Filtering (CF)

1 Introduction

Service Oriented Architecture (SOA) has become a promising paradigm in system engineering. Many systems are built by integrating services as their basic units of building. With many service providers, we witness a proliferation in the number of services and selecting the right service amongst the many providing similar functionality is a challenging task. To optimize, one approach,

© IFIP International Federation for Information Processing 2023
Published by Springer Nature Switzerland AG 2023
G. A. Papadopoulos et al. (Eds.): ESOCC 2023, LNCS 14183, pp. 55–69, 2023.
https://doi.org/10.1007/978-3-031-46235-1_4

services are selected based on their Quality of Service (QoS) attributes (i.e. non-functional properties, such as response time, throughput, etc.). However, some QoS attributes are not stable, as they are declared by the service provider. For example, in the well-known real QoS dataset WSDREAM [43], the response time attribute fluctuates around a range of [0 s-20 s]. So predicting dynamic QoS attributes is a crucial task that has gained research interest in the last decade.

In a dynamic environment, a user may receive different QoS values from the same service due to changes in the service load (number of clients) and network conditions (e.g. congestion) along with time, so time is considered a crucial factor that affects the accuracy of prediction. In response, time-aware Collaborative Filtering (CF) methods have been proposed for predicting QoS in such environments. The recent research witnessed a clear orientation toward utilizing these types of methods for QoS prediction, actually various reasons caused this orientation: first, they have achieved a remarkable improvement in the prediction accuracy due to their ability to augment various contextual information related to users and services, [29,33,49]. Second, they have proved their usability in different applications in the service computing field such as service selection, composition, adaptation, and fault tolerance [50]. Third, they have the ability to leverage large historical data to make predictions with respect to current or future times. Lastly, they can accommodate the recent changes in the dynamic environment, such as new incoming QoS values or new incoming users and services.

Due to the aforementioned points, we performed a comprehensive literature review that tackled time-aware QoS prediction in CF methods. Our review was performed in a systematic manner, we searched four known digital scientific libraries, including IEEExplore, Springer, ScienceDirect, and ACM. The review included studies published in the years between 2011 and 2022. Two inclusion criteria were used to limit the scope of this review which were: the inclusion of studies that proposed a time-aware QoS prediction method, and the proposed method should be a CF one. In the first criterion, a method was considered time-aware if it predicted QoS with respect to the current time or if it forecasted QoS in the future time. In the second criterion, a method was considered CF if it exploited data of other users and services when making predictions.

In the end, we identified a total of 40 prominent studies that reflect the state-of-the-art. We categorized them thematically into three categories: 1)time-aware neighborhood CF, 2) time-aware model-based CF, and 3) time-aware hybrid approaches. To the best of our knowledge, this is the first literature review that is dedicated to time-aware CF methods, the previous work in CF discussed time-aware methods within the general context of other types. The specialization in our review is beneficial for researchers who seek comprehensive state-of-the-art time-aware methods. Indeed, we identified the main research challenges that face researchers in time-aware CF, and we provided potential research directions that guide researchers for further research in this area.

The rest of the review is organized as follows: Sect. 2 presents the related work. Section 3 describes our classification and the approaches under each category. Section 4 discusses research challenges and directions. Finally, we conclude our work in Sect. 5.

2   Related Work

CF methods have received the attention of researchers in the last decade. There are several studies that reviewed and summarized these methods. These studies are general and not dedicated to any specific type, however, this literature review is dedicated only to the time-awareness CF methods, and to the best of our knowledge there are no reviews that have been conducted in this field. However, we will discuss these general studies according to their relevance to the topic.

In [45], the authors provided a survey about Web Service QoS prediction via CF, they categorized these methods in two levels: at the first level, they used the general categorization as neighborhood, model-based, and hybrid, at the second level the methods under each general category were further categorized according to what type of contextual data they incorporated, such as location, time or other. In addition, they discussed the forefront research issues like adaptability, credibility, and privacy-preserving.

The work in [7] also provided a survey about QoS Web service prediction methods, the authors categorized methods into the known general categories: neighborhood, model-based, and hybrid. A special section was dedicated to time-aware collaborative methods, where they discussed a set of popular methods in a nutshell. In [22], the authors provided an overview of the Web service recommendation system, they differentiated between recommendations and predictions. They also provided explanations of different types of CF, like user-based, item-based, model-based, personalized, and location-aware.

Another approach that accounts for time in service selection is the time series forecasting approach. This approach can statistically forecast the QoS values in the future, famous methods in this type are the Moving Average (MA) method, AR (Auto Regressive), ARIMA (Auto Regressive Integrated with Moving Average). However, this approach is not a CF-based approach, since it works for each individual pair of user-service, so it is out of the scope of this review. Despite this point, we found that some of the hybrid CF methods utilized the time series method. In the following study [27] the authors provided a comprehensive survey about QoS time series modeling and forecasting. They selected a set of studies and discussed issues like the addressed problem, the proposed approach, the considered performance measure, and the QoS time series dataset, also they discussed the insufficiency of these studies.

3   Time-Aware Collaborative Filtering (CF) Methods: Review

Time-aware CF methods are classified thematically into three categories: time-aware neighborhood methods, time-aware model-based methods, and time-aware hybrid methods. This classification of CF corresponds to the different time-awareness aspects of QoS prediction. The following subsections present the literature review of the different methods for each.

3.1   Time-Aware Neighbourhood Collaborative Filtering

The methods under this section used the traditional CF computation in both similarity and prediction measurements, however, to be time-aware methods they have to capture the dynamic change of QoS similarity over time. The time-aware similarity can be computed using one of two approaches: first, using the time decay function as a weighting major for the effectiveness of QoS values, and second, using the time interval slots approach. Next, we provide more details about the studies under each approach.

Time Decay Approach. The authors in [8] used an exponential decay function whose value decreases as the time span between two related QoS increases or as the time span between the current time and two related QoS increases. They alleviated the data sparsity problem by using the random walk algorithm, which discovered the indirect user and service similarities. However, authors in [35] argued that using non-linear decay functions alone is not sufficient for evaluating the effectiveness of QoS values, so they designed a hybrid decay function, of both linear and non-linear. Similarly, the study in [6] has used the exponential time decay function, but a novel idea is added, which aims to increase weights for QoS values that seemed to be too small or too large in user similarity calculation. They also modeled the correlation between user and service locations before calculating the similarity in order to increase prediction accuracy.

Time Interval Approach. The time interval approach was used with average similarity computation. This method divides the historical QoS data into time slots and created a matrix of users and services in each slot. It computes similarity in each time slot and the final value of similarity at the current time is the average of similarities in all time slots. In a study done in [37], the authors calculated user and service similarity in a static number of time slots determined by a variable named d, which was a parameter used to reduce the searching space. The same authors extended their work and introduced a time and location-aware method in [38]. Their new method used location-based clusters of users and services in order to alleviate scalability problems. In [14], the authors tried to improve the work done in [37]. They used a clustering approach that determined dynamically the size of time slots instead of being static.

Another work in [39] introduced a novel approach named CluCF. This work extended the studies [37,38]. The authors alleviated the data sparsity problem. They converted the sparse user, service, and time tensor into a high-density user-service matrix, this matrix was converted into userCluster-service matrix and user-serviceCluster matrix. The clustering was based on location data. In the end, a hybrid prediction with weighted parameters is computed from both user and service predictions. In this method, the clusters can be updated when new users or services are introduced, however, it had a trade-off between scalability and prediction accuracy.

Later on, [20,29] improved the final similarity measure by using weighting functions and this achieved a better improvement over the average similarity measure used in the aforementioned studies. So first, in [20], a new approach was used to calculate the service similarity in the historical data. They used CAN-DECOMP/PARAFAC (CP) tensor decomposition to alleviate the data sparsity problem, and they assigned weights to global and temporal neighborhood services. Second, in [29], the user and service similarities were measured in a set of time slots, to compute the final similarity, the authors used a weighted decay function, which emphasized the similarity effect of recent time slots. In addition, they introduced a novel approach that searched for the most similar user in each time slot.

3.2 Time-Aware Model-Based Collaborative Filtering

Time-aware model-based methods represent a large number of studies in CF methods. They depend on training a model with a large set of historical QoS data. The trained model can be used later for predicting QoS. They are further classified into three subcategories: latent factors methods, clustering, machine learning methods, and deep learning methods.

Latent Factors Methods. Latent factors methods are based on the assumption that the user-service matrix can be factorized into low-rank latent factor matrices, by utilizing these matrices the missing QoS can be predicted. It is worth noting that all studies in this section used latent factorization, however, some of them also used traditional CF or clustering in addition to latent factorization.

In the year 2011, Y. Zhang et al. [43] introduced the first time-aware CF method which was named WSPred. This method created a tensor of three dimensions: user, services, and time. In order to predict missing QoS data, it performed a tensor factorization that learned the latent factors of users, and services in specific time intervals. The main contribution of their work was the data used in the tensor, which was real data that had been collected and used for the first time. It is known now as WSDREAM dataset2 [46] and it had become a well-known benchmark in the research community.

Later on, similar work was introduced in [41]. The authors used a Non-negative Tensor Factorization (NTF) approach. The approach used CANDE-COMP/PARAFAC (CP) factorization with consideration to the non-negativity property of QoS data. It decomposed the user, service, and time tensor into three non-negative latent matrices to get an approximation for the temporal QoS values. Moreover, the approach was evaluated using their own collected dataset, which was a tensor of size $343 \times 5817 \times 32$ user-service-time.

The same authors introduced another work in [40]. They used a triadic factorization approach on a user, service, and time tensor. The novelty in their approach was providing a mechanism to reduce the memory space needed to store the sparse data in the high dimensional tensor. To do so, they proposed two methods: Tucker Decomposition (TD) and the coordinate approach, the former achieved a remarkable memory space reduction. They evaluated their approach using a tensor of size $408 \times 5473 \times 56$ user-service-time.

One of the main limitations in studies [40,41,43] was making predictions offline, which means once the models are trained, they are unable to deal with new incoming QoS data. To overcome this limitation, the study in [42] proposed an Incremental Tensor Factorization (ITF) method, the ITF is based on the incremental approach of Singular Value Decomposition (SVD) and Tucker Decomposition (TD). The new approach had the ability to update prediction when new QoS data arrives while preserving the scalability and space efficiency properties. It was evaluated on a tensor of size: 408 users and 5,473 Web services at 240 time periods, and it achieved higher accuracy than the offline methods.

In [50], the authors used Adaptive Matrix Factorization (AMF) method that made QoS prediction for candidate services in run-time service adaptation. A set of well-designed steps were followed to achieve the requirements of accuracy, efficiency, and robustness. The method performed matrix factorization for each time slot, with the ability to learn online and to update its parameters using adaptive weights as new QoS data arrives or as new users and services come.

In [21], the authors used a hybrid method of both traditional neighborhood CF and latent factors in order to increase prediction accuracy. In the traditional neighborhood CF part, they used a service-based similarity measure that distinguished between static and temporal QoS attributes. In the latent factor part, they used CANDECOMP/PARAFAC (CP) decomposition on the user, service, and time tenor. The final prediction was a weighted addition of the two parts.

In [17], the study used the CP factorization of user-service-time tensor by applying non-negativity constraint on QoS data. The important contribution of this study was improving the prediction accuracy by several steps including a linear bias for both user, service, and time to model the temporal changes in data, using multiplicative learning rule for parameter optimization, and using of altering direction method in the training process.

In [34], authors provided an outlier resilient prediction method that used Cauchy loss for measuring the prediction errors. However, they extended their method by providing time-aware prediction by using CP factorization approach. Also, they added the non-negativity constraint on QoS data, which caused them to use the Multiplicative Updating (MU) algorithm to optimize the parameters.

In [28], the authors modeled the effect of temporal changes on service recommendation at three levels: users, services, and preferences. They used a latent factor decomposition that had a bias shifting for each one of the mentioned levels. They used the implicit feedback from users, which was collected on their own dataset. In [16], an adaptive matrix factorization approach was used to model the interactions between users and services in a specific time slot. The enhancement, in this approach, was the addition of temporal smoothing of the prediction, which accounted for the dependency between QoS in adjacent time slots. In [49], a model named CARP was proposed, the model can be used for offline and online predictions. The method used K-means clustering to cluster the invocation records, where each cluster represented a specific context and a cluster may contain a set of time slots. In order to alleviate the data sparsity problem, they aggregated invocation records from different time slots in the same cluster. Lastly, a matrix factorization approach was used to predict the final reliability value.

In order to improve the prediction accuracy, other studies incorporated context data like the location of users and services. Incorporating such context data to cluster users and services may help in alleviating the data sparsity problem. Moreover, it can help in improving the final prediction accuracy due to the implicit correlation between time and location that must be considered when making predictions. An example of these studies is the study in [36], where the authors created a tensor of multi-dimensions(user, service, time, location, and QoS property) and used a tensor decomposition method to predict missing QoS values. Another study is [4], which created local clusters of users and services based on location information, it performed a hierarchical tensor decomposition in two types of tensors: the location-based local tensors and the general global tensors. Finally, in [19], a unified and generalized approach was contributed. The approach created a tensor of five dimensions(user, service, time, location, and QoS property). It used tensor decomposition to predict QoS. The prediction loss was minimized using iRPROP+ optimization method, which produced accurate prediction results.

Clustering and Machine Learning Methods. Several studies have used clustering and machine learning approaches in QoS prediction. Clustering is usually used as a data pre-processing step to alleviate the scalability and data sparsity problems. It is not sufficient alone to perform QoS prediction, so other methods like linear regression and QoS averaging are merged with the approaches in this section. Below is a summary of these studies.

In [24], a method named CLUS was proposed, it predicted reliability attribute for ongoing services. The method performed a K-means clustering of invocation records into three steps: environmental variable (network load) clustering, user-specific clustering, and service-specific clustering. The final prediction was done by cluster-based computations that used the averaging of the reliability values. In addition, the authors used a linear regression model for making predication.

In [31], the authors provided a novel method that first predicted the QoS at the current time by calculating the average of the historical QoS data in a pre-determined time interval, then a K-means clustering approach was used to make clusters of similar users and services. The authors used the average value of the resulting clusters to make user and service-based predictions, lastly, a linear weighted addition of the two predictions was used.

In [11], the authors proposed a method of two steps: first, it filled in missing QoS values in the historical QoS time slots. This was done by employing clustering to compute user and service similarity, the missing QoS was then calculated by averaging the weighted similarity for both users and services. Second, it predicted QoS in the current time slot by using the averaging of the calculated historical QoS data.

The method in [2] generated temporal patterns that represented a series of user invocations for each service, after smoothing the pattern, a clustering approach was used to cluster the generated temporal patterns. The final prediction of missing QoS was done using a polynomial fitting function.

In [30], a novel approach called lasso was proposed, this method treats the QoS as a general regression problem. It used lasso regularization to overcome the sparsity of the QoS data. In addition, it used the location of users and services to improve prediction accuracy. This model also can accommodate newly incoming QoS and provide up-to-date predictions. In [12], a Weighted Support Vector Machine (WSVM) was used. This approach treated the problem of QoS prediction as a linear regression problem but in a high dimensional space. It used an exponential weighting function to give high weights for recent data. A sliding window approach was used to generate data for training.

Deep Learning Methods. To distinguish from traditional machine learning methods, this section describes methods that used deep learning approaches, including neural networks and their derivations.

In [33], the authors proposed a novel method called PLMF. The method improved the prediction accuracy by employing Long Short-Term Memory (LSTM), which is a type of Recurrent Neural Network (RNN). It performed online learning and continuously trained with newly coming QoS data by using a moving sliding window. The model used matrix factorization, where the latent factors of both users and services were learned using a personalized LSTM.

The study in [32], proposed a method that used a matrix called QI, which was generated from integrating invocation records with QoS observation matrix. By using matrix factorization, the method captured the user preferences and service features matrices. An LSTM was used to predict the QoS values at each time slice of 64 time intervals, from which, the top N Web services were recommended to the user.

Despite that LSTM has the ability to model long-term dependency between QoS data, it has the problem of vanishing gradient, which may stop the learning process in the neural network. In order to overcome this limitation, the study in [47] proposed a method that used a Projected Factorization Machine (PFM) and Gated Recurrent Unit (GRU). The PFM was used to capture the non-linear interaction in a user, service, and time tensor, and the GRU was used to model the long-term dependency between sequential historical QoS records. A combination of the two predictions was adopted.

A similar method was proposed in [44] which used Generalized Tensor Factorization (GTF) to model the static relationship between user, services, and time. Indeed, it used a Personalized Recurrent Gated Unit (PRGU) to model the long-term dependency. A maximum activation function was used to combine the two predictions.

Other studies utilized the ability of deep learning in inferring the complex relationships between different input features, they used neural networks to model the correlation between time and location as two important context data in the prediction. In the study [48] two methods named STCA-1 and STCA-2 were proposed. In these methods, the spatial and temporal features of services and users were extracted and entered into hierarchical neural networks. The networks were composed of multiple important layers, for example, an interaction layer was used to identify the first and second-order features. Attention layers were used to assign more weights to spatial features which made this model more interpretable than other models.

In [13], a method named QSPC was introduced. It utilized two inputs: the request context and the temporal information. These inputs were fed to a multi-layers neural network. One of the important layers in this network was the LSTM layer, which captured the temporal information into a set of service requests using a static time window. The final output consisted of the prediction of multiple QoS attributes, in their case, response time and throughput. In [15], another method MtforSRec was proposed which accounted for static and dynamic QoS data. It used a factorization machine to model the static feature of QoS and a bi-directional LSTM to model the dynamic features. A softmax layer was used to give the final recommendations from the combined predictions.

In [51], a method named DeepTSQP was proposed. It integrated features computed from the traditional similarity measures with binary features. For QoS prediction, it used the GRU model which helped in modeling the temporal dependency and in mining the implicit features in user-service interactions. This method achieved good prediction accuracy compared with the methods covered in this review.

3.3 Time-Aware Hybrid Collaborative Filtering Methods

A number of recent studies combined the CF methods with other methods, such as time series models and their derivations. Usually, this hybridization is done to improve prediction accuracy, these studies can be summarized as follows.

In [9], the authors proposed a hybrid method that combined ARIMA model and traditional CF. ARIMA was used to generate time series for each Web service, however, ARIMA can't correct itself timely by taking new observations as feedback. To overcome this limitation, KALMAN filtering was used. The authors employed CF to capture user side effects by using user-based similarity. Lastly, they added two predictions for the final output.

In [5], a method was presented that also combined CF with ARIMA. The method first applied traditional CF to predict missing QoS for the past and current Point In Time(PIT). This method used two types of user similarities: global similarity with attenuation function, and user invocation similarity with edit distance measure. In the second step of prediction, ARIMA method was used to forecast QoS for the future PIT. The final Web services recommendation was done using Multi-Criteria Decision Making (MCDM).

In [18], the authors proposed a method that combined time series analysis with cloud model theory based on the CF approach to predict unknown QoS. The QoS data was transformed into time series that represented different cloud models for different time periods. The similarity between models was measured using two novel methods namely, orientation and dimension similarity, which improved the final similarity computation. This method also used weights for every period using the fuzzy analytic hierarchy method.

4   Research Challenges and Directions

As we stated earlier, incorporating invocation time in QoS prediction for Web services is a crucial issue that must be considered in order to provide an accurate prediction. However, several challenges face researchers when they create time-aware prediction methods, which can be summarized in the following points:

Data Sparsity. In reality, a user usually invokes a limited number of services, so the QoS values of the un-invoked services remain unknown forming what is called the data sparsity problem. This problem becomes more critical when building time-aware methods since it will occur in multi-time slots during user-service interactions. Several studies, in the literature, came up with several sparse-tolerant solutions such as using random walk algorithm [8], using data aggregation [49], or using clustering [39]. However, this challenge is still unsolved and there is room for more innovative ideas to mitigate it.

Deficiency in Incorporating other Context Data Correctly. Time is one of the factors that affect prediction accuracy, however, other contextual factors such as the location of users or services, and environmental factors also play a role in prediction accuracy. The important point here is the understanding of the correlation between the time factor and other factors. This is considered a kind of context reasoning that can be inferred by observing and analyzing the historical QoS values in the datasets. Several studies' attempts can help in investigating datasets, on this issue, such as [46] and [26]. In fact, models must be built based on observations and evidence that would interpret context data correlation. This will help in generating true context-aware models that have high prediction accuracy.

The Deficiency in Providing Up-to-Date Predictions. It is very important for time-aware to be updated continuously as new QoS data is coming. The majority of methods discussed in this review are offline methods (i.e. all QoS data are collected before the training phase). The accuracy of the offline methods deteriorates as time advances since they ignore new QoS observations that may carry changes in users, service similarities, or changes in context. Another important point, here, is that in a dynamic environment, the number of users and services also change over time. In reality, new users or services may appear, or current users and services may be disconnected. However, to address this challenge two solutions exist: first **re-training the offline model periodically**, re-training is required to accommodate new real-time QoS observations and new users or services. The limitation of this solution is the expensive time spent in re-training and testing the models as in [24,39,49]. Second **building adaptive online models**, these models can adapt to changes timely and can provide accurate up-to-date predictions. The premise of these models is that no need to train the whole model, however, there are limitations to this solution, for example, in online clustering models, there is always a trade-off between accuracy and scalability. Also, the online latent factor and deep learning models need special techniques that use moving sliding window and Adam or SGD optimizer to enable the online incremental training [13,33]. However, this incremental training is a modern trend that needs further exploration of many issues such as computational complexity, resource consumption, stability, and maintainability.

Optional Research Directions. There are several research directions that researchers may work on in order to increase the accuracy of time-aware methods, from these we mention the following:

Creating Generalised Methods. Most of the research methods attempted to increase their accuracy with respect to a limited number of known datasets commonly used in the experiments. However, this may result in creating data-biased methods which produce inaccurate results when they are evaluated on large-scale datasets [3]. Hence, there is room for enhancements here, for example: testing these methods using other different real datasets, applying them in real environments in the industry, or integrating them with real applications that need QoS prediction.

Creating Unified Methods. The majority of the current methods incorporated one or two contextual data, like being location-aware or time-aware, or both. The more contextual data used by the prediction method the higher accuracy it provides [23]. To this end, some methods are oriented toward building a unified framework, which can be extended to include new contextual data without changing the model's internal structure. In fact, this will release researchers from updating or creating models to support new types of contextual data. In these models, contextual data, like service semantic or load, environmental conditions, user-specific context, etc. can be combined into one unified model. In addition, these unified models may be extended to support multi-QoS factor predictions, such as predicting response time, throughput, and reliability at the same time, which is expected to increase prediction accuracy [19].

Creating New Datasets. The majority of studies in this review utilized the WSDREAM dataset [46]. Although this dataset is a real dataset, it has several limitations. First, the used Web services are SOAP-based, so it would be helpful to include other recent types of Web service, such as Restful API, providing other types may bring other research challenges in QoS prediction for cloud, mobile, and IoT fields. Second, the size of this dataset is considered small, so creating a larger dataset is an important need to keep up with the huge increase in the number of Web services in the real world. Third, this dataset records QoS values such as response time and throughput independently in different datasets, this forms a limitation to research that attempt to conduct multi-predictions. Including QoS attributes in a synchronous manner will bring about new research issues.

Performing Empirical Studies. Performing empirical studies in the field of time-aware CF methods is considered an important need. However, until the time of writing this review, there are no empirical studies in this field. In fact, most of the studies, in this review, have deficiencies in selecting the baseline methods for comparison, they may compare their methods with non-time-aware methods or with a small number of time-aware methods. So an empirical study is needed to provide a clear picture of the performance of these methods at computational and prediction accuracy levels. Moreover, most of the studies, in this review, discussed the accuracy of their approach without reporting any information about their computational complexity. Researchers who are interested in this direction can benefit from empirical studies that have been conducted in the time series field, like [25], where the authors compared (23) methods and proved that Genetic Programming (GP) had better accuracy than ARIMA. Similarly, [10] compared time series methods with some machine learning methods. Another less comprehensive one is in [1] where authors compared less complicated time series methods. However, for CF, one may compare several well-known deep learning methods or several online methods, or any other combinations. Surely, this comparison will help in selecting the right method either in academic or industrial fields.

5   Conclusion

In this paper, we performed a comprehensive review of time-aware Web service QoS prediction for CF methods. We identified a total of forty (40) studies from four known relevant digital libraries: IEEExplore, Springer, ScienceDirect, and ACM. We provided a thematic classification of these reviews into 1)time-aware neighborhood CF 2) time-aware model-based CF and 3) time-aware hybrid approaches. We thoroughly analyzed the reviews under each classification and we identified research challenges. We found a number of key outstanding research challenges including data sparsity, lack of study of some important service prediction context data, and lack of providing up-to-date service predictions.

A number of limitations of these approaches have been identified, including their limited ability to provide updated predictions, expensive computation on re-training for offline methods, limited details on computational complexity, limited interpretability of results, especially for deep learning methods, a limited study of service and user context and QoS factors, and so forth. The review also suggested a number of potential research directions that need to be explored to address some of the outstanding research challenges. This review may provide a thorough guide for researchers in this field.

References

1. Cavallo, B., Di Penta, M., Canfora, G.: An empirical comparison of methods to support qos-aware service selection. In: Proceedings of the 2nd International Workshop on Principles of Engineering Service-Oriented Systems, pp. 64–70 (2010)
2. Chen, L., Ying, H., Qiu, Q., Wu, J., Dong, H., Bouguettaya, A.: Temporal Pattern Based QoS Prediction. In: Cellary, W., Mokbel, M.F., Wang, J., Wang, H., Zhou, R., Zhang, Y. (eds.) Web Information Systems Engineering – WISE 2016, pp. 223–237. Springer, Cham (2016). https://doi.org/10.1007/978-3-319-48743-4_18
3. Chen, Z., Sun, Y., You, D., Li, F., Shen, L.: An accurate and efficient web service QoS prediction model with wide-range awareness. Futur. Gener. Comput. Syst. **109**, 275–292 (2020)
4. Cheng, T., Wen, J., Xiong, Q., Zeng, J., Zhou, W., Cai, X.: Personalized web service recommendation based on QoS prediction and hierarchical tensor decomposition. IEEE Access **7**, 62221–62230 (2019)
5. Ding, S., Li, Y., Wu, D., Zhang, Y., Yang, S.: Time-aware cloud service recommendation using similarity-enhanced collaborative filtering and Arima model. Decis. Support Syst. **107**, 103–115 (2018)
6. Fan, X., Hu, Y., Zheng, Z., Wang, Y., Brézillon, P., Chen, W.: CASR-TSE: context-aware web services recommendation for modeling weighted temporal-spatial effectiveness. IEEE Trans. Serv. Comput. **14**(1), 58–70 (2017)
7. Ghafouri, S.H., Hashemi, S.M., Hung, P.C.: A survey on web service QoS prediction methods. IEEE Transactions on Services Comput. **15**(4), 2439–2454 (2020)
8. Hu, Y., Peng, Q., Hu, X., Yang, R.: Time aware and data sparsity tolerant web service recommendation based on improved collaborative filtering. IEEE Trans. Serv. Comput. **8**(5), 782–794 (2014)
9. Hu, Y., Peng, Q., Hu, X., Yang, R.: Web service recommendation based on time series forecasting and collaborative filtering. In: 2015 IEEE International Conference on Web Services, pp. 233–240. IEEE (2015)
10. Hussain, W., Hussain, F.K., Saberi, M., Hussain, O.K., Chang, E.: Comparing time series with machine learning-based prediction approaches for violation management in cloud SLAs. Futur. Gener. Comput. Syst. **89**, 464–477 (2018)
11. Jin, Y., Guo, W., Zhang, Y.: A time-aware dynamic service quality prediction approach for services. Tsinghua Sci. Technol. **25**(2), 227–238 (2019)
12. Kai, D., Bin, G., Kuang, L.: A time-aware weighted-SVM model for web service QoS prediction. In: Wang, S., Zhou, A. (eds.) CollaborateCom 2016. LNICST, vol. 201, pp. 302–311. Springer, Cham (2017). https://doi.org/10.1007/978-3-319-59288-6_27
13. Li, B., Ye, C., Yu, X., Zhou, H., Huang, C.: Qos prediction based on temporal information and request context. SOCA **15**(3), 231–244 (2021)
14. Li, J., Wang, J., Sun, Q., Zhou, A.: Temporal influences-aware collaborative filtering for qos-based service recommendation. In: 2017 IEEE International Conference on Services Computing (SCC), pp. 471–474. IEEE (2017)

15. Li, M., Lu, Q., Zhang, M., Liang, X.: A multi-task service recommendation model considering dynamic and static QoS. In: 2019 IEEE International Conference on Parallel & Distributed Processing with Applications, Big Data & Cloud Computing, Sustainable Computing & Communications, Social Computing & Networking (ISPA/BDCloud/SocialCom/SustainCom), pp. 760–767. IEEE (2019)
16. Li, S., Wen, J., Luo, F., Ranzi, G.: Time-aware QoS prediction for cloud service recommendation based on matrix factorization. IEEE Access **6**, 77716–77724 (2018)
17. Luo, X., Wu, H., Yuan, H., Zhou, M.: Temporal pattern-aware qos prediction via biased non-negative latent factorization of tensors. IEEE transactions on cybernetics **50**(5), 1798–1809 (2019)
18. Ma, H., Zhu, H., Hu, Z., Tang, W., Dong, P.: Multi-valued collaborative QoS prediction for cloud service via time series analysis. Futur. Gener. Comput. Syst. **68**, 275–288 (2017)
19. Ma, Y., Wang, S., Yang, F., Chang, R.N.: Predicting qos values via multi-dimensional qos data for web service recommendations. In: 2015 IEEE International Conference on Web Services, pp. 249–256. IEEE (2015)
20. Meng, S., et al.: Temporal-sparsity aware service recommendation method via hybrid collaborative filtering techniques. In: Pahl, C., Vukovic, M., Yin, J., Yu, Q. (eds.) ICSOC 2018. LNCS, vol. 11236, pp. 421–429. Springer, Cham (2018). https://doi.org/10.1007/978-3-030-03596-9_30
21. Meng, S., et al.: A temporal-aware hybrid collaborative recommendation method for cloud service. In: 2016 IEEE International Conference on Web Services (ICWS), pp. 252–259. IEEE (2016)
22. Puri, A.S., Bhonsle, M.: A survey of web service recommendation techniques based on QoS values. International Journal (2015)
23. Shen, L., Pan, M., Liu, L., You, D., Li, F., Chen, Z.: Contexts enhance accuracy: on modeling context aware deep factorization machine for web API QoS prediction. IEEE Access **8**, 165551–165569 (2020)
24. Silic, M., Delac, G., Srbljic, S.: Prediction of atomic web services reliability for QoS-aware recommendation. IEEE Trans. Serv. Comput. **8**(3), 425–438 (2014)
25. Syu, Y., Kuo, J.Y., Fanjiang, Y.Y.: Time series forecasting for dynamic quality of web services: an empirical study. J. Syst. Softw. **134**, 279–303 (2017)
26. Syu, Y., Wang, C.M.: An empirical investigation of real-world QoS of web services. In: International Conference on Services Computing, pp. 48–65 (2019)
27. Syu, Y., Wang, C.M.: QoS time series modeling and forecasting for web services: a comprehensive survey. IEEE Trans. Netw. Serv. Manage. **18**(1), 926–944 (2021)
28. Tian, G., Wang, J., He, K., Hung, P.C., Sun, C.: Time-aware web service recommendations using implicit feedback. In: 2014 IEEE International Conference on Web Services, pp. 273–280. IEEE (2014)
29. Tong, E., Niu, W., Liu, J.: A missing qos prediction approach via time-aware collaborative filtering. IEEE Trans. Services Comput. **15**(6), 3115–3128 (2021)
30. Wang, X., Zhu, J., Zheng, Z., Song, W., Shen, Y., Lyu, M.R.: A spatial-SQos prediction approach for time-aware web service recommendation. ACM Trans. Web (TWEB) **10**(1), 1–25 (2016)
31. Wu, C., Qiu, W., Wang, X., Zheng, Z., Yang, X.: Time-aware and sparsity-tolerant QoS prediction based on collaborative filtering. In: 2016 IEEE International Conference on Web Services (ICWS), pp. 637–640. IEEE (2016)
32. Wu, X., Fan, Y., Zhang, J., Lin, H., Zhang, J.: QF-RNN: Qi-matrix factorization based RNN for time-aware service recommendation. In: 2019 IEEE International Conference on Services Computing (SCC), pp. 202–209. IEEE (2019)

33. Xiong, R., Wang, J., Li, Z., Li, B., Hung, P.C.: Personalized LSTM based matrix factorization for online QoS prediction. In: 2018 IEEE International Conference on Web Services (ICWS), pp. 34–41. IEEE (2018)
34. Ye, F., Lin, Z., Chen, C., Zheng, Z., Huang, H.: Outlier-resilient web service QoS prediction. In: Proceedings of the Web Conference 2021, pp. 3099–3110 (2021)
35. Yin, G., Cui, X., Dong, H., Dong, Y.: Web service evaluation method based on time-aware collaborative filtering. In: Yin, H., et al. (eds.) Intelligent Data Engineering and Automated Learning – IDEAL 2013, pp. 76–84. Springe, Berlin, Heidelberg (2013). https://doi.org/10.1007/978-3-642-41278-3_10
36. You, M., Xin, X., Shangguang, W., Jinglin, L., Qibo, S., Fangchun, Y.: QoS evaluation for web service recommendation. China Commun. 12(4), 151–160 (2015)
37. Yu, C., Huang, L.: Time-aware collaborative filtering for QoS-based service recommendation. In: 2014 IEEE International Conference on Web Services, pp. 265–272. IEEE (2014)
38. Yu, C., Huang, L.: A web service QoS prediction approach based on time-and location-aware collaborative filtering. SOCA 10(2), 135–149 (2016)
39. Yu, C., Huang, L.: Clucf: a clustering CF algorithm to address data sparsity problem. SOCA 11(1), 33–45 (2017)
40. Zhang, W., Sun, H., Liu, X., Guo, X.: Incorporating invocation time in predicting web service QoS via triadic factorization. In: 2014 IEEE International Conference on Web Services, pp. 145–152. IEEE (2014)
41. Zhang, W., Sun, H., Liu, X., Guo, X.: Temporal QoS-aware web service recommendation via non-negative tensor factorization. In: Proceedings of the 23rd International Conference on World wide web, pp. 585–596 (2014)
42. Zhang, W., Sun, H., Liu, X., et al.: An incremental tensor factorization approach for web service recommendation. In: 2014 IEEE International Conference on Data Mining Workshop, pp. 346–351. IEEE (2014)
43. Zhang, Y., Zheng, Z., Lyu, M.R.: WSPred: A time-aware personalized qos prediction framework for web services. In: 2011 IEEE 22nd International Symposium on Software Reliability Engineering, pp. 210–219. IEEE (2011)
44. Zhang, Y., Yin, C., Lu, Z., Yan, D., Qiu, M., Tang, Q.: Recurrent tensor factorization for time-aware service recommendation. Appl. Soft Comput. 85, 105762 (2019)
45. Zheng, Z., Xiaoli, L., Tang, M., Xie, F., Lyu, M.R.: Web service QoS prediction via collaborative filtering: a survey. IEEE Trans. Serv. Comput. 15(4), 2455–2472 (2020)
46. Zheng, Z., Zhang, Y., Lyu, M.R.: Investigating QoS of real-world web services. IEEE Trans. Serv. Comput. 7(1), 32–39 (2012)
47. Zhou, J., Guo, X., Yin, C.: Recurrent factorization machine with self-attention for time-aware service recommendation. In: 2020 6th International Conference on Big Data Computing and Communications (BIGCOM), pp. 189–197. IEEE (2020)
48. Zhou, Q., Wu, H., Yue, K., Hsu, C.H.: Spatio-temporal context-aware collaborative QoS prediction. Futur. Gener. Comput. Syst. 100, 46–57 (2019)
49. Zhu, J., He, P., Xie, Q., Zheng, Z., Lyu, M.R.: Carp: context-aware reliability prediction of black-box web services. In: 2017 IEEE International Conference on Web Services (ICWS), pp. 17–24. IEEE (2017)
50. Zhu, J., He, P., Zheng, Z., Lyu, M.R.: Online QoS prediction for runtime service adaptation via adaptive matrix factorization. IEEE Trans. Parallel Distrib. Syst. 28(10), 2911–2924 (2017)
51. Zou, G., et al.: Deeptsqp: temporal-aware service QoS prediction via deep neural network and feature integration. Knowl.-Based Syst. 241, 108062 (2022)

Enhanced Time-Aware Collaborative Filtering for QoS Web Service Prediction

Ezdehar Jawabreh[1,2]([envelope]) [ID] and Adel Taweel[1] [ID]

[1] Department of Computer Science, Birzeit University, Birzeit, Palestine
{eajawabreh,ataweel}@birzeit.edu
[2] Palestine Polytechnic University, Hebron, Palestine
ezdehar@ppu.edu

Abstract. Predicting Quality of Service (QoS) is an essential task in Service Oriented Computing (SOC). In service selection, choosing the right services is a crucial step to achieve high system stability and user satisfaction. Considerable research has been conducted in the last decade to develop accurate prediction methods. Among these are the time-aware Collaborative Filtering (CF) methods, which utilize the QoS values recorded across multiple time periods (slices). However, they suffer from low accuracy due to adopting inaccurate measures, such as averaging old collected QoS or averaging user (or service) similarity values. In this paper, we propose a time-aware method (ETACF) that uses an exponential time-decay function for quantifying the effectiveness of time slices according to their temporal recency. Experiments were conducted in order to evaluate the accuracy of the proposed method. Results show that the developed method achieves a significant improvement in prediction accuracy (decreased NMAE by 9.8%) when compared with the state-of-art methods.

Keywords: Web service · QoS · time-aware prediction · Collaborative Filtering (CF)

1 Introduction

Nowadays, software development witnesses a transition from traditional software development to one that heavily utilizes components and services distributed over the Internet. This led to the emergence of the Service Oriented Architecture (SOA), in which services are widely used in many fields, such as Web development, cloud computing, IoT, and many others. However, the increasing number of available services over the Internet makes choosing the optimal service a significant challenge. A selected service should satisfy both user's functional and non-functional requirements. The latter is known as Quality of Service (QoS), and it has become a distinguished feature among many equally functional candidate services. Usually, some QoS attributes are considered service provider dependent, such as cost, while others are more dependent on the user and network environment [3,19], such as response time and throughput attributes.

© IFIP International Federation for Information Processing 2023
Published by Springer Nature Switzerland AG 2023
G. A. Papadopoulos et al. (Eds.): ESOCC 2023, LNCS 14183, pp. 70–83, 2023.
https://doi.org/10.1007/978-3-031-46235-1_5

Obtaining accurate values for user-dependent QoS values is a critical task in the service selection problem. Several traditional ways were used to obtain these values, such as using the QoS values announced by the service provider in the Service Level Agreement(SLA), but this is considered inaccurate since the QoS values may change over time. Another way is testing candidate services manually by users to evaluate their QoS values, this approach is also not feasible, time-consuming, and expensive. As a result, a number of QoS prediction methods have been proposed to provide a personalized prediction. The Collaborative Filtering (CF) method is one that is mostly used in this field.

The premise of CF method is to employ QoS values obtained from collaborators (users), when they invoke services, to make predictions for others. The similarity between users or services is an essential factor in this method, since users who gained similar values in the past are likely to get similar values in the future [19]. However, several problems faced CF prediction methods, such as scalability, data sparsity, and the more important one that is tackled in this paper, is the dynamics in user characteristics and network environments over time. To mitigate these problems, methods have started optimizing similarity computations by utilizing contextual information, such as the location of the users and services in the location-aware methods [16], and the invocation time in the time-aware methods [5,11].

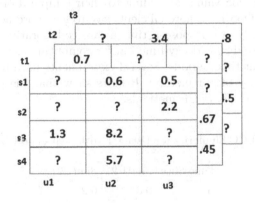

Fig. 1. User-Service QoS matrix (u: user, s: service, t: time)

Time-aware CF methods utilize large amounts of historical data collected at different time slices (periods). Figure 1 shows a matrix of QoS values obtained when users invoked a set of services at different temporal slices. The numbers in the matrix could represent any QoS attribute, such as response time or throughput. Accounting for temporal changes in user and service similarity has a good impact on producing an accurate prediction. However, many methods produced prediction of QoS by averaging the past values taken from all time slices [10,11]. Other methods have, also, used the averaging method for calculating time-aware similarity [14,15]. Using these methods may produce inaccurate results, since they assign an equal degree of importance for each QoS regardless of their temporal order. However, for some QoS attributes, such as response time, the latest values will reflect the true status of the system and hence should contribute more to predicting the QoS of concern. Indeed, several recent studies [4,13,19] have proved empirically that utilizing recent values significantly increased the accuracy of the prediction.

Table 1 lists a simple toy example to illustrate the importance of this idea, which shows the similarity measures for user U1 with respect to two other users: U2, and U3 at different time slices t1, t2, t3 and t4, where t1 represents the recent time slice. These similarities are continuous numbers in the range [−1,1], that Pearson Correlation Coefficient (PCC) may be used to compute them, where larger values mean greater similarity. Indeed, they could represent similarities in response time QoS or any other attribute. If the average similarity measure is used to compute the similarity of U1 with respect to these two users then this will produce an equal similarity value of 0.51, which is considered an inaccurate similarity indication in our case. As shown, in the recent slices, U3 became less similar to U1 than U2, this could happen for example due to a change in U3 location or a change in the network environment. Thus, this dynamic change in the surrounding environment must be reflected in our similarity computation in order to provide accurate QoS prediction.

In this paper, we propose a time-aware prediction method that determines the effectiveness of QoS values according to their temporal order. Our method utilizes the recent QoS in a more efficient way to get more accurate similarity measures. Specifically, we propose a time-aware collaborative filtering method that uses an optimized time decay function for computing user and service similarities over different time periods. Several experiments have been conducted to evaluate the accuracy of our method. Results show that the proposed method outperforms the state-of-art CF methods.

Table 1. PCC Similarity for User U1 with respect to U2 and U3

Time Slice	Sim(U2)	Sim(U3)
t1	0.8	0.2
t2	0.75	0.3
t3	0.3	0.7
t4	0.2	0.85

The rest of this paper is organized as follows: Sect. 2 presents the related work, and Sect. 3 shows the details of the proposed method with the formal mathematical formulation. Section 4 describes the conducted experiments to validate the proposed method and the results of the experiments. Section 5 discusses and concludes our work.

2   Related Work

CF is one of the effective methods that is widely adopted in research to make QoS predictions. Mainly, it is divided into two types: model-based and memory-based [3,19]. The model-based approach builds a model from the historically collected QoS data, which is used later to predict missing QoS values. However, the memory-based approach, or sometimes it is called the neighborhood approach, utilizes the information of similar users or services in making QoS predictions. The memory-based approach can be divided into three types: user-based [9], item-based [8], and a hybrid of the two types [18]. Our investigated approach in this paper is a hybrid memory-based approach.

In [18], the authors proposed a hybrid method that used Pearson Correlation Coefficient (PCC) in making two predictions, the first one is a user-based prediction (UPCC) and the other is Item (Service) IPCC prediction [8]. The method is known as WSRec. It used confidence weights to balance between the two predictions, the final prediction is a linear addition of the weighted predictions. Usually, this hybrid prediction achieved better results than employing UPCC or IPCC methods separately. Another hybrid method, called RACF, was introduced in [12], in which authors proposed a ratio-based approach to compute both users and services similarity; they also suggested a novel item-based method for making a final prediction. To improve the accuracy of QoS prediction, several studies have also integrated contextual information. In [1], the authors proposed a hybrid method called RegionKNN. The method employed, for the first time, the geographical location of users and services in similarity computation. In [7], authors proposed a location-based Matrix Factorization approach that utilized the similarities in user and service locations to eliminate the effect of the cold start problem. In another work, [15] the authors created location-based clusters of users and services in order to alleviate the scalability problem of the memory-based approach.

Time is another important contextual factor that is widely employed in the research for improving QoS prediction. WSPred [17] is known to be the first time aware CF method, proposed by Y. Zhang et al, in the year 2011. This method performed factorization of a user, services, and time tensor in order to predict missing QoS data over specific time intervals. However, in memory-based approaches, time is integrated using different techniques at similarity and prediction levels. In [4], authors used the time decay technique to model the temporal effect of service invocation's time in computing user (or service) similarity. They stated two principles for QoS contribution in similarity and prediction computations. Their principles utilized the QoS values that have a close timestamp, and the QoS values that were obtained recently.

A similar usage of time decay is done in [2], where authors model temporal similarity changes along with a weighted effect for similar ratings. Other approaches used the time-interval technique in similarity computation. For example in [10], the authors proposed a method that combined the average value of QoS computed from a set of historical time intervals with weighted time-aware similarity; their approach has achieved a higher prediction accuracy compared with other time-aware methods. In [14], the authors proposed a method, called TACF, that computed an average time-aware similarity of a set of a predetermined number of historical time intervals. Actually, this approach suffers from limitations, such as the oscillation in prediction accuracy as the number of time intervals is increased and another limitation represented in the static setting of the parameter that determines the number of time intervals to be considered for making the prediction. An extension to this work is done in [6], where authors used a clustering approach to dynamically determine the number of time intervals.

In this paper, we introduce a new approach that combines the time-interval technique for similarity computation with the time decay function for quantifying the temporal effectiveness of the computed similarity. Our approach is an enhanced version of TACF approach, thus named ETACF, in which we eliminate the effect of bad prediction that occurred due to the use of the average similarity measure. As we stated before, the average similarity is considered an inaccurate measure for computing time-aware similarity, since it does not reflect the last changes in the real environment. Next, we will explain the details of our approach.

3   Proposed ETACF Method

This section describes the details of our proposed method, along with a clarification of the mathematical formulation that was implemented in each step.

3.1   Notations and Definitions

We define a set of notations and definitions that will be used in the rest of this paper, as follows.

Notations

- $U = \{u_1, u_2, \dots, u_m\}$ is set of users for web services, u_i denotes a user, where $(1 \leq i \leq m)$.
- $S = \{s_1, s_2, \dots, s_n\}$ is set of web services, s_d denotes a service, where $(1 \leq d \leq n)$.
- $R(u, s) = \{r_{u,s} | u \in U, s \in S\}$ is user-service matrix, where $r_{u,s}$ represents the QoS value of the u user when they invoked the s service.
- $T_j = \{t_1, t_2, t_3, \dots, t_j\}$ is a time interval consists of j number of time slices, and t_k denotes a time slice where $(1 \leq k \leq j)$

Definitions

- Target User: a user attempts to invoke a service whose QoS value is currently missing.
- Target Service: a service that a target user wants to invoke, and its QoS value is missing for this user.

3.2   QoS Model Description

Our approach for QoS prediction builds on the Time-Aware Collaborative Filtering (TACF) algorithm proposed in [14]. The QoS prediction in the TACF original method is done through three main steps as follows:

- Compute the service similarity between target service s and the other services at j number of time slices. This step produced a set of most N similar services to the target one, named $TopN_S$.
- Compute user similarity for the target user by using the $TopN_S$ similar services computed in the previous step. This step produced a set of most similar users to the target one, named $TopN_U$.
- Predict the missing QoS for the target user based on $TopN_U$ similar users produced in the previous step.

We will denote our new approach as Enhanced TACF (ETACF), for simplicity. Worth to note that our new approach predicts the QoS in the current time slice t_1 by utilizing a number of historical time slices in the User-Service QoS matrix. Next, we will introduce a detailed description of each step of the new proposed algorithm.

Service Similarity Computation. This is a crucial step in any CF prediction algorithm, which calculates the similarities between the target service and all other services; different measures can be used to calculate this similarity, one of the commonly used measures is Pearson Correlation Coefficient (PCC) [18], which is defined by Eq. 1.

$$sim(s,f) = \frac{\sum_{u \in U'} (r_{u,s} - \bar{r}_s)(r_{u,f} - \bar{r}_f)}{\sqrt{\sum_{u \in U'} (r_{u,s} - \bar{r}_s)^2} - \sqrt{\sum_{u \in U'} (r_{u,f} - \bar{r}_f)^2}} \tag{1}$$

where U' represents the set of users who invoked both services s and f, and $\bar{r}_s$ and $\bar{r}_f$ represent the average QoS value of s and f services invoked by users in U', respectively.

In order to eliminate the effect of services that may have few similar values with the target service, but are not actually similar, we used a weight for similarity computation adapted from [18], which is defined by Eq. 2.

$$w = \frac{2 \times |U(s) \cap U(f)|}{|U(s)| + |U(f)|} \tag{2}$$

where $|U(s)|$ and $|U(f)|$ are the number users who invoked services s and f, respectively. So the final PCC similarity measure between two services will be computed by Eq. 3.

$$sim'(s,f) = w \times sim(s,f) \tag{3}$$

Time-Aware Service Similarity Using Time Decay Function
The service similarity is computed for a specific number of time slices in the QoS

matrix. Our approach introduces a new contribution that uses an exponential time decay function to weight the service similarity for each time slice according to its temporal order. The principle we adopted here is that: recent time slices should contribute more to prediction. To realize this, we designed an exponential time decay function, as in Eq. 4.

$$f(k) = e^{-\alpha.k} \tag{4}$$

where k denotes the order of the time slice in the time intervals set T_j, such that recent time slices that have small values for k will have larger effectiveness in prediction making. Indeed, the decay function has, also, α parameter, which is a positive time decay constant used to control the speed of decaying in the assigned weights. Our algorithm treats this constant as a hyperparameter whose value is tuned experimentally to fit the available QoS values. In Sect. 4, we will show how its value is selected to produce the best prediction.

By augmenting this time decay function in the calculation, the final time-aware service similarity in time interval set T_j will be calculated by Eq. 5.

$$sim_{T_j}(s, f) = \frac{\sum_{t_k \in T_j} f(k) \times sim'_{t_k}(s, f)}{\sum_{t_k \in T_j} f(k)} \tag{5}$$

where sim'_{t_k} is the time-aware similarity in time slice t_k, such that $t_k \in T_j$, and $(1 \leq k \leq j)$. Finally, we select the $TopN_S$ similar services to the target. This set of services will be used in the next step of the algorithm.

User Similarity Computation. User similarity is measured based on the $TopN_S$ similar services computed in the previous step. In the same way, PCC [9] is used to compute user similarity as defined in Eq. 6.

$$sim(u, v) = \frac{\sum_{s \in S'} (r_{u,s} - \overline{r}_u)(r_{v,s} - \overline{r}_v)}{\sqrt{\sum_{s \in S'} (r_{u,s} - \overline{r}_u)^2} - \sqrt{\sum_{s \in S'} (r_{v,s} - \overline{r}_v)^2}} \tag{6}$$

where S' represents the set of services invoked by both users u and v, and $\overline{r}_u$ and $\overline{r}_v$ represent the average QoS value of u and v users who invoked services in S', respectively.

A weight is assigned to this similarity in order to eliminate the effect of dissimilar users [18], as in Eq. 7.

$$w = \frac{2 \times |S(u) \cap S(v)|}{|S(u)| + |S(v)|} \tag{7}$$

where $|S(u)|$ and $|S(v)|$ are the number services which invoked by users u and v, respectively. So the final user similarity is calculated as in Eq. 8.

$$sim'(u, v) = w \times sim(u, v) \tag{8}$$

Time-Aware User Similarity Using Time Decay Function
Similarly, we compute the user similarity for a specific number of time slices,

and the time decay function is used to give more effectiveness for the recent time slice, so the final user similarity computed in time interval T is defined in Eq. 9.

$$sim_{T_j}(u,v) = \frac{\sum_{t_k \in T_j} f(k) \times sim'_{t_k}(u,v)}{\sum_{t_k \in T_j} f(k)} \quad (9)$$

Where sim'_{t_k} is the time-aware similarity in a specific time slice t_k, such that $t_k \in T_j$, and $(1 \leq k \leq j)$

Finally, we select the $TopN_U$ similar users to the target. This set of users will be used for making predictions in the next step of the algorithm. Worth to note here that we apply the positive similarity constraint on $TopN$ to avoid selecting neighbors with negative similarity values, thus, the goal of this constraint is to improve the prediction accuracy.

QoS Prediction. After calculating the $TopN_U$ similar users, the prediction for the current value $q_{u,s,t1}$ that represents QoS value of the target user u on the target service s is calculated using a weighted sum for every similar user in $TopN_U$ as defined in Eq. 10.

$$q_{u,s,t1} = \frac{\sum_{v \in TopN_U} sim_{T_j}(u,v) \times q_v}{\sum_{v \in TopN_U} sim_{T_j}(u,v)} \quad (10)$$

4   Evaluation and Results

To evaluate the accuracy of the proposed method, a number of key factors need, first, to be determined and optimized. Thus, to do so, we conducted a set of experiments, which then their determined values are used to optimize the proposed method. More specifically, we conducted experiments to answer the following questions:

- What are the optimal weights imposed by the time decay function for best prediction?
- What is the impact of time decay function on the proposed method (ETACF), compared to the baseline TACF and other baseline methods?
- What is the impact of time interval parameter T_j on prediction accuracy (i.e. the impact of the number of time slices used for prediction making)?
- What is the impact of $TopN$ parameter on the prediction accuracy?

4.1   Experiments Setup

To evaluate our method, we used the real-world data set WSDream2 [20]. This data set contains real values for two QoS attributes, which are response time and throughput. In this paper, our experiments were run on the Response Time (RT) data set. Response time data set is a matrix of size: $142 \times 4500 \times 64$

($users \times services \times timeslices$). The details statistics of this data set are shown in Table 2. Indeed, in our experiments, we randomly removed QoS values to generate matrices of different data densities. This helps in simulating the real situation and in proving the validity of our model. Details of parameter settings are shown in Table 3. In each experiment, we randomly chose 100 user-service pairs that QoS values are missing to make a prediction, the experiments were repeated multiple times and the average Normalized Mean Absolute Error (NMAE) is taken as the final results, details of results with different parameter settings will be shown in Sect. 4.3.

Table 2. Response Time WSDREAM2 dataset

Statistics	Values
Num. of Records	30287611
Num. of Service Users	142
Num. of Web Services	4500
Num. of Time Slots	64
Interval of Time Slots	15 min
Mean of Response-Time	3.165 s
Scale of Response Time	0–20 s

Table 3. Parameter's Setting

Parameter	Description	Values
MD	Density of RT matrix	$\{0.30, 0.20, 0.10\}$
$TopN$	Top Similar Users(Services)	$\{10, 20, 30, 40, 50\}$
α	Time Decay constant	$\{1, 1.5, 2, 2.5, 3\}$
T_j	Time interval	$j = \{2, 4, 6, 8\}$

4.2   Evaluation Metrics

Evaluation metrics are used to measure the deviation of the predicted QoS from the actual one. Different metrics can be used. Equation 11 shows the Mean Absolute Error (MAE) metric [14].

$$MAE = \frac{\sum_{u,s,t_1} |ar_{u,s,t_1} - pr_{u,s,t_1}|}{N} \tag{11}$$

where ar_{u,s,t_1} denotes actual QoS values of user u on Web service s in the first time interval t_1 and pr_{u,s,t_1} denotes the predicted QoS values of Web service

s observed by user u also in t_1. N denotes the number of predicted values. The lower value of the MAE, means higher prediction accuracy. Since the QoS values of Web services in response time data set come from different ranges, the Normalized Mean Absolute Error (NMAE) metric [14] is considered more interpretative in this case. NMAE is defined as in Eq. 12.

$$NMAE = \frac{MAE}{\sum_{u,s,t_1}(ar_{u,s,t_1})/N} \tag{12}$$

In this paper, NMAE was adopted as the final metric to measure prediction accuracy.

4.3   Controlling Time Decay Function Weights

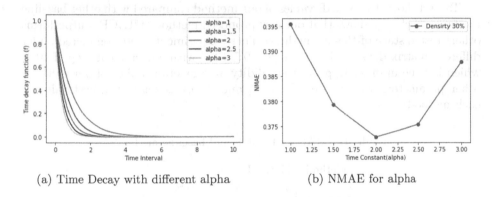

(a) Time Decay with different alpha   (b) NMAE for alpha

Fig. 2. Time Decay Function

The time decay function has two important parameters: the temporal parameter k. Its value denotes the temporal sequence of the time slices, such that the older slice will have larger k values. The second parameter is the time constant alpha (α). This parameter determines the speed of decaying in weights and it should be adjusted in a way that produces the best accuracy. To this end, we conducted several experiments. Initially, we tried to figure out how the decaying will be in the first eight-time slices. Figure 2a shows the resulting time decay exponential curves for alpha values in the range [1,3] and increment step of 0.5. From these curves, we can notice that a larger value for α results in faster decay in weights.

In the next step, we experimentally tested the suggested range for α on the RT data set and measure NMAE for each value. We adjusted the model parameters as follows: $T_j = T_2$, $TopN = 30$, and MD $= 30\%$. Results are shown in Fig. 2b. We can conclude that when $\alpha = 2$ we obtained the minimum NMAE. For this reason, we chose the value of α to be 2. This means that the speed of decaying in weights is best to be a median one.

4.4   Evaluating Performance of Proposed Method (ETACF) Using Decay Function

The following baseline methods have been used to evaluate the performance of our proposed method:

- UPCC (user-based collaborative filtering using PCC) [9]: this method uses the information of similar users for prediction making.
- IPCC (item-based collaborative filtering using PCC) [8]: this method uses the information of services for prediction making.
- WSRec [18]: this method is a hybrid one that combines UPCC with IPCC in prediction making.
- TACF (time-aware collaborative filtering) [14]: this method is the one we extend in this paper, it is a time-aware method that uses both user and service similarities in making predictions.

Table 4 shows the NMAE values of our method compared with other baseline methods. It clearly shows that our new proposed method (ETACF) outperforms others tested state-of-the-art methods. These experiments were conducted under different matrix densities in the range [30%,10%] with a decrement step of 10%, which is done in order to prove the validity and generalizability of our method; other parameters settings were $T_j = T_2$ and $TopN$ is set to the best value in each method.

Table 4. NMAE for ETACF and baseline methods

Method	Matrix Density		
	30%	20%	10%
UPCC	0.5622	0.5998	0.6718
IPCC	0.6532	0.6831	0.6939
WSRec	0.5620	0.5984	0.6601
TACF	0.4172	0.5064	0.6394
ETACF	**0.4018**	**0.4856**	**0.5823**

To evaluate the impact of introducing a time decay function compared with the original TACF method, we conducted another series of experiments at different time intervals in the range $[T_2, T_8]$ with an increment step of 2 and MD = 30%. As Fig. 3 shows, the original TACF has low prediction accuracy and suffers from oscillations as T_j value is increased, actually. These limitations were mentioned by the authors of the original method and we noticed them when we implemented their method. However, clearly, we can notice that introducing the time decay function in our proposed ETACF method had two positive effects in that: first, it smoothed the oscillations along with the increment of T_j, and second, it improved the prediction accuracy. So our new method is considered a significant enhancement to the original method.

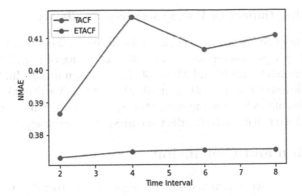

Fig. 3. Comparison of Performance

4.5 Evaluating Impact of Time Slices

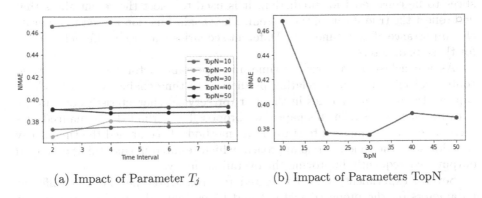

(a) Impact of Parameter T_j (b) Impact of Parameters TopN

Fig. 4. Impact of Parameter T_j and TopN

To evaluate the effect of number of time slices used in QoS prediction, i.e., in other words, the effect of the parameter T_j, we conducted a set of experiments with T_j value in the range $[T_2, T_8]$ with increment of 2. The experiments were repeated for different values of $TopN$ parameter at MD = 30% as shown in Fig. 4a. We can notice that in either value of $TopN$ our method achieves a steadiness in prediction accuracy. The steadiness begins from $T = T_4$, which is because the time decay function assigns tiny weights to intervals larger than T_4. In fact, this achieved our initial goal in that recent time intervals should contribute more in the prediction making while the effect of old intervals should be eliminated to gain more prediction accuracy. So in our case considering a larger value for parameter T_j will not achieve a considerable difference in the prediction accuracy due to the weights imposed by the time decay function.

4.6 Evaluating Impact of Users/Services Similarity

To investigate the effect of users (or services) similarity on the proposed method, i.e., the impact of $TopN$ parameter, we tested different values of $TopN$ in the range of [10,50] with increment step 10 and MD = 30%. As shown in Fig. 4b, the minimum NMAE was achieved at $TopN$ = 30. A small value for $TopN$ will not bring a suitable number of similar users for making predictions, and a large value will bring fewer similar users, which will negatively affect the prediction accuracy.

5 Discussion and Conclusion

In the section above, we conducted several experiments to validate the proposed method. The results proved that our method enhanced the prediction accuracy. Several parameters such as $TopN$, T_j, and weights imposed by the time decay function have to be studied carefully in order to get the best prediction. The $TopN$ is used to control a number of similar users/services that will contribute to prediction, at some optimal point, the method will generate the best prediction, for example, 30 in our case. The T_j parameter determines the number of time slices to be considered for prediction, it is used to select the recent slices that will reflect the true status of the system. The weight function is used to quantify the importance of each time slice. Different scenarios may need different settings for these parameters.

As a conclusion, we consider time an important factor for inferring valid contextual information, so relating prediction to time enables CF methods to capture the dynamic changes in the user (or service) characteristics and in the network environment. In this paper, we proposed a method that enhanced prediction accuracy compared to state-of-art methods. It combined the time-decay function with the time-interval approach, which resulted in smoothing predicted outputs, consequently improving the overall accuracy.

Several experiments were conducted to investigate the effect of different parameters on the proposed method and to evaluate the performance of our method. Results show the proposed method (ETACF), achieved better NMAE than state-of-the-art.

As a future work, the effect of different contextual data, for example, location of users or services, on prediction accuracy will be investigated in different contextual setups. Additionally, other types of time-decay functions, such as linear or a hybrid of exponential and linear functions, will be investigated.

References

1. Chen, X., Liu, X., Huang, Z., Sun, H.: Regionknn: a scalable hybrid collaborative filtering algorithm for personalized web service recommendation. In: 2010 IEEE International Conference on Web Services, pp. 9–16. IEEE (2010)
2. Fan, X., Hu, Y., Zheng, Z., Wang, Y., Brézillon, P., Chen, W.: CASR-TSE: context-aware web services recommendation for modeling weighted temporal-spatial effectiveness. IEEE Trans. Serv. Comput. 14(1), 58–70 (2017)

3. Ghafouri, S.H., Hashemi, S.M., Hung, P.C.: A survey on web service QoS prediction methods. IEEE Trans. Serv. Comput. **15**(4), 2439–2454 (2020)
4. Hu, Y., Peng, Q., Hu, X., Yang, R.: Time aware and data sparsity tolerant web service recommendation based on improved collaborative filtering. IEEE Trans. Serv. Comput. **8**(5), 782–794 (2014)
5. Hu, Y., Peng, Q., Hu, X., Yang, R.: Web service recommendation based on time series forecasting and collaborative filtering. In: 2015 IEEE International Conference on Web Services, pp. 233–240. IEEE (2015)
6. Li, J., Wang, J., Sun, Q., Zhou, A.: Temporal influences-aware collaborative filtering for QoS-based service recommendation. In: 2017 IEEE International Conference on Services Computing (SCC), pp. 471–474. IEEE (2017)
7. Ryu, D., Lee, K., Baik, J.: Location-based web service QoS prediction via preference propagation to address cold start problem. IEEE Trans. Serv. Comput. **14**(3), 736–746 (2018)
8. Sarwar, B., Karypis, G., Konstan, J., Riedl, J.: Item-based collaborative filtering recommendation algorithms. In: Proceedings of the 10th International Conference on World Wide Web, pp. 285–295 (2001)
9. Shao, L., Zhang, J., Wei, Y., Zhao, J., Xie, B., Mei, H.: Personalized QoS prediction for web services via collaborative filtering. In: IEEE International Conference on Web Services (ICWS 2007), pp. 439–446. IEEE (2007)
10. Tong, E., Niu, W., Liu, J.: A missing QoS prediction approach via time-aware collaborative filtering. IEEE Trans. Serv. Comput. **15**(6), 3115–3128 (2021)
11. Wu, C., Qiu, W., Wang, X., Zheng, Z., Yang, X.: Time-aware and sparsity-tolerant QoS prediction based on collaborative filtering. In: 2016 IEEE International Conference on Web Services (ICWS), pp. 637–640. IEEE (2016)
12. Wu, X., Cheng, B., Chen, J.: Collaborative filtering service recommendation based on a novel similarity computation method. IEEE Trans. Serv. Comput. **10**(3), 352–365 (2015)
13. Xiong, R., Wang, J., Li, Z., Li, B., Hung, P.C.: Personalized LSTM based matrix factorization for online QoS prediction. In: 2018 IEEE International Conference on Web Services (ICWS), pp. 34–41. IEEE (2018)
14. Yu, C., Huang, L.: Time-aware collaborative filtering for QoS-based service recommendation. In: 2014 IEEE International Conference on Web Services, pp. 265–272. IEEE (2014)
15. Yu, C., Huang, L.: A web service QoS prediction approach based on time-and location-aware collaborative filtering. SOCA **10**(2), 135–149 (2016)
16. Yu, C., Huang, L.: CluCF: a clustering CF algorithm to address data sparsity problem. SOCA **11**(1), 33–45 (2017)
17. Zhang, Y., Zheng, Z., Lyu, M.R.: WSPred: a time-aware personalized QoS prediction framework for web services. In: 2011 IEEE 22nd International Symposium on Software Reliability Engineering, pp. 210–219. IEEE (2011)
18. Zheng, Z., Ma, H., Lyu, M.R., King, I.: QoS-aware web service recommendation by collaborative filtering. IEEE Trans. Serv. Comput. **4**(2), 140–152 (2010)
19. Zheng, Z., Xiaoli, L., Tang, M., Xie, F., Lyu, M.R.: Web service QoS prediction via collaborative filtering: a survey. IEEE Trans. Serv. Comput. **15**(4), 2455–2472 (2020)
20. Zheng, Z., Zhang, Y., Lyu, M.R.: Investigating QoS of real-world web services. IEEE Trans. Serv. Comput. **7**(1), 32–39 (2012)

Comparison of Performance and Costs of CaaS and RDBaaS Services

Piotr Karwaczyński[1]([⊠]), Mariusz Wasielewski[1], and Jan Kwiatkowski[2] [iD]

[1] Sygnity S.A., Strzegomska 140a, 54-429 Wrocław, Poland
{pkarwaczynski,mwasielewski}@sygnity.pl
[2] Wrocław University of Science and Technology, Wybrzeże Wyspiańskiego 27, 50-370 Wrocław, Poland
jan.kwiatkowski@pwr.edu.pl

Abstract. Public clouds like AWS, Azure, GCP, and OCI offer a range of services including Container as a Service (CaaS) and Relational Database as a Service (RDBaaS). From the perspective of an IT system provider there is a notable lack of information on the overall performance that can be achieved when using specific configurations of these interdependent CaaS and RDBaaS services. To address this issue and avoid incorrect architectural assumptions, it was decided to empirically evaluate the combined performance offered by CaaS and RDBaaS services, considering their hardware configurations selected based on a predetermined cost constraint.

The experiments were conducted in two stages. The first stage was aimed at narrowing down the set of investigated CaaS and RDBaaS services. Using the measurements collected in the second stage, a statistical analysis was performed, comparing the performance achieved in the cloud environments with the performance obtained in the on-premise environment, taking cost constraints into account.

The experiments conducted for the cloud services provided insights into their limitations and performance, enabling informed architectural decisions during the design of complex IT systems. The results of the analysis confirmed that the performance obtained for the studied combinations of services and their associated costs significantly varied among the different cloud providers.

Keywords: Cloud Service · CaaS · RDBaaS · Performance · Cost

1 Introduction

Public clouds, such as AWS, Azure, GCP, or OCI, offer a plethora of services. Among them are services that enable the execution of containers (CaaS, Container as a Service) and services providing relational databases (RDBaaS, Relational Database as a Service). Each of these services has a pricing model dependent on various configuration parameters, including the allocated hardware resources. From the perspective of IT system providers, it can be stated that there is a lack of information regarding the performance

© IFIP International Federation for Information Processing 2023
Published by Springer Nature Switzerland AG 2023
G. A. Papadopoulos et al. (Eds.): ESOCC 2023, LNCS 14183, pp. 84–99, 2023.
https://doi.org/10.1007/978-3-031-46235-1_6

that can be collectively achieved for specific configurations of interacting CaaS and RDBaaS services. Without such information, making architectural decisions during the design of complex information systems that utilize cloud services, while operating under a limited budget, is a highly risky endeavor.

To mitigate the risk of making incorrect architectural assumptions, it was decided to empirically evaluate the combined performance offered by CaaS and RDBaaS services, considering hardware configurations (vCPU, RAM) selected based on a predetermined cost constraint. The maximum cost of cloud configurations was arbitrarily set at 70% of the known (estimated) cost of the on-premise environment. The CaaS services encompassed both Kubernetes-based solutions and proprietary cloud provider solutions. Among the available RDBaaS services, those providing database systems based on MSSQL, Oracle, MySQL, and PostgreSQL were selected.

In each CaaS service, the same Docker image containing a test application was deployed. Upon execution, the application performed several typical, elementary business operations and recorded their execution times. Additionally, the cost of using each environment in which the experiment was conducted was estimated.

The experiments were conducted in two stages. The first stage aimed to preliminarily narrow down the set of investigated services. In the second stage, based on the results of repeated measurements, a statistical analysis was performed to compare the performance achieved in the cloud environments with the performance obtained in the on-premise environment, taking cost constraints into account.

The conducted experiments provided knowledge about the limitations and performance of selected cloud services. The analysis results confirmed that the performance achieved for the investigated combinations of services and their associated costs significantly varied among different cloud providers. It is also worth emphasizing that the most expensive services did not always prove to be the most efficient.

The study begins with a literature review that focuses on the characterization of cloud services, specifically in terms of performance and costs. Following this, the objective, motivation, and research question for the conducted experiments are formulated. In the subsequent sections the preparation and planning phase are extensively described, the analysis procedure is detailed, and the execution of the experiments is summarized. Finally, the results of the statistical analysis are presented along with the discussion, which is followed by the conclusions drawn from the obtained findings.

2 Related Work

Over the past decade, attempts have been made to comprehensively characterize clouds and their services, including their performance and usage costs. In particular, a thorough approach proposed by the Cloud Services Measurement Initiative Consortium, based on the Service Measurement Index (SMI) [1, 2], can be mentioned. SMI is a structure of features and associated attributes and measures that can be used for comparing cloud services. Unfortunately, the consortium suspended its work in 2014, and the initially promising concept of SMI did not progress to the standardization stage.

A contemporary attempt at a comparative assessment of clouds in terms of performance and costs is the Cloud Transparency Platform developed by Cloud Mercato, a company researching the cloud services market [3]. Among the information provided in one place, the platform offers primarily performance benchmark results, such as GB5 (single, multi), Sysbench CPU, and iPerf, as well as information on service costs. The presented information pertains to preconfigured virtual machines (IaaS) offered in cloud computing and does not encompass PaaS services. Similar approach addressing the performance of IaaS model is given in SPEC Cloud Benchmark [4].

Another current approach to characterizing IaaS cloud services based on their cost and responsiveness is the Application Performance and Price Index (APPI) [5, 6]. This index requires assuming certain subjective values that express acceptable levels of response time and the cost of using a virtual machine from the user's perspective.

A comprehensive review of publications presenting methods and performance measurement results in the field of cloud computing is [7]. The researchers present methodological principles that measurements for cloud environments should adhere to, and subsequently evaluate the quality of measurements carried out by the research community in the cloud computing domain in relation to these principles. The conclusions presented in the article regarding the need for and quality of measurements in cloud environments align with our observations. When designing our own measurement experiments, we relied on the guidelines provided by the authors.

A non-functional aspect of cloud solutions that must be considered when designing systems utilizing cloud computing services is the cost of their usage. In practice, determining "how much it will cost" for implementation in a PaaS or SaaS model proves to be a non-trivial task. Cost control in cloud utilization remains a significant challenge for its users [8].

The aspect of cost calculation in cloud usage is currently a widely discussed topic. In [9], the author analyzes and compares cost models of IaaS services. In the next step, a method is proposed to determine the parameter values of these models in such a way that the service provider maximizes revenue. The customer's perspective of cloud services is presented in [10]. The author observes that besides the costs directly resulting from the service pricing, the customer incurs many additional costs associated with using the cloud. These costs are often invisible during the decision-making process of adopting cloud services.

In [11], the authors present the problem of optimal selection of cloud services by an application provider running in the cloud with the aim of minimizing costs while maintaining the required QoS levels. Like in the aforementioned studies, in this case the authors also focus on IaaS services. As they note: "the comprehensive charging model for the cloud computing environment becomes even more complex when it includes PaaS and SaaS charging models."

In practice, utilizing cloud services limited to the IaaS model is impractical. The rich range of managed PaaS services allows for faster solution delivery while reducing the administrative overhead associated with deploying and maintaining middleware software. The distinctive feature of this study is the cost and performance analysis of a solution utilizing PaaS services from the categories of CaaS and RDBaaS.

3   Goal and Motivation

The goal of this research was to compare the performance provided by CaaS and RDBaaS services in AWS, Azure, GCP, and OCI clouds with the performance of the on-premise reference environment, considering the costs, in the context of designing a high-performance IT system that utilizes containerization and a relational database.

The research question that was sought to be answered was: *Can CaaS and RDBaaS services deliver performance that is not inferior to the on-premise reference environment while keeping the costs of the cloud environment at a level no higher than 70% of the on-premise environment costs?*

The primary motivation for undertaking the research presented in this paper was the difficulties encountered in estimating the performance and costs that arose in Sygnity's business practice. The research question stated above was formulated in 2019 while preparing the solution architecture for a tender process for the implementation of a national IT system worth tens of millions of euros.

4   Experiment Planning

4.1   Investigated Cloud Services

The experiment was conducted using managed CaaS and RDBaaS services available in AWS, Azure, GCP, and OCI clouds (Table 1). The CaaS services included both Kubernetes-based solutions and cloud provider-specific solutions. Among the available RDBaaS services, those that provided database systems based on MSSQL, Oracle, MySQL, and PostgreSQL were selected.

For each of the cloud services, computational resources (primarily CPU type) were selected in a way that best matched the resources of the reference environment. This task proved to be challenging due to: (1) highly diverse and simultaneously limited resource pools available in the clouds, (2) imprecise information provided by cloud providers regarding the utilized resources. It was not possible to find an exact match of the same processor as the one in the on-premise environment for any of the cloud services. However, for most services, compatible processors at the platform level (Intel Xeon Cascade Lake) were selected.

4.2   On-Premise Reference Environment

The reference environment consisted of two Dell PowerEdge R740 servers (application and database), built on Intel Xeon Gold 6226R CPUs, located in the Sygnity company's data center in Wrocław. Both servers were connected directly (point-to-point) by Ethernet 3×1 Gbps network, with RTT below 1ms.

Four database management systems have been installed on the database server: 1) Oracle 21c Enterprise Edition, 2) MSSQL Server 2019 Developer Edition, 3) PostgreSQL 14, and 4) MySQL Community Server 8.0.27 for Linux. The configurations of the installed DBMS have not been optimized.

Table 1. The investigated CaaS and RDBaaS services

Cloud	CaaS	RDBaaS
AWS	· AppRunner · ECS (Elastic Container Service) + EC2 (Elastic Compute Cloud) · ECS + Fargate · EKS (Elastic Kubernetes Service)	· Aurora MySQL · Aurora PostgreSQL · RDS MSSQL EE · RDS MySQL · RDS Oracle EE · RDS PostgreSQL
Azure	· AKS (Azure Kubernetes Services) · AppServices · ContainerApps · Container Instances	· MySQL · PostgreSQL · SQL Database – MSSQL Provisioned · OADB-TP[a] on Shared Exadata (multicloud)
GCP	· CloudRun · AppEngine Flexible · GKE (Google Kubernetes Engine)	· CloudSQL MySQL · CloudSQL PostgreSQL · CloudSQL MSSQL EE
OCI	· OKE (Oracle Kubernetes Engine)	· MySQL · MySQL HW · OADB-TP on Shared Exadata · OADB-TP on Dedicated Exadata

[a]OADB-TP = Oracle Autonomous Database, workload type: Transaction Processing.

4.3 Benchmark Software

The experiments utilized a fragment of commercial MDM-class software [12] offered by Sygnity for electric energy market enterprises. The selected functionality is *transmission of profile data* which consists of the following elementary business operations:

1. Retrieving daily profiles of electrical energy consumption with a 15-min resolution from the measurement database.
2. Validating the retrieved data against business rules.
3. Transforming the data into the expected data model for the recipient.
4. Archiving the resulting message in the database.

A daily profile of electrical energy consumption consists of 96 records containing the following: the value of the measured energy, the date and time to which the reading corresponds, and the status of the measured value. Consumption profiles are recorded in relation to uniquely identifiable Points of Energy Consumption (PEC). A single PEC refers to a point in the power grid or a recipient's address where the measurement of energy products (such as consumed or generated active electrical energy) takes place through appropriate devices (meters).

The *transmission of profile data* service was chosen due to the following features:

– It significantly strains computational resources in production deployments.
– It is highly susceptible to parallelization.
– It belongs to the set of core functionalities of the MDM system.

The code was written using Microsoft.NET technologies: C#, Entity Framework, Task Parallel Library, and then prepared for deployment in various environments by encapsulation in a Docker container. It was given the working name *Spectra.API*[1].

The *Spectra.API* application was used to assess the performance of cloud and on-premise environments in which it was deployed. Performance was defined as the profile data transmission rate, expressed in seconds per million transmitted records.

4.4 Cost Estimation of Cloud Environments

The typical time resolution of billing data is one hour, while the conducted experiments sometimes lasted less than a minute. Being unable to measure the incurred costs, it was decided to estimate them.

When considering the utilization of RDBaaS/CaaS services for building an MDM system, it is reasonable to assume that these services operate continuously, allowing business processes to be executed at any given time. With this in mind, it was decided to estimate the monthly costs associated with using them, based on the official price lists of their providers. The assumptions made for the cost estimation can be found in Table 2.

Table 2. The fundamental factors influencing the cost of cloud services

Cost factor	Assumptions
Geographic region	Poland or the region closest to Poland
Usage duration	3-year commitments, corresponding to the accepted 3-year depreciation period for on-premise servers
Computational resources	To standardize the results: 1 OCPU (OCI) = 2 vCPU (other clouds)
Disk type	SSD
High availability	No high availability
Backup	No backup services
Network traffic	Excluded from cost estimations (free intra-zone; negligible from/to Internet)
Currency conversions	A unified currency conversion rate: 1EUR = 1USD = 4.5PLN

The annual workload dynamics for a given MDM deployment should not change significantly within the assumed 3-year perspective, as it primarily relies on a relatively stable number of hosted PECs. Concerning the daily workload dynamics, the anticipation is that certain peaks will arise (e.g. during working hours, due to long-running batch jobs). These peaks might present opportunities for cloud cost optimizations. Nonetheless, it was decided to omit such application-specific optimizations to maintain the analysis and conclusions on a more general level.

---

[1] Version number 43863 was used in the experiments. For those interested in reproducing or expanding upon the conducted experiments, the application image and its API specification may be provided upon email request.

4.5   Cost Estimation of On-Premise Environment

The cost estimations of the on-premise environment included: server acquisition costs, colocation costs, administration costs, and licensing costs.

The cost of the servers was determined based on a competitive procurement process conducted in Q1 2022. Assuming a 3-year depreciation period, the monthly cost of the servers was calculated as 1/36 of their net price.

To estimate the costs of colocation and server administration, a Request for Information (RFI) was issued to the market, encompassing the fixed cost of colocation for two Dell PowerEdge R740 servers including Internet connection and energy consumption, and the fixed cost of server administration, including server software administration (OS, DBMS). Based on the received responses, the monthly net cost of colocation and server administration was estimated.

The cost of MSSQL and Oracle licenses was calculated according to official price calculators.

4.6   Experiment Scenario

CaaS and RDBaaS services can be run on different computational resources. To compare their performance with the on-premise environment, it would be sufficient to use analogous resources. However, it was decided to broaden the scope of experiments to gain a broader perspective on the performance and costs of using cloud services. For this purpose, a predetermined set of technical configurations, labeled KT1-KT8, was adopted. The KT8 configuration corresponds, in terms of the number of vCPUs and RAM, to the configuration of on-premise servers. KT1 represents the minimum configuration, based on 1 vCPU. The remaining configurations are arbitrarily selected intermediate configurations between KT1 and KT8. CaaS services, due to the computational power required for data processing, have a minimum number of vCPUs in each configuration greater than that of RDBaaS environments. The amount of RAM for RDBaaS services was determined based on the size of the largest table storing profile data for 100,000 PECs for 1 month.

The selection of groups of pairs of services for comparison based on performance was decided to be limited to the same DBMS. For each tested pair of services U_C and U_{DB}, and for each test configuration KT from the set {KT1-KT8}, the following generic experiment scenario was planned:

1. Prepare a relational database: enable the U_{DB} database service, configure it with the test configuration KT, create database, populate the database tables with test data.
2. Launch the application: enable the U_C service, configure it with the test configuration KT, launch the Spectra.API container image, and configure the connection between the Spectra.API application and the prepared database.
3. Perform the experiment:
   a. Execute the *transmission of profile data* functionality 11 times.
   b. For each execution, measure the performance.
   c. Save the measurement results, excluding the results of the first execution.
4. Calculate the profile data transmission rate statistics for the experiment: the normalized, average profile data transmission rate $\bar{x}$ and its variance S_x^2.

4.7 Hypotheses

To compare the performance offered by pairs of CaaS and RDBaaS cloud services with the performance of the on-premise reference environment, two hypotheses were formulated:

Hypothesis H^1: Equal profile data transmission rate in the cloud and on-premise, with the null hypothesis stated as:

H_0^1: The average rate in the cloud is the same as in on-premise.

Against the alternative hypothesis:

H_A^1: The average rate in the cloud is different from in on-premise.

Hypothesis H^2: Better profile data transmission rate in the cloud compared to on-premise, with the null hypothesis stated as:

H_0^2: The average rate in the cloud is not better than in on-premise.

Against the alternative hypothesis:

H_A^2: The average rate in the cloud is better than in on-premise.

5 Analysis Procedure

For each series of data transmission time measurements, the conformity of the collected data with the normal distribution was verified using the Shapiro-Wilk test. Adequate statistical tools were employed for the verification of assumed hypotheses, depending on the results of the normality test for the compared samples.

5.1 Occurrence of Normal Distribution in the Compared Samples

If both compared samples confirmed conformity with the normal distribution, the statistical equality of variances in these samples was examined. For this purpose, the Fisher-Snedecor test with a two-sided critical region was utilized. Depending on the test result, an appropriate test comparing the mean values in both samples was applied.

Equal Variances. In this case, the t-Student test for independent groups with equal variances was used. The test statistic in this test is expressed by the formula:

$$t = \frac{\bar{x}_1 - \bar{x}_2}{\sqrt{\frac{(n_1-1)S_{x_1}^2 + (n_2-1)S_{x_2}^2}{n_1+n_1-2}\left(\frac{1}{n_1} + \frac{1}{n_2}\right)}} \tag{1}$$

and the degrees of freedom is:

$$DF = n_1 + n_2 - 2 \tag{2}$$

where:

n_1 – the number of included series of measurements for the on-premise experiment.

$S_{x_1}^2$ – the variance of the sample of normalized on-premise profile data transmission rates.

n_2 – the number of included series of measurements for the cloud experiment.

$S_{x_2}^2$ – the variance of the sample of normalized cloud profile data transmission rates.

In the case of the hypothesis H^1 of equality, the critical value of the statistic for a two-sided critical region was used, whereas in the case of the hypothesis H^2 of a better performance, the critical value of the statistic for a right-sided critical region was used.

Unequal Variances. In this case, the t-Student test for independent groups with the Cochran-Cox adjustment [13] was used. The test statistic in this test is expressed by the following formula:

$$t = \frac{\bar{x}_1 - \bar{x}_2}{\sqrt{\frac{S_{x_1}^2}{n_1} + \frac{S_{x_2}^2}{n_2}}} \tag{3}$$

and the approximate degrees of freedom [14] is:

$$DF = \frac{\left(\frac{S_{x_1}^2}{n_1} + \frac{S_{x_2}^2}{n_2}\right)^2}{\left(\frac{S_{x_1}^2}{n_1}\right)^2 \frac{1}{n_1-1} + \left(\frac{S_{x_2}^2}{n_2}\right)^2 \frac{1}{n_2-1}} \tag{4}$$

In the case of the hypothesis H^1 of equality, the critical value of the statistic for a two-sided critical region was used, whereas in the case of the hypothesis H^2 of a better performance, the critical value of the statistic for a right-sided critical region was used.

5.2 Lack of Normal Distribution in the Compared Samples

To analyze cases where there is a lack of conformity with the normal distribution in either sample, the Mann-Whitney U test [15, 16] was anticipated. This non-parametric test utilizes ranks assigned to individual observations, making it more appropriate to compare the medians of both samples rather than their means. However, since all the samples exhibited conformity with the normal distribution, the use of the Mann-Whitney U test was unnecessary for the analysis.

6 Experiment Execution

The experiment was conducted in two stages. The first stage aimed to narrow down the set of investigated services. As a result, the following services were excluded from further investigation due to the following reasons:

- Configuration limitations: some services could not offer performance comparable to the reference environment.

  - AWS: AppRunner (max. 2 vCPU); ECS + Fargate (max. 16 vCPU)
  - Azure: AppServices (max. 8 vCPU); ContainerApps (max. 2 vCPU); Container Instances (max. 4 vCPU)
  - GCP: CloudRun (max. 8 vCPU)

- Unstable operation of Spectra.API.

- MySQL: Regardless of the cloud provider or on-premise environment, we encountered unexpected issues resulting in the failure of the tested solution. During high multi-threaded workload, operations were interrupted by ambiguous exceptions from MySQL, often preventing the collection of measurement results. We made various attempts to improve stability, including using different MySQL access libraries, testing changes to DBMS configuration parameters and connection parameters. Despite these efforts, the situation did not improve.

- More expensive compared to functionally and performance-wise similar alternatives available in the same cloud.

  - AWS: Aurora PostgreSQL (59% more expensive than RDS PostgreSQL); EKS (9% more expensive than ECS, while operating on the same EC2 instances)
  - GCP: AppEngine Flexible (over 3 times more expensive than GKE)
  - OCI: Oracle Autonomous Database on Dedicated Exadata (66% more expensive than OADB on Shared Exadata)

As a result of the presented exclusions, a total of 9 pairs of services were included into the second stage (Table 3). For each of the pairs, the technical configuration as the maximum number of vCPUs was selected for each service in such a way that the total costs did not exceed 70% of the costs of the on-premise environment based on the same DBMS (Table 3, # vCPU columns).

Table 3. Pairs of CaaS and RDBaaS services qualified for the second stage

Cloud	CaaS		RDBaaS	
	Service	# vCPU	Service	# vCPU
AWS	ECS+EC2	32	RDS PostgreSQL	16
	ECS+EC2	16	RDS MSSQL EE	8
	ECS+EC2	32	RDS Oracle EE	8
Azure	AKS	32	PostgreSQL	16
	AKS	32	SQL Database – MSSQL Provisioned	20
	AKS	32	OADB-TP on Shared Exadata (multicloud)	16
GCP	GKE	32	CloudSQL PostgreSQL	28
	GKE	22	CloudSQL MSSQL EE	8
OCI	OKE	32	OADB-TP on Shared Exadata	16

Finally, for the prequalified pairs of CaaS and RDBaaS services running on fixed technical configurations, the experiments were conducted according to the scenario. Based on the collected data, statistical hypothesis tests were performed.

7 Analysis

The performance data collected for each DBMS in all tested environments is summarized in Table 4. During the experiments conducted for the GKE configuration in combination with PostgreSQL, the results did not exhibit conformity with a normal distribution (p-value of 0.0207 at a predetermined significance level of 0.05). A decision was made to repeat the experiment three times. The predominance of positive results in this additional series indicated that the initially obtained result was a random deviation. Ultimately, the results obtained in the first experiment of the additional series, which showed conformity with a normal distribution, were included in the analysis. This ensured that all gathered data followed a normal distribution, enabling more reliable comparisons (e.g., means instead of medians).

Table 4. Performance of cloud and on-premise environments

DBMS	CaaS	RDBaaS	Mean [s]	Std. Dev. [s]
MSSQL	ECS	RDS MSSQL EE	0.1805	0.0294
	AKS	SQL Database – MSSQL Provisioned	0.1821	0.0246
	GKE	CloudSQL MSSQL EE	0.2922	0.0159
	on-premise	MSSQL DE	0.1516	0.0269
Oracle	ECS	RDS Oracle EE	0.1719	0.0265
	AKS	OADB-TP on Shared Exadata (multicloud)	0.2245	0.0434
	OKE	OADB-TP on Shared Exadata	0.1300	0.0379
	on-premise	Oracle EE	0.1469	0.0277
PostgreSQL	ECS	RDS PostgreSQL	0.1664	0.0383
	AKS	PostgreSQL	0.1446	0.0182
	GKE	CloudSQL PostgreSQL	0.1075	0.0261
	on-premise	PostgreSQL	0.2277	0.0186

For comparing cloud environments with reference on-premise environments, the t-Student test for independent groups was mostly employed. An exception was the configuration based on AWS in conjunction with PostgreSQL, where, due to statistically different variances, the t-Student test for independent groups with the Cochran-Cox adjustment was utilized. In Table 5 information on the results of verifying the statistical hypotheses for the considered test configurations is given.

Table 5. Results of hypothesis verification (at a significance level of 0.05)

DBMS	CaaS	Degrees of freedom	Test value	Hypothesis H^1		Hypothesis H^2	
				Crit. Value	Reject	Crit. Value	Reject
MSSQL	ECS	18	−2.29	2.10	Y	1.73	N
	AKS	18	−2.64	2.10	Y	1.73	N
	GKE	18	−14.24	2.10	Y	1.73	N
Oracle	ECS	18	−2.07	2.10	N	1.73	N
	AKS	18	−4.77	2.10	Y	1.73	N
	OKE	18	1.14	2.10	N	1.73	N
PostgreSQL	ECS	13	4.55	2.16	Y	1.77	Y
	AKS	18	10.09	2.10	Y	1.73	Y
	GKE	18	11.86	2.10	Y	1.73	Y

8   Discussion

During the analysis of the gathered data, it was found that in most cases of cloud solutions, the observed performance of individual experiments did not concentrate around the mean (except for the GKE configuration combined with MSSQL). Conversely, the performance distribution for on-premise environments presented a completely different scenario, where the performance of individual experiments typically centered around the mean (except for the MSSQL-based configuration). To better illustrate the observed performance characteristics of each environment, violin plots depicting the distribution of observations were used. These plots were supplemented with graphical information in the form of error boxes indicating the mean value and its standard error. The white-colored plot represents the results achieved in the on-premise environment. The graphs of the violin plots were accompanied by a presentation of the costs associated with the attained performance. The reference value (represented by a dashed line) is 70% of the costs incurred in the on-premise experiments.

The implementation utilizing MSSQL proved to be slower in all analyzed cloud environments compared to on-premises (Fig. 1). The performance of the experiment was notably lower when utilizing GCP GKE. The remaining analyzed environments, despite achieving poorer results, exhibited comparable performance. All cloud environments utilized nearly the entire available budget. In most cases, the observed performance did not concentrate around the mean.

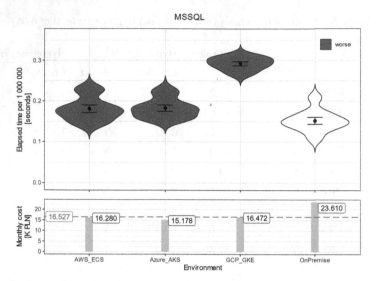

Fig. 1. Comparison of performance for a given cost level. Selected DBMS: MSSQL

Cloud solutions based on Oracle database did not statistically differ from the on-premises solution in most cases, except for Azure AKS (Fig. 2). Comparable performance to on-premises, with the lowest cost, was achieved in AWS ECS. This configuration also exhibited performance the most centered around the mean. The remaining two environments showed low performance stability and clear bimodal distribution.

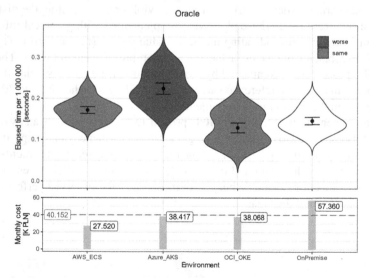

Fig. 2. Comparison of performance for a given cost level. Selected DBMS: Oracle

In the case of the PostgreSQL engine, better performance was achieved in all analyzed cloud environments compared to on-premises (Fig. 3). However, the observed performance is the least stable (with highly bimodal distributions) across all cloud environments. In terms of costs, this database exhibits the largest percentage differences in costs between environments. The best performance, albeit at the highest costs, was achieved when utilizing GCP GKE.

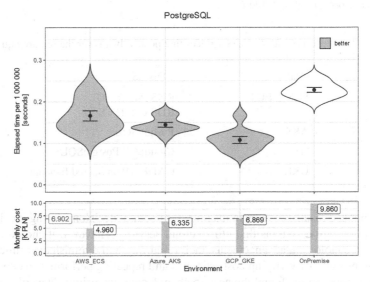

Fig. 3. Comparison of performance for a given cost level. Selected DBMS: PostgreSQL

The lack of concentration of observations around the means and the presence of bimodal distributions in cloud environments are intriguing. The reasons behind such behavior have not been definitively determined. We speculate that it may be attributed to (1) the resource allocation behavior of virtualization employed by cloud providers and (2) resource utilization optimization practices adopted by cloud providers. These assumptions are supported by the performance fluctuations observed in the data collected during a single experiment. However, the information gathered does not allow for conclusive inferences to be drawn.

During each experiment, a predetermined number of repetitions (10) was arbitrarily conducted. This number was based on the assumed acceptable measurement error, which was defined as a 25% difference between the maximum and minimum performance values observed in each series conducted in the reference environment. In our case, the estimation of this error resulted in 0.038 s. With such a level of standard error of the mean, the minimum common sample size for experiments in all environments was determined to be 7 (the maximum value from the minimum sample sizes for each test environment). Since 10 observations were collected, there was no need to repeat the experiments with a larger sample size. However, it cannot be ruled out that adopting a different acceptable estimation error for the mean could lead to different results in verifying the stated statistical hypotheses.

9 Conclusions and Future Work

The conducted experiments and analysis of the results provided a positive answer to the research question formulated in the "Goal and Motivation" section. By using CaaS and RDBaaS services, it is possible to achieve performance that is no worse than in the on-premise reference environment, while keeping the costs of the cloud environment at a level not higher than 70% of the on-premise costs. The pairs of services that meet this condition are presented in Table 6.

Table 6. Pairs of CaaS and RDBaaS services that positively answer the research question

Cloud	CaaS	RDBaaS
AWS	ECS + EC2	RDS PostgreSQL RDS Oracle EE
Azure	AKS	PostgreSQL
GCP	GKE	CloudSQL PostgreSQL
OCI	OKE	OADB-TP on Shared Exadata

The obtained results serve us in making architectural decisions during the design of complex information systems that utilize cloud services. However, it should be noted that due to technological advancements, their reliability will diminish over time. This is not a rapid process: by verifying cost estimates and repeating performance experiments after a year, we have not found the need to change our conclusions. Nevertheless, after 2–3 years, we anticipate repeating the experiments for selected pairs of services.

Acknowledgments. Part of this work has been funded by the European Regional Development Fund under the Smart Growth Operational Programme (contract number POIR.01.01.01-00-0112/21-00), www.sygnity.pl/dotacje.

The authors would like to thank all members of the Sygnity Spectra project for their contribution to the development of the test application, construction of research environments and conducting experiments.

References

1. Siegel, J., Perdue, J.: Cloud services measures for global use: the service measurement index (SMI). In: Annual SRII Global Conference (2012). https://doi.org/10.1109/SRII.2012.51
2. Garg, S.K., Versteeg, S., Buyya, R.: A framework for ranking of cloud computing services. Future Gener. Comput. Syst. **29** (2013). https://doi.org/10.1016/j.future.2012.06.006
3. Cloud Mercato's Manifesto. https://dochub.cloud-mercato.com/manifesto/. Accessed June 2023
4. SPEC Cloud IaaS 2018. https://www.spec.org/benchmarks.html. Accessed Aug 2023
5. Fraś, M., Kwiatkowski, J., Staś, M.: A study on effectiveness of processing in computational clouds considering its cost. In: Proceedings International Conference on Information Systems Architecture and Technology – ISAT 2019 (2019). https://doi.org/10.1007/978-3-030-30440-9_25

6. Kwiatkowski, J., Fraś, M.: A cost based approach for multiservice processing in computational clouds. In: Proceedings 22nd International Conference on Enterprise Information Systems (ICEIS) (2020). https://doi.org/10.5220/0009780304320441

7. Papadopoulos, A.V., et al.: Methodological principles for reproducible performance evaluation in cloud computing. IEEE Trans. Software Eng. **47**(8) (2019). https://doi.org/10.1109/TSE.2019.2927908

8. Cloud Computing Study. Market report, Foundry, form. IDG Communications (2022)

9. Dimitri, N.: Pricing cloud IaaS computing services. J. Cloud Comp. **9**(14) (2020). https://doi.org/10.1186/s13677-020-00161-2

10. Makhlouf, R.: Cloudy transaction costs: a dive into cloud computing economics. J. Cloud Comp. **9**(1) (2020). https://doi.org/10.1186/s13677-019-0149-4

11. Stupar, I., Huljenic, D.: Model-based cloud service deployment optimisation method for minimisation of application service operational cost. J. Cloud Comp. **12**(23) (2023). https://doi.org/10.1186/s13677-023-00389-8

12. Sumic, Z., Harrison, K.: Magic quadrant for meter data management products. Market report, Gartner (2018)

13. Cochran, W.G., Cox, G.M.: Experimental Designs. 2nd edn. Wiley (1957)

14. Satterthwaite, F.E.: An approximate distribution of estimates of variance components. Biometrics Bull. **2**(6), 110–114 (1946). https://doi.org/10.2307/3002019

15. Mann, H., Whitney, D.: On a test of whether one of two random variables is stochastically larger than the other. Ann. Math. Stat. **18**(1), 50–60 (1947). https://doi.org/10.1214/aoms/1177730491

16. Wilcoxon, F.: Some rapid approximate statistical procedures. Ann. N. Y. Acad. Sci. **52**(6), 808–814 (1950). https://doi.org/10.1111/j.1749-6632.1950.tb53974.x

Service Orchestration

Horizontal Scaling
of Transaction-Creating Machines
for Blockchains

Ole Delzer[1], Ingo Weber[2], Richard Hobeck[1], and Stefan Schulte[3(✉)]

[1] Technische Universität Berlin, Berlin, Germany
ole.delzer@campus.tu-berlin.de, richard.hobeck@tu-berlin.de
[2] Technical University of Munich & Fraunhofer Gesellschaft, Munich, Germany
ingo.weber@tum.de
[3] Christian Doppler Laboratory for Blockchain Technologies for the Internet of
Things, Institute for Data Engineering, Hamburg University of Technology,
Hamburg, Germany
stefan.schulte@tuhh.de

Abstract. The increasing popularity of blockchains raises the question
of how to improve their scalability. While researchers are exploring ways
to scale the on-chain processing of transactions, the scalability of the
off-chain creation of transactions has not been investigated yet. This is
relevant for organizations wishing to send a high volume of transactions
in a short time frame, or continuously. Especially for blockchain implementations such as Ethereum which require transactions to include so-
called nonces, horizontally scaling transaction creation is non-trivial. In
this paper, we propose four different approaches for horizontal scaling of
transaction creation in Ethereum. Our experimental evaluation examines
the performance of the different approaches in terms of scalability and
latency and finds two of the four proposed approaches feasible to scale
transaction creation horizontally.

1 Introduction

Since the advent of smart contracts, blockchains have been explored as a foundation for decentralized applications (dapps) and multi-party business processes [2].
Early blockchain platforms, like Bitcoin, offered maximum transaction throughput rates between 3 and 15 transactions per second (tps) initially [11]. Transaction throughput is widely discussed as a factor impeding the scalability of
blockchain applications [8]. This very limited throughput scalability motivated
numerous proposals of consensus algorithms and blockchain platforms, including
Ripple with 1 500 tps [1] and the RedBelly Blockchain with 30k tps [3].

In some blockchain use cases, organizations may need to send a high volume
of transactions in a short time frame, or continuously. This includes among
others manufacturers of high-volume products, e.g., in application scenarios like
traceability of food or pharmaceutical products. To register each product with

© IFIP International Federation for Information Processing 2023
Published by Springer Nature Switzerland AG 2023
G. A. Papadopoulos et al. (Eds.): ESOCC 2023, LNCS 14183, pp. 103–118, 2023.
https://doi.org/10.1007/978-3-031-46235-1_7

an individual identifier (ID) on a blockchain, per 100 million transactions that need to be processed per day, a throughput of approx. 1 158 tps results (assuming 1 transaction per ID).

However, conventional approaches to creating transactions do not scale easily, within a single machine, to such throughput rates.[1] Thus there is a need to scale transaction-creating machines horizontally, i.e., using more (or fewer) machines to create transactions, as opposed to vertical scaling, i.e., using a faster/stronger machine, which is limited by the maximal speed/power of that single machine. This is non-trivial, since blockchains typically require a unique identifier for each transaction; the unique identifier is required to prevent replay attacks. For instance, in Ethereum, this is achieved with the so-called *nonce*, essentially a sequence number for transactions created by a given sender account. The combination of sender account and nonce is unique. Horizontal scaling of a function that relies on a shared variable is in general not a new topic, but the specific setting for blockchain transaction creation allows for different solution approaches than other settings. To the best of our knowledge, this is the first paper formulating and addressing this problem.

In this paper, we propose four alternative approaches for achieving such scalability, in part making use of the specifics of the environment like employing smart contracts. We implement the approaches and conduct experiments to study and contrast the properties of the four approaches, particularly in terms of scalability, latency, and fairness. Summarizing the evaluation results, we find that one approach only scales sub-linearly, and another one is typically less preferable than a third. In our experiments, the remaining two approaches scale well, offer high tps, and – with suitable parameter setting – achieve good fairness regarding the distribution of transaction inclusion latency.

The remainder of the paper is structured as follows. After discussing related work in Sect. 2, we present the four alternative approaches in Sect. 3. The evaluation is presented in Sect. 4, and the results are discussed in Sect. 5 before Sect. 6 concludes.

2   Related Work

In 2016, Croman et al. were among the first to scientifically explore ways for scaling blockchains [4]. They also explained why earlier methods for scaling – increasing the block size so that more transactions can be included in a single block while decreasing the inter-block time – are limited. That is why other, more drastic changes are necessary to enable scalability to industrial use cases. Another early paper by Vukolić [9] discussed different proposals for blockchain scalability, including the option to rely on alternatives to Proof-of-Work (PoW).

---

[1] For an individual use case, alternative architectures can be designed; however, we here address the general class of problems where *high throughput in transaction creation* is required. Layer 2 technologies are often no viable solution, if the goal is to create persistent records on a blockchain.

Taking into account the popularization of smart contracts in Ethereum, Dickerson et al. [5] proposed that miners speculatively process transactions (and thereby execute smart contracts) concurrently. If conflicts arise, the affected contracts are rolled back and serially re-executed. The resulting execution schedule is populated alongside the mined block so that validators can execute the smart contracts in parallel deterministically.

Early blockchain protocols achieved only a limited number of tps. For instance, Bitcoin achieves ca. 7 tps. PoW-based Ethereum achieved 15 tps in 2018 [1] and could, due to increased block "size" and frequency at the time of writing, achieve a theoretical 120 tps. More recent protocols achieve higher numbers, e.g., the RedBelly Blockchain achieved 30k tps in a globally distributed network [3], with the authors stating that the bottleneck in this experiment was the load generation, which is in the focus of our work. Importantly, the possible tps are primarily affected by the applied consensus mechanism. The usage of PoW naturally leads to a low tps, while (Delegated) Proof-of-Stake (PoS) enables increasing the tps to higher numbers. For instance, Ethereum 2.0 applies PoS, and aims at 200k to 300k tps.

The discussed approaches mainly aim at increasing the transaction throughput of blockchains and therefore only consider the *on-chain* transaction processing by miners and validators. For the client-side of dapps, i.e., for the creation of transactions, these approaches are not applicable.

Furthermore, the area of blockchain benchmarking is also relevant to the work at hand. Benchmarking of blockchains with regard to scalability and general performance has been an important research topic in recent years [10]. For instance, Gervais et al. [7] present a simulation framework for analyzing security and performance constraints of PoW blockchains. Dinh et al. [6] implement BLOCKBENCH, which is a framework used to analyze private blockchains. For this, respective workloads are defined. Finally, Hyperledger Caliper[2] is used to benchmark the performance of Hyperledger-based blockchains. To the best of our knowledge, none of the discussed solutions takes into account the off-chain creation of transactions. Therefore, the work at hand could be used in order to extend existing frameworks and simulators.

3 Approaches

In this section, we describe our four different approaches to horizontally scale transaction creation. All four approaches are designed to accept requests from applications, which may be distributed over the available transaction (TX) creating machines, e.g., by a load balancer component. These TX creating machines operate as part of the off-chain backend, which interacts with on-chain backend components like smart contracts.

---

[2] https://hyperledger.github.io/caliper/, accessed 2023-08-10.

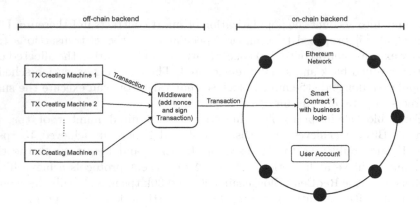

Fig. 1. Approach 1: Externalizing the nonce setting and signing the transaction in a separate, dedicated *middleware*.

3.1   Approach 1

The first approach is arguably the most straight-forward one. As depicted in Fig. 1, the on-chain backend consists of a smart contract and a user account. The smart contract implements the business logic, e.g., a registry of product IDs. The user account represents an organization, e.g., the producer of high-volume goods for which individual IDs are needed, and is used to create transactions which call the smart contract. The off-chain backend includes the TX creating machines as per above, and a *middleware* component between the TX creating machines and the blockchain system. The middleware receives transaction objects from the TX creating machines. These transaction objects are transmitted to the middleware without the nonce. The middleware then adds the current nonce, signs the transaction on behalf of the Ethereum user account, and forwards it to the Ethereum network. Note that the TX can only be signed once the nonce has been set. This design allows us to keep track of the nonce locally at the middleware. We only fetch the current nonce of our user account from the Ethereum network once at startup and store it as a local variable. Then, we simply increment it by one every time the middleware finalizes a new transaction. Since the nonce is irrelevant when the transaction object is first created, we can horizontally scale the TX creating machines without concern for the nonce.

The downside of this approach is that, while transactions can be created concurrently from multiple machines, the middleware is a singleton: setting the nonce and signing the transactions are done on a single machine. There will be a limit regarding the number of transactions the middleware can process per second, which will conceivably pose a bottleneck.

3.2   Approach 2

Figure 2 depicts our second approach. Here, we circumvent the nonce problem by equipping each TX creating machine with its own user account to sign transactions. This way, all machines can keep track of their individual nonce in a local variable. They can create transactions completely independent from each other, which allows for easy scaling without synchronization in the off-chain backend.

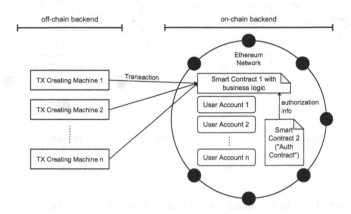

Fig. 2. Approach 2: Allocating an individual account to each TX creating machine

However, using multiple accounts introduces a new problem concerning *authorization*: the smart contract containing the business logic has to be able to decide which invocations to accept (cf. the Embedded Permission pattern [12]). In all other approaches, we use a single designated user account, so the smart contract simply checks if a transaction originates from this account. In contrast, here we want to dynamically scale our TX creating machines according to the current workload, hence the number of accounts that should be permitted to send transactions to our smart contract cannot be static. It must be possible to increase or decrease the number of authorized accounts as needed, and the smart contract needs to be able to verify the authorization of the accounts.

We achieve this by introducing a second smart contract, which we refer to as *Auth Contract*. The Auth Contract maintains a list of the addresses of all authorized user accounts. It offers a function to check if a specific address is contained in this list, i.e., belongs to an authorized user account. The list can be updated dynamically with a dedicated *master account*. Upon being invoked, our first smart contract containing the business logic calls the Auth Contract to check whether the transaction's sender account is authorized. Only then will the business logic of our first smart contract be executed; otherwise, an error is logged and no other state change takes place. The disadvantages of this approach are the extra complexity introduced by using a variable number of distinct user accounts, and slightly higher gas usage (for deploying the Auth Contract, updating the variables, and conducting the checks). The list containing the authorized accounts' addresses has to be updated whenever the number of TX creating machines changes, and the key pairs for all accounts have to be managed well.

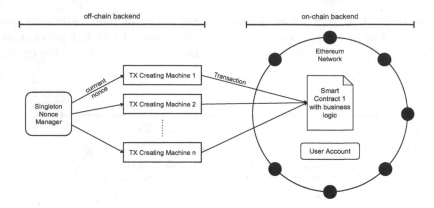

Fig. 3. Approach 3: Outsourcing the nonce management

3.3   Approach 3

For Approach 3, to horizontally scale our TX creating machines, we outsource the nonce management to a new singleton component called *Nonce Manager* (see Fig. 3). As a singleton, there is only one instance that is shared by all TX creating machines. So instead of maintaining the current nonce's value locally at the TX creation machines, it is only stored at the Nonce Manager. Every time the TX creating machines create a new transaction, they request a nonce value from the Nonce Manager. The Nonce Manager then responds with the value of its nonce counter and increments it by one afterwards. The TX creating machine sets the nonce to the received value for the new transaction, which is then signed and sent to the Ethereum network.

The disadvantage of this approach is that it entails a service invocation every time a transaction is created. This will presumably increase the time it takes to create a transaction, thereby decreasing the tps. The impact will likely depend on the network latency between a TX creating machine and the Nonce Manager and the load of the latter: the Nonce Manager is shared by all TX creating machines, and naturally subject to limited bandwidth and computing power. The Nonce Manager also poses a single point of failure. However, the Nonce Manager only implements the functionality of a data store containing a single key-value pair, so it should be feasible to achieve high performance and resiliency.

3.4   Approach 4

As we can see in Fig. 4, Approach 4 is quite similar to Approach 3: We also externalize nonce management to a dedicated singleton Nonce Manager. But instead of having the TX creating machines requesting the nonce from the Nonce Manager for every new transaction individually, we use the Nonce Manager to allocate *nonce contingents* to the machines.

For example, say we use a contingent size of $c = 100$ and the current nonce value stored in the Nonce Manager is 1 500. If a particular TX creating machine A

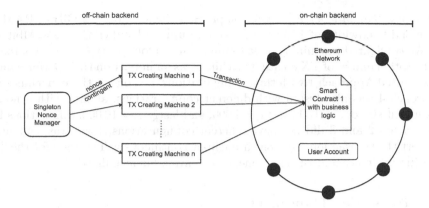

Fig. 4. Approach 4: Assigning *nonce contingents*

requests the next nonce contingent from the Nonce Manager, the latter responds with the contingent of nonces 1 500 to 1 599. The Nonce Manager then increments the current nonce by the contingent size of $c = 100$, so the new value is 1 600. A can now start to create transactions with nonces from 1 500 to 1 599. Afterwards, A requests another contingent from the Nonce Manager and the cycle repeats.

This will lead to situations where, for example, another TX creating machine B creates transactions with nonce 1 600 and above while A has not yet used all nonces between 1 500 and 1 599, i.e., there are nonces lower than 1 600 yet unused. For transaction creation itself, this is not a problem. But once it is sent to the Ethereum network, a transaction with a nonce that is higher than a yet-unused nonce has to wait in the miner's transaction pool – until all lower nonce values are used in a mined or pending transaction. Hence, larger contingent sizes will increase the expected waiting time (latency) of the transactions and also lead to a higher variance in the distribution of waiting times. The advantage compared to Approach 3 is that the frequency and volume of requests to the Nonce Manager is much lower when requesting whole nonce contingents instead of single nonces, which allows the Nonce Manager to serve more TX creating machines.

4   Evaluation

In our experimental setup, up to three TX creating machines are used on individual VMs. The private Ethereum network, consisting of a single Geth node, was operated on another, separate VM. To allow high transaction throughput, the node was operated with the consensus mechanism Proof-of-Authority (PoA), at 400 M gas per block, and an inter-block time of 5 s, resulting theoretically in up to 3 800 tps. This proved sufficient for all the experiments we conducted, i.e., the blockchain was not the bottleneck. There also was a separate VM for the middleware in Approach 1 and for the Nonce Manager in Approaches 3 and 4, respectively. We use Microsoft Azure as cloud computing platform. All VMs were of the size *Standard_A1_v2*, which comprises a single vCore[3], 2 GiB of RAM, a download bandwidth of 1 500 Mbit/s and an upload bandwidth of 250 Mbit/s.

We configured the mining node to mine a new block every 5 s. For Approach 1, the total number of TX creating machines has an impact on their performance, so we tested Approach 1 with three configurations, i.e., one to three machines m. Approach 4 was also tested with different configurations, at first with a nonce contingent size of $c = 100$, then $c = 1\,000$, and lastly, $c = 10\,000$. Simulations for Approaches 2 and 3 did not have different configurations. Load was simulated to exert the transaction creation throughput continuously. The code for the TX creating machines and the experiments are available at Gihub[4].

4.1 Transaction Throughput

In this section, we discuss the evaluation of the transaction throughput of our approaches to scale TX creating machines. Throughput, in this case, refers to how many transactions are created per second (tps).

Figure 5 shows a comparison of the total transaction throughput, i.e., the transaction throughput of all machines combined, between the four approaches. We can see that Approach 1 performed the worst. Even with $m = 3$ TX creating machines running simultaneously, this approach yielded a median of only about 680 tps. Also, the increase in throughput is sub-linear with a growing number of machines. In contrast, all the other approaches achieved significantly higher throughput rates, with medians ranging from 980 up to 1 045 tps. It appears that the middleware used in Approach 1 already poses a severe bottleneck when we only use a small number of machines. We observed the highest throughput for Approach 2 with 1 045 tps (median). That corresponds to our expectations because the TX creating machines in Approach 2 can locally keep track of the current nonce. In contrast, Approaches 3 and 4 regularly have to make external requests to the Nonce Manager. Still, the difference in performance between Approaches 2, 3 and 4 is only marginal. It is especially notable that the median transaction throughput for Approach 3 with 1 030 tps was only slightly smaller than that of Approach 2, even though the TX creating machines had to make a request to the Nonce Manager for every single transaction they created. Figures 5 and 6 show a similar spread of the distributions for all settings, with two exceptions: Approach 1, $m = 3$ and Approach 4, $c = 10\,000$. The former is clearly suboptimal, and does not warrant further discussion, while the latter is of interest and this setting will be discussed in detail in Sect. 4.2.

Figure 6 shows the transaction throughputs per machine for the different approaches and configurations. Here, we can see even more clearly that the middleware in Approach 1 becomes a bottleneck as soon as we try to horizontally scale transaction creation. When only a single transaction-machine was running, Approach 1 achieved a median throughput of 435 tps, the highest observed throughput across all machines and configurations. The reason for this is that

---

[3] Intel Xeon Platinum 8272CL CPU @ 2.60 GHz.
[4] https://github.com/OleDe/ethereum-tx-scaling.

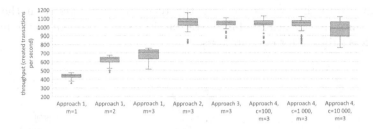

Fig. 5. Comparison of the total transaction throughput

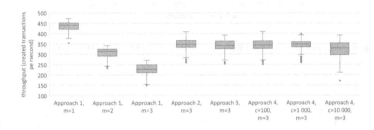

Fig. 6. Comparison of the transaction throughput per machine

the machines in Approach 1 do not have to sign the transactions, but instead only create and forward "unfinished" transactions to the middleware. For all other approaches, the machines are themselves responsible for signing the transactions, which leads to lower performance in the individual machine. However, once we consider $m = 2$ TX creating machines, the throughput per machine of Approach 1 drops to a median of 307 tps. At $m = 3$ machines, Approach 1 only offers a median throughput per machine of 230 tps, which is significantly lower compared to the other approaches, whose median throughput rates per machine range from 323 tps to 348 tps.

Summarized, Approaches 2, 3 and 4 offer adequate throughput rates that increase proportionally when adding more TX creation machines. For Approach 1, on the other hand, the middleware poses a bottleneck when scaling horizontally, so its throughput does not increase proportionally when the number of machines is increased. For all four approaches, the throughput was mostly stable, i.e., the variance of the throughput over time was low. In addition, the load was distributed evenly across all active machines; no single machine had significantly higher/lower throughput than others during the same run.

4.2 Latency and Waiting Periods

In this section, we examine the transactions' latency, measured as *waiting periods*. With the term *waiting period* we describe the time it takes from a transaction's creation at the TX creating machine to it being included in the Ethereum

blockchain. Note that we do not use the term *commit time* from the literature [11], since that is measured from transaction announcement to the network,
which is less suitable for our purposes.

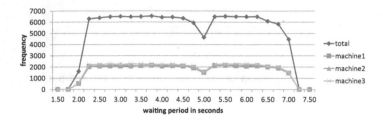

Fig. 7. Approach 2: Aggregated waiting periods with bin sizes of 0.25 s

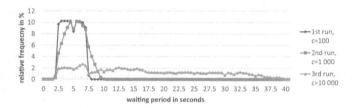

Fig. 8. Approach 4: Aggregated waiting periods with bin sizes of 0.5 s for different
contingent sizes

Figure 7 shows the distribution of waiting periods for Approach 2; observations for Approaches 1 and 3 were almost identical, hence the following also
applies to them. The shortest (longest) observed waiting periods were at approximately 1.8 (7) s, respectively. In-between this interval, the waiting periods follow
roughly a uniform distribution. This was to be expected, because we continuously create new transactions while creating new blocks and thereby including
transactions in the blockchain every 5 s. Hence, the length of the interval also
approximately corresponds to the configured inter-block time of 5 s. On average,
it took 4.4 s from a transaction's creation to its inclusion in the blockchain.

The frequency of observed waiting periods noticeably drops at the 5-second-
mark, as can be seen in Fig. 7. Through further testing, we could confirm that
this drop depends on the configured inter-block time, i.e., when changing the
inter-block time to a specific value, the drop could then be observed around that
new inter-block time. Given that the behavior of Ethereum clients is not in our
focus, we did not investigate this particularity further.

Figure 8 compares the distribution of waiting times of Approach 4 for contingent sizes of $c = 100$, $c = 1\,000$ and $c = 10\,000$. In general, the observed waiting
periods were lower when smaller contingent sizes were used, because assigning
nonce contingents leads to situations where transactions with higher nonces have

already reached the transaction pool of our Ethereum node, while some transactions with smaller nonces have not yet been created. The transactions with the higher nonces then have to wait in the queue until all transactions with lower nonces have been created and sent to the Ethereum node as well. For larger nonce contingents, this effect intensifies and the average length of the waiting period increases.

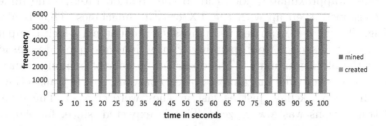

Fig. 9. Approach 2: Comparison between the number of created transactions and the number of transactions included in the blockchain over intervals of 5 s

For a contingent size of $c = 100$, the distribution of waiting periods is similar to that of Approaches 1, 2 and 3. The observed waiting periods range from 1.8 to 7.2 s. Within this interval, they approximately follow a uniform distribution, except for the drop in frequency around the 5-second-mark which we also observed for the other approaches. When increasing the contingent size to $c = 1\,000$, the average length of the waiting periods already slightly rises. But for contingent sizes of $c = 10\,000$, we observe a drastic upsurge, with transactions waiting up to 40 s from their creation to being included. With a transaction throughput of about 330 tps on average, the TX creating machines are fast enough to completely deplete a whole contingent for $c = 100$ and $c = 1\,000$ within the 5 s inter-block time. But for $c = 10\,000$, a machine needs about 30 s until it has used all nonces of a contingent. Accordingly, for larger contingent sizes, the inter-block time is less and less the determining factor for a transaction's estimated waiting period, but instead the average time it takes for all transactions with lower nonces to also reach the miner.

Nevertheless, as long as the contingent size is not configured to be overly large, Approach 4 offers comparable latency/waiting periods to the other approaches. Across all approaches, waiting periods were low and independent from the TX creating machine from which a transaction originated.

4.3   Performance of the Mining Node

In this section, we present additional data regarding the inclusion of transactions in the blockchain and the status of our miner in general. Like in Sect. 4.2, we first discuss results for the first three approaches and then regard Approach 4 separately. Again, Approaches 1, 2 and 3 behaved very similarly, hence Figs. 9 and 10 are representative for Approaches 1 and 3 despite being based on data from Approach 2.

Figure 9 depicts a comparison between the number of created transactions and the number of transactions included in the blockchain over intervals of 5 s, respectively. Again, we chose 5 s as the size for the intervals because it corresponds to the inter-block time. We can see that both the mining rate and the creation rate are quite stable, with no noteworthy fluctuations. In addition, the mining rate is approximately identical to the creation rate, so the miner was able to constantly keep up with the TX creating machines. That is also visible in Fig. 10, where we can see the transaction count per block compared to the size of the transaction pool (pending transactions and queued transactions) right after the block was mined. The observed number of pending transactions did not increase over time but almost stayed constant, so the transactions were included in the blockchain just as fast as they were created. The number of queued transactions was always zero. This is expected, since, for Approaches 1–3, the transactions are always created in sequence according to their nonces. Therefore, we observed no instance of a transaction with a higher nonce being in the transaction pool before a transaction with a lower one, at the points of observation.

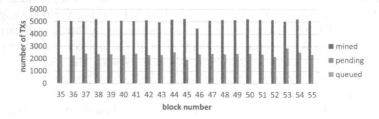

Fig. 10. Approach 2: Transaction count per block compared to the number of pending and queued transactions right after the block was mined

The same does *not* apply for Approach 4, especially for larger contingent sizes, as can be seen in Fig. 11. While the transaction creation rate is fairly stable, the contingent size of $c = 10\,000$ led to heavy, periodic fluctuations for the rate at which transactions are included in the blockchain. Here, we observed a standard deviation of $\sigma = 3\,800$.

The reason for these fluctuations can be seen in Fig. 12: when using larger contingent sizes c, transactions with higher nonces remain in the transaction pool longer, in the *queued* status. They have reached the Ethereum node but cannot be included (or "mined") because not all transactions with lower nonces have yet been created and sent to the Ethereum node. The maximum possible number of these temporarily "missing" transactions is of course higher for larger contingent sizes c. More specifically, with $m = 3$ TX creating machines running at roughly the same speed, the maximum is at $2c$. The higher the value of c, the longer it takes the TX creating machines to create all the missing transactions, and the longer the queued transactions with the higher nonces have to wait and their number is building up. Eventually, when all missing transactions have been created and sent to the Ethereum node, the queued transactions can be included in the blockchain. Therefore, they are shifted to the *pending* status all at once. They are then included in the next block (or in the next multiple blocks, if their combined amount of gas is higher than the gas limit for a single block) to be mined and become a part of the blockchain. As a result, the mining rates are periodically fluctuating above and below the creation rates in Fig. 11. The theoretical maximum of simultaneously queued transactions is also $2c$, assuming we have $m = 3$ TX creating machines with the same throughput.

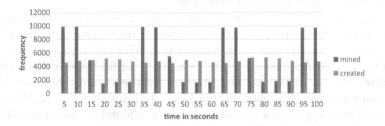

Fig. 11. Approach 4, $c = 10\,000$: Comparison between the number of created transactions and the number of transactions included in the blockchain over intervals of 5 s

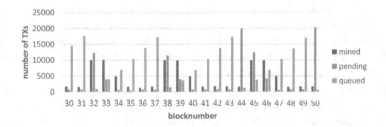

Fig. 12. Approach 4, $c = 10\,000$: Transaction count per block compared to the number of pending and queued transactions right after the block was mined

5 Discussion

Overall, the first approach, where we add the nonce at a dedicated singleton middleware, displayed the weakest scalability. While the transaction throughput increased proportionally for additional TX creating machines in Approaches 2, 3, and 4, this was not the case for Approach 1. Instead, the throughput increase caused by adding additional machines quickly declined, so scaling from two to three machines only increased throughput by 10.8 %. When scalability is a main objective, Approach 1 should likely be avoided.

In contrast, Approach 2 displayed a much more favorable performance, with a very stable throughput that sufficiently increases when adding TX creating machines. The key advantage of Approach 2 is that the TX creating machines do not depend on any other component to set the nonce or to forward transactions to the Ethereum Node, which is why it offered the overall highest throughput of 1 045 tps. As a downside, Approach 2 requires supplying a distinct Ethereum Account for each TX creating machine and a slightly higher gas usage. This might introduce higher complexity for dynamically scaling the number of machines and for realizing authentication and authorization. In summary, Approach 2 is a solid design choice to implement horizontal scalability for TX creating machines, provided that using multiple Ethereum accounts or higher gas usage are acceptable in a given context.

For Approach 3, it is harder to give a clear recommendation. During our simulation run with three TX creating machines, the transaction throughput of our implementation was similar to Approach 2. With an average of 1 030 tps, it even outperformed Approach 4 – albeit slightly – for all three tested contingent sizes. However, the singleton Nonce Manager will eventually become a bottleneck when too many TX creating machines are running concurrently, so both Approach 3 and Approach 4 cannot be scaled indefinitely. The big disadvantage of Approach 3 is that the TX creating machines will have to make c-times as many requests to the Nonce Manager as they would in Approach 4. This means the Nonce Manager will become a bottleneck in Approach 3 considerably sooner, so the maximum number of machines running concurrently is drastically higher in Approach 4. In contrast to the other approaches, if the contingent size c is too large, Approach 4 is suboptimal in terms of latency, and particularly the distribution of waiting times, which can be understood as *fairness*. By selecting a smaller c, this issue can be avoided. Given these points, Approach 4 should generally be preferred over Approach 3, even though the average throughput was slightly higher for Approach 3.

Approaches 2 and 4 are both decent choices for implementing horizontal scaling of transaction creation, and they offer very similar performance. However, while Approach 2 requires a way to deal with account management and authorization (see Sect. 3.2), Approach 4 necessitates implementing an additional component – the Nonce Manager – which poses a single point of failure, so there need to be adequate measures for mitigation and recovery. For a given context, the choice comes down to finding the better trade-off between the drawbacks and advantages, in most contexts likely between Approaches 2 and 4.

6   Conclusion

Following the increased throughput scalability of blockchain systems, high-volume applications with a single participant issuing thousands of tps become possible. However, the horizontal scaling of transaction-creating machines has received little attention in research to date. We study this subject and propose four approaches to this end. Prototypical implementations of the approaches allow us to evaluate them experimentally. Our work demonstrates that it is feasible to horizontally scale transaction creation, and two of the approaches – Approaches 2 and 4 – achieve both good scalability and fair latency distributions. Approach 2 introduces additional complexity because it requires on-chain account management and slightly higher gas usage, but it offers the highest throughput. Approach 4 relies on the Nonce Manager, which could become a single point of failure, and achieved a throughput only slightly below that of Approach 2.

In future work, we want to take into account the failure of transactions and ordering constraints on the incoming requests. We so far assumed that there are no dependencies between transactions other than the nonce of their associated Ethereum account. However, business logic might require transactions to be processed in a specific sequence, and that sequence would then need to be accounted for when setting the nonces. This case should be researched more, as it might require changes to the transaction creation approaches, or even render Approach 4 unsuitable. Last but not least, we have not regarded the batching of transactions so far.

Acknowledgements. The financial support by the Austrian Federal Ministry for Digital and Economic Affairs, the National Foundation for Research, Technology and Development as well as the Christian Doppler Research Association for the Christian Doppler Laboratory for Blockchain Technologies for the Internet of Things is gratefully acknowledged.

References

1. Bach, L.M., Mihaljević, B., Žagar, M.: Comparative analysis of blockchain consensus protocols. In: International Convention on Information and Communication Technology, Electronics and Microelectronics (MIPRO), pp. 1545–1550. IEEE (2018)
2. Bratanova, A., et al.: Blockchain 2030: a look at the future of blockchain in Australia. Technical report, Data61, CSIRO, Brisbane, Australia (2019)
3. Crain, T., Natoli, C., Gramoli, V.: Red belly: a secure, fair and scalable open blockchain. In: IEEE Symposium on Security and Privacy (SP), pp. 466–483. IEEE (2021)
4. Croman, K., et al.: On scaling decentralized blockchains. In: Clark, J., Meiklejohn, S., Ryan, P.Y.A., Wallach, D., Brenner, M., Rohloff, K. (eds.) FC 2016. LNCS, vol. 9604, pp. 106–125. Springer, Heidelberg (2016). https://doi.org/10.1007/978-3-662-53357-4_8
5. Dickerson, T., Gazzillo, P., Herlihy, M., Koskinen, E.: Adding concurrency to smart contracts. In: ACM Symposium on Principles of Distributed Computing, pp. 303–312. ACM (2017)
6. Dinh, T.T.A., Wang, J., Chen, G., Liu, R., Ooi, B.C., Tan, K.: BLOCKBENCH: a framework for analyzing private blockchains. In: 2017 ACM International Conference on Management of Data, pp. 1085–1100. ACM (2017)
7. Gervais, A., Karame, G.O., Wüst, K., Glykantzis, V., Ritzdorf, H., Capkun, S.: On the security and performance of proof of work blockchains. In: 2016 ACM SIGSAC Conference on Computer and Communications Security, pp. 3–16. ACM (2016)

8. Khan, D., Jung, L.T., Hashmani, M.A.: Systematic literature review of challenges in blockchain scalability. Appl. Sci. **11**(20), 9372 (2021)

9. Vukolić, M.: The quest for scalable blockchain fabric: proof-of-work vs. BFT replication. In: Camenisch, J., Kesdoğan, D. (eds.) iNetSec 2015. LNCS, vol. 9591, pp. 112–125. Springer, Cham (2016). https://doi.org/10.1007/978-3-319-39028-4_9

10. Wang, R., Ye, K., Xu, C.-Z.: Performance benchmarking and optimization for blockchain systems: a survey. In: Joshi, J., Nepal, S., Zhang, Q., Zhang, L.-J. (eds.) ICBC 2019. LNCS, vol. 11521, pp. 171–185. Springer, Cham (2019). https://doi.org/10.1007/978-3-030-23404-1_12

11. Weber, I., et al.: On availability for blockchain-based systems. In: IEEE International Symposium on Reliable Distributed Systems, pp. 64–73. IEEE (2017). https://doi.org/10.1109/SRDS.2017.15

12. Xu, X., Pautasso, C., Zhu, L., Lu, Q., Weber, I.: A pattern collection for blockchain-based applications. In: European Conference on Pattern Languages of Programs, pp. 1–20. ACM (2018)

Uncovering Effective Roles and Tasks for Fog Systems

Maximilian Blume[✉], Sebastian Lins, and Ali Sunyaev

Karlsruhe Institute of Technology (KIT), Karlsruhe, Germany
maximilian.blume@partner.kit.edu

Abstract. Fog computing has evolved as a promising paradigm to overcome challenges of edge and cloud computing for use cases such as autonomous driving and virtual reality demanding low latency and the handling of large data loads. The design of fog systems between the cloud and edge opens a large space of possible tasks that fog nodes can take, such as (pre-)processing data or providing advanced security measures for networks. The question remains which tasks a fog system should effectively fulfill to meet the objectives of a specific use case and its requirements. We address this question by developing a hierarchy of standardized tasks and roles (defined as effective sets of recurring tasks for fog systems) based on the analyses of implemented and proposed fog systems from 105 research articles. Researchers and practitioners can leverage this hierarchy to select effective fog roles for use cases and mitigate conceptual ambiguity related to fog computing.

Keywords: Fog Computing · Fog Nodes · Fog Tasks · Fog Roles

1 Introduction

Fog computing describes an additional compute, storage, and networking layer, consisting of so-called fog nodes that reside between a centralized cloud infrastructure and decentralized edge devices [1]. Fog computing gains increasing traction as promising computing paradigm that can solve shortcomings of cloud and edge systems for novel use cases such as Autonomous Driving (AD) and Virtual Reality (AR) with challenging latency, bandwidth, and energy-consumption requirements [2]. Recent examples of larger scale fog system implementations have proven the benefit of an additional, intermediate IT infrastructure layer, such as connected tools that offload data to fog nodes while charging their battery to save energy and reduce cost of edge devices [3].

A fog system can take over tasks from both edge devices and the cloud to offer digital services and enable innovative IT use cases. There are many options to set up fog systems and manifold roles that these systems can take over in an IT landscape. Here, a role is referred to as an effective set of recurring tasks that a fog system performs to fulfill the objectives of a specific use case as intermediary between central cloud services and distributed edge devices. The portfolio of potential roles for a fog system ranges from

© IFIP International Federation for Information Processing 2023
Published by Springer Nature Switzerland AG 2023
G. A. Papadopoulos et al. (Eds.): ESOCC 2023, LNCS 14183, pp. 119–135, 2023.
https://doi.org/10.1007/978-3-031-46235-1_8

simple processing support services for edge sensors up to a fog hub that offers complex processing, networking, and security services close to the edge [4].

However, developers and system designers currently struggle to identify and select appropriate roles due to the novelty of fog computing and the low maturity of the application domain [5]. Selecting viable fog roles is crucial because the effectiveness and suitability of a role for fog systems interdepends with the use case and its requirements. More importantly, developers and designers must set up fog systems differently for each role. For example, a smart power grid that requires very low latency to handle emergency requests demands a fog system that performs orchestration tasks to prioritize emergency requests for processing at available fog nodes [6]. For smart grid IT system designers, it is then difficult to assess if the fog system should also manage the network, take over security-related tasks, or focus on processing and orchestrating tasks only. Similar, a use case with mobile edge devices and fog nodes requires a multi-layer, central overarching fog system that is managing the network and guarantees consistent target addresses for every entity [7]. In contrast, static edge devices allow the deployment of a one-layer flat hierarchy of fog nodes [8]. Hence, the design of a fog system depends on the use case dictating what the fog system can, need, or cannot do.

Under consideration of the use case requirements (e.g., latency, resilience, data load), fog system developers must make well-founded decisions regarding the system architecture and technical specifications. For an informed decision, designers and developers require both a better understanding of (1) potential fog system roles that real-world implementations and experiments proved as being effective for their use case, and (2) how the assignment of a role to their fog system will affect the fulfillment of use case requirements. Unfortunately, the terminology of roles, related tasks and implementations of fog systems are diverse and not standardized because manifold fog systems are currently under development in many industries and use cases with varying requirements [9]. Accordingly, it is difficult for practitioners to identify viable fog system roles from literature or implementations that match their use case and that could provide suggestions on the fog system design. Practitioners can hardly oversee their design choices and expected effects until they understand how fog roles and tasks relate to use cases, the fulfillment of use case requirements, and required system architectures. The full value of fog systems may stay untapped in case of ineffective design choices.

Related research on discussing fog system tasks and roles consists of descriptive surveys, taxonomies, and reference architectures each contributing a specific perspective on the structuring of fog systems. Partly, research on tasks proposes very specific tasks defined from a technical perspective (e.g., [9, 10]). Alternatively, other literature on tasks defines generic fog node tasks such as offering Software as a Service [11]. While all of them contribute to a better understanding of fog nodes, prior studies do not discuss effective sets of tasks (i.e., roles) that fog systems usually fulfill. Related research on roles describes very specific roles based on one or a few similar use cases without standardizing certain parts of the role (e.g., [4, 12]). Further, research often defines roles based on the industry where the fog system is applied in (e.g., [13]), although fog systems may fulfill similar tasks under similar requirements in different industries. Overall, prevalent research agrees that the standardized description of fog applications still is immature (e.g., [5]). Besides, existing fog research uses terminologies for tasks and roles ambiguously so that fog systems for similar roles cannot be compared easily [9]. We therefore target to answer the following research question: *What are common tasks and roles of fog systems?*

We address this problem by developing a fog task-role hierarchy. Applying a top-down and bottom-up literature review, we analyzed existing research on tasks and roles and iteratively aggregated and defined both tasks and roles based on actual and proposed fog systems to build a hierarchy and support the semantic standardization and categorization of fog systems. In this use-case-centric hierarchy, roles are on the highest level and combine one or several tasks that itself encompass more specific sub-tasks. In total, we identified six fog system roles, namely processing assistance, security enforcer, network controller, smart processing support, edge manager, and hub, comprising four key tasks and ten sub-tasks. Practitioners and researchers can leverage the hierarchy (and the categorized articles) as foundation for the design of new fog systems that build upon existing knowledge.

2 Theoretical Background

2.1 Fog Computing

CISCO was one of the first that introduced the concept of fog computing to support edge devices with separate physical nodes providing additional compute, storage, and networking capabilities in a geographically close position [1]. We define the layer of fog nodes together with its relations to adjacent edge or cloud layers and interacting end users as fog system. With that, we interpret fog systems as socio-technical constructs to highlight individuals and technologies interacting in order to fulfill a use case's objectives [14]. A fog system has entities such as edge devices, fog nodes or cloud services that can request or fulfill tasks or end users that can only request tasks. Fog nodes itself can have processing, storage, and networking resources [1]. As edge devices, we interpret any sensors, mobile devices, vehicles, etc. that have capabilities to sense and/or act, deployed at the edge of a network, often with direct contact to users.

Fog nodes enhance the cloud infrastructure in a continuum of both varying geographic distance and extent of capabilities because fog nodes can be either placed directly next to edge devices or in larger distances to support a higher number of devices in a specific area [15]. Thereby, fog nodes can process data and workloads from the edge with much lower latency compared to the cloud [16]. For instance, network service providers can enhance roadside units (RSUs) across a city with additional processing capabilities to take over the resource-intensive task of sensor fusion and object detection for several vehicles [7]. Besides improving latency, fog nodes can reduce data loads that need to be sent to the cloud by aggregating and filtering data received from the edge [17]. For use cases with sensitive data, fog systems can also enhance privacy across the system keeping data and its processing close to their creation and usage [18].

2.2 Related Research on Roles and Tasks in Fog Computing

Being placed between edge devices and the cloud, a fog node can take over tasks from both layers. Tasks thereby describe categories of (recurring) activities that need to be done by one or several fog nodes to fulfill the purpose of the whole edge, fog and cloud system in the context of a specific use case [10]. In that sense, tasks can be both direct processing support for the edge or cloud as well as supporting activities like ensuring a balanced load across the system. For instance, a fog node task can be the real-time analysis of sensor data to detect abnormalities [19] or the authentication for new fog nodes joining the system [20]. Tasks can be inherently defined in nodes when setting up the fog system (e.g., constantly optimize routing tables [21]) or flexibly submitted by entities (e.g., users request sensor data aggregation [22]). We define a "job" as the specific instantiation of a task, that is, a runtime manifestation of a fog node doing something. A fog system can consist of one or more physically separated fog nodes that can individually either fulfill all or individual tasks related to the assigned fog system role. We therefore do not apply roles for individual fog nodes but interpret the totality of fog nodes in a specific use case as a fog system fulfilling one role.

Existing research on structuring tasks either takes a detailed technical perspective on specific tasks or defines high-level task categories. For instance, Mahmud et al. [10] define tasks that fog nodes could do to provide a benefit for specific technical applications, among others, act as a server in content-delivery networks to cache content close to edge. Ahmed et al. [11] define more generic categories of tasks for fog nodes such as the provision of a certain function as a service. Yousefpour et al. [9] provide a detailed summary of potential software modules and activities that need to be defined for an extensive fog system to function, such as the load balancing between nodes or the placement of virtual machines. While prior research contributes valuable details on the potential implementation of fog systems, they rather take a technical perspective instead of a use-case-centric perspective and do not discuss effective sets of tasks that a fog system can, cannot or should do depending on the use case.

Initial research on fog roles largely focuses on an anecdotal description of specific roles but neglects to generalize roles across use cases and contexts. For instance, Naha et al. [4] and Nath et al. [12] define industry-specific roles for fog systems based on existing fog architectures but neglect to discuss similarities of the defined roles or to standardize facets of the roles. Mouradian et al. [13] differentiate fog systems as per industry, helping designers to select an effective fog system. Nevertheless, fog systems in different industries may fulfill the same tasks under similar requirements, for example, signal processing for healthcare sensors and for smart grid sensors that both need to work very reliably and recognize deviations or potential threats in an instant. A comparison of roles and tasks across industries thus might provide further insights, such as conditions when roles are generalizable and when not. Especially, since best practices for fog systems in one industry may not be easily transferred to other industries although the underlying tasks may be similar. Habibi et al. [5] similarly state that the description of fog applications still has a low maturity and lacks standardized components. We argue that the structuring of roles and tasks for fog systems need to be led by generic and industry-agnostic use cases to provide guidance for the design and comparison of fog systems, contributing to a constant evolution of their implementation.

3 Research Approach

3.1 Literature Search

We performed a descriptive literature review to identify tasks and combine them into roles, following guidance on conducting literature reviews [23, 24]. We focused on conference and journal articles published in IEEE Xplore, EBSCOhost, ScienceDirect, ACM Digital Library, and ProQuest to cover relevant literature in the domain of cloud, fog, and edge computing. For our research objective to conceptualize a fog-specific task-role hierarchy, we combined a top-down and bottom-up approach. From a top-down perspective, we searched for articles discussing fog system tasks and roles (search string: Title (fog AND (role or task)) NOT (scheduling* OR prioritization* OR offloading* OR allocation* OR placement* OR distribution*). Due to the generic use of the terms "role" and "task", we only selected literature having these terms in their document title ensuring a focus on the investigation of roles or tasks for fog computing. We also focus our research on the setup of fog systems and less on the detailed processing operations of fog systems, and therefore excluded literature related to task scheduling, prioritization, etc. From a bottom-up perspective, we searched for specific fog implementations to incorporate how fog systems are setup or planned to be setup to fulfill certain tasks and roles (search string: (fog AND (network OR system OR computing) AND (architecture OR design OR setup)). This bottom-up approach enabled us to examine proposed fog systems and derive respective tasks and roles, while gathering data on how the fog system is implemented to meet use case requirements.

In total, we found 553 articles that we checked for relevancy. We removed 4 books, 76 duplicates, 51 articles focusing on other topics than fog computing (e.g., literature discussing biological fog such as [25]), 104 articles applying a generic fog architecture, 168 articles focusing on the processing operations of fog systems, 26 articles providing a survey or taxonomy of fog computing, and 19 articles focusing on Radio Access Networks (RAN). We excluded generic fog architectures as they discuss potential applications but not specifically what and how fog systems can take over certain tasks, and RAN-focused articles as they focus on very specific details of fog computing technologies, for instance, network transmission bandwidth allocation [26]. We thoroughly analyzed the remaining 105 articles to extract descriptions of tasks or roles for fog systems and their technical system setups. Notably, analyzed articles focus on setting up new fog systems rather than retrofitting existing or legacy IT systems with a fog system.

3.2 Literature Analyses

We followed a structured coding approach to iteratively identify, structure, and refine tasks and roles for fog nodes and systems [27]. Starting with the fog implementation-focused articles identified with the bottom-up approach, one author coded every task that a fog node was designed to fulfill and noted a title, description, and its source. For instance, Taherizadeh et al. [28] propose a fog system that processes data, prioritizes processing tasks and assigns tasks to fog nodes depending on their utilization. The author coded three tasks and added a role consisting of these tasks named "Processing and resource manager". For the following articles that he coded, he either defined a new task if an activity described by the article's authors was not already in the list of tasks, or adapted tasks to standardize the description of similar activities for fog nodes. For instance, he combined the task of "process container" and "process virtual machine" to "process virtualized job" and distinguished that task from "process data" as the former demands more flexibility and imposes higher requirements. To reach sufficient abstraction and standardization, the team of authors aggregated tasks and developed a structure of tasks and sub-tasks, for instance, summarizing all activities like data aggregation, filtering, etc. under the sub-task "process data" belonging to the task "processing". In total, we coded 227 activities that we aggregated into four tasks and ten sub-tasks.

To identify roles, we either assigned a role proposed by the article for certain tasks, or defined a new role per article depending on the proposed tasks that the fog system fulfills. We iteratively reviewed all identified roles and their assigned tasks to aggregate and standardize roles across cases and contexts. For instance, we re-named the role "edge controller" to "edge manager" catering for the fact that assigned fog systems do not only have the capability to control edge devices but also manage security activities. We also identified optional tasks that a role can but does not have to fulfill. For the role "smart support", for example, we identified several proposed fog systems that also track suspicious activities to identify and stop attacks and added this sub-task as optional to the role. Overall, we found that a fog system usually fulfills one of six roles.

We also documented the use-case specifics of each role. For instance, we recognized that a fog system fulfilling the role of "processing assistance" is rather used for use cases with a stable data load and static system setup without any external entities to join the system. Once loads become more volatile and emergency jobs appear that require immediate processing (e.g., in smart power grids to control energy production and consumption [6]), fog systems rather fulfill the role of "smart support" that includes the prioritization and monitoring of edge and fog layer.

4 Fog Node Tasks

We uncovered four key tasks that fog nodes address: *processing, orchestration, securing,* and *networking*. Table 1 summarizes the uncovered fog node tasks and sub-tasks. The entire coding table can be accessed at: https://www.researchgate.net/publication/373194 959_Uncovering_Effective_Roles_and_Tasks_for_Fog_Systems.

Notably, for securing, we did not include basic security measures as sub-tasks, such as an individual fog node running a firewall to ensure protection of each computing resource in an untrusted network. We rather focused on fog nodes acting as dedicated security enforcer for the entire IT system and performing advanced security operations on top of basic security operations being always needed for operation.

Analogously, we did not include basic networking activities (e.g., one-time setup of routers and switches to connect edge, fog and cloud in a semi-static way with fixed IP addresses and (sub-) network affiliations) but focused on the networking sub-tasks to enable mobility support of edge devices and fog nodes or optimization of networking. For instance, if edge devices such as autonomous vehicles constantly move larger distances, they connect to different base stations over time, thereby changing sub-networks. To keep track of the location of a car and the routing path to reach it, fog nodes can monitor and

Table 1. Fog node tasks and sub-tasks with a description and examples.

Task	Sub-task	Description	Examples
Processing	Offer Software-as-a-Service (SaaS) to process data	Process data and store or forward the outcomes (only the data for processing is submitted to the fog node)	Sensors spread across a city section send traffic data to a fog node for aggregation and providing recommendations to autonomous vehicles for preferred routes [29]
	Offer Platform- or Infrastructure-as-a-Service (PaaS/ IaaS) to process virtualized jobs	Run containers and VMs on demand and follow flexibly defined instructions (data and instructions are submitted to the fog node)	Underutilized autonomous vehicles act as fog node with virtualized resources to flexibly fulfill end user or other edge device requests [30]
Orchestration	Prioritize jobs from different participants	Manage a queue of jobs from different participants, assess criticality, and assign jobs according to their position in the queue	Central fog node collects all processing jobs in a smart building, prioritizes jobs according to their criticality and assigns the jobs to processing fog nodes [31]
	Administer resources of all participants	Monitor all available processing resources from participants and current and predicted jobs, and distribute jobs according to quality-of-service requirements	Central fog node monitors the utilization of all participating fog nodes in real-time to assign jobs to underutilized nodes or outsource jobs to the cloud if all fog nodes are highly utilized [28]

(continued)

Table 1. (*continued*)

Task	Sub-task	Description	Examples
Securing	Manage internal and external attacks	Track traffic and activities across the system to prevent, identify, and stop malicious behavior and external or internal attacks	Central fog node collects all traffic across a city-wide fog system and looks for often repeating requests to block related IPs and prevent DDoS attacks [32]
	Manage identities of all participants	Manage all devices, nodes, users, etc. in terms of their registration, authentication, emergency control, trust-management, etc	Central fog node hosts a registry of participating edge devices, fog nodes, and cloud services in the fog system so that every resource needs to authenticate with this node before it can submit, e.g., a processing request [22]
	Preserve data and location privacy	Implement mechanisms preserving data/location privacy across the fog system with role-based access-control and encryption	Fog node encrypts data from sensors before sending it through the internet to processing fog or cloud nodes [33]
	Ensure non-repudiation and immutable traceability	Host infrastructure to track participants and activities reliably and consistently	Fog nodes host distributed ledger and mining infrastructure to document each transaction in the fog system [34]

(*continued*)

Table 1. (*continued*)

Task	Sub-task	Description	Examples
Networking	Manage network connections within and adjacent to the fog system	Manage connections among edge, fog, and cloud resources dynamically and handle mobility of nodes and the handover of jobs (fog node acts as a software-defined networking controller)	Fog node tracks mobile edge device position and movement and informs adjacent fog node in case there is an ongoing job processed by a fog node for the edge device that need to be handed over to another node closer to the device [35]
	Distribute traffic within the fog system	Monitor traffic across the whole network and optimize connections, communication strategy, and handovers accordingly	Fog node continuously assess the network topology and related traffic to optimize routing paths towards short distances and low energy consumption [21]

update routing tables and target addresses across the system. In addition, fog nodes can predict the sub-network changes of edge devices and, in case of an ongoing processing job from a moving edge device placed at a local fog node, prepare the handover of such job to the next closest fog node of that edge device.

5   Fog System Roles

We structured six fog system roles in a hierarchy along the identified tasks and sub-tasks (see Fig. 1). Each role represents a fog system that fulfills one or several tasks and related sub-tasks (i.e., indicated by the width of a role´s bar in Fig. 1).

The structure is based on the logic that depending on the tasks a fog system fulfills, a role is assigned. For example, if a fog system fulfills a sub-task from processing, orchestration and securing, it does not take both the roles smart processing support and security enforcer but only the role smart support. Roles thereby describe common sets of (sub-) tasks that we identified in articles from our literature review. In the following, we briefly describe each role, exemplary applications, and the use case conditions under which the role can be effectively used for the fog system.

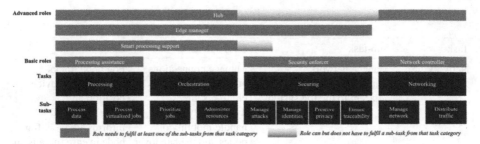

Fig. 1. Fog system roles and related (sub-) tasks they consist of

5.1 Basic Fog System Roles

Processing Assistance. A fog system fulfilling the role *processing assistance* focuses on the processing of data in a pre-defined way or processing of virtualized jobs (e.g., containers, VMs). Every fog node in the system supports one or several edge devices and can also take over tasks from the cloud or end users. For example, a fog system can support a smart city to locally process sensor data for the identification of immediate threats with very low latency (e.g., [36, 37]). Potential implementations of *processing assistance* reach from transformation of data into standardized formats for central nodes to process the data [37] up to a multi-layer fog architecture in which lower nodes do basic analyses and forward the data to higher level nodes for complex analyses [36]. Favorable use case conditions for the role *processing assistance* are constant data loads and unchanging jobs together with low latency requirements that cannot afford any prioritization or assignment steps of the data before it can be processed. Moreover, *processing assistance* allows for a low-cost setup as all fog resources focus on processing without overhead tasks such as the monitoring of resources or the prioritization of jobs.

Security Enforcer. To fulfill the role *security enforcer*, a fog system takes over one or several advanced security-enhancing tasks to support edge devices. For instance, a fog system can constantly monitor and filter traffic to detect suspicions IP addresses and manage (DDoS) attacks [18] for a large number of connected IoT devices. Alternatively, fog systems can manage the identities and authentication for edge devices [38] or support preserving privacy by encrypting data close to the edge [33]. By that, fog nodes take over energy-consuming security tasks for energy-restricted edge devices and pool resources to achieve higher cost-efficiency. Fog systems taking over advanced security tasks require use cases with high security requirements (e.g., healthcare patient data) or a high risk of significant damages if attacks are recognized too late or not mitigated (e.g., in IoT production settings) while additional data processing or orchestrations capabilities are not required at the edge.

Network Controller. The role *network controller* requires a fog system to manage the mobility of edge devices that change networks over time or manage highly volatile network loads. The former can include to track the location of devices, adapt routing tables, and inform other network devices to update accordingly. Potential use cases for fog systems as pure *network controller* include smart vehicle systems that require location-aware fog nodes close to the vehicles to balance the network traffic and avoid congestions [39]. In addition, local fog nodes can track and predict the movements of edge devices and prepare for handover of processing support in the cloud if devices are close to changing networks [35]. For the role *network controller*, fitting use cases require a real-time coordination of moving devices and nodes without the need of further processing or resource orchestration capabilities close to the edge.

5.2 Advanced Fog System Roles

Smart Processing Support. A fog system offering *smart processing support* does not only process data or virtualized jobs but orchestrates jobs and available resources across edge, fog, and cloud. Both processing and orchestration can be either done in the same fog node or in separated nodes. Orchestration ranges from prioritizing, queuing, and assigning of jobs up to the full monitoring of resources, load predictions and balancing as well as resource spin ups and downs. *Smart processing support* can also include the security assessment of submitted jobs before assignment to a processing fog node. A *smart processing support* fog system is often proposed and implemented in closed but volatile infrastructures such as (industrial) IoT (e.g., [40]) or small smart grids (e.g., [6]). It can, for instance, manage cyber-physical power systems and both monitor the power system to notify producers and consumers and orchestrate fog and edge resources [6]. With an overview of all resources, the fog system is able to prioritize tasks in case of urgencies and allows for a better utilization of resources system-wide [28]. Assigning the role *smart processing support* to a fog system is effective for use cases with more resource-intensive and varying jobs as the fog nodes know the system status and can assign jobs accordingly. In addition, at least the role *smart processing support* is required in case highly latency- or safety-critical jobs need to be prioritized to avoid waiting times before they can be processed. Further, the setup of a fog system acting as *smart processing support* with dedicated orchestration fog nodes fits use cases that need to scale fast. In that case, new fog nodes can be easily connected with the orchestration node and start operating faster compared to the role of *processing assistance* in which fog nodes are assigned to a fixed number of edge devices so that the whole topology may need to be changed if the system is scaled up.

Edge Manager. A fog system fulfilling the role *edge manager* extends the role of *smart support* by also addressing tasks related to securing the system. However, the *edge manager* does not always fulfill comprehensive securing tasks. Often, it either manages identities, mitigates attacks, preserves privacy, or ensures traceability of activities. The *edge manager* is applicable across many industries. For instance, a fog system proposed by Núñez-Gómez et al. [41] hosts a distributed ledger setup for others to exchange processing capacity. Such a fog system could be applied in smart cities, IoT, and other settings that require to keep track of microtransactions with many stakeholders that post and fulfill processing requests. A fog system acting as *edge manager* is effective for use cases when a system becomes large and open with the necessity to have external participants in the system with the need of low latency for administration. In that case, the *edge manager* allows for a more dynamic and open system that can, for instance, add or remove third-party devices, nodes, and users flexibly while being live. The additional security measures also reduce risks if the fog system is allowed to control edge devices.

Hub. As *hub*, fog systems additionally manage advanced networking tasks like the handover of jobs for mobile edge devices or the dynamic distribution of traffic. A *hub* often but not always fulfills sub-tasks to secure the fog system. Among them, a hub mostly manages identities or ensures traceability. Smart vehicles are one of the key use cases for the *hub* role as they are mobile per se with large data loads and low latency requirements [7]. To implement a *hub* for smart vehicles, existing infrastructure like roadside units can be enhanced to function as fog nodes for processing with an overarching, city-wide node that manages the network [7, 42]. A *hub* is effective for use cases that either include mobile edge devices or fog nodes or create extensive network traffic and potential congestions. Being close to the devices with location awareness, a *hub* can monitor and predict the devices' positions as foundation for an effective handover of processing jobs. Moreover, local fog nodes can collaboratively ensure up-to-date routing tables for mobile devices so that these can be found anytime. In case of high risks of harm by network congestions, a *hub* can identify and quickly react to sharply increasing traffic by changing routes and data allocation.

6 Discussion

6.1 Principal Findings

We systematically derived four key tasks and ten sub-tasks for fog nodes from 105 articles. Based on often occurring sets of tasks and sub-tasks, we defined a hierarchy with six roles that fog systems can fulfill to support edge devices and cloud services depending on the use case. For each role, we were able to define use case characteristics that point towards the necessity of such role for a fog system. For instance, once a use case does not only entail a closed system (suitable for the roles *processing assistance* or *smart processing support*) but also needs to accommodate for third party participants to join or leave the fog system, fog nodes need to take over security-related tasks such as the authentication of users, nodes, and devices. Accordingly, the fog system needs to either fulfill the roles *edge manager* or *hub* in that case to be effective. For simple use cases with constant loads, stable participants, etc., a fog system fulfilling the role of *edge manager* or *hub* is feasible but may create too much overhead in organizing the system leading to inefficiencies. Our hierarchical structure of roles (see Fig. 1) thereby indirectly indicates not only the most effective role for a specific use case but also highlights further feasible (roles that are above the one in focus in Fig. 1) and unfeasible ones (roles below the one in focus in Fig. 1).

Among the six roles, *processing assistance* appeared the most in the analyzed articles (n = 42), followed by *hub* (n = 18) and *smart processing support* (n = 15). With *processing assistance*, related fog systems fulfill the general idea of fog to directly support edge devices with additional processing close to the edge. It often requires a less extensive architecture and generally fits more use cases than *hub* or *smart processing support*. The role *edge manager* only appears five times indicating that for more extensive use cases, fog systems also take over networking tasks besides securing and rather act as *hub* instead of only *edge manager*. Our review also indicates that the designated roles for fog systems still mostly adhere to the initial idea of fog computing to act as processing support for the edge because of the rather low number of articles proposing the single-task roles *security enforcer* (n = 10) or *network controller* (n = 3). Further tasks for fog systems beyond processing are rather a necessary support function to allow fog nodes fulfilling more extensive use case requirements. Notably, reviewed literature neglects proposing a fog system fulfilling the role *orchestrator* only.

Interestingly, within each role, there are distinct patterns for implementing a fog systems. For instance, articles proposing a fog system fulfilling the role *smart processing support* either apply a centralized (e.g., [21, 43]) or decentralized orchestration (e.g., [40, 44]). Centralized orchestration describes a topology in which one or a few central fog nodes are connected to the edge devices to collect all their processing requests and assign them to available fog nodes on a higher layer. Decentralized orchestration foresees that each fog node is connected to several edge devices, directly receives their processing requests, and only tracks their own utilization and that of adjacent fog nodes. In case of local bottlenecks, fog nodes communicate with adjacent nodes to shift jobs among them. Similar patterns can be found for *processing assistance*. They can be distinguished into single-layer fog systems that can efficiently address homogeneous jobs from edge devices (e.g., [45]) or multi-layer fog systems with more flexibility to address heterogeneous jobs (e.g., [46]). These implementation patterns further substantiate the need to design fog systems according to a specific role taken.

6.2 Implications for Research and Practice

This study uncovers and standardizes four key tasks and ten related sub-tasks that fog nodes can perform in a fog system. We provide descriptions and example implementation references for each (sub-) task and therefore guide future research examining the useful application of fog computing for certain use cases. Second, extending recent research examining fog roles (e.g., [4, 12]), we were able to uncover six industry-agnostic roles that a fog system can take to fulfill use case requirements and objectives. We describe each role with a definition, example implementations, and use-case conditions for an effective application of each role. Third, prior research on fog roles mostly structured fog systems according to the industry they were applied in (e.g., [13]), and did not examine generalizability of roles' facets and the applying fog system. Rather than focusing on industries, we took an overarching, use-case-specific perspective examining effective sets of fog tasks. With that, we were able to define a hierarchy of tasks and roles that supports to organize fog systems according to their similarity. Researchers can use the hierarchy to ground the development of new fog systems on similar systems to improve its design. With this study, we thereby help to mitigate the problem of inconsistent descriptions of fog applications with a low maturity and standardization, raised by prior research (e.g., [5]). For the design of new fog systems, practitioners and researchers can leverage the hierarchy and the recommendations for fog system roles depending on use case requirements to systematically select the appropriate role and related (sub-) tasks for their use case. Since each role requires different system design decisions, our work provides the foundation for developing role-specific system design patterns for fog computing. Finally, for both researchers and practitioners, our hierarchy with (sub-) tasks and roles proposes a standardized terminology of fog systems counteracting the prevalent conceptual ambiguity around fog computing [9].

6.3 Limitations and Future Research

Our study is subject to limitations, paving the way for future research. As our research is based on an extensive literature review with 105 articles and 227 activities coded, we develop our fog task-role hierarchy solely on extant literature without further validation of the results. The literature coding was also conducted mostly by one author, posing the risk of subjective researcher bias. We addressed this limitation by discussing and iterating our results among the team of authors supported by informal discussions with practitioners to indicate the validity and usefulness of our task-role hierarchy. Further research on this topic could include the validation of our results with expert interviews. Another limitation of our research is grounded on the selection of relevant literature. As indicated by overarching surveys, fog computing can be clearly defined and distinguished from other computing paradigms (e.g., [4, 9]). In practice and research though, articles that would fit our definition of fog are published as edge, mist, or mobile computing, limiting our research to a subset of all potentially relevant fog system articles. However, all articles in scope of our research share a similar definition of fog and focus on novel use cases, ensuring that we analyzed theoretically consistent systems. Further research may investigate into specifics of roles for fog and related paradigms. Another promising future research direction based on the principal findings emerges from the identification of fog system implementation patterns within individual roles. Diving deeper into each role and related patterns could allow to develop best practices for the technical implementation of use-case specific fog systems.

6.4 Conclusion

With fog systems being placed between the edge and cloud, they not only impose significant opportunities for IT architects and system designers but also challenge an effective system setup. The multitude of different (sub-)tasks that fog nodes can take over creates burden on the designers to select and combine tasks to fulfill their use case objectives and requirements. We reviewed the extensive body of knowledge on fog computing to uncover common tasks, map them to roles, and develop a task-role hierarchy for fog systems. We contribute to the informed decision of a role for a specific fog system with our task-role hierarchy that allows to categorize existing fog systems and assign effective roles and respective tasks for new fog systems.

References

1. Bonomi, F., Milito, R., Zhu, J., et al.: Fog computing and its role in the internet of things. In: Gerla, M., Huang, D. (eds.) Proceedings of the first edition of the MCC workshop on Mobile cloud computing - MCC 2012, p. 13. ACM Press, New York, NY, USA (2012)
2. Singh, J., Singh, P., Gill, S.S.: Fog computing: A taxonomy, systematic review, current trends and research challenges. J. Parallel Distrib. Comput. **157**, 56–85 (2021)
3. Hassler, M.: NURON – THE COMPLETELY NEW CORDLESS PLATFORM WITH BUILT-IN CONNECTIVITY (2022). https://www.hilti.group/content/hilti/CP/XX/en/company/media-relations/media-releases/Nuron.html. Accessed 11 Jan 2022
4. Naha, R.K., Garg, S., Georgakopoulos, D., et al.: Fog computing: survey of trends, architectures, requirements, and research directions. IEEE Access **6**, 47980–48009 (2018)

5. Habibi, P., Farhoudi, M., Kazemian, S., et al.: Fog computing: a comprehensive architectural survey. IEEE Access **8**, 69105–69133 (2020)
6. Wang, H., Wang, Q., Li, Y., et al.: Application of fog architecture based on multi-agent mechanism in CPPS. In: 2018 2nd IEEE Conference on Energy Internet and Energy System Integration (EI2), pp. 1–6 (2018)
7. Cao, B., Sun, Z., Zhang, J., et al.: Resource allocation in 5G IoV architecture based on SDN and fog-cloud computing. IEEE Trans. Intell. Transport. Syst. **22**, 3832–3840 (2021)
8. Fraga-Lamas, P., et al.: Design and empirical validation of a Bluetooth 5 fog computing based industrial CPS architecture for intelligent industry 4.0 shipyard workshops. IEEE Access **8**, 45496–45511 (2020). https://doi.org/10.1109/ACCESS.2020.2978291
9. Yousefpour, A., Fung, C., Nguyen, T., et al.: All one needs to know about fog computing and related edge computing paradigms. J. Syst. Architect. **98**, 289–330 (2019)
10. Mahmud, R., Kotagiri, R., Buyya, R.: Fog computing: a taxonomy, survey and future directions. In: Di Martino, B., Li, K.-C., Yang, L.T., Esposito, A. (eds.) Internet of Everything. IT, pp. 103–130. Springer, Singapore (2018). https://doi.org/10.1007/978-981-10-5861-5_5
11. Ahmed, A., Arkian, H., Battulga, D., et al.: Fog Computing Applications: Taxonomy and Requirements (2019). http://arxiv.org/pdf/1907.11621v1
12. Nath, S.B., Gupta, H., Chakraborty, S., et al.: A survey of fog computing and communication: current researches and future directions (2018). https://arxiv.org/abs/1804.04365
13. Mouradian, C., Naboulsi, D., Yangui, S., et al.: A comprehensive survey on fog computing: state-of-the-art and research challenges. IEEE Commun. Surv. Tutor. **20**, 416–464 (2018)
14. Chatterjee, S., Sarker, S., Lee, M.J., et al.: A possible conceptualization of the information systems (IS) artifact: a general systems theory perspective. Inf. Syst. J. **31**, 550–578 (2021)
15. Iorga, M., Feldman, L., Barton, R., et al.: Fog computing conceptual model (2018). https://www.nist.gov/publications/fog-computing-conceptual-model
16. Vaquero, L.M., Rodero-Merino, L.: Finding your way in the fog. SIGCOMM Comput. Commun. Rev. **44**, 27–32 (2014)
17. Blume, M., Lins, S., Sunyaev, A.: Understanding Interdependencies among fog system characteristics. In: 2022 IEEE 24th Conference on Business Informatics (CBI), Amsterdam, Netherlands, pp. 126–135 (2022)
18. Qusa, H., Tarazi, J.: Collaborative fog computing architecture for privacy-preserving data aggregation. In: 2021 IEEE World AI IoT Congress (AIIoT), pp. 86–91 (2021)
19. Veeramanikandan, M., Sankaranarayanan, S.: Publish/subscribe broker based architecture for fog computing. In: 2017 International Conference on Energy, Communication, Data Analytics and Soft Computing (ICECDS), pp. 1024–1026 (2017)
20. Razouk, W., Sgandurra, D., Sakurai, K.: A new security middleware architecture based on fog computing and cloud to support IoT constrained devices. In: Proceedings of the 1st International Conference on Internet of Things and Machine Learning. Association for Computing Machinery, New York, NY, USA (2017)
21. Ma, K., Bagula, A., Nyirenda, C., Ajayi, O.: An IoT-based fog computing model. Sensors **19**(12), 2783 (2019). https://doi.org/10.3390/s19122783
22. Kim, W., Chung, S.: User-participatory fog computing architecture and its management schemes for improving feasibility. IEEE Access **6**, 20262–20278 (2018)
23. Webster, J., Watson, R.T.: Analyzing the past to prepare for the future: writing a literature review. MIS Q. **26**, 8–28 (2002)
24. vom Brocke, J., Simons, A., Riemer, K., Niehaves, B., Plattfaut, R., Cleven, A.: Standing on the shoulders of giants: challenges and recommendations of literature search in information systems research. Commun. Assoc. Inf. Syst. **37**, 9 (2015). https://doi.org/10.17705/1CAIS.03709
25. Hao, T., Han, S., Chen, S., et al.: The role of fog in haze episode in Tianjin, China: a case study for November 2015. Atmos. Res. **194**, 235–244 (2017)

26. Roy, D., Dutta, S., Datta, A., et al.: A cost effective architecture and throughput efficient dynamic bandwidth allocation protocol for fog computing over EPON. IEEE Trans. Green Commun. Netw. **4**, 998–1009 (2020)

27. Lacity, M.C., Khan, S.A., Willcocks, L.P.: A review of the IT outsourcing literature: insights for practice. J. Strateg. Inf. Syst. **18**, 130–146 (2009)

28. Taherizadeh, S., Stankovski, V., Grobelnik, M.: A capillary computing architecture for dynamic internet of things: orchestration of microservices from edge devices to fog and cloud providers. Sensors **18**, 2938 (2018)

29. Datta, S.K., Bonnet, C., Haerri, J.: Fog computing architecture to enable consumer centric Internet of Things services. In: 2015 International Symposium on Consumer Electronics (ISCE), pp. 1–2 (2015)

30. Mekki, T., Jabri, I., Rachedi, A., et al.: Towards multi-access edge based vehicular fog computing architecture. In: 2018 IEEE Global Communications Conference (GLOBECOM), pp. 1–6 (2018)

31. Seitz, A., Johanssen, J.O., Bruegge, B., et al.: A fog architecture for decentralized decision making in smart buildings. In: Proceedings of the 2nd International Workshop on Science of Smart City Operations and Platforms Engineering, pp. 34–39, New York, USA (2017)

32. Sundarakantham, K., Shalinie, S.M., Prabavathy, S.: Design of cognitive fog computing for intrusion detection in Internet of Things. J. Commun. Netw. **20**, 291–298 (2018)

33. Zhang, H., Qin, B., Tu, T., et al.: An adaptive encryption-as-a-service architecture based on fog computing for real-time substation communications. IEEE Trans. Industr. Inf. **16**, 658–668 (2020)

34. Mayer, A.H., Rodrigues, V.F., de Costa, C.A., et al.: FogChain: a fog computing architecture integrating blockchain and internet of things for personal health records. IEEE Access **9**, 122723–122737 (2021)

35. Valentini, E.P., Lieira, D.D., Nakamura L.H.V. et al.: MOMMA: a flexible architecture based on fog computing for mobility management. In: 2018 IEEE Symposium on Computers and Communications (ISCC), pp. 964–969 (2018)

36. Tang, B., Chen, Z., Hefferman, G., et al.: A hierarchical distributed fog computing architecture for big data analysis in smart cities. In: Proceedings of the ASE BigData & SocialInformatics 2015, New York, NY, USA (2015)

37. Rampérez, V., Soriano, J., Lizcano, D.: A multidomain standards-based fog computing architecture for smart cities. Wirel. Commun. Mob. Comput. **2018**, 1–14 (2018). https://doi.org/10.1155/2018/4019858

38. Barik, R.K., Dubey, H., Mankodiya, K.: SOA-FOG: secure service-oriented edge computing architecture for smart health big data analytics. In: 2017 IEEE Global Conference on Signal and Information Processing (GlobalSIP), pp. 477–481 (2017)

39. Khan, A.A., Abolhasan, M., Ni, W.: 5G next generation VANETs using SDN and fog computing framework. In: 2018 15th IEEE Annual Consumer Communications & Networking Conference (CCNC), pp. 1–6 (2018)

40. Ungurean, I., Gaitan, N.C.: Software architecture of a fog computing node for industrial internet of things. Sensors **21**, 3715 (2021)

41. Núñez-Gómez, C., Caminero, B., Carrión, C.: HIDRA: a distributed blockchain-based architecture for fog/edge computing environments. IEEE Access **9**, 75231–75251 (2021)

42. Zhang, W., Zhang, Z., Chao, H.-C.: Cooperative fog computing for dealing with big data in the internet of vehicles: architecture and hierarchical resource management. IEEE Commun. Mag. **55**, 60–67 (2017)

43. Madumal, M.B.A.P., Atukorale, D.A.S., Usoof, T.M.H.A.: Adaptive event tree-based hybrid CEP computational model for Fog computing architecture. In: 2016 Sixteenth International Conference on Advances in ICT for Emerging Regions (ICTer), pp. 5–12 (2016)

44. Hassan, S.R., Ahmad, I., Nebhen, J., et al.: Design of latency-aware iot modules in heterogeneous fog-cloud computing networks. Comput. Mater. Continua. **70**, 6057–6072 (2022)
45. Abbas, A., Asghar, A., Khattak, H.A., et al.: Fog based architecture and load balancing methodology for health monitoring systems. IEEE Access **9**, 96189–96200 (2021)
46. Souza, A., Izidio L., Rocha, A., et al.: Sapparchi: an architecture for smart city applications from edge, fog and cloud computing. In: 2019 IEEE International Smart Cities Conference (ISC2), pp. 262–267 (2019)

Cooperative Virtual Machine Placement

José G. Quenum[1]($\boxtimes$) and Samir Aknine[2]

[1] Namibia University of Science and Technology, Windhoek, Namibia
`jquenum@nust.na`
[2] Université Claude Bernard - Lyon 1, Lyon, France
`samir.aknine@univ-lyon1.fr`

Abstract. Server virtualisation has played a preponderant role in cloud computing success todate. It controls hardware resource access and management for computing, storage and networking in cloud environments. There have been several approaches for virtual machine placement based on reinforcement learning, bin packing, game theory, multi-objective non-linear optimisation and other heuristics. This paper proposes a cooperative virtual machine (VM) placement approach based on commitments made in a prior coalition formation phase. Based on these commitments and the availability of resources, we use a heuristic to place new VMs. Using the coalition structure, we narrow the space for candidates during a placement, reducing the computation cost of a VM placement. We evaluated our approach and compared it to existing methods.

Keywords: Virtual Machine Placement · Coalition Formation · Resource Allocation

1 Introduction

The success of cloud computing in recent years is attributable to several technological developments, including *virtualisation* [16]. It creates an abstraction layer over physical hardware resources to increase the scalability of systems and reduce the cost of their underlying infrastructure. There are generally three types of virtualisation technologies: *full virtualisation*, which uses a hypervisor (e.g., `Xen` [3], `KVM` and `VMware ESX` [17]), to manage and monitor access to the hardware resources; *para virtualisation*, where the host operating system (OS) is modified to inter-operate with the hypervisor through hypercalls, and finally, *host virtualisation*.

One of the functions a hypervisor fulfils is to *allocate* hardware resources to newly spawned VMs and monitor their usage. This research focuses on three types of resources: *CPU* and *memory* for computationally intensive workloads and *secondary storage* (e.g., disk) for I/O-intensive workloads. Virtualisation resource allocation (VM placement) addresses the issue of mapping the hardware resources on a physical machine (PM) to the workloads in a VM or transferring the VM from one PM to another when the source PM is under or over-utilised.

© IFIP International Federation for Information Processing 2023
Published by Springer Nature Switzerland AG 2023
G. A. Papadopoulos et al. (Eds.): ESOCC 2023, LNCS 14183, pp. 136–150, 2023.
https://doi.org/10.1007/978-3-031-46235-1_9

It uses different variants of *scheduling* (and *load balancing*) algorithms [2]. A VM is often created to execute one or several tasks, resulting in one of the following workloads: burst, batch, IO- and CPU-intensive. Hypervisors must provision and allocate hardware resources to enable VMs to use various strategies to execute their tasks. For example, VMware ESX uses a resource *commitment* strategy (e.g., memory overcommit for memory allocation), while Hyper V uses a dynamic allocation (e.g., dynamic memory) based on the actual resource usage by the existing VMs. Despite all these fine-grained allocation strategies, when the physical resources dwindle within a hypervisor, the execution slows down, or an increased latency can be observed. As a workaround and to guarantee that the resources will be available when needed, some hypervisors may lease their spare resources at a discount price (e.g., spot instance in EC2, low-priority VM in Azure and preemptible and spot VMs in Google Computing Engine). We argue that one approach to enhance these techniques is to extend the resource allocation to several hypervisors and place the VM in the adequate host(s) when needed. Several VM placement or migration algorithms have been proposed in the past with techniques ranging from *bin packing* and related heuristics (see [7]) to various predictive schemes (queueing theory, Markov models, ensemble techniques, see [13]) and other metaheuristics and optimisation techniques (see [9,18]).

A VM placement mechanism should fulfil several objectives, including maximizing the profitability for the infrastructure provider (e.g., cloud provider), guaranteeing a level of performance for the user based on an agreed-upon service level agreement (SLA), and ensuring energy efficiency, reliability and locality within a VM. *Dynamic* VM placement algorithms face an additional challenge; the new host identification should complete fast to allow a timely execution of the user request. Our intuition in this paper is to reduce the computation time of the VM placement by narrowing the search space using a coalition structure built from a prior negotiation among the agents (hypervisors). A coalition structure is a partition of the complete set of agents into different groups. Each group, a *coalition*, represents a set of agents committed to cooperating for resource sharing when the need arises. When a user submits a new request to the system, and the agent the request is addressed to fails to allocate the necessary resources, we start two parallel processes. The first one searches for a suitable host among the coalition members, while the second looks for a host outside the coalition. The second process is stopped as soon as a host is found among the coalition members. From a list of candidates (hosts with available resources), a suitable host has the least amount of available resources. We assume that coalitions are generally of reasonable size, which searches for a host faster.

The remainder of the paper is structured as follows. Section 2 presents our coalition formation mechanism, while Sect. 3 discusses our VM placement method. Section 4 discusses an evaluation of our approach. The related work is discussed in Sect. 5. Finally, Sect. 6 concludes the paper and presents future directions.

2   Coalition Structure for Virtual Machine Placement

The value of a coalition depends on the agreements between its members, i.e., the sum of the hardware resources they can share. Thus, before the coalition formation, we ran an automated negotiation between the hypervisors (agents).

2.1   Automated Negotiation

The automated negotiation algorithm is a multilateral negotiation. However, because eventually the commitments are *bilateral*[1], we implement our negotiation protocol as a collection of independent[2] time-bounded bilateral negotiations. The domain of each negotiation is the set of hardware resources that agents can share. A portion of the hardware resources at an agent's disposal is reserved for sharing to foster cooperation. Moreover, our approach focuses on computationally-intensive workloads, which consume more CPU and memory, and I/O-intensive workloads, which consume more storage. As such, during the negotiations, the offers and counter-offers organise resources in two packages: P_1 for computationally-intensive tasks and P_2 for I/O-intensive ones.

An agent A is represented as a tuple $< P, R, \hat{R}, G, \bar{A}, \overset{\circ}{A} >$ where P (*Pref*) represents the preferred package (P_1 or P_2) of the agent, R (*Resources*) represents all the resources available to the agent and how much it can share with other agents, $\hat{R}$ (*Reserved*) represents the resources to be shared with other agents, G (*Guarantees*) represents the resources other agents will share with the agent, $\bar{A}$ (*Agreements*) represents all final agreements reached after the negotiations, and $\overset{\circ}{A}$ (*Allocations*) corresponds to the resources allocated during the execution.

Algorithm 1 details the negotiation protocol. It uses several primitives, which we highlight here. The *send* primitive delivers messages from one agent to another, while the *fetch_message* primitive fetches new messages from an agent's message queue. The *generate_request* primitive creates a new message whose content is a request, a special message content that indicates for each package the requested shareable percentage (an offer of some sort) and the deadline of the subsequent negotiation. Similarly, *generate_counter_offer* produces a new message of type **counter_offer**. The content of the message specifies the revised percentage of resources that the agent is ready to share at that point of the negotiation. For an agent handling a message during the negotiation, the *update_agreements* primitive updates the *Agreements* attribute of the agent by recording a new agreement, a tuple containing the shareable percentage for each package, the direction of the commitment (provider or consumer), and the other agent involved in the negotiation. Moreover, the initiator of a negotiation uses the *evaluate_and_reply* primitive to evaluate a counteroffer and decides whether to accept it or not. The *has_capacity_and_pref* primitive checks whether a negotiation participant has the required resources and the suitable package preference to

---

[1] This is due to how the placement and migration algorithms are currently set up.

[2] Although these bilateral negotiations run independently, there is a limit to the resources they can commit to sharing.

Algorithm 1. Negotiation Protocol

    Input: Initiator   `/Initiator of the negotiation`

    Input: Agents   `// List of agents`

    Output: Agreements

1   *initiate_negotiation*(Initiator, Agents)

2   **while** *true* **do**

3   *handle_message*(Initiator)

4   **return** Agreements

5

6   **Function** *initiate_negotiation* (initiator,   agents)

7   req := *generate_request*(initiator)

8   pending := agents

9   **repeat**

10   send(req, *select_provider*(agents, pending))

11   **until** pending = $\emptyset$

12

13   **Function** *handle_message* (initiator)

14   msg := *fetch_message*()

15   agent := msg.*destination*

16   **if** agent = initiator **then**

17   **if** msg.type = **accept** **then**

18   *update_agreements*(msg)

19   **else**

20   **if** msg.type = **counter_offer** **then**

21   *evaluate_and_reply*(msg)

22   **else**

23   **if** *expired*(msg) **then**

24   send(**reject**, initiator)

25   **else**

26   **if** *has_capacity_and_pref*(msg, agent) **then**

27   send(**accept**, initiator)

28   *update_agreements*(msg)

29   **else**

30   c_offer = *generate_counter_offer*()

31   send(c_offer, initiator)

---

accommodate a request. Finally, the *select_provider* primitive selects a potential participant which has not been contacted yet to initiate a negotiation. To initiate a negotiation (see Algorithm 1, lines: 6–11), an agent acting as a consumer issues a request to each potential provider, asking the provider to commit to a fraction of its shareable resources. For example, for a consumer A_i, the request looks as follows: $req^{A_i} = (P_1 : 10.0; P_2 : 20.3; deadline : 10000)$. This request indicates that A_i expects a provider evaluating the request to commit 10% of its shareable CPU and memory and 20.3% of shareable storage resources. The deadline[3] of the negotiation, or at least the response from the provider, is due in 10 min. Once a negotiation is initiated, the initiator or an agent participating in the negotiation monitors its message queue and handles incoming messages. The *handle_message* function (lines 13–31) fulfils that functionality. When an agent A_j receives the message req^{A_i}, it takes one of the following decisions: (1) if the deadline of the negotiation has elapsed, it rejects the request; (2) if the agent can accommodate the request and is willing to, it accepts the request and updates its commitments (`Reserved` attribute); (3) if, due to prior commitments, she cannot share any more resources, it rejects the request; (4) if not, it makes a counteroffer about the fraction it can provide. If the response to the request is a `reject`, A_i ends the negotiation for both participants. If, on the contrary, it is an `accept`, A_i updates its `Guarantees` and `Agreements` attributes and ends the negotiation for both participants. Finally, with a `counter-offer`, A_i evaluates the messages and accepts, rejects or carries on by making another counteroffer.

In short, a rejected offer ends the bilateral negotiation. Similarly, an accepted offer concludes the negotiation, with both participants updating their agreement lists. Finally, during the time set for the negotiation, alternating offers are exchanged by both parties to reach a possible agreement. Once all bilateral negotiations are completed, we use the agreements reached by the agents to group them optimally.

Although the initial request in a bilateral negotiation starts with a random offer, the rationality of the overall negotiation lies in the fact that the evaluation of the request is based on the provider's current capabilities. Furthermore, when the provider makes a counteroffer, it is accepted or rejected since the consumer assumes that the value in the counter offer reflects the actual capabilities of the agent.

By way of example, we use a set of ten agents whose resources, including shareable resources (**S***), are presented in Table 1. Figure 1 depicts the agreements the agents reached after the negotiation phase. For example, `MLion` agreed to share its storage with `WWolf` (3.0%) and `GEagle` (4.0%). Similarly, `Boar` agreed to share 15.0% of its CPU and memory with `WWolf` and expects 8.0% of storage from `AFox`.

---

[3] Note that we use a *physical clock* value for the sake of simplicity in this example. Actually, due to the distributed nature of our algorithm, we use a time limit and a *vector clock* (logical clock).

Table 1. Ten-Agent Example

Name	P_1			P_2	
	cpu	memory	S*	storage	S*
GEagle	10000	256	10.0	30000	11.0
MLion	35000	1024	25.0	7000	7.0
SLeopard	44000	4096	10.5	96000	9.5
Hyaena	15000	512	12.0	96000	11.0
SWolf	35000	2048	12.0	70000	7.0
WWolf	70000	8192	7.0	96000	12.0
AMuskox	35000	256	6.0	70000	8.0
PBear	48000	512	9.0	96000	10.9
AFox	57000	4096	14.0	96000	12.0
Boar	70000	4096	15.0	96000	10.0

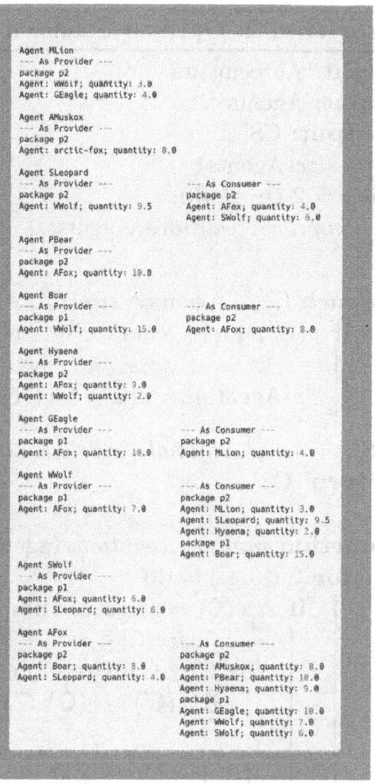

Fig. 1. Negotiation agreements

2.2 Optimal Coalition Structure

A coalition represents a group of agents constituted to allow these agents to coordinate and cooperate in the execution of several complex tasks [15]. The partition of the set of agents into exhaustive and disjoint coalitions in order to maximise the overall outcome is a *coalition structure*. More formally, let $\mathcal{A} = \{A_1, A_2, \ldots, A_n\}$ be the set of agents and v be a characteristic function[4] ($v : 2^{\mathcal{A}} \to \mathbb{R}$), a coalition structure over $\mathcal{A}$ is a set $\{C_1, C_2, \ldots, C_\ell\}$ such that:

$$C_i \neq \emptyset \cdot C_i \cap C_j = \emptyset \cdot \bigcup_{i=1}^{\ell} C_i = \mathcal{A} \text{ with } i \text{ and } j \in \{1, 2, \ldots, \ell\}.$$

Our optimal coalition structure generation is derived from the ODSS algorithm presented in [5]. More specifically, our algorithm focuses[5] on the IDP part of the method presented in [5].

Our characteristic function assigns to each coalition C_i the sum of the values of the resources shared by its members, i.e., determines the quantity

---

[4] v assigns a utility value to a coalition of agents in $\mathcal{A}$.

[5] Although data centres may employ multiple hypervisors, their number is not as high as the number of agents used in a typical coalition formation problem.

Algorithm 2. Optimal Coalition Structure Generation

    Input: Agreements   // All agreements
    Input: Agents   // List of agents
    Output: CS*   //Optimal coalition structure
1 n := $size$(Agents)
2 **for** $\imath = 2$ **to** $\frac{2n}{3}$ **do**
3     $improve\_coalitions$(Agents, $\imath$)

4
5 **foreach** $C'' \subset$ Agents $\wedge$ $size(C'') \in [1, \frac{n}{2}]$ **do**
6   **if** $v(C'') + v($Agents $\setminus C'') > v($Agents$)$ **then**
7   // Update grand coalition
8       $v($Agents$) := v(C'') + v($Agents $\setminus C'')$
9 CS* := $select\_optimal\_coalition\_structure()$
10 **return** CS*
11
12 **Function** $improve\_coalitions$ (agents, coal_size)
13   **for** $C \subset$ agents **do**
14   **if** $size(C) =$ coal_size **then**
15        $s_C := size(C)$
16   **for** $C' \subset C \wedge size(C') \in [1, \frac{s_C}{2}]$ **do**
17   **if** $v(C') + v(C \setminus C') > v(C)$ **then**
18   //Update coalition C's value
19            $v(C) := v(C') + v(C \setminus C')$

---

corresponding to the shared fraction for each type of resource and applies a unit price to extract the value.

Algorithm 2 summarises our optimal coalition structure generation. In Algorithm 2, the *size* primitive returns the size of a set: the number of its elements. As well, the *select_optimal_coalition_structure* primitive evaluates all coalition structures and selects the optimal one.

Algorithm 2 follows three steps. In the first step (lines 2–3), for each coalition $C_\imath$ of size ranging between 2 and $\frac{2n}{3}$, we split the coalition if doing so improves its value (see the *improve_coalitions* function (lines 12–19)):

$$\exists C_j \subset C_\imath, 1 \leq |C_j| \leq \frac{|C_\imath|}{2}, v(C_j) + v(C_\imath \setminus C_j) > v(C_\imath).$$

In the second step (lines 5–8), for any coalition whose size does not exceed half of the grand coalition ($\mathcal{A}$) size, we split $\mathcal{A}$ if doing so improves its utility:

$$\forall C, C \subset \mathcal{A}, 1 \leq |C| \leq \frac{|\mathcal{A}|}{2}, v(C) + v(\mathcal{A} \setminus C) > v(\mathcal{A}).$$

Finally, in the third step, we select *the optimal coalition structure*. To this end, we generate and evaluate the partitions based on the updated values. Then, we select the complete set of partitions with the highest value.

Following the example discussed in Sect. 2.1, the coalition structure generated by applying Algorithm 2 is as follows: {{AMuskox, SLeopard, Boar, Hyaena, Wwolf, SWolf}, {MLion, PBear, GEagle, AFox}}.

3 Virtual Machine Placement

The VM placement algorithm aims to identify which agent is best suited to host a VM given its current needs (in terms of workload). We use a request symbolising a demand for new hardware resources (CPU, memory and storage) to represent a workload. A request is addressed to an agent and may result in spawning a new VM or extending the hardware resources allocated to an existing VM. We consider three options: (1) the agent to which the request is addressed has the capacity and, therefore, handles the request; (2) if not, we turn to the members of the agent's coalition and select one that does not violate its commitments; (3) finally, if no member of the coalition can host the placement, we turn to the rest of the agents, looking for one with enough resources without violating its commitments. In our approach, we consider two scenarios: handling a single request and clustering multiple requests to be handled in bulk.

When an agent receives a request, we first check if the agent has the capacity to allocate the resources, i.e., the agent has the CPU, memory and storage resources required for the request. When the agent does not possess the required resources, we use a three-dimensional[6] *bin packing* algorithm [4,19] to determine which other agent should fulfil the request and host the related VM. Bin packing belongs to the family of multi-dimensional, multi-container packing problems. Given a set $\mathcal{H}$ of agent (hypervisor) type, each with a cost c_ℓ and a variable capacity (or hardware resources) W_ℓ. Given a set R of workload requests, each with a weight ω_i. The purpose is to allocate n request items to many agents such that the sum of the costs of the agent types is minimised. We formulate the variable-size multi-dimensional bin packing problem in Eq. (1). The equation includes two variables: x_{ij} and $y_{j\ell}$. x_{ij} indicates whether a request i is allocated to agent j. Furthermore, $y_{j\ell}$ determines if agent j is of type ℓ.

---

[6] The three dimensions represent the attributes of a request: cpu, memory and storage.

$$\min \sum_{j=1}^{n} \sum_{\ell=1}^{m} c_\ell \cdot y_{j\ell}$$

$$\text{s.t.} \quad \sum_{j=1}^{n} x_{ij} = 1 \quad \text{for } i = 1, \ldots, n$$

$$\sum_{\ell=1}^{m} y_{j\ell} \leq 1 \quad \text{for } j = 1, \ldots, n \tag{1}$$

$$\sum_{i=1}^{n} \omega_i \cdot x_{ij} \leq \sum_{\ell=1}^{m} W_\ell \cdot y_{\ell j} \quad \text{for } j = 1, \ldots, n$$

$$x_{ij} \in \{0, 1\} \quad \text{for } i, j = 1, \ldots, n$$

$$y_{j\ell} \in \{0, 1\} \quad \text{for } j = 1, \ldots, n \text{ and } \ell = 1, \ldots, m$$

Algorithm 3 summarises our bin packing algorithm. It uses the online *best-fit* heuristic [8]. The latter selects the agent with the tightest capacity (the least available resources) when possible. To improve the performance of our bin packing algorithm, we use a binary search tree (an AVL tree [1]), where we store the agents ordering (in increasing order) them based on their available resources. In Algorithm 3, the *violate_commitment* primitive determines whether allocating the request to an agent violates the agreements it reached during the negotiation, factoring in the allocations done by the agent so far. From lines 2–3, the algorithm tries to allocate the resources to the addressee. If unsuccessful, it then looks for a host among the coalition members (lines 6–15). When both options fail[7], the algorithm attempts a placement outside the coalition (lines 17–26). When the host is a coalition member or an agent outside the coalition, and a prior VM was previously spawned to handle the workload, there is a need to migrate the VM (see Le [11]). As an illustration of Algorithm 3, we submitted the request $W_{req}^1 = (\text{CPU} : 100, \text{memory} : 85, \text{storage} : 65)$ 100 times to agent Hyaena. After the agent handled the first five requests, all subsequent requests were handled by members of its coalition: {SWolf, AMuskox, SLeopard, Boar}. An important observation made during this experiment is as follows. If all the requests were different workloads of the same initial VM, the VM would be migrated from one hypervisor to another. However, some of these workloads, although running on the same VM, might be independent. As such, there is a need for a finer-grained migration policy. For example, a migration could occur only when a workload is related to a running process that can no longer be executed on a VM due to resource limitations. This, in turn, implies that a VM could exploit hardware resources from different hypervisors. A smart migration policy could coordinate this transfer until the workloads stabilise.

---

[7] In fact, the non coalition part is processed in parallel to the coalition part and will be cancelled when a coalition member is found.

Algorithm 3. Virtual Machine Placement

    Input: Agents   `// List of agents`

    Input: Coal   `//Coalition of the addressee`

    Input: Addressee   `// Agent`

    Input: Req   `// Request`

    Output: Host*   `// Placement host`

```
 1  Host = nothing
 2  if has_capacity (Addressee, Req) then
 3  │   Host* := Addressee
 4  else
 5  │   th₁ := START process_non_coal(Agents, Coal, Req)
 6  │   coal_avl := generate_bst(Coal \ {Addressee})
 7  │   coal_size := |coal_avl|
 8  │   for rk = 1 to coal_size do
 9  │   │   ag := coal_avl[rk]
10  │   │   if has_capacity (ag, Req)  ∧ ¬violate_commitment (ag, Req) then
11  │   │   │   Host* := ag
12  │   │   │   STOP th₁
13  │   │   │   break
14  │   │   else
15  │   │   └   continue
16  return Host*
17  Function process_non_coal (all_agts, coal, req)
18  │   coal_avl₁ := generate_bst(all_agts \ coal)
19  │   coal_size₁ := |coal_avl₁|
20  │   for rk₁ = 1 to coal_size₁ do
21  │   │   ag₁ := coal_avl₁[rk₁]
22  │   │   if has_capacity (ag₁, req)  ∧ ¬violate_commitment (ag₁, req) then
23  │   │   │   return ag₁
24  │   │   else
25  │   │   └   continue
26  │   return nothing
27
28  Function has_capacity (ag, req)
29  │   return ag.resources > ag.allocations + req
30
31  Function generate_bst (agents)
32  │   avlt := new AVLTree{Agent, Float}()
33  │   for ag ∈ agents do
34  │   └   insert(avlt, (ag, evaluate_capacity(ag)))
35  │   return avlt
36
```

When multiple requests are sent to an agent, we introduce a *beam search* heuristic to address these limitations. First, the requests are sorted from largest to smallest. For each agent type (based on its capacity), we define several subsets of the requests that can be allocated to it. We then evaluate the subsets and choose the one with the highest cluster of requests. We proceed with the next agent type until all the requests have been fulfilled. Different strategies can be considered for selecting the agent type. For example, select the least tight agent type, i.e., randomly select an agent among those with the highest capacity.

The energy consumption of the VM placement can be modelled following Chinprasertsuk and Gertpol [6]. There are two possible outcomes for the VM placement procedure. The energy consumption is limited to the computational load of Algorithm 3, or it involves an additional cost for transferring the VM. Energy quantification in a data centre is a rather complex task. It does not just focus on the energy drawn by the computational tasks. It also involves the cooling system, the energy used while the equipment is idle. For the sake of simplicity, we will assume here that these additional quantities represent a *constant*. A more fine-grained analysis could consider the cooling energy as a factor of the computational load. Equation (2) presents the power draw during the VM placement with no migration[8]. In Eq. (2), ϑ represents a constant that includes the power draw during idle time and other activities. η represents a factor of the power draw during the active time, and ρ_p a power consumption quantifier bounded between the idle power draw and the maximum power draw. Finally, cpu_load_{pl} is the CPU load corresponding to Algorithm 3. Consequently, the energy consumed during the VM placement is defined in Eq. (3); the migration occurs between *start* and *end*.

$$\mathsf{p}_{pl1}(t) = \vartheta + \eta \times \rho_p \times cpu\_load_{pl}(t) \tag{2}$$

$$\mathsf{E}_{pl1} = \int_{start}^{end} \mathsf{p}_{pl1}(t)\, dt \tag{3}$$

4   Evaluation

The approach presented in this paper is structured around three components. First is an automated negotiation component, where agents use a sequence of message exchanges to agree on resource sharing. The computational complexity of the negotiation procedure is *polynomial*. Assuming there are N agents in the system, each agent will evaluate its resources $N - 1$ times and exchange at most $3(N - 1)$ messages to reach an agreement with other agents. The second component is the optimal coalition structure generation. Its complexity is exponential ($O(3^n)$[9]). Finally, the last component in our approach is the VM placement algorithm. The latter completes in $n \log n$ steps. In summary, the first

---

[8] In the case of a migration an additional storage cost should be factored in.

[9] This follows from the computational complexity of IDP.

two components of our approach, executed offline overall, have an exponential complexity, while the last component, executed online, has a time complexity of $n \log n$.

Furthermore, we implemented the approach discussed in this paper in Julia[10] and evaluated the performance of each algorithm. We ran the evaluations in Julia 1.9 on an Apple M1 Pro chip with ten (10) cores. Figures 2a to 2c present the execution performance histograms for Algorithms 1 to 3, respectively. For Figs. 2b and 2c, our evaluation uses 10000 samples and 2307 samples for Fig. 2a. Each histogram records the minimum, maximum, mean, median and standard deviation of the corresponding algorithm's execution time. On average, our automated negotiation algorithm takes 2.16 ms, while the coalition formation takes 159.92 μs to complete. At runtime, the VM placement algorithm takes 4.08 μs to complete. The reduced time of the VM placement algorithm is due to the reduced number of agents involved in the search.

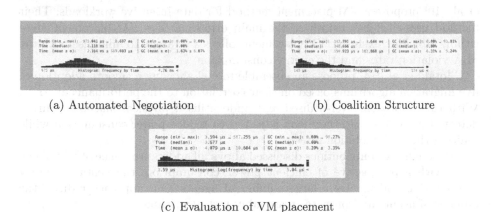

(a) Automated Negotiation   (b) Coalition Structure

(c) Evaluation of VM placement

Fig. 2. Evaluations

We compared our approach to various strategies presented in [7]. For example, Table 2 shows the performance (in nanoseconds) of our approach compared to the modified worst fit decreasing VM placement (MWFDVP). The table shows a different number of agents (with the number of agents in the coalition). Although both approaches perform almost similarly, our approach performs slightly better.

5   Related Work

Xiao et al. [20] propose an automated resource management system that avoids the overload of physical machines and guarantees energy efficiency. The approach uses skewness to measure the discrepancies in physical machine utilisation

---

[10] https://julialang.org.

Table 2. Comparison with MWFDVP

Number of Agents	Our Approach	MWFDVP
5(2)	288.603	320.887
10(5)	303.409	493.340
15(5)	431.950	275.332
20(8)	304.888	388.817
25(10)	607.955	494.845

and corrects the load distribution. It also includes a load prediction algorithm to anticipate the workload submission to the data centre. Finally, this approach mitigates resource scarcity by dynamically migrating the VM from one hypervisor to another. However, this assumes centralised coordination of the hypervisors. Kim et al. [10] propose a VM placement method for data-intensive workloads. Their method uses disk bandwidth as the main criterion. The VM placement algorithm, *Min-Max* exclusive VM placement, offers a strategy to minimise both the SLA violation rates and the energy consumption.

Motaki et al. [14] propose an ensemble model allowing a smooth adoption of live migration algorithms based on their correlation to the performance metrics. With this approach, over-utilised and underutilised physical machines can be detected optimally, and their load adjusted to reduce power consumption while limiting the SLA violation rates.

Although the contributions discussed above all address the issue of VM placement with a perspective of efficient power consumption, they entail a costly computation and involve a large number of agents. Our approach reduces the number of agents and proposes reasonably fast algorithms.

6   Conclusion

This paper proposes a new approach for virtualisation resource allocations using prior commitments between hypervisors (agents). The approach integrates an automated negotiation component followed by a coalition formation and a VM placement. The VM placement ensures the workload is distributed across all the active hypervisors. Reducing the set of agents participating in the placement algorithm tremendously reduces the algorithm's execution time. Furthermore, our approach guarantees energy efficiency thanks to the workload distribution among the hypervisors.

Our approach maximises the profitability of the infrastructure provider by optimising the hardware resource usage that satisfies almost all user workload requests. It limits SLA violations by ensuring that a hypervisor hosting a VM possesses the hardware resources to run the underlying workloads. Finally, thanks to our VM placement heuristic, we reduce the idle time of hypervisors and thus promote energy efficiency.

In the future, we wish to extend the approach in three directions. First, we wish to introduce more realistic metrics (e.g., a distance function like in [12]) to measure the optimality of the placement. Second, we wish to introduce a *proactive* VM placement component to adapt to dynamic scenarios. For example, when a hypervisor remains underutilised for a long time, it might be better to migrate all its workload and switch it off. In that case, the commitments need to be re-evaluated and updated. Moreover, in case of failure of a hypervisor, the existing commitments need to be re-evaluated, and the workloads migrated optimally. Finally, elongate and contextualise the VM migration time to support independent workloads of the same VM supported by resources from various hypervisors.

References

1. Amani, M., Lai, K.A., Tarjan, R.E.: Amortized rotation cost in AVL trees. CoRR abs/1506.03528 (2015). http://arxiv.org/abs/1506.03528
2. Asyabi, E., Sharifi, M., Bestavros, A.: ppxen: a hypervisor CPU scheduler for mitigating performance variability in virtualized clouds. Future Gener. Comput. Syst. **83**, 75–84 (2018). https://doi.org/10.1016/j.future.2018.01.015
3. Barham, P., et al.: Xen and the art of virtualization. SIGOPS Oper. Syst. Rev. **37**(5), 164–177 (2003). https://doi.org/10.1145/1165389.945462
4. Brandão, F., Pedroso, J.P.: Bin packing and related problems: general arc-flow formulation with graph compression. Comput. Oper. Res. **69**, 56–67 (2016). https://doi.org/10.1016/j.cor.2015.11.009. https://www.sciencedirect.com/science/article/pii/S0305054815002762
5. Changder, N., Aknine, S., Ramchurn, S.D., Dutta, A.: ODSS: efficient hybridization for optimal coalition structure generation. In: The Thirty-Fourth AAAI Conference on Artificial Intelligence, AAAI 2020, The Thirty-Second Innovative Applications of Artificial Intelligence Conference, IAAI 2020, The Tenth AAAI Symposium on Educational Advances in Artificial Intelligence, EAAI 2020, New York, NY, USA, 7–12 February 2020, pp. 7079–7086. AAAI Press (2020)
6. Chinprasertsuk, S., Cortphol, S.: Power model for virtual machine in cloud computing. In: 2014 11th International Joint Conference on Computer Science and Software Engineering (JCSSE), pp. 140–145 (2014). https://doi.org/10.1109/JCSSE.2014.6841857
7. Chowdhury, M.R., Mahmud, M.R., Rahman, R.M.: Implementation and performance analysis of various VM placement strategies in CloudSim. J. Cloud Comput. **4**(1), 1–21 (2015). https://doi.org/10.1186/s13677-015-0045-5
8. Coffman, E.G., Csirik, J., Galambos, G., Martello, S., Vigo, D.: Bin packing approximation algorithms: survey and classification. In: Pardalos, P.M., Du, D.-Z., Graham, R.L. (eds.) Handbook of Combinatorial Optimization, pp. 455–531. Springer, New York (2013). https://doi.org/10.1007/978-1-4419-7997-1_35
9. Filho, M.C.S., Monteiro, C.C., Inácio, P.R.M., Freire, M.M.: Approaches for optimizing virtual machine placement and migration in cloud environments: a survey. J. Parallel Distrib. Comput. **111**, 222–250 (2018). https://doi.org/10.1016/j.jpdc.2017.08.010
10. Kim, M.-H., Lee, J.-Y., Raza Shah, S.A., Kim, T.-H., Noh, S.-Y.: Min-max exclusive virtual machine placement in cloud computing for scientific data environment. J. Cloud Comput. **10**(1), 1–17 (2021). https://doi.org/10.1186/s13677-020-00221-7

11. Le, T.: A survey of live virtual machine migration techniques. Comput. Sci. Rev. **38**, 100304 (2020). https://doi.org/10.1016/j.cosrev.2020.100304. https://www.sciencedirect.com/science/article/pii/S1574013720304044
12. López, J., Kushik, N., Zeghlache, D.: Virtual machine placement quality estimation in cloud infrastructures using integer linear programming. Software Qual. J. **27**(2), 731–755 (2018). https://doi.org/10.1007/s11219-018-9420-z
13. Masdari, M., Zangakani, M.: Green cloud computing using proactive virtual machine placement: challenges and issues. J. Grid Comput. **18**(4), 727–759 (2019). https://doi.org/10.1007/s10723-019-09489-9
14. Motaki, S.E., Yahyaouy, A., Gualous, H.: A prediction-based model for virtual machine live migration monitoring in a cloud datacenter. Computing **103**(11), 2711–2735 (2021). https://doi.org/10.1007/s00607-021-00981-3
15. Rahwan, T., Jennings, N.R.: An improved dynamic programming algorithm for coalition structure generation. In: Padgham, L., Parkes, D.C., Müller, J.P., Parsons, S. (eds.) 7th International Joint Conference on Autonomous Agents and Multiagent Systems (AAMAS 2008), Estoril, Portugal, 12–16 May 2008, vol. 3, pp. 1417–1420. IFAAMAS (2008). https://dl.acm.org/citation.cfm?id=1402887
16. Rodríguez-Haro, F., et al.: A summary of virtualization techniques. Procedia Technol. **3**, 267–272 (2012). https://doi.org/10.1016/j.protcy.2012.03.029. https://www.sciencedirect.com/science/article/pii/S2212017312002587. The 2012 Iberoamerican Conference on Electronics Engineering and Computer Science
17. Scroggins, R.: Virtualization technology literature review. Glob. J. Comput. Sci. Technol. (2013). https://computerresearch.org/index.php/computer/article/view/317
18. Sudhakar, Saravanan: A survey and future studies of virtual machine placement approaches in cloud computing environment. In: Proceedings of the 2021 6th International Conference on Cloud Computing and Internet of Things, CCIOT 2021, pp. 15–21. Association for Computing Machinery, New York (2021). https://doi.org/10.1145/3493287.3493290
19. Wei, L., Lai, M., Lim, A., Hu, Q.: A branch-and-price algorithm for the two-dimensional vector packing problem. Eur. J. Oper. Res. **281**(1), 25–35 (2020). https://doi.org/10.1016/j.ejor.2019.08.024. https://www.sciencedirect.com/science/article/pii/S0377221719306770
20. Xiao, Z., Song, W., Chen, Q.: Dynamic resource allocation using virtual machines for cloud computing environment. IEEE Trans. Parallel Distrib. Syst. **24**(6), 1107–1117 (2013). https://doi.org/10.1109/TPDS.2012.283

Edge Computing

A Multi-pronged Self-adaptive Controller for Analyzing Misconfigurations for Kubernetes Clusters and IoT Edge Devices

Areeg Samir$^{(\boxtimes)}$ (ID), Abdo Al-Wosabi (ID), Mohsin Khan (ID),
and Håvard Dagenborg (ID)

Universitetet i Tromsø - Norges arktiske universitet, Hansine Hansens veg 18,
9019 Tromsø, Norway
`areeg.s.elgazazz@uit.no`

Abstract. Kubernetes default configurations do not always provide optimal security and performance for all clusters and IoT edge devices deployed, making them vulnerable to security breaches and information leakage if misconfigured. Misconfiguration leads to a compromised system that disrupts the workload, allows access to system resources, and degrades the system's performance. To provide optimal security for deployed clusters and IoT edge devices, the system should detect misconfigurations to secure and optimize its performance. We consider that configurations are hidden, as they are some sort of secret key or access token for an external service. We aim to link the clusters and IoT edge devices' undesirable observed performance to their hidden configurations by providing a multi-pronged self-adaptive controller to monitor and detect misconfigurations in such settings. Furthermore, the controller implements standardized enforcement policies, demonstrating the controls required for regulatory compliance and providing users with appropriate access to the system resources. The aim of this paper is to introduce the controller mechanism by providing its main processes. Initial evaluations are done to assess the reliability and performance of the controller under different misconfiguration scenarios.

Keywords: Misconfiguration · Monitor · Detection · RBAC · IoTs
Edge Devices · Clusters · Markov Processes

1 Introduction

Misconfiguration is unsecured default configurations or incorrect configuration(s) within the parameters of the system components (i.e., system clusters, IoT edge devices) that violate a configuration policy and may lead to vulnerabilities that affect the system's workload and performance at different system levels. At the edge level, a misconfigured edge device opens the potential for security breaches. For instance, if an edge device runs with default privileges or the same privileges

© IFIP International Federation for Information Processing 2023
Published by Springer Nature Switzerland AG 2023
G. A. Papadopoulos et al. (Eds.): ESOCC 2023, LNCS 14183, pp. 153–169, 2023.
https://doi.org/10.1007/978-3-031-46235-1_10

as the application, vulnerabilities in any system's component can be accidental (e.g., remote SSH open) or intentional (e.g., backdoor in component). At the application level, a misconfigured container (e.g., network port open) allows an attacker to exploit the Docker API port that escalates the attack to other containers and hosts. At the cluster level, misconfigurations in core Kubernetes components (e.g., API server, Kubelet, Kube-proxy) lead to the compromise of complete clusters, severely impacting system performance. To optimize a system's performance, system resources (e.g., CPU, memory) should be maximized for a workload; however, knowing the right limits to set for smooth application performance with different resource settings can be tricky. Large cloud service providers (e.g., Google, Microsoft, Amazon, Netflix) experienced misconfigurations that resulted in a vulnerable system [11,25]. The management of configurations has been explored in the literature [3,4,8], however, the complexity of misconfigurations arose from a large number of configuration parameters, their correlations, and dependencies makes the reasoning about the misconfigurations difficult.

This paper extends the work in [20,21] by proposing more details about a self-adaptive controller that detects misconfigurations of edge devices and clusters. The proposed controller is based on Hierarchical Hidden Markov Models (HHMMs), which we chose to (1) map the observed failure in metrics variations (e.g., CPU, Network, Memory, Workflow, Response Time) to the hidden misconfigurations in edge devices and system clusters. (2) Track the path of misconfiguration to show its impact on performance and workload. Furthermore, the controller extension implements standardized enforcement policies, demonstrating the controls required for regulatory compliance, and providing users with appropriate access to the system resources by extending the HHMMs to restrict access to our system and prevent security policy violations. The objective of this paper is to introduce the controller in terms of its architecture and processing activities, focusing on performance and reliability concerns. The remainder of this paper is organized as follows. Section 2 presents the research challenges. Section 3 discusses a use-case. Section 4 introduces the self-adaptive controller phases. Section 5 evaluates the controller. Sections 6 and 7 conclude the article and present the future direction of the work.

2   Research Challenges

Managing the misconfiguration of Kubernetes clusters and edge devices offers several challenges, such as: **Workload Misconfiguration:** containers have built-in configuration settings to determine the amount of CPU and memory resources they use (via resource requests and limits). These settings in essence override some auto-scaling capabilities of the underlying platform and can lead to under-provision of the workloads, which causes performance issues, or over-provision, which can lead to dramatic inefficiency and cost overruns. For example, a container may run with more security permissions than required and escalate its own privileges, e.g., root-level access, which consumes considerable resources to fix and cause system downtime. A single workload may require significant configuration to ensure a more secure and scalable application [18,23,26].

Resource-Limit: misconfigurations of Kubernetes workloads often involve inefficient provisioning of compute resources, leading to an over-sized bill for cloud computing. To maximize CPU efficiency and memory utilization for a workload, teams need to set resource limits and requests. But knowing the right limits to set for smooth application performance can be tricky [2,10,13].

Dependency between System Components: while many tools are available for configuration scanning, there are some challenges ahead of them: (a) some configuration processes are done manually, which could lead to a risk of user error [19,22,27] (b) Configuration dependencies between different system components are passed manually as configuration parameters, which could lead to a complex set of CI/CD pipelines that is difficult to maintain [6,7,12].

Shared-Configurations: A configuration can be used by multiple applications that are themselves managed by different teams. While a configuration's name (key) stays the same across environments, a configuration's value varies across environments, which makes configuration changes hard to test, as changing a shared configuration requires coordination across teams, coordinated testing, and coordinated deployment [12,13,19,29].

Configuration Change Late Check: While some configuration parameters may be checked when used in specific tasks at startup time, other parameters may not be checked or used. These parameters might have errors that wouldn't be detected until they showed up later (e.g., error handling). Before deploying, the configuration parameters must be validated to optimize system performance, which is a time-consuming task, and failing to validate a change could lead to undesirable downtime.

3   The System Under Observation - A Healthcare Use-Case

Our system comprises hierarchical components with different configurations, resources, and policies. Components include gateways, sensors, services (e.g., monitor heart rate), edge devices, clusters, nodes, containers, and system users (e.g., healthcare participants), including their roles and access control to manage and control sensors and actuators attached to the system, as shown in Fig. 1.

At the edge layer, misconfiguration (e.g., lack of authentication and authorization [15]) could affect device monitoring and allow an attacker to inject or modify data to reprogram the device. At the fog layer, misconfiguration at the cluster level (e.g., vulnerable product version [14,16], no parameter validation [17]) could allow an attacker to gain root-level access to the host and exploit system processes. At the cloud layer, misconfiguration, such as enabling anonymous access to blob containers in cloud storage, might result in the leakage of sensitive information. In such settings, participants linked to the system may experience anomalous behavior or threats that stress the system and its performance. Hence, we differentiated between the types of observation concerning misconfiguration and performance degradation: **error** that refer to a misconfig-ured system component, which is unknown and hidden from the participants and could lead to **threats** such as distributed denial of service attacks that target the configuration of the component to impact the trust established between the IoT devices and the system. Error and its consequences of threats can lead to anomalous or faulty behavior **anomaly/fault**, which is hidden from the partic-ipants (i.e., overload and abnormal flow of information characterizing stealthy threat strategies conditioned on the system model and the control policy). Such settings are observed by the occurrence of an observed **failure** (e.g., saturated resources) emitted from the settings of hidden components.

4   Self-adaptive Controller

This section presented the main phases of the controller. The controller adopted the Monitor, Analysis, Plan, Execute, and Knowledge (MAPE-K) architecture for self-adaptive systems and consists of (1) *Monitoring* that collects performance data; (2) *Detection and Identification* that analyzes detected misconfigurations and vulnerabilities in edge device(s) and container-based cluster and identifies its type. To control access from edge devices to system components, we extended HHMM to manage constraints in role-based access control. Models are imple-

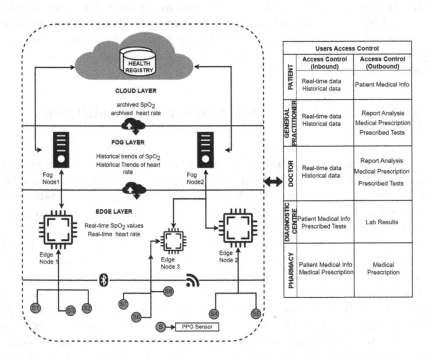

Fig. 1. Hierarchical Interaction between System Components, Participants, and The Access Control

mented at the gateway to collect and transmit measurements from the edge device to the fog.

4.1   Phase 1: System Components Monitor

We checked the normality of the workload of the components under observation using the Spearman rank correlation coefficient to estimate the dissociation between the observations emitted (failures) and the amount of flow (hidden workload). To achieve that, we wrote an algorithm that is used as a general threshold to highlight the occurrence of faults in managed components (for more details, see [21]). The controller checked the configuration settings against the benchmarks of Azure Security, CIS Docker, and Kubernetes to detect any mismatch between the settings and the requirements of secure deployment in components.

4.2   Phase 2: Access Control Policy Management

We controlled the information flow from/to the system by managing the interaction of participants with the system. Each participant has allowed actions and roles to access nodes and services of the system (see Fig. 1). We identified a list of the roles and actions of the participants, which has a set of access variables for each participant, such as the roles, actions, access to the API, the authorizations they have, the permissions, the boundaries of the permissions, and the conditions. The permission limit defines the maximum permissions granted to participants and roles using an enumeration-type action with two values (true and false). If the permission action is true, then the permission is allowed; otherwise, it is rejected. Moreover, we assumed that if no information flow policy is specified in the domain, the inbound and outbound flow will be set if the policy has any outbound rules. The policies in the observed system do not conflict as they are addictive. We extended our HHMM model with a set of controlling labels made up of tags, each of which stands for a specific integrity issue (private data) and outlines the information flow allowed. We define a role-based access space and a set of policies for each participant to allow specific participants access to specific system services. The access control policies are specified in the form of YAML format by writing a script that defines a template for generating YAML definitions based on the external policies. The script iterates over each policy, fills in the template with policy details, and accumulates the generated YAML. The script writes the accumulated YAML to an output file that is applied to the Kubernetes cluster and ensures that the translated policies are properly enforced.

System Component and Participants Role we specified a set of labels made up of tags to represent certain integrity (private data) and secrecy issues (sanitized data) to manage system components and access of participants from medical devices. Tags outline information flows by regulating the sensitive flow of information, such as patient personal information and related medical reports/outcomes. Tags correlate objects, such as patient and data items, with the secrecy and integrity flow constraints required to formulate a policy. Each tag is decomposed into a pair $\langle c, s \rangle$ of concern and a specifier. For example, the pair $\langle medical, Patient432 \rangle$ symbolizes Patient432's health information. We defined all data records of a particular type without listing all potential tags, as shown in Fig. 2. Each tag has one or more subtag connections defined for any concern and specifier. For example, a tag $T_0 = \langle c, s \rangle$ is a subtag of tags $T_{\{1,0\}} = \langle c, * \rangle$ and $T_{\{1,1\}} = \langle *, s \rangle$, which are in turn subtags of the tag $T_2 = \langle *, * \rangle$ as shown in Fig. 3. In addition to the tags, every participant has an access variable Λ that expresses (1) the access role AR: read R, write W, update U or combination of them (see Fig. 2), (2) access status AS successful $Approval$ or $Fail$, (3) device id DID (see Fig. 4), (4) device type DTY, (5) component label $Cabel$ (i.e., node label), (6) component type $Comty$ either ($node$, $container$, or $services$), (7) component id $ComID$ to access node, container or service, (8) user id $UserID$, and (9) data access type DAT either $PatientMedicalInfo$, $ReportAnalysis$, $PrescribedTests$, $MedicalPrescription$, and/or $LabResults$. The state space is a set of $\Lambda = \{AR, AS, DID, DTY, Cabel, ComID, UserID, DAT\}$. To define the maximum permissions granted to participants, a set of access boundaries is defined based on conditions and actions. The access boundaries take effect only if all conditions are satisfied. The access boundaries are accompanied by an enumeration type that takes true or false as a value to permit or reject access to the system. For each component and participant, we specify access control permissions as follows.

Access Control Permission for each type of component $Comty$, each participant $Participant\{p\}$ $Doctor$, $Patient$, GP, $DigCen$, or $Pharmacy$ has two label constraints (secrecy and integrity). The secrecy label restricts the read operation (i.e., incoming data flow), for example, $Sec(Participant\{Patient\}) = \{DAT, UserID\}$. The integrity label constrains the write operation (i.e., outgoing data flow), for example, $Int(Participant\{Patient\}) = \{Approval, DID, DTY\}$. The status of these two labels specifies the security context of accessing a specific component by a specific participant. For example, $Patient$ and $PatientMedicalInfo$ tags with the type of data accessed 'DAT' are presented in the hospital process to obtain patient data $Sec(Participant\{p\})$ according to (1).

$$\forall p \in Participantp\ \exists!\,(Sec(Participantp) \wedge Int(Participantp)),$$
$$where\ (Sec()\ and\ Int()) \supset \Lambda, \exists!\,(DID \wedge DTY)\ ForEvery\ Patient, \wedge \quad (1)$$
$$\iff DID \subset Comty$$

To ensure integrity consistency between groups, our system only accepts data from authorized medical devices based on the confirmation of approval of a patient and gives access to a specific node $Int(Participant\{Patient\}) = \{Approval, HeartMon24329, N21\}$ as shown in Fig. 4, and according to the rule in (2).

$$E1 \rightarrow E2, if\ Sec(E1) \precsim Sec(E2) \wedge Int(E2) \precsim Int(E1) \quad (2)$$

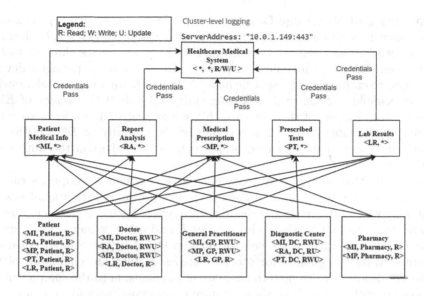

Fig. 2. Role-Based Access Control

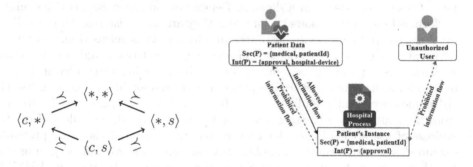

Fig. 3. Tag and Sub-Tags Relations   **Fig. 4.** Information Flow Access Constraints

A decision rule $\Omega = \{AccessGranted, PerformManagement\}$ is added to allow certain actions in the access role (read, write, or update information) and to provide system-wide enforcement of the information flow policy, as shown in Fig. 2. The decision rule represented a generated probability distribution $\mu T_{ins}(Comty)$ from a type of component $Comty$, which is labeled $Cabel$, with specific actions at a time instant T_{ins} as shown in (3).

$$\omega = \begin{cases} AccessGranted, PerformManagement \ If \\ Comty \in \{AR, AS, DID, DTY, ComID, UserID, DAT\} \\ AccessDenied, \ Otherwise \end{cases} \quad (3)$$

Addition of New Edge Device to adapt the controller to accept new data from a new device, we introduced entities E with actions and events. Each entity has participants and sensors that interact with system nodes through mobile applications/interfaces and medical devices. Here, $E1$ (e.g., patient's device) has access to entity $E2$ (e.g., specific node '$N21$') with any preorder relationship $\precsim$. For example, $E2$ can read data from entity $E1$ only if the secrecy of $E1$ is preorder (i.e., subset) of the secrecy of $E2$, while entity $E1$ can write to entity $E2$ only if the integrity of $E2$ is preorder of the integrity of $E1$. Entities are registered in a domain with credentials to be validated upon the authorized participant's request.

Domain Management we define a *domain* as a named grouping structure with a particular function. The *domain* represents an organizational system cluster (s) with participants associated with devices. Each domain maintains its policies to control interactions with entities E and other domains. The *domain* indicates that if either of its policies returns $\Omega = AccessGranted$, then the information flow is granted for specific entities E with an annotation of the sequence, denoted X. To map the domain of participants to the components of the system without requiring them to store these mappings and to manage the workload of the system under observation, each component with a component label $Cabel$ is registered in a domain. Depending on the policy, entities might perform actions in other domains for which they are not registered. Thus, to allow domains controlling the circumstances in which data is released and in which information can be accessed, we considered that entities could communicate with the system through a combination of the following three identifiers: (a) other nodes that are allowed (exception: a node cannot block access to itself), (b) namespaces that are allowed, and (c) IP blocks (exception: traffic to and from the node where a running container is always allowed, regardless of the IP address of the node). Hence, for each entity, we computed the most probable extended annotation considering (Len, SN) at time tim. We defined Len as the length of the graph sequence and SN as the number of states of the HHMM. We constructed a directed cyclic graph in which every path has a start vertex device id DID and an end vertex component id $ComID$ corresponding to an annotation of the sequence X of that path (e.g., $path1 : DID_1 > Cl_1 > N21$; $path2 : DID_2 > Cl_1 > N22$; $path3 : DID_1 > Cl_1 > N23$). On the contrary, for every annotation of X, there is a path with specific properties. For example, $X_{i=1} = \{path1, tim, \Omega, Participant\{p\}, \Lambda\}$. We considered that the only allowed connections in the graph are those from the containers and nodes in our domains under some containers and policies, which do not conflict, as they are addictive. Hence, for a connection from a source node to a destination node, both the inbound and outbound flow policy on the source node and the destination node must allow the connection. If either side does not allow the connection, the connection will be rejected. If no information flow policy is specified in the domain, then by default, the inbound flow will always be set, and the outbound flow will be set if the policy has any outbound rules. Each information flow policy permits participants to access the system's components in a Namespace. Each policy includes a type list *PolicyType*, which may include inbound, outbound, or both in a namespace. The *PolicyType* indicates whether the given policy applies to the inbound flow to one or more selected nodes (s), the outbound flow from one or more selected nodes (s), or both. If no *PolicyType* are specified in a Namespace, then by default, inbound and outbound will be set if the policy has any outbound rules, and all inbound and outbound flows are not allowed to and from nodes in the Namespace. Participants access the system according to a request that includes the username, the requested action, and the object affected by the action. The request is authorized if the existing policy for a Namespace declares that the participants have permission to complete the requested action (write, read, update, or combination of them).

Our intention is not to prescribe action sequences for participants. Instead, we provide mechanisms to control the system's access actively, according to the flow of information from the participants, through adaptation and conditional access to the system components. Once access to the system is secured, the controller moves on to the next phase.

4.3   Phase 3: Misconfiguration Detection

We use HHMM [5] to model the hierarchical structure of our system and map the hidden misconfiguration settings from the observer to the performance metric. We choose HHMM because every component, along with its dependence on configuration settings, can be represented as a set of hierarchically interlinked HMMs, as shown in Fig. 5.

The components of our system under observation have a hierarchical structure. The system consists of one or more clusters Cl (root state) that are composed of a set of nodes N (internal states) that host containers C (substates) with one or more deployed services S (production state) as a component of the application. Each component emits observations, which are emissions of failures from a component resource. Each component has configuration settings. The node assigns requests to its containers, communicating at the same node or externally. A service could be deployed in several containers simultaneously, and a container is defined as a group of one or more containers that constitute one service. The system has more than one cluster $Cl^{j=1}$ and has internal states $N_i^{j=2}$, which represent our virtual machines (nodes) with horizontal i and vertical j. Each node has a substate C_i^{j+1} that represents our containers (e.g., C_1^3 at vertical level 3 and horizontal level 1). Each container has deployed services S_i^{j+2} that emit Observations Space OS_n, which reflects a sequence of workload fluctuations for CPU, Memory, Network, and Response time. The fluctuation is associated with the saturation of observed computing resources to be either H: High, L: sLow, or N: Normal, more details in [21]. This fluctuation is associated with a probability that reflects the state transition status from AF (Abnormal Flow) to NL (Normal Flow) at a failure rate $\Re$, which indicates the number of failures emitted from our Cluster Space (ClS) over a period of time. ClS consists of a set of Ns, containers C, and services S. The edge direction indicates the information flow and the dependency between states.

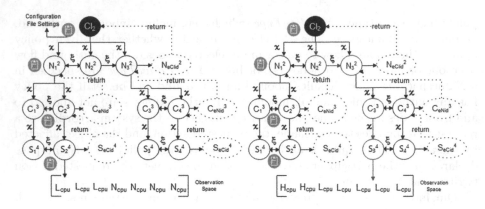

Fig. 5. Misconfiguration Detection in Multi-Clusters System(s) Using HHMM

For example, $N_1^2 = \{C_1^3, C_2^3\}$, N_2^2, $N_3^2 = \{C_3^3, C_4^3\}$, $C_1^3 = \{S_1^4\}$, $C_2^3 = \{S_2^4\}$, $C_3^3 = \{S_3^4\}$, $C_4^3 = \{S_4^4\}$.

For each participant in a specific *domain* with $X_i = \{path_i, tim, \Omega, Participantp, \Lambda\}$ where $\Omega = \{Access\ Granted\}$, our system calls its nodes to enter their containers and services $N_1^2 = \{C_1^3, C_2^3\}, N_2^2$, $N_3^2 = \{C_3^3, C_4^3\}$, $C_3^3 = \{S_1^4, S_2^4, S_3^4, S_4^4\}$. Here, each service emits observations and transits to its final state S_{eCid}^4 to end the transition for the services and to return the control to its calling parent C_2^3, as shown in (4) and (5). The same process is followed, however, to make a horizontal transition to C_2^3 to obtain the observations at the container level. Once the horizontal transition is completed, the transition goes to the end state C_{eNid}^3 to make a vertical transition to the state N_1^2. Once all transitions are achieved under this node, the control returns to N_3^2, as shown in Fig. 5. The model is trained by calculating the probabilities of the parameters to obtain a hierarchy of abnormal flow path $AF_{seq} = \{Cl, N_2^2, N_3^2, C_3^3, S_3^4\}$, which is affected by the misconfigured component (N_2^2) and might cause a threat, as shown in (6). Here, we recursively calculate $\Im$, which is ψ for a time set ($\bar{t} = \psi(t, t + k, S_i^j, S^{j-1})$), where ψ is a state list, which is the index of the most probable production state to be activated by S^{j-1} before activating S_i^j. $\bar{t}$ is the time when S_i^j was activated by S^{j-1}. The δ is the likelihood that the most probable state sequence generates $(O_t, \cdots, O_{(t+k)})$ by recursive activation. τ is the transition time at which S_i^j was called by S^{j-1}. Once all recursive transitions are returned to Cl_w, we get the most probable hierarchies starting from Cl_w the production states in the T period by scanning the state list ψ, the likelihood of states δ and the transition time τ. The same previous steps are taken for each cluster where w refers to the cluster number $w = \{1, 2, \cdots, m\}$. We correlated each state with time to know its activation time, its activated substates, and the time at which the control returns to the calling state to have more information about the occurrence time and dependency of the misconfiguration. In the end, a sequence of anomalous hierarchical states is obtained. We compared the detected hierarchies with the observed ones to detect the misconfigured state and its impact on the flow of information. The detected path with the lowest probabilities will be considered the vulnerable path with misconfigured states and abnormal flow. For example, the observed failure $L_{Network}$ is associated with a vulnerable abnormal flow path $AF_{seq} = \{Cl, N_2^2, N_3^2, C_3^3, S_3^4\}$ that is affected by N_2^2.

$$\Upsilon_S = \max_{(1 \leq r \leq S_i^j)} \left\{ \delta(\bar{t}, t+k, S_r^j, S_i^j) a_{S_{eC_i}^j}^{S_i^j} \right\} \tag{4}$$

$$\Im_S = \max_{(1 \leq y \leq S^{j-1})} \left\{ \delta(t, \bar{t}-1, S_y^j, S^{j-1}) a_{S_{eC_y}}^{S^{j-1}} \Upsilon_S \right\} \tag{5}$$

$$AF_{seq} = \max_{Cl_{(1 \leq w \leq m)}} \left\{ \delta(T, Cl_w), \tau(T, Cl_w), \psi(T, Cl_w) \right\} \tag{6}$$

5   Evaluations

This section assesses the detection and role-based access control, focusing on the measurement of performance and reliability.

5.1   Detection Evaluation

Assessment1: Simulation Environment

Environment Settings: The testing environment is built with Python. It runs on VMware and consists of three nodes (i.e., VM instances), which are for (1) VM1: the Healthcare application that handles patient data. The VM1 is connected to an edge gateway device that acts as a local hub for data aggregation and processing. The edge gateway collects data from the IoT device and transmits the collected data to VM1 for further processing. The device communicates with the edge gateway through Wi-Fi. Edge devices with similar functionality are grouped and allocated to a respective group. For VM1, we created a patient application on the edge device that generates patient information using the Python Faker and paho-mqtt libraries and transmits the information to VM1. The edge gateway is presented by the MQTT client, which establishes a connection to the gateway's IP address and port. (2) VM2: correctly configured container-based cluster node, and (3) VM3: controller. For each node, we implemented a set of containers and services. Each node is equipped with Linux OS (Ubuntu 18.10 version), a VCPU, and 2GB of VRAM. The virtual platform is allocated to a physical PC equipped with Windows 11, Intel Core i7-1260P 2.10 GHz, and 32 GB of RAM. Around 30 namespaces are created, each with 4 microservices (pods) used for performance measurements and assigned the same number of network policies. The number of policies created was 900, which were ordered, managed, and evaluated using Calico, Open Policy Agent, and Styra DAS, respectively. A set of agents was installed to collect data on CPU, memory, network, changes in the file system (i.e., no flow issued to the component), patient health information, device operation status, device id, and system components service status. The agent adds a data interval function to determine the time interval to which the collected data belong. The agent is configured to connect to the system automatically with the valid credentials of the system users for authentication. The Datadog tool is used to obtain a live data stream for the running components and to capture the request-response tuples and associated metadata. Prometheus is used to group the collected data and to store them in a time series database using Timescale-DB.

Table 1. Detection Evaluation

Models	RMSE	PFD	Recall	Accuracy
HHMM	0.3299	0.4050	95.01%	94%
CRFs	0.4023	0.4208	92.86%	92%

Edge Device Configuration Errors: We installed K3s on a Raspberry Pi 3 Model B+ and set up a single node Kubernetes cluster. We created three configuration errors. The first one is an 'empty configuration file' that makes the device have trouble starting modules. The second one is 'enabling unnecessary port', in which the YAML configuration defines a pod with a single container running the Nginx image. The container is configured to expose three ports: 80, 443, and 8080. The third one deployed a container image 'Simulated Hospital[1]' that generates patient data. The YAML image file is configured to allow privilege escalation.

Container-based Cluster Configuration Error Scenarios: We write our configuration files using YAML. Privilege escalation configuration errors were deployed, such as Privilege Escalation Flaw and Privilege Escalation Flaw and Redeployment Fail [20]. The configuration files of the components are stored in GitOps version control to simplify the rollback of configuration changes. We use Kube-Applier to fetch our declarative configuration files for our clusters from the Git repository.

Performance Evaluation: The model was trained on the collected data and on the configuration error scenarios all at once. The performance of the detection model is evaluated by the root mean square error (RMSE) and the probability of false detection (PFD), which are the metrics commonly used to assess the accuracy of the detection. The RMSE measures the differences between the detected value and the one observed by the model. A lower RMSE value indicates a more effective detection scheme. The PFD measures the number of components normally detected that have been misdetected as anomalies by the model. A lower PFD value indicates a more effective detection scheme. The efficiency of the model is compared to Conditional Random Fields (CRFs); see Table 1. We noticed that the computation of CRFs is harder than that of the HHMM. The results show

---

[1] https://github.com/google/simhospital.

that the performance of the proposed detection is better than that of the CRF, as it correctly detected misconfigurations with around 95% recall and 94% accuracy with few false positives, which occur due to some ports being identified as insecure (e.g., insecure docker registry 5000). A false positive occurred at the edge level due to a condition identified in the YAML rule that is based on a fixed threshold without taking into account personal variations that could affect normal ranges of vital signs (e.g., $condition : heart\_rate > 100$).

Assessment2: Real-World Scenario

Learning Settings: The controller is further trained in some of the misconfigurations that allow an escalation of privileges to the host [15,16]. We evaluated the detection performance by comparing the HHMM with the HMM and measuring their log-likelihood. We ran each model for a maximum of 10 iterations with a random start and an approximate training period ranging from 164 s to 9 min with two layers of HHMM. The size of our generated data set was approximately 10 MB with a period of 6 months. We selected a subset of the data set of around 4.3 MB mainly related to the types of misconfiguration mentioned above to train the models and provide more targeted and specialized training data sets. We trained the models on different hidden state numbers (8, 16, 32, 64) and evaluated their performance. The data are divided into 70% training data and 30% testing data, more details on the environment settings in [20].

Performance Evaluation: In the training data, the log-likelihood of the HHMM was around -63 with 8 states, which increased with increasing number of states to -50 with 10 states and -20 with 30 states. The HMM was -30 with eight states, -20 with 10 states, and reached -15 with 30 states. On the test data, the log-likelihood of HHMM gradually increased from -50 with 8 states to a peak of -5 with 30 states. Then the model increased slightly with increasing number of states, while the HMM fluctuated to -65 with 8 states, -50 with 10 states, and -60 with 30 states. After that, the HMM decayed to -70 with increasing numbers of states. We observed that HHMM outperforms HMM in different states. With a decreasing number of states, both models show good performance. However, with an increasing number of states, HHMM performance shows better results, whereas HMM performance gradually decays, showing a symptom of overfitting as its likelihood drops from training data to testing data. This returns to the larger capacity of the HHMM, which allows the model to adapt to new changes and to be less prone to overfitting.

5.2 Rule-Based Access Control Performance Evaluation

Test Settings: We created access control roles for system participants with different roles and different access levels, as shown in Fig. 2. We evaluated the performance of rule-based access control under misconfiguration by giving the Pharmacy the Doctor role. This misconfiguration violates the principle of privileged access and leads to security breaches or unauthorized access. We use NetPerf and iPerf to measure network latency. The NetPerf is configured with a

200-second test duration and a goal of 99% confidence that the measured mean values are within ±2.5% of the real mean values. The iPerf is configured with a 30-second duration of the test, a 5-second reporting interval, and 3 numbers of parallel user threads to use, in which each thread will initiate a separate connection to the server. To constitute unauthorized access to the system, we define the rule that a pharmacy can write and update patient data. We implemented a trace file with 5000 requests that correspond to 15 min of workload. The trace file is generated using OpenTelemetry and Jaeger in Kubernetes. We generated several unauthorized access attempts from the Pharmacy due to the misconfiguration. We focussed on measuring the overhead latency of network performance during the creation of several network access policies.

Performance Evaluation: We created a cluster with two namespaces: "users-namespace" and "healthcare-namespace" with 4 microservices (pods) for each. We created an access control policy that assigns to the pharmacy the "edit" ClusterRole, which allows for write and update access to resources within the "healthcare-namespace". We measured unauthorized access to the application. The average access was about 3100 access attempts per 2 min with CPU and memory loads 80% and 75%, respectively. We measured the performance overhead for network latency by increasing the number of policies from 100 to 900 policies by 100 policies at a time. We created some policies, one that allows traffic communication between pods and gave it the highest order, and the other one, a policy that disallows traffic between pods, and we gave it the lowest order. We increase the number of policies to measure network performance in terms of latency. Our goal is to enforce a network policy that restricts communication between these namespaces. Hence, the pods in the "users-namespace" namespace can only communicate with pods in the "healthcare-namespace" namespace on a specific port while denying all other traffic and on specific roles. We created a misconfiguration that violates the principle of privileged access in the "users-namespace" namespace by assigning the user "pharmacy" the "cluster-admin" ClusterRole, which grants the pharmacy full access including the ability to modify resources and update other patient's data at least. During the evaluation, the network performance shows an unremarkable impact on latency while increasing the number of policies. The latency was almost stable, from 70 microseconds with 100 policies to 85 microseconds with 900 policies. Due to the misconfiguration of the network policy, the pods within the nodes were able to communicate with resources that should be restricted. We created another VM (VM4) with 4 pods to communicate with VM1 to measure the latency of the pods between the nodes. We stress the resources of VM4 with Locust with a waiting time between requests of 5 to 15 ms. The latency for the pods' communications between the nodes was higher than that for the pods' communication within the node. It increased from 250 microseconds with 100 policies to 280 microseconds with 900 policies. This leads to shared resources and direct communications between the pods on the same network, resulting in lower latency.

From the results obtained, we conclude that system performance is directly affected by configuration errors. The higher the number of configuration errors, the more likely the system will experience performance degradation.

6   Related Work

Existing frameworks have paid limited attention to the critical role of efficient management of misconfiguration in edge devices and clusters [1,4,24]. The work in [19] conducted an empirical study with 2,039 Kubernetes manifests to categorize the security misconfiguration and quantify it. Another work [3] presented a performance-centric configuration framework for containers on Kubernetes that gives unified key-value data, including configurations and metrics, to analysis plugins by providing a built engine for processing defined rules in analysis plugins. However, those techniques are time-consuming to come up with good result quality and are unmanageable with large datasets. The techniques suffer from catching every code defect and are limited when it comes to addressing issues in complex, multi-component applications, especially in scale and load balance environments. The work in [27] focused on detecting configuration errors at the startup time by analyzing the source code and generating the configuration checking code. However, this technique cannot handle the interaction between the configuration parameters. An analysis of misconfigurations and their associated code blocks helps in detecting which parts of the system code are associated with configuration parameters. This could be achieved by deriving the specification of the configurations by designing a custom control and data flow analysis targeting the configuration-based code [9,28], based rule [22], or based inference. However, those ways are highly specialized as some of them only focus on security, are not simple to write and maintain, are geared towards a host only instead of container images and edge devices, and can result in false positives or false negatives. Unlike our work, previous techniques are (1) limited in the types of configuration errors that can be detected, (2) Focus on detecting misconfiguration based on the type inference of the source code. (3) lack of adaptable detection that works on configurations inherited from different systems or incorrect settings that fall into normal ranges.

7   Conclusions and Future Work

The paper presented a controller that detects misconfigurations of container-based clusters and edge devices in hierarchical computing environments. The controller mapped observable quality concerns onto hidden settings to track misconfiguration paths and enforced access to informational constraints derived from healthcare legislation. The controller used the Hierarchical HMM mechanism and extended its mechanism to propose an access control policy model to increase the flexibility of role-based access control so that users can gain access to resources with regard to the model constraints, and the permissions could be adjusted based on user and environment conditions. Compared with other techniques, the evaluation presented the ability of the controller to detect misconfigurations with few false positive instances and promised log-likelihood. The purpose of the paper is to introduce the controller mechanism by providing its main processes and evaluations to assess its reliability and performance.

In the future, our objective is to carry out more experiments to confirm the results concluded, highlight the difference between the controller detection and other misconfiguration tools, improve the security of the access control model to handle system failure, and expand the evaluation of access control and policy rules.

References

1. Alspach, K.: Major vulnerability found in open source dev tool for kubernetes (2022). https://venturebeat.com/security/major-vulnerability-found-in-open-source-dev-tool-for-kubernetes/
2. Assuncao, L., Cunha, J.C.: Dynamic workflow reconfigurations for recovering from faulty cloud services, vol. 1, pp. 88–95. IEEE Computer Society (2013)
3. Chiba, T., Nakazawa, R., Horii, H., Suneja, S., Seelam, S.: Confadvisor: a performance-centric configuration tuning framework for containers on kubernetes, pp. 168–178 (2019)
4. Fairwinds: Kubernetes benchmark report security, cost, and reliability workload results (2023). https://www.fairwinds.com/kubernetes-config-benchmark-report
5. Fine, S., Singer, Y., Tishby, N.: The hierarchical hidden Markov model: analysis and applications. Mach. Learn. **32**, 41–62 (1998)
6. Gantikow, H., Reich, C., Knahl, M., Clarke, N.: Rule-based security monitoring of containerized environments. In: Ferguson, D., Méndez Muñoz, V., Pahl, C., Helfert, M. (eds.) CLOSER 2019. CCIS, vol. 1218, pp. 66–86. Springer, Cham (2020). https://doi.org/10.1007/978-3-030-49432-2_4
7. Haque, M.U., Kholoosi, M.M., Babar, M.A.: Kgsecconfig: a knowledge graph based approach for secured container orchestrator configuration, pp. 420–431. Institute of Electrical and Electronics Engineers Inc. (2022)
8. Hicks, M., Tse, S., Hicks, B., Zdancewic, S.: Dynamic updating of information-flow policies, pp. 7–18 (2005)
9. Hu, Y., Huang, G., Huang, P.: Automated reasoning and detection of specious configuration in large systems with symbolic execution, pp. 719–734 (2020)
10. Kermabon-Bobinnec, H., et al.: Prospec: proactive security policy enforcement for containers, pp. 155–166. Association for Computing Machinery, Inc. (2022)
11. Lakshmanan, R.: Microsoft confirms server misconfiguration led to 65,000+ companies' data leak (2022). https://thehackernews.com/2022/10/microsoft-confirms-server.html
12. Mahajan, V.B., Mane, S.B.: Detection, analysis and countermeasures for container based misconfiguration using docker and kubernetes, pp. 1–6. Institute of Electrical and Electronics Engineers Inc. (2022)
13. Moothedath, S., et al.: Dynamic information flow tracking for detection of advanced persistent threats: a stochastic game approach. arXiv:2006.12327 (2020)
14. NVD: Cve-2019-5736 (2019). https://nvd.nist.gov/vuln/detail/CVE-2019-5736
15. NVD: Cve-2019-6538 (2019). https://nvd.nist.gov/vuln/detail/CVE-2019-6538
16. NVD: Cve-2020-10749 (2020). https://nvd.nist.gov/vuln/detail/cve-2020-10749

17. NVD: Cve-2022-0811 (2022). https://nvd.nist.gov/vuln/detail/cve-2022-0811
18. Pranata, A.A., Barais, O., Bourcier, J., Noirie, L.: Misconfiguration discovery with principal component analysis for cloud-native services, pp. 269–278. Institute of Electrical and Electronics Engineers Inc. (2020)
19. Rahman, A., Shamim, S.I., Bose, D.B., Pandita, R.: Security misconfigurations in open source kubernetes manifests: an empirical study. ACM Trans. Softw. Eng. Methodol. 1–37 (2023)
20. Samir, A., Dagenborg, H.: A self-configuration controller to detect, identify, and recover misconfiguration at IoT edge devices and containerized cluster system, pp. 765–773 (2023)
21. Samir, A., Ioini, N.E., Fronza, I., Barzegar, H., Le, V., Pahl, C.: A controller for anomaly detection, analysis and management for self-adaptive container clusters. Int. J. Adv. Softw. **12**, 356–371 (2019)
22. Santolucito, M., Zhai, E., Dhodapkar, R., Shim, A., Piskac, R.: Synthesizing configuration file specifications with association rule learning. Proc. ACM Program. Lang. **1** (2017)
23. Sorkunlu, N., Chandola, V., Patra, A.: Tracking system behavior from resource usage data, vol. 2017-Sept, pp. 410–418 (2017)
24. Taft, D.K.: Armo: misconfiguration is number 1 kubernetes security risk (2022). https://thenewstack.io/armo-misconfiguration-is-number-1-kubernetes-security-risk/
25. Venkat, A.: Misconfiguration and vulnerabilities biggest risks in cloud security: report (2023). https://www.csoonline.com/article/3686579/misconfiguration-and-vulnerabilities.html
26. Wang, T., Xu, J., Zhang, W., Gu, Z., Zhong, H.: Self-adaptive cloud monitoring with online anomaly detection. Futur. Gener. Comput. Syst. **80**, 89–101 (2018)
27. Xu, T., Jin, X., Huang, P., Zhou, Y.: Early detection of configuration errors to reduce failure damage, pp. 619–634. USENIX Association (2016)
28. Zhang, J., Piskac, R., Zhai, E., Xu, T.: Static detection of silent misconfigurations with deep interaction analysis. Proc. ACM Program. Lang. **5**, 1–30 (2021)
29. Zhang, J., et al.: Encore: exploiting system environment and correlation information for misconfiguration detection, pp. 687–700 (2014)

Adaptive Controller to Identify Misconfigurations and Optimize the Performance of Kubernetes Clusters and IoT Edge Devices

Areeg Samir$^{(\boxtimes)}$ and Håvard Dagenborg

Universitetet i Tromsø - Norges arktiske universitet, Hansine Hansens veg 18, 9019 Tromsø, Norway
areeg.s.elgazazz@uit.no

Abstract. Kubernetes default configurations do not always provide optimal security and performance for all clusters and IoT edge devices deployed, affecting the scalability of a given workload and making them vulnerable to security breaches and information leakage if misconfigured. We present an adaptive controller to identify the type of misconfiguration and its consequence threat to optimize the system behavior. Our work differs from existing approaches as it is fully automated and can diagnose various errors on the fly. The controller is evaluated in terms of quality and accuracy of identification. The results show that the controller can identify around 90% of the total number of configuration values with a reasonable average identification overhead.

Keywords: Misconfiguration · Threats · Identification · IoTs · Clusters · Markov Processes · Security · Performance

1 Introduction

Misconfiguration is an incorrect configuration(s) within the parameters of system components (i.e., system clusters, IoT edge devices) that may lead to vulnerabilities and affect system workload and performance at different levels. At the edge level, a misconfigured edge device opens the potential for security breaches. For instance, if an edge device runs with default privileges or the same privileges as the application, vulnerabilities in any system's component can be accidental (e.g., remote SSH open) or intentional (e.g., backdoor in component). At the application level, a misconfigured container (e.g., network port open) allows an attacker to exploit the Docker API port that escalates the attack to other containers and hosts. At the cluster level, misconfigurations in core Kubernetes components (e.g., API server, Kubelet, Kube-proxy) lead to the compromise of complete clusters that cause network latency overheads, CPU throttling, or container to run out of memory. The management of configurations has been

G. A. Papadopoulos et al. (Eds.): ESOCC 2023, LNCS 14183, pp. 170–187, 2023.
https://doi.org/10.1007/978-3-031-46235-1_11

explored in the literature [2, 4, 8, 10, 15]. However, the complexity of misconfigurations does not arise only from a large number of configuration parameters, but also from their correlations and dependencies. The paper proposes a real-time misconfiguration identification controller based on the fine-grained configuration type category. The paper is organized as follows. Section 2 provides a background of some concepts used in the paper. Section 3 presents related research. Section 4 provides examples of misconfigurations that motivate the paperwork. Section 5 presents the methodology followed to analyze misconfigurations and explains the identification of configuration errors and their threats as a consequence according to the identified configuration error cases. Section 6 evaluates the controller and discusses the reported results. Section 7 concludes the paper and presents the future direction of the work.

2   Background

Misconfigurations can lead to a variety of security threats and vulnerabilities. This section gives an introduction to the configuration and Hidden Markov Model that can be used to analyze the behaviors of the system components to identify potential threats.

2.1   Configurations

Configurations are a list of entries or parameters, in terms of key-value pairs, a list, and a map, that define the configurations for an object (e.g., cluster, node, pod, container, service, user) and manage its deployment. Configurations are stored in a configuration file that contains basic information about a cluster, and are written in a user-friendly YAML syntax format that is called 'manifest'. The configuration file is stored in version control before being pushed to the cluster to simplify the rollback of a configuration change, aids cluster recreation and restoration. The configuration file has to contain four main entries, which are apiVersion (i.e., used to create the Kubernetes object), kind (e.g., Pod, Deployment, Service, Job, or DemonSets), metadata (unique properties of an object such as name, namespace, and label entries), and spec (i.e., specification, defines the operation of an object and depends upon the apiVersion). Kubernetes cluster uses configuration files to create an object based on a set of defined configurations. By concentrating on developing YAML configuration management, we can reduce configuration errors and vulnerabilities, resulting in improved cluster security and stability.

2.2   Hidden Markov Model

A Hidden Markov Model (HMM) is a statistical model that is used to describe a system that evolves over time and generates observable data sequences. It is widely applied in various fields, such as security. An HMM consists of two main components: (1) hidden states, which are the underlying, unobservable states of the system that transition from one state to another over time. The system is assumed to be in one of these hidden states at any given time. (2) Observable emissions, which are the observable outcomes associated with each hidden state. These observations are what we can measure or observe, and they provide information about the underlying hidden states. HMMs are often used for threat detection and anomaly detection to identify patterns of behavior that deviate from normal or expected behavior, which could indicate potential threats or attacks. Thus, utilizing the HMM-based detection system provides a comprehensive threat identification strategy specifically for attacks caused by configuration errors.

3   Related Work

Configuration error analysis is crucial for maintaining the stability, performance, and security of a system. Current frameworks have not focused sufficiently on the essential aspect of effectively handling misconfigurations in edge devices and clusters [4,22]. Since most tools work with predefined constraint templates, unlike our work, the following techniques lack of an adaptive misconfiguration identification that works with different types of errors, which makes configuration management a challenging task, especially when considering heterogeneous hardware and software stacks in cluster and edge environments.

To optimize and manage the configurations of containers running in a Kubernetes cluster, configuration framework solutions with a focus on performance are presented [2,23]. These solutions focused on detecting configuration errors by analyzing the source code and generating the configuration check code. Maintenance overhead can occur with large data sets and can be time-consuming in multicomponent applications, especially in scale and load-balance environments. In such complex environments, there are often multiple layers of configuration, including their configuration parameters and interactions, leading to more complexity [23]. For example, configuring network policies involves defining how pods communicate with each other and other endpoints. An incorrect combination of policies can inadvertently block traffic or create security vulnerabilities.

In addition, misconfigurations can have detrimental effects in scenarios where load balancing and resource allocation are critical. For example, setting too high memory or CPU limits for a particular service might cause contention for resources among different services running on the same infrastructure [1]. Incorrect configurations can lead to bottlenecks in data traffic at the network level and open suspicious flows in the system [10]. Rules-based security techniques are used to detect misconfigurations and optimize system performance [5,9], however, checking every constraint is time-consuming and can lead to more errors. An analysis of misconfiguration helps to detect which parts of the system are associated with configuration parameters. This could be achieved by deriving the specification of the configurations by designing a custom control and data flow analysis targeting the configuration-based code [6,24], based rule [20], or based inference [25]. However, those ways are highly specialized, as some of them only focus on security, they are not simple to write and maintain, and they are geared towards a host only instead of container images and edge devices, which might result in the occurrence of false positives or false negatives.

4   Motivation Examples

Any configuration error (Misconfiguration) can lead to privilege escalation, containers running as root, and other critical vulnerability issues that have negative consequences on security, efficiency, reliability, and performance. For example, some wireless access points may have outdated or insecure wireless security services enabled (e.g., WEP or WPS) by default. Such standards could allow attackers within range of the device to gain access to the network. Since data are also often transmitted via an insecure protocol (e.g., FTP, HTTP, etc.) by default, some of it may be exposed to an attacker with such access. If credentials or encryption keys are captured, the initial access gained through these default settings could lead to further access to systems within the network or the ability to read encrypted data. For example, suppose that we have a cluster with three nodes that do not act as host control planes. Cluster nodes have some pods and a set of deployed containers with privilege and access control settings, such as privilege access (e.g., *allowPrivilegeEscalation*), as shown in Fig. 1. This setting controls whether a process can gain more privileges than its parent process, and it is always true when the container is run as privileged, or has *CAP_SYS_ADMIN*. Here, a user root inside a container will have the same access as the root on the host system, allowing an attacker with root access in the container to gain access to the nodes, steal the secrets of their running containers, and exploit flaws in the cluster. The severity of the attack is highly rated with a score of 7.0 according to the level of severity of the CVE.

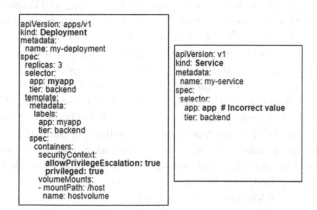

Fig. 1. Setting-Value Dependency Cascading Failure in YAML

In addition, any incorrect value might create a failure that can be cascaded if the failure in one component or resource setting impacts other dependent components or resources. For example, as shown in Fig. 1, the service should reference the *Deployment* with the *selector* field, specifying the labels that correspond to the deployment pod. However, the *selector* field is given an incorrect value. The *selector* field is set to *app: app* in the *Service*, which does not match the value of the label *app: myapp* used in the *Deployment*. This wrong value enables *Service* to incorrectly target deployment pods. Such settings cause service discovery and routing failures as the service cannot correctly track the deployment pod to establish dependency between the two resources.

To identify the type of misconfiguration, we extracted the configuration error settings of the anomalous component only to reduce the complexity of identification, as shown next.

5 The Proposed Approach

This section extends the controller misconfiguration analysis phases (monitor, detection) to identify the type of misconfigurations and their threat consequence based on the output of the detection phase in [17].

5.1 Methodology of Misconfigurations Analysis

To analyze misconfigurations, the controller has 4 main phases, which are monitor, detection [17], identification, and recovery [18]. This paper aims to introduce the identification phase.

We ran the controller on a set of manifest YAML files to inspect configuration errors in edge devices and clusters and sent a warning message for any deviations from the configuration settings; more details are given in [17]. The YAML manifest files were inspected on the basis of Kind and APIVersion keys using Kubernetes utilities. We received warning messages for configuration parameters violating specified rules with approximately 36,709 configuration errors containing around 2090 unique errors from 3000 apps. Many of those errors were simple misconfigurations that could be avoided by developers, such as edge device default settings (e.g., accounts passwords) were not changed, or sensitive medical data being leaked due to the enabling of privilege escalation. We also found several errors which have serious consequences such as the port of the etcd server (Kubernetes database) not encrypted and accessible via plain HTTP, the failure to update software patches, the system network as KubePi was not configured properly or the pod was constantly crashing in an endless loop. Only 1087 apps, among the apps studied, had no configuration errors.

Based on that, we identified the categories of misconfigurations in the manifests and the sensors that were on our device by getting a reference to the sensor service to list all the sensors on the device of type. We focus on analyzing the configurations defined in the application manifest file, including components, enforced permissions, exported attribute values, and intent filters. We focus on the most common misconfigurations that negatively impact system components' workload and cause performance degradation on performance metrics (application domain metrics and system-specific metrics).

The metrics are kept within acceptable limits using dynamic thresholds to avoid degradation of system performance and maintain continuous delivery [19].

We collected data from the metrics into a two-dimensional matrix which formed our data set; the columns refer to the metrics, and the rows refer to the components. Then we derived the relationship between the performance of the components, the workload, and the misconfigurations to detect the misconfigurations for the applications deployed in the hierarchical system settings [17]. The controller detects the hierarchical path(s) that show anomalous behavior (e.g., overload) and tracks the misconfigured components under the constraints of the extracted configurations. We checked the configuration security settings and detected misconfigurations in the vulnerable path. For edge devices, the configuration check was performed on authorized devices that had legal access to the system and were assigned to authorized participants. The detection is based on statistical learning that can detect misconfigurations based on the learned configuration settings and can be used for real-time misconfiguration detection to quickly reduce the negative imprint on the system. The following represents the steps of misconfiguration detection [17] and identification by the controller:

Training Phase. During the training phase, the configurations are collected in terms of labeled training sets to train the controller. The controller learns the patterns and relationships between various configuration settings and their corresponding outcomes to characterize correct and incorrect configurations. For example, if a certain setting is known to cause conflicts or performance issues, the controller learns to identify such patterns. **Feature extraction:** Relevant settings are extracted from the configuration data, such as specific settings, parameters, or dependencies. These features provide the input for the controller. **Model training:** The controller is trained using the extracted features to identify the patterns and rules associated with the correct configurations and detect deviations that can indicate errors. **Real-time detection:** Once the controller is trained, it can monitor and analyze the new configuration settings in real time. When a new configuration is encountered, the controller evaluates it against the learned rules and patterns to detect any misconfiguration; more details are given in [17]. **Prompt error detection and mitigation:** When a configuration error or anomaly is detected, an alert is generated to prompt corrective action as our proposed recovery process in [18]. **Continuous learning and improvement:** The controller continues to learn from new configurations and adapts to changing settings or emerging errors to improve its detection capabilities and accuracy over time. The result of the detection is used to identify the type of misconfiguration to locate its root cause through the configuration error-failure cases and the identification phase, as shown in the following sections. The phase aims to track the dependency between misconfigurations in edge devices and clusters of the system to show its impact on performance and workload, and to demonstrate the impact of misconfigurations on resource vulnerability.

5.2   Configuration Error-Failure Cases

To identify the type of misconfigurations, we focused on identifying common security misconfigurations (Errors) in Kubernetes, Azure, and Docker Swarm that negatively cause anomalous workload (Fault) and dramatically saturate monitoring metrics (Failure) of system components. We achieved this by focusing on misconfigurations reported in 2023 and 2022 by the CVE, NIST, OWASP, Fairwinds, ENSA, CIS Docker, and Kubernetes benchmarks. We targeted those benchmarks, as they provide a systematic analysis that addresses key architectural vulnerabilities and platform dependencies of such tools. The benchmark used artifacts reported by DevOps, Azure, Kubernetes, Google Kubernetes Engine, Docker Swarm, Amazon Elastic Kubernetes Service, Oracle, Google Cloud, Microsoft, and Alibaba practitioners. The benchmarks go through two stages of consensus review and evaluation of the results of security misconfigurations that alter the dependability, security, and cost of more than 150,000 workloads from hundreds of businesses.

We classified the types of misconfiguration into cases and we linked hidden settings of configuration errors and their faults in the system under observation to their observed failures, which are sequences of observations emitted by system resources. The type of misconfiguration falls under three main error failure cases: (1) IoT edge failure is due to a device failure that occurred during run-time or during provision and deployment. Edge device misconfigurations were classified as impaired communications, indicating limited communication between the device and the service, or non-sensor data, indicating that a device has communication with the service but only reports partial sensor data. (2) application failure is due to a pod or container failure, and (3) node or cluster failure relates to a core component failure. We used the IEEE Standard Classification for Software Anomalies [7] to analyze observed failures in multiple dimensions: Failure ID (unique identifier for the failure type and its category), Failure Description (describe an observed behavior), Failure Analysis (describe and analyze failure's root-cause), and Failure Severity (in percentage) relating to the system performance and reliability in terms of the objectives that were not met by the observed metrics and benchmarks. We used Key Performance Indicators (KPIs) to determine whether the motoring metrics met the maintenance goals and the system's performance (e.g., resource utilization, latency, response time, network congestion, throughput). The higher the value, the more severe the impact on system performance will be [3, 21].

The following cases refer to observed failures that are either emitted by an administrative operation internal to Kubernetes, Azure, and Docker Swarm or emitted by a trigger external to them as follows:

IoT Edge Cases. It refers to IoT edge failure that occurs during run time or during provision and deployment such as:

Case 1: Sudden Stop of the Edge Device. Failure ID: $Conf_{EC1}$. Failure Description: The edge device stopped for a specific period (e.g., minutes) after running successfully. The logs indicated that the device failed to connect to the IoT hub via AMQP or WebSocket and that the edge device existed. Failure Analysis: A misconfiguration of the host network prevented the edge agent from reaching the network. The agent attempted to connect over AMQP (port 5671) or WebSockets (port 443) as the edge device runtime set up a network for each module to communicate, either using a bridge network or NAT. Failure Severity: 70%.

Case 2: Empty Configuration File. Failure ID: Conf_{EC2}. Failure Description: The device has trouble starting the modules defined in the deployment. Only the edge agent is running, but it continually reports empty configuration files. Failure Analysis: The device may have trouble with the resolution of the DNS server name within the private network. Failure Severity: 20%~30%.

Case 3: Edge Hub Failure. Failure ID: Conf_{EC3}. Failure Description: The Edge Hub module does not start. Failure Analysis: Some process on the host machine has bound a port to which the edge hub module is trying to bind. The Edge hub maps ports 443, 5671, and 8883 for use in gateway scenarios. The module fails to start if another process has already bound one of those ports. Failure Severity: 20%~30%.

Case 4: Default Credentials. Failure ID: Conf_{EC4}. Failure Description: The default accounts/passwords of the edge device are not changed. Failure Analysis: Using vendor-supplied defaults for accounts and passwords could allow attackers to brute-force and gain unauthorized access to the system. Failure Severity: 98%~99%.

Application Cases. It refers to the occurrence of failure due to the failure of a pod or container as follows:

Case 1: Privilege Escalation Flaw and Redeployment Fail. Failure ID: Conf_{AC1}. Failure Description: Sensitive medical data was leaked. Failure Analysis: An Azure function (e.g., SCM_RUN_FROM_PACKAGE) gave access to the remapped root and allowed privilege escalation to the root level. Failure Severity: 80%~90%.

Case 2: Privilege Escalation Flaw. Failure ID: Conf_{AC2}. Failure Description: Sensitive medical data was leaked. Failure Analysis: A docker engine function option (e.g., users-remap) gives access to the remapped root and allows privilege escalation to the root level. Failure Severity: 80%~90%.

Case 3: Unauthenticated Connection. Failure ID: Conf_{AC3}. Failure Description: Kubernetes labels are not validated or incorrectly typed. Failure Analysis: Privilege access to Kubelet, which allows unexpected routing from service target selectors. Failure Severity: 40%~60%.

Case 4: Outdated Package and Flow Unpatched. Failure ID: Conf_{AC4}. Failure Description: The software is outdated and flaws are unpatched. Failure Analysis: Failure to update software patches as part of the software management process, allowing attackers to inject malicious code into the application. Failure Severity: 80%~90%.

Case 5: Loop Crash. Failure ID: Conf_{AC5}. Failure Description: The pod is constantly crashing in an endless loop and cannot be started. Failure Analysis: A server cannot load the configuration file due to a typo in a configuration file system. Failure Severity: 80%~90%.

Core Components Cases. It indicates the occurrence of a failure at a node or cluster level.

Case 1: Spike Traffic Received by System. Failure ID: Conf_{CC1}. Failure Description: System services do not work properly and its resources are excessively saturated. Failure Analysis: Distributed Denial of Service (DDOS) attack prevents access to the system network, as KubePi is not configured correctly. Failure Severity: 98%~99%.

Case 2: Data Leakage. Failure ID: Conf_{CC2}. Failure Description: Sensitive medical data was leaked. Failure Analysis: The deployment of highly sophisticated malware leads to compromise of sensitive medical data. Ingress allowed unauthorized users to access and update all secrets in the cluster. Failure Severity: 98%~99%.

Case 3: Anonymous Authentication. Failure ID: Conf_{CC3}. Failure Description: Unauthenticated requests can be sent to Kubelet, as its configuration is not set properly, which saturated the system resources. Failure Analysis: The misconfigured Kubernetes core component gave unauthorized access to the entire cluster. Failure Severity: 80%~99%.

Case 4: Non-Secure Cluster Transmittance. Failure ID: Conf_{CC4}. Failure description: The etcd server port (Kubernetes database) is unencrypted and accessible over plain HTTP. Failure Analysis: The etcd process on the master node exhausts all memory, as the etcd cluster is left without authentication, allowing a DDOS attack to gain unauthorized access to a system. Failure Severity: 80%~99%.

At the end of this step, misconfiguration description profiles for the cases are created and stored to be used in the identification phase along with the output of the detection phase, which provides the path of the hierarchical anomalous misconfigured components that are affected by specific components.

5.3 Misconfiguration Identification Phase

The controller uses the output of the detection phase as input for the identification phase. For example, $AnomalousPath = \{Cluster > Node_{22} > Node_{23} > Container_{33} > Service_{43}\}$ is a hierarchy anomalous path that is affected by $Node_{23}$ with the vertical level index 2 and horizontal level index 3 in the graph, respectively. On the basis of that, we initialized a model with the configuration settings of the anomalous states and observations obtained. The model is created with a graph length of states $ConfLeng = (Conf_{ij}, .., Conf_{Nj})$ and the length of observations $FLeng = \{F_1, .., F_T\}$, which are stored in a matrix $ConfMat[ConfLeng, FLeng]$. To show the dependency between misconfigurations, each $Conf_{ij}$ represents the misconfigured settings that belong to the anomalous state that has vertical i and horizontal j levels. For each $Conf_{ij}$, as shown in Fig. 2, we checked the type of misconfiguration, which is hidden from the observer considering the state level in the defined failure-error cases $(Conf_{EC}, Conf_{AC}, Conf_{CC})$.

The configuration settings (key-value pairs) were extracted from the manifest of the anomalous state based on the Kind and API version objects. A state check function denoted SC checks the misconfigured settings against centrally managed correct configuration settings stored in Knowledge storage. We iterated through the manifest settings to check the key-value pairs. For each pair, we calculated the confidence score taking into account the type of key with (p-value $\leqslant 0.05$) to validate our hypothesis against the difference between manifests. A low confidence score indicates a difference between the configuration settings for the anomalous state. The difference between the configuration obtained from the anomalous state (actual state) and the correct configuration (desired state) represents the incorrectly configured state that is likely to be targeted for exploitation by attackers. For the desired state, management data from the configuration settings were recorded, such as privilege, default accounts and their passwords, unnecessary ports, certificates, unpublished URLs, validation rules, default namespace, and version (e.g., deprecated API).

In case the misconfiguration is not defined within the cases, the controller records the new characteristics of the misconfiguration type and assigns unique identifiers (i.e., Failure ID, Label, component relationship information, and case type) to the selected items. The identification result is stored in the knowledge storage to enhance the identification process.

5.4 Threat Type Identification Under Misconfiguration

We are mainly concerned with threats that occur due to misconfiguration and cause data breaches and information leakages, such as botnets, ransomware, amplification, flooding, and protocol exploration. We created description profiles for each type of threat that include information about the threat (type, description, source, technique, configuration setting relation, and mitigation). We considered that the types of threats are hidden; thus, we employed the Hidden Markov Model (HMM) [16] to predict hidden threats because of its ability (1) to capture dynamic patterns by allowing the hidden states to transition between different states, reflecting changes in threat behavior. (2) to establish a baseline of normal behavior and then identify deviations from this baseline as potential threats. (3) update the model in the future to adapt to changing threat landscapes. (4) to incorporate data from multiple sources.

The controller maps the anomalous path obtained from the detection phase $(Cluster > Node_{22} > Node_{23} > Container_{33} > Service_{43})$ to a set of states $(St1 > St2 > St3 > St4 > St5)$ to be fed to the model. Then, it adds a start

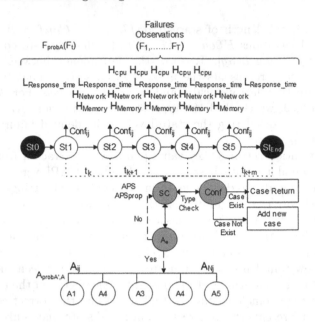

Fig. 2. Misconfigurations and Threats Identification Type

state $St0$ and an end state St_{End} to the abnormal path $(St0 > St1 > \cdots > St5 > St_{End})$ to capture the entire information flow within that path. The controller checks the existence of a threat A_e using the SC function. If a threat exists, the model checks its type A_i according to the observations emitted (A_1: botnet, A_2: flood, A_3: amplification, A_4: protocol exploit, A_5: ransomware). For each threat A, we initialize the parameters of the state of the model A_i and the observations $F_{\{1,\cdots,T\}}$ through a graph length of the threat states APN and observation length T to track the duration of the threat states and identify them in a timely manner.

The probability of A_i is calculated assuming that a threat starts in the initial state $St1$ and might spread from one state to another. The probabilities of A_i and observations $F_{\{1,\cdots,T\}}$ are stored in matrix ATI. We calculate the probability F by summing the previous forward path probability of the previous time step $t-1$, weighted by their transition probabilities $Aprob_{A',A}$, and multiplying by the observation probability $Fprob_A(F_t)$. We sum the probabilities of all possible threats $\{A_i, \cdots, A_N\}$ that could generate the observation sequence $F_{\{1,t+1,\cdots,T\}}$. Each A represents the probability of being in A_i after seeing the first F_t observations, as shown in Algorithm 1.

Algorithm 1 Identify The Type of Threat

APS: Get abnormal path states $APS()$
APSprop: Get portability of abnormal path states $APSprop()$
APN: Threat states length
Store portability of A at time T in matrix $ATI[A, T]$
for each state aps from 1 to APS_{length} **do**
    for each portability $apsprop$ from 1 to $APSprop_{length}$ **do**
      if SC is Threat **then**
        for each state A from 1 to APN **do**
          $ATI[A, 1] \leftarrow \pi_A \times F_A(F_1)$
        end for
        for each time step t from 2 to T **do**
          for each state A from 1 to APN **do**
            $ATI[A, t] \leftarrow \sum_{A'=1}^{APN} ATI[A', t-1] \times Aprob_{A', A} \times Fprob_A(F_t)$
          end for
          $ATIprob \leftarrow \sum_{A=1}^{APN} ATI[A, T]$
        end for
        return $ATIprob$
      end if
    end for
end for

Transition probabilities equal to 0 are omitted since not all previous states contributed to the forward probability of the current state. Each St has a probability value reflecting the probability of a given abnormal behavior. The assumption is that a sufficiently low probability (abnormal flow) value indicates a potential threat. The decision is made by calculating a threat score $Threat_{Score}$ for each St and the whole abnormal path ($St1 > St2 > St3 > St4 > St5$). As shown in (1)–(3), the $Threat_{Score}$ for St is derived from the probability values returned by the detection model $\wp$ associated with St. The threat score value is calculated using a weighted sum $\sum_{St=1}^{w}$. The weight ω associated with the model is represented by ω_{RPV}, while M_{RPV} is the probability value returned by the model. The probability M_{RPV} is subtracted from 1 ($1 - M_{RPV}$) because a value close to zero indicates a threat that should produce a high threat score. The weight ω is calculated considering the state transition probability of the type of hidden threat $Aprob_{ij}$ and the observation probability $Fprob_t$. The highest threat score is stored, and then the threshold is set to an adjustable percentage higher than the maximum score obtained, so that a user can adjust the sensitivity of the state check in terms of the number of false positives and the expected detection accuracy. The state is marked as vulnerable when $Threat_{Score}$ exceeds a predefined threshold. Once we identify the type of threat, the model transits to the next state to check the existence and type of potential threat for that state (if any); otherwise, the model returns to the state check SC to check the next state.

The process is repeated until we reach the end of the abnormal path $St5$. Then the model progresses to the end state St_{End}, ending the threat identification process. The derived hidden types of misconfiguration and threat are shown in Table 1.

$$Threat_{Score} = \sum_{St=1}^{w} \omega_{RPV} \times \wp \qquad (1)$$

$$\omega = \sum_{RPV \in AI_{models}} Fprob_t \times Aprob_{ij} \qquad (2)$$

$$\wp = (1 - M_{RPV}) \qquad (3)$$

Table 1. Misconfiguration and Threat Identification

Abnormal Flow Path	St1 > St2 > St3 > St4 > St5
Vulnerable Component	St2
Misconfigured Component	N_{23}
Misconfiguration Type	$Conf_{CC3}$
Threat Type	A_1

6   Evaluations and Results Analysis

This section evaluates the identification of the controller, focusing on measuring its performance in terms of quality and accuracy.

6.1   Environment Settings Description

The controller ran on a virtual machine equipped with Linux OS (Ubuntu 18.10 version), a VCPU, and 2 GB of VRAM. The virtual platform is allocated to a physical PC equipped with Windows 11, Intel Core i7-1260P 2.10 GHz, and 32 GB of RAM. A set of agents was installed to collect data on CPU, memory, network, and changes in the file system (i.e., no flow issued to the component). The agent adds a data interval function to determine the time interval to which the collected data belong. The Datadog tool is used to obtain a live data stream for the running components and to capture the request-response tuples and associated metadata. Prometheus is used to group the collected data and store them in a time series database using Timescale-DB. The size of our generated data set was approximately 10 MB with a period of 6 months. We selected a subset of the data set of around 4.3 MB mainly related to the types of misconfiguration mentioned in Misconfiguration Scenarios to train the models and provide more targeted and specialized training data sets. Data are divided into 70% training data and 30% testing data. More details about environment evaluation settings can be found in [17].

6.2   Misconfiguration Scenarios

We trained our models during the evaluation on some of the types of misconfiguration identified that allow privilege escalation at IoT edge device level [12] and at the container cluster level [11,13,14]. These types of errors excessively consume the usage of system resources (CPU, memory, network) as they dramatically increase the request latency and decline the request rate. The configuration files of the components are stored in GitOps version control to simplify the rollback of configuration changes.

6.3   Threat and Workload Scenarios

The threat scenario is based on the misconfiguration scenarios that lead to vulnerability in IoT edge devices and Kubernetes. The aim is to simulate the attack that could occur due to misconfiguration. The controller performance was tested in hybrid traffic, combining attack data generated by the tools at different levels. At the edge level, the IoT-Flock tool is used to generate normal and abnormal flow (threat) of IoT edge devices in a real-time network. At the container level, a Distributed Internet Traffic Generator (D-ITG) tool is used to generate normal and abnormal flow at the network, transport, and application layers with various packet sizes and a variety of probability distributions. We used OWASP-ZAP to simulate an attacker's attempt at vulnerable containers.

6.4   Identification Assessment

Assessment1: Identification Quality and Accuracy. We extracted around 2090 real-world Kubernetes configuration files from version control repositories such as GitLab and GitHub, with 550 and 1540 files, respectively. The settings of the extracted files were valid in terms of format and syntax. We focus on the types of misconfiguration related to the misconfiguration cases mentioned in the paper that lead to system performance degradation, which were 279 and 1016 true positive configuration errors from GitLab and GitHub, respectively, identified by the controller. The controller reported other configuration errors; however, in this evaluation, we focused only on errors due to privilege escalation. Around 181 configuration errors in the true positives reported were due to privilege escalation, 109 from GitHub, and 72 from GitLab. The controller reported 16 false alarms, which occurred due to incorrectly skipping conditional instructions affected by the configuration value such as non-existent paths (e.g. invalid image repository path), unreachable IP addresses, or referencing a non-existent-configmap. Hence, to measure the quality of the identification process, we split the normal behavior sequences into correct configurations using a sliding window and then further learn the controller. For testing, the first step is to split the test sequence into small segments and to calculate the probability under normal behavior. We analyzed the results with different window sizes (in hours) and state transitions by computing the Configuration Error Rate (CER), which divides the total number of unequal key-value pairs of data elements by the total number of data elements from one component to quantify the number identification error made by the controller with respect to the actual values. The total CER was approximately 10%, indicating that the model incorrectly identified 10% of the total elements.

Assessment2: Identification Overhead. We measured the controller's performance baseline metrics (e.g., throughput, latency, CPU, memory, response time) under normal settings without configuration errors, workload, and without a configuration error detection mechanism enabled. The normal settings were approximately 70% and 35% for CPU and memory, respectively, the average response time was between 100 and 170 microseconds per request, 100 transactions/second of throughput, and 130 milliseconds of latency. We created the configuration error [13] at the container cluster level, which severely saturated the system resources to be 95% and 76% for CPU and memory, respectively, the average response time of 600 microseconds, the transaction per second of throughput, and the latency of 500 milliseconds. We measured the identification overhead as the time needed to identify the misconfigurations by measuring the execution time before and after the controller invocation. The average identification time taken by the controller was 301.8 milliseconds, which returned to the network and file-related checks.

6.5   Misconfiguration Identification Accuracy Under Threats

We measured the accuracy of the model identification under different misconfigurations (Test1 [13], Test2 [14], and Test3 [12]), threat and workload test scenarios, and under various window sizes during the learning process. We calculate the threat ratio (TR) to count the number of components identified as compromised due to misconfiguration during time intervals to the total number of components of the system and report the result as a percentage. As shown in Table 2, the TR under different tests represents a specific diversity. When the size of the sliding window is greater than 6, the TR improves, but the relationship between the size of the data set and the threat ratio is not always linear. Hence, to ensure accurate and unbiased identification, we measured TR under different model transitions along the test scenarios. For each transition, we applied the same data set used in the baseline transition to analyze the changes in the TR between the baseline transition and the other model's transitions. As shown in Table 3, the model transitions significantly indicate a change in identification effectiveness, which indicates an improvement in threat identification performance. To confirm the reported results, we further evaluated the unbiased performance of the model transitions based on the number of true positives, false positives, and false negatives of identification to measure precision, recall, and F1-score. The identification precision, recall, and F1-score were 0.950, 0.932, and 0.974 respectively. The recall gives an interesting insight into the performance of the controller in relation to the number of false identifications. It is important to note that the reported results were delivered according to the type of test scenarios for misconfiguration, threat, and workload, and the data set used to learn the model.

Table 2. Threat Ratio with Different Windows Size in Hours

Windows Size	3	6	9	12
TR of Test1	8.17	5.49	3.07	0.21
TR of Test2	74.31	65.03	52.01	54.24
TR of Test3	43.09	54.29	45.24	35.09

Table 3. Threat Ratio Under Model Transitions

Transition Model	Baseline-Transition	Transition 1	Transition 2
TR of Test1	31.39	5.49	5.93
TR of Test2	74.01	54.88	55.93
TR of Test3	64.79	43.65	40.03

7   Conclusions and Future Work

The paper presented a controller for analyzing misconfigurations of container-based clusters and edge devices in a hierarchical computing environment. The aim is to propose the identification mechanism of the controller by defining a set of configuration error cases that result in the emission of failures observed through system performance metrics. The controller identifies the root cause of the configuration error and its consequence threats to optimize the system's behavior to update configurations and prevent their future occurrences. The paper evaluated the performance of the controller, focusing on accuracy and quality. The results show that the controller can deliver a performance improvement under different transitions with 0.950 precision.

In the future, we will provide technical details on the collection criteria, quality, and diversity of the data set as the scope of this paper is to present the identification phase mechanism. We plan to conduct comprehensive security assessments to evaluate the proposed controller and compare its performance against existing mechanisms under various types of configuration errors. We aim to integrate the controller into the Kubernetes workflow and CI/CD pipeline to catch invalid configurations and potential security vulnerabilities before deployment to maintain secure and reliable Kubernetes-based applications. Implement a control strategy to track configuration changes and validate configurations before applying changes to production clusters to improve cluster security and stability. Combine multiple metrics to improve the accuracy of threat identification.

References

1. Assuncao, L., Cunha, J.C.: Dynamic workflow reconfigurations for recovering from faulty cloud services, vol. 1, pp. 88–95. IEEE Computer Society (2013)
2. Chiba, T., Nakazawa, R., Horii, H., Suneja, S., Seelam, S.: Confadvisor: a performance-centric configuration tuning framework for containers on Kubernetes, pp. 168–178 (2019)
3. CWE: Common weakness enumeration category: Configuration (2023). https://cwe.mitre.org/data/definitions/16.html
4. Fairwinds: Kubernetes benchmark report security, cost, and reliability workload results (2023). https://www.fairwinds.com/kubernetes-config-benchmark-report
5. Gantikow, H., Reich, C., Knahl, M., Clarke, N.: Rule-based security monitoring of containerized environments. In: Ferguson, D., Méndez Muñoz, V., Pahl, C., Helfert, M. (eds.) CLOSER 2019. CCIS, vol. 1218, pp. 66–86. Springer, Cham (2020). https://doi.org/10.1007/978-3-030-49432-2_4
6. Hu, Y., Huang, G., Huang, P.: Automated reasoning and detection of specious configuration in large systems with symbolic execution, pp. 719–734 (2020)
7. of the IEEE Computer Society, S.E.S.C.: IEEE standard classification for software anomalies (ieee 1044–2009) (2010)
8. Lakshmanan, R.: Microsoft confirms server misconfiguration led to 65,000+ companies' data leak (2022). https://thehackernews.com/2022/10/microsoft-confirms-server.html
9. Mahajan, V.B., Mane, S.B.: Detection, analysis and countermeasures for container based misconfiguration using docker and Kubernetes, pp. 1–6. Institute of Electrical and Electronics Engineers Inc. (2022)
10. Moothedath, S., et al.: Dynamic information flow tracking for detection of advanced persistent threats: a stochastic game approach, June 2020. arXiv:2006.12327
11. NVD: Cve-2019-5736 (2019). https://nvd.nist.gov/vuln/detail/CVE-2019-5736
12. NVD: Cve-2019-6538 (2019). https://nvd.nist.gov/vuln/detail/CVE-2019-6538
13. NVD: Cve-2020-10749 (2020). https://nvd.nist.gov/vuln/detail/cve-2020-10749
14. NVD: Cve-2022-0811 (2022). https://nvd.nist.gov/vuln/detail/cve-2022-0811
15. Pranata, A.A., Barais, O., Bourcier, J., Noirie, L.: Misconfiguration discovery with principal component analysis for cloud-native services, pp. 269–278. Institute of Electrical and Electronics Engineers Inc., December 2020
16. Rabiner, L., Juang, B.H.: An introduction to hidden Markov models. IEEE ASSP Mag. **3**(1), 4–16 (1986)
17. Samir, A., Dagenborg, H.: A self-configuration controller to detect, identify, and recover misconfiguration at IoT edge devices and containerized cluster system, pp. 765–773 (2023)
18. Samir, A., Dagenborg, H.: Self-healing misconfiguration of cloud-based IoT systems using Markov decision processes, pp. 244–252 (2023)
19. Samir, A., Ioini, N.E., Fronza, I., Barzegar, H., Le, V., Pahl, C.: A controller for anomaly detection, analysis and management for self-adaptive container clusters. Int. J. Adv. Softw. **12**(3&4), 356–371 (2019)
20. Santolucito, M., Zhai, E., Dhodapkar, R., Shim, A., Piskac, R.: Synthesizing configuration file specifications with association rule learning. Proc. ACM Program. Lang. **1**(OOPSLA), 1–20 (2017)
21. Scarfone, K., Mell, P.: The common configuration scoring system (CCSS): metrics for software security configuration vulnerabilities. NIST interagency report, p. 7502 (2010)

22. Wang, S., Li, C., Hoffmann, H., Lu, S., Sentosa, W., Kistijantoro, A.I.: Understanding and auto-adjusting performance-sensitive configurations, vol. 53, pp. 154–168. Association for Computing Machinery, March 2018
23. Xu, T., Jin, X., Huang, P., Zhou, Y.: Early detection of configuration errors to reduce failure damage, pp. 619–634. USENIX Association (2016)
24. Zhang, J., Piskac, R., Zhai, E., Xu, T.: Static detection of silent misconfigurations with deep interaction analysis. Proc. ACM Program. Lang. **5**, 1–30 (2021)
25. Zhang, J., et al.: Encore: exploiting system environment and correlation information for misconfiguration detection, pp. 687–700 (2014)

Streamlining XR Application Deployment with a Localized Docker Registry at the Edge

Antonios Makris[1]([✉])(ID), Evangelos Psomakelis[1](ID), Ioannis Korontanis[1](ID),
Theodoros Theodoropoulos[1](ID), Antonis Protopsaltis[2,4](ID), Maria Pateraki[3,4](ID),
Zbyszek Ledwoń[5], Christos Diou[1](ID), Dimosthenis Anagnostopoulos[1](ID),
and Konstantinos Tserpes[1,3](ID)

[1] Department of Informatics and Telematics, Harokopio University, Athens, Greece
{amakris,vpsomak,gkorod,ttheod,cdiou,tserpes}@hua.gr
[2] University of Western Macedonia, Kozani, Greece
antonis.protopsaltis@oramavr.com
[3] National Technical University of Athens, Athens, Greece
[4] ORamaVR, Heraklion, Greece
maria@oramavr.com
[5] Orbital Knight, Warsaw, Poland
zledwon@orbitalknight.com

Abstract. In recent years, containerization is becoming more and more popular for deploying applications and services and it has significantly contributed to the expansion of edge computing. The demand for effective and scalable container image management, however, increases as the number of containers deployed grows. One solution is to use a localized Docker registry at the edge, where the images are stored closer to the deployment site. This approach can considerably reduce the latency and bandwidth required to download images from a central registry. In addition, it acts as a proactive caching mechanism by optimizing the download delays and the network traffic. In this paper, we introduce an edge-enabled storage framework that incorporates a localized Docker registry. This framework aims to streamline the storage and distribution of container images, providing improved control, scalability, and optimized capabilities for edge deployment. Two demanding XR applications are employed as use cases to experiment with the proposed solution.

Keywords: edge · cloud · containers · storage · registry · docker · kubernetes

1 Introduction

Recently, the rapid emergence of XR applications, including Augmented, Virtual, Mixed Reality and Holography has revolutionized the way users interact with digital content, providing immersive and engaging experiences in diverse

© IFIP International Federation for Information Processing 2023
Published by Springer Nature Switzerland AG 2023
G. A. Papadopoulos et al. (Eds.): ESOCC 2023, LNCS 14183, pp. 188–202, 2023.
https://doi.org/10.1007/978-3-031-46235-1_12

domains. However, these applications present several challenges that are profoundly intertwined with the fundamental nature of their respective types. From a network standpoint, they establish a novel category of services in which conventional best-effort and simple traffic differentiation approaches prove inadequate to satisfy their stringent demands. Even when considering the advances of 5G, these applications pose a huge challenge to the network and the entire computation infrastructure.

One option to meet such demanding requirements is by leveraging Edge computing [9]. Edge computing has gained considerable traction in both industry and academia in recent years and it is widely recognized as a critical facilitator for addressing the ever-increasing strict requirements of next-generation applications [10,13]. Edge computing has emerged as a promising paradigm able to avoid network bottlenecks, overcome communication overheads, and reduce the data transfer delay, as the computational load is moved to the edge of the network, thus leveraging the computational capabilities of the edge nodes [14,15]. However, the seamless delivery of XR applications on resource-constrained edge devices, poses unique challenges due to limited network bandwidth, latency constraints, and intermittent connectivity [16]. Additionally, the size of XR application images is often significant, and downloading these images from remote repositories can put a burden on the limited network bandwidth and introduce significant latency.

In order to address these challenges, one approach is to leverage localized registries. A localized registry serves as a local cache on container images, enabling edge nodes/devices to retrieve these images from nearby storage instead of fetching them over the network. By deploying a localized registry at the edge nodes, the burden of downloading these large application images from remote repositories can be alleviated. This results in faster and more efficient application deployment as well as significantly lower latency. This is crucial for meeting the stringent latency constraints of XR applications, ensuring smoother and more responsive user experiences. Additionally, a localized registry provides resilience in environments with intermittent connectivity. Edge environments often face connectivity issues, and accessing remote repositories can be challenging. By relying on a localized registry, uninterrupted application delivery can be ensured.

This paper presents and evaluates a hybrid distributed edge-enabled storage framework spread across heterogeneous edge and cloud nodes with considerations on performance (QoS), emphasizing on the resolution of the problem of data distribution and offloading based on application's requirements. A Localized Docker Registry (LDR) is provided which serves as a crucial component, addressing the need to bring application images closer to the edge while minimizing network traffic and image download durations. LDR is based on the Docker registry technology with Kubernetes orchestration, a MinIO object storage backend and a set of automated deployment and configuration scripts. This integration enables LDR to deploy and scale the Docker registry automatically while maintaining centralized control over various configuration options. Additionally, an image synchronization daemon, called Registry Sync Daemon (RSD) waits for trigger messages that instruct it to populate the LDR with new images.

Subsequently, all nodes within the corresponding edge cluster gain access to these updated images through the LDR, enabling rapid deployment of the associated services. By employing this configuration, we gain the ability to finely adjust the back-end storage, strategically positioning the images in optimal physical locations based on the specific requirements of each use case. As a result, LDR streamlines the storage and distribution of container images, offering enhanced control, scalability, and optimized edge deployment capabilities. The proposed framework is examined in two XR use case scenarios, specifically Collaborative VR medical training and Multiplayer Mobile Gaming. The evaluation reveals a significant reduction in application deployment time, indicating the positive impact of the proposed solution.

The rest of the paper is organized as follows. Section 2 serves as a literature review in the field of employing local registries for storing application images in edge computing environments. Section 3 describes in detail the system architecture of the proposed framework, outlining the various components it comprises. Section 4 introduces the XR use cases while Sect. 5 presents the experimental evaluation of the proposed solution. Finally, Sect. 7 summarizes the merits of our work and highlights some perspectives that require further attention in the future.

2   Related Work

With containerization being widely adopted as the microservice approach in cloud computing [11], a growing body of research is investigating the potential benefits of using local registries to store Docker application images. The primary objective is to speed up container deployment by reducing the time required for image downloads.

Boubendir et al. [3] proposed a platform that utilizes container agents to federate IT and network resources located at the edge outside an operator's infrastructure. They estimate the deployment time for slices, which includes on-boarding each Docker onto infrastructure nodes from a Docker registry on the operator gateway. Deployment time varies according to network performance with deployment taking less than 16 s using a 100 Mbps Ethernet LAN but up to 3 h for a remote registry over a 10 Mbps link. To reduce deployment time to 3 min in this scenario, the authors suggested deploying registry relays locally at the edge.

While remote registries can result in substantial waiting and downloading times for platforms, local registries situated on the edge can operate on hosts with constrained resources while handling numerous image pulling and pushing requests. To overcome prolonged times associated with downloading application images from remote registries, some platforms adopt a hybrid approach of both remote and local registries. Gupta et al. [7] introduced a solution that utilizes containerization techniques for deploying and managing deep learning models, providing benefits such as low latency, data privacy, and minimal space requirements. During their study, an edge server retrieved images from a centralized registry and stored them in a local registry. This allowed the edge server to fulfill future requests for the same model from the local registry, thereby reducing download times.

To address the issue of registry scalability and reduce pull delay at the edge, Gazzetti et al. [5] introduced a streamed deployment approach. This approach involves the use of a singular device, known as the Gateway, which engages with the cloud and retrieves images on behalf of nearby devices. Subsequently, these images are disseminated among these devices in a peer-to-peer fashion, resulting to reduced delays, minimized network usage, and enhanced scalability.

Platforms and tools can use local registries at the edge to reduce image download speed, but strategic placement is necessary when dealing with many nodes. Knob et al. [4] proposed a new deployment solution for distributing container registries on an edge topology using a community-based placement algorithm that optimizes registry distribution in a relation graph. The proposed solution employs a two-phase algorithm to generate communities and designate a central node as the host for the new registry. This approach showcases enhanced performance, achieving over a 70 percent reduction in total instantiation time. Furthermore, it effectively minimizes the occurrence of non-started containers, even when employing only two registries.

Becker et al. [2] presented EdgePier, a fully decentralized container registry for edge sites that uses peer-to-peer connections to reduce deployment times. EdgePier facilitates the exchange of image layers without relying on centralized orchestration entities. Evaluations indicate that it can enhance provisioning times by up to 65 percent compared to a standard registry, even when dealing with limited bandwidth. This advantage became increasingly prominent as the sizes of the images expanded.

Littely et al. [8] proposed a distributed architecture to solve the issues of high waiting and downloading times associated with remote registries and resource limitations of local registries. The architecture utilizes individual registry nodes, which eliminates the need for separate storage backends, simplifies scaling, and enables efficient caching strategies. By forming a consistent hashing ring, the registry nodes establish a mechanism to identify each other using Zookeeper. This enables clients to directly communicate with the registry nodes, facilitating the retrieval of images through direct requests.

Zheng et al. [17] presented Wharf, a middleware that distributes Docker images across a distributed file system to decrease storage usage, network load, and job completion times in a cluster. They optimized the synchronization of global state accesses and employed Wharf to partition Docker's runtime state in order to achieve faster image retrievals by up to 12 times compared to utilizing Docker on local storage. CoMICon [12] is another example that showcases the usage of a decentralized multi-agent approach with storage-aware nodes to improve high availability and load balancing in localized image registries. This approach offers a range of features, such as the ability to store and delete images in partial layers, facilitating efficient transfers of image layers between registries, and enabling distributed image retrieval during the startup of containers.

3   System Architecture

The proposed framework is based on Kubernetes (K3s)[1], MinIO[2] and Prometheus[3] technologies. Kubernetes is an open-source system for automating deployment, scaling, and management of containerized applications. A lightweight Kubernetes distribution built for IoT & Edge computing is used, called K3s. K3s is a highly available, certified Kubernetes distribution designed for production workloads in unattended, resource-constrained, remote locations or inside IoT appliances. As a storage solution, an open-source framework created by IBM is utilized, called MinIO. MinIO is an inherently decentralized and highly scalable peer-to-peer solution which is designed to be cloud native and can run as lightweight containers managed by external orchestration services such as Kubernetes. It supports a hierarchical structure in order to form federations of clusters and it has been proven as a valid candidate for an edge data storage system [1]. MinIO writes data and metadata together as objects, eliminating the need for a metadata database. In addition, MinIO performs all functions (erasure code, bitrot check, encryption) as inline, strictly consistent operations. The result is that MinIO is exceptionally resilient. Moreover, it uses object storage over block storage so it is in fact a combination of the two systems, preserving the lightweight distributed nature of block storage while providing the plethora of metadata and easy usage of the object storage. Unlike other object storage solutions that are built for archival use cases only, MinIO is designed to deliver the high-performance object storage that is required by modern big data applications. In addition, MinIO provides both a web-based GUI and an AWS S3 compatible API library. The Kubernetes Dataset Lifecycle Framework (DLF) provided by IBM's Datashim[4] is employed on top of MinIO, allowing the edge storage component to be used as a mountable virtual disk drive. A detailed description of the DLF is provided in Sect. 3.1. In addition, Prometheus is responsible for collecting monitoring data about the real time performance of the nodes and the component as a whole to analyze the behaviour of different applications and optimize the cluster architecture, the options, and the data distribution. Finally, a localized Docker registry (LDR) is provided in order to move application images closer to the edge and limit network traffic and image download times. LDR hosts the Docker images and employs Kubernetes containerization in order to provide its services, creating a new pod that is able to connect to the Minio storage backend. In addition, LDR creates a set of secrets that allows the secure communication between the registry and its clients using the HTTPS protocol and a basic authentication scheme. A detailed description of the LDR is provided in Sect. 3.2. Figure 1 presents a conceptual overview of the proposed framework, highlighting the components utilized in an illustrative scenario featuring a K3s cluster consisting of two nodes.

---

[1] https://k3s.io/.
[2] https://min.io/.
[3] https://prometheus.io/.
[4] https://datashim.io/.

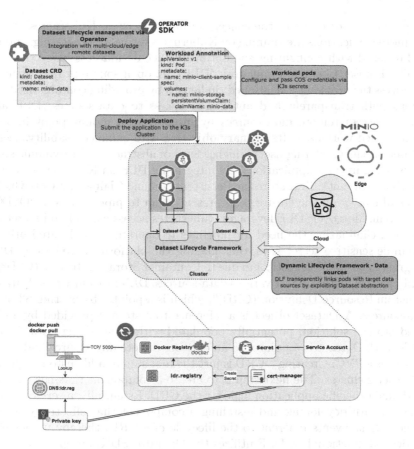

Fig. 1. Conceptual overview of the proposed framework

3.1 Kubernetes Dataset Lifecycle Framework

The hybrid cloud/edge environment is swiftly emerging as the favored approach for organizations seeking the perfect mix of scalability, performance, and security. Therefore, it has become customary for organizations to utilize a combination of on-premises data centers (private cloud), and cloud/edge solutions from multiple providers to store and manage their data. Nevertheless, many obstacles arise when applications have to access the data. Developers are required to have knowledge of the precise location of data, while also managing the appropriate credentials to access the designated data sources containing their data. In addition, access to cloud/edge storage is often completely transparent from the cloud management standpoint and it is difficult for infrastructure administrators to monitor which containers have access to which cloud storage solution. Despite the widespread promotion of containerized components and microservices as the ideal solution for efficient storage deployment and management in hybrid edge/cloud infrastructure, containerization makes it more difficult for the workloads to access the shared file systems. Currently, there are no established resource types to represent the concept of data-source on Kubernetes. As more and more applications are running on Kubernetes for batch processing, end users are burdened with configuring and optimizing the data access [6].

The Dataset Lifecycle Framework (DLF), an open-source project, is utilized to address the previously mentioned challenges by providing containerized applications with transparent and automated access to data-sources. DLF allows users to access remote data-sources by integrating a mount point into their containerized workloads. Its primary objective is to enhance usability, security, and performance, offering users a higher level of abstraction for dynamic storage provisioning in their applications. By integrating DLF on Kubernetes pipelines, it is able to mount object stores as Persistent Volume Claims (PVCs), which are pieces of storage in the cluster, and present them to pipelines as a POSIX-like file system. Moreover, DLF leverages Kubernetes access control and secret management, eliminating the need for pipelines to operate with elevated privileges or handle sensitive secret keys, thus making the platform more secure. DLF is designed to be cloud-agnostic and due to Container Storage Interface (CSI)[5], it is highly extensible to support various data-sources. DLF introduces the Dataset as a Custom Resource Definition (CRD)[6], which is a pointer to existing S3 or NFS data-sources. A Dataset object is a reference to a storage provided by a cloud-based storage solution, potentially populated with pre-existing data. In other words, each Dataset is a pointer to an existing remote data-source and is materialized as a PVC. Creating a CRD is just the first step to add custom logic in the Kubernetes cluster. The next step is to create a component that has embedded the domain-specific application logic for the CRD. Essentially, a service provider is tasked with developing and installing a component that effectively responds to the various events inherent to the lifecycle of a CRD, thereby implementing the desired functionality. DLF utilizes the Operator-SDK, an open-source component of the Operator Framework[7], which provides the necessary tooling and automation in the development of these components in an effective, automated, and scalable way. Its main functionality is to respond to the creation or deletion of a new Dataset and materialize the specific object.

3.2   Localized Docker Registry

The localized Docker registry (LDR) is creating a Docker image registry inside each MiniCloud, taking Docker and VM images near the edge devices. A Mini-Cloud is a set of interconnected resources that are available at the edge and can host instances of application components. This functionality acts as a proactive caching mechanism by optimizing the download delays and the network traffic. The port of the LDR as well as its credentials are pre-configured using the generalized configuration file that is packed with the proposed edge storage solution.

---

[5] https://kubernetes-csi.github.io/docs/.

[6] https://kubernetes.io/docs/tasks/extend-kubernetes/custom-resources/custom-resource-definitions/.

[7] https://operatorframework.io/.

After the successful deployment of the LDR, an image synchronization daemon, called Registry Sync Daemon (RSD), is started in another container and waits for triggering messages that instruct it to populate the LDR instance with new images. Then each node in the same egde cluster gains access to these new images through the LDR, allowing them to quickly deploy the associated services.

LDR is based on the Docker registry technology in order to store and distribute container images. It combines the official Docker registry image[8] with Kubernetes orchestration, a MinIO object storage backend and a set of automated deployment and configuration scripts. This enables LDR to automatically deploy and scale the Docker registry as needed while centrally controlling the configuration options such as communication protocols, SSL certificates, credentials, connection ports and others. This configuration also enables us to fine-tune the back-end storage, placing the images at the optimal physical locations according to the needs of each use case. The VM images are handled as objects, stored in a MinIO bucket and accessed either using the S3 API it provides, its web interface or the DLF functionality the LDR has added on top of MinIO, making the buckets available as mountable virtual disks.

RSD is a synchronization mechanism that can take decisions about image pre-loading in real time. In detail, it can monitor a Kafka message broker topic in real time, waiting for triggering messages about new or updated images. In addition, it also exposes an API endpoint that allows manual triggering of a pre-loading task. When a pre-loading task is initiated, RSD is trying to access the target image, using any pre-registered credentials if needed. If it successfully accesses the image, it starts replicating it to its host Minicloud using the deployed LDR instance. In the scenario where the image corresponds to a container, it will be deployed within the Docker Registry section of the LDR. Conversely, if the image is a VM image, it will be replicated in the appropriate MinIO bucket. In addition, RSD also provides a wide set of API endpoints that enable users to trigger various tasks or get information about available images, provided functionalities and status of running tasks.

4   Use Cases

The proposed framework has been deployed and evaluated in the context of two European funded projects; CHARITY[9] and ACCORDION[10]. These projects offer a wide set of real life use cases that provide ample opportunity for testing and evaluating the proposed solution. In this section we provide a brief overview of two use cases.

4.1   Collaborative VR Medical Training

The collaborative Virtual Reality (VR) use case addresses an experiential medical training simulation, via a gamified, multi-user VR platform, namely ORa-

---

[8] https://hub.docker.com/_/registry.

[9] https://www.charity-project.eu/.

[10] https://www.accordion-project.eu/.

maVR (OVR) MAGES SDK [18], that is based on the Unity game engine. As the VR Head-mounted Displays (HMDs) are generally of limited processing power and storage resources, this use case offloads the most demanding Unity pipeline processes to powerful, in terms of CPU, GPU and memory, edge resources. The remote-rendering network application, deployed on the edge, is responsible for maintaining the game logic of the virtual scenario, synchronizing all in-game VR user interactions in real time, performing physics computations, image rendering, encoding and streaming. To achieve multi-user collaboration in the same VR session, the edge application broadcasts all VR scene transformation data to other edge nodes, serving other users that may be situated in various geolocations, through Photon Relay server. The VR HMD application is responsible for receiving, decoding and projecting the rendered images and for capturing and transmitting user event data. In VR applications, optimal Quality of Experience (QoE) must be maintained at all times, in order to ensure user immersion in the virtual environment. To achieve such QoE, minimal latency and high bandwidth are critical factors in this demanding distributed VR pipeline, which may be alleviated by intelligent data handling and network transactions, through high speed networks, for streaming. Figure 2 presents the high level architecture of the collaborative VR use case.

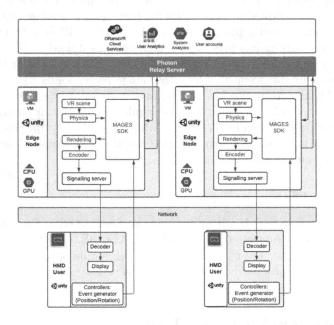

Fig. 2. Collaborative VR medical training high level architecture

The presented solution is actively aiding the deployment, migration and scaling of the collaborative VR medical training application, by using pro-active data caching near the edge node, which hosts the remote-rendering network application. The application, which is packaged into a VM image (grey boxes in Fig. 2), needs to be dynamically deployed in an edge server, which is a machine with high-end CPU, GPU, and memory resources, physically located near the HMDs. This means that to deploy the remote-rendering application, the VM image should be fetched and executed in minimal time, while the HMD user is initiating the VR session.

4.2 Multiplayer Mobile Gaming

The second use case is owned by Orbital Knight[11], a Polish based mobile game development company. The use case concerns the deployment of a multiplayer mobile game that runs on Android smart devices and involves a big number of concurrent players, up to 100, that share the same session. The primary difficulty faced in this use case pertains to the substantial amount of ongoing, real time data exchanges required to synchronize a large number of players. As every action taken by players within the game must be communicated to the game server and subsequently transmitted to each individual player's device, the objective is to update the game's state and the visuals displayed on their screens. To accomplish effective coordination and reduce network and processing delays, it is essential to dynamically scale out the game servers in real time as additional players join a session. This means that the new servers need to be deployed near the edge devices as fast as possible in order to counter any overcrowded servers that are causing delays to a game session. A high level architecture of this use case and its scaling capabilities is presented in Fig. 3.

5   Experimental Evaluation

The experimental evaluation of LDR was conducted having the scope of the presented use cases in mind. Nevertheless, the results gathered can be generalized and they can be used to estimate the contributions of the LDR to other possible use cases. The selected use cases were selected due to their distinct features and specific requirements. In detail, the collaborative VR use case requires a substantial VM image, approximately 25 GB in size, to be deployed near the end users, which in this case are the HMDs. On the other hand, the multiplayer mobile gaming use case needs multiple small files, sized less than 3 MB, to be exchanged in real time between multiple participating nodes.

---

[11] https://www.orbitalknight.com.

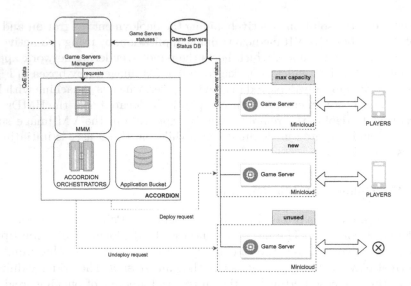

Fig. 3. Multiplayer Mobile Game architecture

Throughout the pilot evaluations of the collaborative VR medical training application, the retrieval of the 25GB-sized VM image from a remote repository resulted in substantial network congestion, causing delays in both the image download and other concurrent network operations. By positioning the VM image within the LDR on the same edge node before initiating a new VR session request, the transfer delay was minimized, since the deployment of the new VM was performed from a local instead of a remote repository. In detail, the pilot evaluations were conducted on three different locations; a) Italy, b) Greece and c) Poland. Each location had one Minicloud that contained one windows node acting as the Kubernetes master and 1 to 3 HMDs acting as the client nodes. Since the Miniclouds were constructed for the pilot evaluations RSD was configured to pre-load the OVR images into the LDR of these Miniclouds. In the initial tests, without the LDR pre-loading, the deployment time of the application was over 10 min and in cases it even reached 20 min. Using the pre-loading of LDR this dropped to 1–2 min, depending on the Minicloud. This means that LDR achieved a deployment time up to 10 times faster than raw Kubernetes deployment.

The second use case, the multiplayer mobile gaming, does not preserve any data during its sessions so the edge storage solution has little to no contributions to offer. Nevertheless, the LDR solution offers significant support in minimizing both the network load and the deployment time of new game servers by strategically placing the game server Docker images near the edge nodes that will host them, before they are actually needed. In detail, each Minicloud has one storage node that is located physically close to the edge nodes that can host game servers. By placing the Docker image at the storage node of a MiniCloud, the edge storage solution minimizes both the network load and the image download time for all other nodes in the same MiniCloud. This advantage is derived from the physical proximity of the MiniCloud nodes and the high-quality connection between them. The evaluation performed during the pilot phase yielded impressive results as presented in Fig. 4. Throughout the evaluation, data files essential for the game engine's functionality, each smaller than 3 MB in size, were exchanged in real time between the remote game servers and the Minicloud clients.

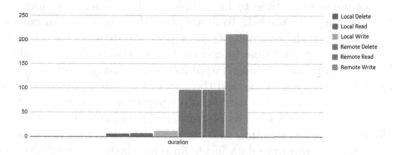

Fig. 4. LDR evaluation results for small files

6 Discussion

6.1 Semi-automated Deployment and Off-Loading

In the context of the presented solution, a set of bash and yaml scripts have been developed that handle all the configuration, installation and deployment processes that need to be contacted before and after the MinIO workers are deployed. These configurations include firewall rules, DNS settings, package installations and security checks that take into account the setup environment, the architecture and resources of the physical machines and the software involved. These tasks enable the semi-automatic deployment of the proposed edge storage solution, forming complex pipelines that in most other cases are performed manually by a system administrator. This ensures that scaling can be performed seamlessly on each cluster, regardless of the underlying physical machines that act as nodes. In addition, off-loading of data can be achieved by "ordering" more instances of the MinIO worker to be deployed on more nodes and adding them in the same MinIO cluster in real time.

6.2 Relation to Research Questions

At present, numerous research questions pertaining to edge storage solutions are being actively investigated. These questions include the intelligent data placement in computing networks, the pro-active and intelligent caching of data, the minimization of resource waste and the maximization of resource efficiency and the harmonization of IoT network diversity. The current research efforts and the devised framework comprehensively address the majority of these research questions by providing a complete edge storage solution that takes into account the present issues in IoT edge networks and the vast number of data transactions that continuously happen between them. Pro-active and intelligent caching of data are two questions that also trouble the academic community and the industry for a very long time. This pertains to the replication or migration of data in advance, ensuring their availability for immediate usage when the need arises. This reduces operational waiting times as I/O and network operations, which usually take much more time to be completed than processing does, are performed before they are needed. To accomplish this objective, an edge storage system must possess the capability to anticipate the demand for a specific data packet with sufficient lead time to execute the necessary data operations prior to its actual requirement. Modern approaches are using machine learning in order to profile the applications and the users of a system, extracting patterns of behaviour that hint at the future data operations. The presented solution utilizes Kubernetes (K3s) as an orchestrator, which enables us to define certain node affinity and node selection rules that aid the selection of storage workers and the placement of the data inside an edge cluster. The affinity rules are relaxed rules that are instructing Kubernetes to prefer nodes that are meeting most of the affinity rules specified. On the other hand, selection rules are strict and instruct Kubernetes to deploy the storage workers on nodes that fulfill all of the selection rules. These rules can be dynamically set either by a network administrator or by an automated mechanism such as an intelligent agent or a machine learning model that can estimate the most efficient placement of storage workers. Harmonization of IoT network diversity concerns the definition of a uniform way of handling the various IoT devices that can be part of an edge cluster. An IoT edge network is like a living organism. The parts that comprise it can change at any given time either because they do not wish to be part of the network anymore, due to hardware or software malfunction, scaling out and in operations, or any other event that introduces or removes devices across the device-edge-cloud continuum. K3s is compatible with most devices that run windows or unix-based operating systems. This enables the administrators to create generalized deployment scripts that handle the deployment, configuration, undeployment and re-deployment of the storage workers. These generalized scripts are highly configurable and can be edited in real time by higher level scripts and automated mechanisms adding more layers of intelligence and automation to these deployment and configuration processes. In addition, DLF provides a uniform way of accessing the data, using the local file system of each device, eliminating the need of customized solutions for each new device that becomes a member of the device-edge-cloud continuum.

7   Conclusion

Despite the immersive experiences that next-generation applications provide across various domains, they face numerous challenges closely tied to their inherent characteristics. To address these challenges, edge computing plays a vital role as it enables meeting the demanding requirements of these applications. However, deploying XR applications on edge devices with limited resources presents specific obstacles, including constraints in network bandwidth, limitations in latency, and intermittent connectivity. In this paper, we introduce a hybrid distributed edge-enabled storage framework that integrates a localized Docker registry. This registry utilizes Docker registry technology with Kubernetes orchestration, along with a MinIO object storage backend and automated deployment and configuration scripts. The inclusion of LDR streamlines the process of storing and distributing container images, providing improved control, scalability, and optimized deployment capabilities at the edge. The experimental evaluation conducted using two XR use cases demonstrates a noteworthy reduction in application deployment time, thus confirming the positive effects of the proposed solution. As part of our future work, we aim to explore intelligent image synchronization techniques that dynamically update the localized Docker registry based on usage patterns and application demands.

Acknowledgment. The research leading to these results received funding from the European Union's Horizon 2020 research and innovation programme under grant agreement No 871793 (project ACCORDION), No 101016509 (project CHARITY) and No 101057821 (RELEVIUM). The paper reflects only the authors' views. The Commission is not responsible for any use that may be made of the information it contains.

References

1. Baresi, L., Mendonça, D.F.: Towards a serverless platform for edge computing. In: 2019 IEEE International Conference on Fog Computing (ICFC), pp. 1–10. IEEE (2019)
2. Becker, S., Schmidt, F., Kao, O.: Edgepier: p2p-based container image distribution in edge computing environments. In: 2021 IEEE International Performance, Computing, and Communications Conference (IPCCC), pp. 1–8 (2021)
3. Boubendir, A., et al.: Federation of cross-domain edge resources: a brokering architecture for network slicing. In: 2018 4th IEEE Conference on Network Softwarization and Workshops (NetSoft), pp. 415–423 (2018)
4. Dias Knob, L.A., Faticanti, F., Ferreto, T., Siracusa, D.: Community-based placement of registries to speed up application deployment on edge computing. In: 2021 IEEE International Conference on Cloud Engineering (IC2E), pp. 147–153 (2021)
5. Gazzetti, M., Reale, A., Katrinis, K., Corradi, A.: Scalable Linux container provisioning in fog and edge computing platforms. In: Heras, D.B., Bougé, L. (eds.) Euro-Par 2017. LNCS, vol. 10659, pp. 304–315. Springer, Cham (2018). https://doi.org/10.1007/978-3-319-75178-8_25
6. Gkoufas, Y., Yuan, D.Y.: Dataset lifecycle framework and its applications in bioinformatics. arXiv preprint arXiv:2103.00490 (2021)
7. Gupta, N., Anantharaj, K., Subramani, K.: Containerized architecture for edge computing in smart home: a consistent architecture for model deployment. In: 2020 International Conference on Computer Communication and Informatics (ICCCI), pp. 1–8 (2020)
8. Littley, M., et al.: Bolt: towards a scalable docker registry via hyperconvergence. In: 2019 IEEE 12th International Conference on Cloud Computing (CLOUD), pp. 358–366 (2019)

9. Makris, A., et al.: Cloud for holography and augmented reality. In: 2021 IEEE 10th International Conference on Cloud Networking (CloudNet), pp. 118–126. IEEE (2021)
10. Makris, A., Psomakelis, E., Theodoropoulos, T., Tserpes, K.: Towards a distributed storage framework for edge computing infrastructures. In: Proceedings of the 2nd Workshop on Flexible Resource and Application Management on the Edge, pp. 9–14 (2022)
11. Makris, A., Tserpes, K., Varvarigou, T.: Transition from monolithic to microservice-based applications. Challenges from the developer perspective. Open Res. Eur. **2**, 24 (2022)
12. Nathan, S., Ghosh, R., Mukherjee, T., Narayanan, K.: Comicon: a co-operative management system for docker container images. In: 2017 IEEE International Conference on Cloud Engineering (IC2E), pp. 116–126 (2017)
13. Sabella, D., et al.: Edge computing: from standard to actual infrastructure deployment and software development. ETSI White paper, pp. 1–41 (2019)
14. Satyanarayanan, M.: The emergence of edge computing. Computer **50**(1), 30–39 (2017)
15. Shi, W., Cao, J., Zhang, Q., Li, Y., Xu, L.: Edge computing: vision and challenges. IEEE Internet Things J. **3**(5), 637–646 (2016)
16. Theodoropoulos, T., et al.: Cloud-based XR services: a survey on relevant challenges and enabling technologies. J. Netw. Netw. Appl. **2**(1), 1–22 (2022)
17. Zheng, C., et al.: Wharf: Sharing docker images in a distributed file system. In: Proceedings of the ACM Symposium on Cloud Computing, pp. 174–185. SoCC '18, Association for Computing Machinery, New York, NY, USA (2018)
18. Zikas, P., et al.: Mages 4.0: accelerating the world's transition to medical VR training. arXiv preprint arXiv:2209.08819 (2022)

PhD Symposium

Towards Cloud Storage Tier Optimization with Rule-Based Classification

Akif Quddus Khan[1]([⊠]), Nikolay Nikolov[2], Mihhail Matskin[3], Radu Prodan[4], Christoph Bussler[5], Dumitru Roman[2,6], and Ahmet Soylu[6]

[1] Norwegian University of Science and Technology – NTNU, Gjøvik, Norway
akif.q.khan@ntnu.no
[2] SINTEF AS, Oslo, Norway
[3] KTH Royal Institute of Technology, Stockholm, Sweden
[4] University of Klagenfurt, Klagefurt, Austria
[5] Robert Bosch LLC, Sunnyvale, CA, USA
[6] OsloMet – Oslo Metropolitan University, Oslo, Norway

Abstract. Cloud storage adoption has increased over the years as more and more data has been produced with particularly high demand for fast processing and low latency. To meet the users' demands and to provide a cost-effective solution, cloud service providers (CSPs) have offered tiered storage; however, keeping the data in one tier is not a cost-effective approach. Hence, several two-tiered approaches have been developed to classify storage objects into the most suitable tier. In this respect, this paper explores a rule-based classification approach to optimize cloud storage cost by migrating data between different storage tiers. Instead of two, four distinct storage tiers are considered, including premium, hot, cold, and archive. The viability and potential of the approach are demonstrated by comparing cost savings achieved when data was moved between tiers versus when it remained static. The results indicate that the proposed approach has the potential to significantly reduce cloud storage cost, thereby providing valuable insights for organizations seeking to optimize their cloud storage strategies. Finally, the limitations of the proposed approach are discussed along with the potential directions for future work, particularly the use of game theory to incorporate a feedback loop to extend and improve the proposed approach accordingly.

Keywords: Storage tiers · cloud · optimization · StaaS · cloud storage

1 Introduction

Cloud computing, in general, and cloud storage, in particular, have experienced exponential growth in recent years [15,20,21]. Organizations have increasingly embraced cloud services to meet their computing needs. According to Gartner, 85% of enterprises are expected to adopt a cloud-first approach by 2025 [19]. The use of cloud storage, i.e., Storage-as-a-Service (StaaS) [11], instead of

© IFIP International Federation for Information Processing 2023
Published by Springer Nature Switzerland AG 2023
G. A. Papadopoulos et al. (Eds.): ESOCC 2023, LNCS 14183, pp. 205–216, 2023.
https://doi.org/10.1007/978-3-031-46235-1_13

local storage, has the potential to provide more flexibility in terms of scalability, fault tolerance, and availability. Cloud storage systems (e.g., Amazon S3, Azure Blob Storage, Google Cloud Storage) offer very large storage with high fault tolerance, addressing several big data-related storage concerns [24]. When it comes to object storage services, leading cloud service providers (CSPs) such as Microsoft Azure, Google Cloud, and Amazon S3, offer four different storage tier options and pricing policies tailored to their specific data storage and access requirements. This presents an opportunity for users to optimize their StaaS cost. For example, Google Cloud Storage provides not only hot and cold storage tiers but also premium and archive tiers. The pricing structure varies across these tiers, with the hot tier offering lower access prices but higher storage cost, while the cold tier offers higher access prices but lower storage costs. This means that for data objects with infrequent access, storing them in the cold tier can result in lower expenses compared to the hot tier. As a result, StaaS users can strategically migrate their data, i.e., can do storage tier optimization from the hot tier to the cold tier when access demands decrease, reducing the overall cost.

Storage tier optimization is the process of organizing data into different tiers based on its usage and performance requirements [2]. This can help improve storage performance and efficiency by ensuring that the most frequently accessed data is stored on the fastest media, while less frequently accessed data can be stored on slower, less expensive media. There are many different ways to implement storage tiering. One common method is to use a storage array that has multiple tiers of storage media, such as high-performance flash storage, mid-range spinning disk drives, and low-cost nearline or offline storage. The storage array can then automatically move data between tiers based on its usage patterns [1]. Another common method of storage tiering is to use a software-defined storage solution [8]. These solutions typically provide a more flexible and scalable approach to storage tiering than traditional storage arrays. Software-defined storage solutions can also be used to tier data across multiple physical storage locations, such as on-premise and cloud storage.

In this paper, we focus on moving data between different tiers at a single location. Storage tier optimization can be a complex process, but it can offer significant benefits in terms of performance, efficiency, and cost savings. By planning and implementing a storage tiering strategy, organizations can improve the performance of their storage infrastructure and reduce their storage costs. To this end, in this paper, we explore storage tier optimization for cost-effective data storage using a rule-based classification approach that takes into account four storage tiers instead of just two, is lightweight, does not require intense computing resources, is platform-independent, and is fast. We propose a set of rules for calculating a score or priority score and define a threshold to classify each object stored in cloud storage into premium, hot, cold, or archive tiers. We demonstrate the viability and potential of the proposed approach against a synthetic dataset of 1TB by getting a significant reduction in storage cost. We discuss the limitations of the proposed approach and provide directions for improvement, particularly through expanding the proposal with the use of game theory, to incorporate a feedback loop in the process of storage object classification.

The rest of the paper is structured as follows. Section 2 provides an overview of cloud storage cost elements, while Sect. 3 presents the rule-based classification approach. Section 4 discusses the results and limitations and proposes the use of game theory for storage object classification. Section 5 provides a summary and discussion of related works. Finally, Sect. 6 concludes the paper and presents future work.

2   Cloud Storage Cost

The five major elements of cloud storage cost include: 1) data storage; 2) network usage; 3) transaction; 4) data retrieval; and 5) data replication/migration [5]. Table 1 shows the actual prices of different cost elements of cloud storage by using Google Cloud[1,2] as an example.

Table 1. Cost of data storage by Google Cloud in a single region, Europe - Warsaw (europe-central2) - data collected on 12 May 2023.

Cost Element	Premium	Hot	Cold	Archive
Official term	Standard	Nearline	Coldline	Archive
Storage cost ($ n GBn month)	0.023	0.013	0.006	0.0025
GET Request ($ per 1,000)	0.0004	0.001	0.01	0.05
PUT Request ($ per 1,000)	0.005	0.01	0.02	0.05
Data Retrieval ($n GB)	0	0.01	0.02	0.05
Network Usage ($n GB)	0	0.01	0.02	0.05
Minimum Duration(days)	None	30	90	365
Latency	Low[a]			
Durability	99.999999999%[b]			
Availability	Multi-region: >99.99% Dual-regions: >99.99%Regions: 99.99%	99.95% 99.95% 99.9%	99.95% 99.95%99.9%	99.95% 99.95%99.9%

[a]Time to first byte typically tens of milliseconds.
[b]https://cloud.google.com/blog/products/storage-data-transfer/understanding-cloud-storage-11-9s-durability-target

2.1   Storage Cost

Storage cost refers to the cost of storing data in the cloud. It is charged on a per-GB-per-month basis. Each storage tier has different pricing. It also depends on the amount of data being stored. Some CSPs offer block-rate pricing, i.e., the larger the amount of data, the lower the unit costs are [14]. For example, there is a certain cost for data between 0 and 50 TB, and then for some tiers, it might be cheaper for over 50 TB of data. However, in this paper, we do not take that into account when calculating cost estimates.

---

[1] https://cloud.google.com/storage/pricing.
[2] https://cloud.google.com/storage/docs/storage-classes.

2.2   Network Usage Cost

The quantity of data read from or sent between the buckets is known as network consumption or network usage. Data transmitted by cloud storage through egress is reflected in the HTTP response headers. Hence, the term network usage cost is defined as the cost of bandwidth out of the cloud storage server. It is charged on a per-GB basis. In addition to that, network cost also vary based on the amount of data transferred, as it offers different slabs for different amounts of data. The higher the amount of data transferred, the cheaper the cost will be.

2.3   Transaction Cost

Transaction cost refers to the costs for managing, monitoring, and controlling a transaction when reading or writing data to cloud storage [16]. When it comes to data storage, cloud storage providers charge for the amount of data transferred over the network and the number of operations it takes. Transaction costs deal with the number of operations. These costs are associated with managing, monitoring, and controlling a transaction when reading or writing data to cloud storage.

2.4   Data Retrieval

Data retrieval fees refer to the charges incurred when retrieving or accessing data from a storage system or service. In various cloud storage or object storage platforms, data retrieval fees may apply when retrieving stored files or information. These fees are typically associated with the data transfer or bandwidth used during the retrieval process. Data access frequency in this context is of importance when considering the impact of data retrieval on cost.

2.5   Migration Cost

Different CSPs provide the capability to migrate data objects between tiers throughout their lifecycles, presenting a valuable opportunity for cost optimization. The migration process involves retrieving the complete object from the source tier and subsequently submitting a PUT request to the destination tier to inform it of the impending object. As such, the data migration operation is subject to expenses associated with data retrieval, calculated based on the object size in the source tier, as well as expenses associated with the PUT request in the destination tier.

3   Rule-Based Classification

The term rule-based classification can be used to refer to any classification scheme that makes use of IF-THEN rules for class prediction [23]. In this method, we define rules that assign each object to a storage tier based on specific criteria, such as the frequency of access, the size of the data, and the age of the stored object. For example, we define a rule that assigns objects that are accessed frequently to a high-performance storage tier and those that are accessed less frequently to a lower-performance storage tier. The following are some general rules that are used to determine which characteristics are appropriate for each tier:

1. **Premium tier:** This tier should be used for data with the highest frequency of access, such as data that is accessed continuously or near-continuously and requires the highest levels of performance and durability. For example, mission-critical databases or high-performance computing workloads.
2. **Hot tier:** This tier should be used for data with frequent access patterns, such as data that is accessed daily or weekly and requires fast access times. For example, this might include frequently accessed files, frequently used application data, or logs that require analysis on a regular basis.
3. **Cold tier:** This tier should be used for data with infrequent or irregular access patterns, such as data that is accessed monthly, quarterly, etc. For example, backups, archives, or historical data that is rarely accessed but needs to be kept for long periods of time for compliance or other reasons.
4. **Archive tier:** The archive tier is designed for data that is rarely accessed and has minimal retrieval requirements. It is typically used for long-term storage and compliance purposes. This tier is suitable for data with very infrequent access patterns, such as annually or even less frequently.

3.1 Solution Approach

We first define the weights (W) for each factor (size (Z), access frequency (F), and age (A)) as W_z, W_f, and W_a, respectively. Then the data is defined as a list of dictionaries, where each dictionary represents an object and contains its size, access frequency, and age. Afterwards, the priority score for each object is calculated using the defined weightings using Eq. 1 for size score (α), Eq. 2 for access frequency score (β), Eq. 3 for age score (γ) and Eq. 4 for calculating priority score (λ). The weight (W) of data indicates its priority or significance, allowing for varied importance levels across data objects, often determined by business criteria; for instance, vital data could bear a greater weight, directing it to higher-tier storage. Data size, access frequency, and age serve as pivotal determinants in storage choices, where larger values may entail increased storage costs. Applying the logarithm of these values, such as $\log_{10}(X)$, facilitates data normalization and mitigates the potential dominance of extreme values in classification. This logarithmic transformation ensures a balanced scale for storage tiers, effectively accommodating a wide range of data sizes.

$$\alpha = W_z \times \log_{10}(Z) \tag{1}$$

$$\beta = W_f \times \log_{10}(F) \tag{2}$$

$$\gamma = W_a \times \frac{A}{365} \tag{3}$$

$$\lambda = \alpha + \beta + \gamma \tag{4}$$

In this context,

- Z represents the size of data in Gigabytes (GB);
- F denotes the total number of R/W operations for an object in a specified period of time; and,
- A represents the age of the data in months.

Finally, the objects are divided into groups based on the available storage tiers by iterating over each object and checking if its priority score is greater than or equal to the threshold for each tier. If so, it is added to the corresponding group. Regarding the access frequency, the followings are the nineteen possible windows: hourly, every 2 h, every 3 h, every 4 h, every 6 h, every 8 h, every 12 h, daily, every other day, every 3 days, every 4 days, every week, every 2 weeks, every month, every 2 months, every 3 months, every 4 months, every 6 months, and yearly.

Priority Score Threshold. We set the following priority scores to classify each object into premium, hot, cold, or archive tiers.

- Premium: 1.0
- Hot: 0.7
- Cold: 0.4
- Archive: 0.1

The selection of priority score thresholds for each storage tier aims to balance the trade-offs between data size, access frequency, and age. The premium tier, with a threshold of 1.0, represents the highest priority for critical and frequently accessed data. This tier ensures fast and reliable access to the most valuable information. The hot tier, set at 0.7, accommodates data with slightly lower priority but still significant access requirements. It provides a balance between performance and cost for frequently accessed data. The cold tier, with a threshold of 0.4, caters to less frequently accessed data, offering cost-effective storage without compromising data availability. Lastly, the archive tier, at 0.1, serves as a long-term storage solution for rarely accessed data, providing cost optimization while preserving data retention. These thresholds enable the effective allocation of data to the appropriate storage tiers based on their priority scores, ensuring optimal cost management, while meeting the needs of data access and availability.

3.2   Evaluation

To evaluate the viability and potential of the proposed approach, a software tool has been developed to provide cost estimations based on the values obtained from Google Cloud storage when data is migrated according to the classification performed by the proposed approach.

Dataset Information. Due to limitations in acquiring a real dataset, synthetic data was generated based on publicly available data on Kaggle. It is an access log of a software application deployed on the cloud for a period of almost 2.5 years. Figure 1 shows the access pattern based on the average number of accesses of all objects over the whole storage time period. Additionally, some of the key features of the dataset are as follows:

- Total time of data storage: $A = 871$ days.
- Total number of objects $T_{obj} = 14321$
- Total number of GET Requests: $g(t) = 2906097$
- Total number of PUT Requests: $p(t) = 14321$
- Object size range: 50 MB to 100 MB
- Total data size $Z = 1052.45$ GB

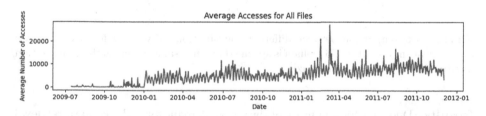

Fig. 1. Data access pattern over the whole time period. Number of accesses on the y-axis and date on the x-axis.

Figure 2 compares the data storage cost if it remained static in one storage tier. The calculation is done keeping in view that the access pattern that objects will follow for the next 871 days will be similar to the first 871 days.

Weights. If 30% weight is set for size, 20% for access frequency, and 50% for the age of the data, the combination of weights would be (0.3, 0.2, 0.5). Generally, the sum of the total weights should be equal to 1. In that case, there are a total of 36 possible combinations of weights. By removing the condition of the sum being equal to 1, we created a total of 286 combinations. Then the priority score was calculated for each combination of weights, and subsequently, the cost was calculated. Out of 286, the cost calculation script returned 169 unique values for the cost. The comparison of cost with those combinations is shown in Fig. 3.

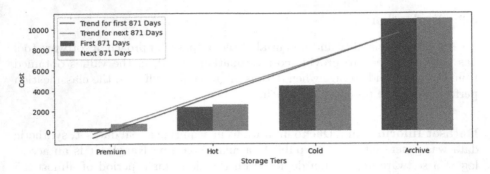

Fig. 2. Comparison of the cost of data storage for the first 871 days with each object having variable age vs. the cost of data storage if it is not moved between tiers for the next 871 days.

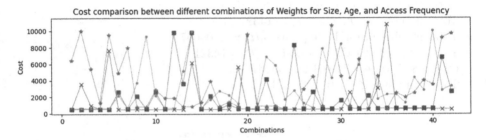

Fig. 3. Cost comparison between different combinations of weights for size, age, and access frequency. Cost in US Dollars is specified on the y-axis, whereas the combination number (#) is shown on the x-axis.

Results. Due to a high number of data access requests and free data retrieval for the premium tier, the cost of the data stored in the premium tier is the cheapest, as shown in Fig. 2. Although when calculating the cost of data storage for the next 871 days, the premium tier shows the highest difference in the cost and is still cheaper than the rest of the tiers because of the low cost of data retrieval in the premium tier. Different costs are calculated using the proposed rule-based classification, and a comparison is presented in Fig. 4. The effectiveness of the weights can vary according to the characteristics of the dataset, hence, for this dataset, the best suitable combination turned out to be size: 20%, access frequency: 80%, and age: 0%. It can be seen that with the proposed rule-based classification technique, the cost of data storage is $473.39. In contrast, if the data is stored in the premium tier for the whole time, the total cost is $694.35 (the cost of data migration is not included in this calculation).

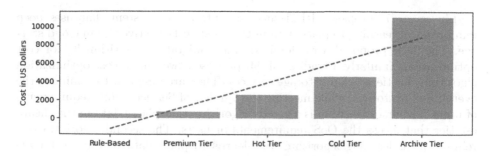

Fig. 4. Cost comparison between rule-based classification and single tiers.

4   Discussion

The proposed rule-based classification approach is lightweight, industry- and platform-independent, and has shown promising results. According to the evaluation, the cost reduction is nearly 32%; even when factoring in the cost of data migration, the difference would be significant. However, it lacks the ability to consider feedback regarding each classification. There is a chance that the classification of a storage object may not be cost-effective, and to enhance the algorithm's performance, it is crucial to incorporate that information as feedback. To tackle this challenge, we suggest utilizing game theory for the classification of storage objects into different tiers.

Game theory is a mathematical framework used to analyze the interactions and decision-making strategies of individuals or agents within a group or system [13]. We propose the use of game theory to optimize the storage tier selection in a multi-agent system, where each agent is responsible for storing and retrieving data. One approach is to use a variant of the multi-armed bandit problem, where the agents are the arms, and the storage tiers are the bandits. One possible implementation of this approach could use the Thompson Sampling algorithm [22], which is a Bayesian approach to the multi-armed bandit problem. In this algorithm, each agent maintains a beta distribution over the storage tiers, where the parameters of the distribution represent the number of successes and failures in selecting a storage tier. The agent selects a storage tier based on the highest sampled value from the distribution. The update of the distribution is done after the storage operation is completed, based on the feedback from the system. Specifically, if the storage cost is lower than the expected cost from the distribution, the parameters of the beta distribution are updated to reflect success.

5   Related Work

Existing related work primarily focuses on two tiers: hot and cold. Hot data is frequently accessed and requires high-performance storage. Cold data is accessed infrequently and can be stored on lower-cost storage.

Liu et al. [7] proposed RLTiering, an auto-tiering system that uses deep reinforcement learning to place data in the most cost-effective tier in cloud storage. They also proposed a randomized online migration algorithm [6] for cost optimization. Similarly, Erradi et al. [4] proposed two online cost optimization algorithms for tiered cloud storage services. They are designed to minimize the overall cost of storage, while meeting the Quality of Service (QoS) requirements of users. The first algorithm is a greedy algorithm that places data in the cheapest tier that meets the QoS requirements of users. The second algorithm is a reinforcement learning algorithm that learns to place data in the most cost-effective tier over time. Alshawabkeh et al. [3] developed an automated and adaptive framework using efficient Markov chain correlation-based clustering to move active data to high-performance storage tiers and inactive data to low-cost/high-capacity storage tiers. This framework can predict workload changes and group similar storage units, enhancing performance, reliability, and availability and reducing cost. On the contrary, we propose an approach to storage tiering that considers four storage tiers: premium, hot, cold, and archive.

Mansouri and Erradi [9], as well as Erradi and Mansouri [4], introduced a series of deterministic online algorithms to address cost reduction in this particular problem. However, the aspect of access frequency, specifically the number of access requests, was not taken into account during their decision-making process. Our approach, however, takes into account three main factors when determining which tier to store an object size, age, and access frequency. Moreover, Zhang et al. [25] investigated how cloud providers can maximize their profits by using hot and cold storage tiers, but our research focuses on how cloud users can minimize their costs by using hot and cold storage tiers. The multi-cloud setting is also introduced by some scientific studies that consider migrating data among multiple clouds for achieving cost-effective geo-distributed workloads [10,17,18]. In [12], Facebook developed a storage tier optimization approach and targeted two storage tiers. In addition to that, their proposed approach made decisions based on the characteristics of the whole bucket. Our algorithm makes decisions on objects rather than buckets, hence proposing a more flexible approach. In addition to that, it is generic, platform- and industry-independent.

6   Conclusion and Future Work

Maintaining data in a single tier continuously is ineffective and expensive. We explored a rule-based approach that examines object metadata and access patterns for storage tier optimization. The rule-based classification was demonstrated to be successful on a synthetic data set and is straightforward and simple to use using $\lambda = \alpha + \beta + \gamma$ for priority score calculations. We also proposed using game theory, which is more complex, to improve the accuracy of the proposed approach. The suggested approach is not platform- or industry-specific and is also not very resource-intensive in terms of computation. It can, therefore, be considered appropriate for a variety of applications. The findings indicate that while developing such an algorithm, it is crucial to take into account the access patterns and metadata of storage items. Additionally, it was demonstrated that by utilizing the suggested approach, storage cost can be decreased.

In the future we aim to extend the proposed approach using game theory to improve the accuracy of our predictions. By using game theory, we can model the interactions between different entities in our system and develop an algorithm that can anticipate their behaviour and make more accurate predictions. In addition, to make the estimations and comparisons more accurate and concise, there is a need for comprehensive mathematical modelling that not only correctly calculates the costs, but also takes into account the followings: 1) network usage cost based on block pricing; 2) data migration costs; and 3) penalty fees if an object is removed before the minimum time period specified for that particular tier. These should be used to generate accurate and concise estimates and comparisons of the cost for different storage options.

Acknowledgments. The first author is a Ph.D. Candidate. This work received partial funding from the projects DataCloud (H2020 101016835), enRichMyData (HE 101070284), Graph-Massivizer (HE 101093202), UPCAST (HE 101093216), and Big-DataMine (NFR 309691).

References

1. What is a storage device hierarchy? (2021). https://www.ibm.com/docs/en/zos/2.2.0?topic=dfsmshsm-what-is-storage-device-hierarchy. Accessed 20 Oct 2023
2. Tier definitions and volume placement optimization (2022). https://www.ibm.com/docs/en/storage-insights?topic=SSQRB8/com.ibm.spectrum.si.doc/tpch_saas_r_volume_optimization_process.htm. Accessed 20 May 2023
3. Alshawabkeh, M., Riska, A., Sahin, A., Awwad, M.: Automated storage tiering using markov chain correlation based clustering. In: Proceedings of the 11th International Conference on Machine Learning and Applications (ICMLA 2012), vol. 1, pp. 392–397. IEEE (2012). https://doi.org/10.1109/ICMLA.2012.71
4. Erradi, A., Mansouri, Y.: Online cost optimization algorithms for tiered cloud storage services. J. Syst. Softw. **160**, 110457 (2020). https://doi.org/10.1016/j.jss.2019.110457
5. Khan, A.Q., et al.: A taxonomy for cloud storage cost. In: Proceedings of the 15th International Conference on Management of Digital Ecosystems. Springer, Cham (2023)
6. Liu, M., Pan, L., Liu, S.: Keep hot or go cold: a randomized online migration algorithm for cost optimization in StaaS clouds. IEEE Trans. Netw. Serv. Manage. **18**(4), 4563–4575 (2021). https://doi.org/10.1109/TNSM.2021.3096533
7. Liu, M., Pan, L., Liu, S.: RLTiering: a cost-driven auto-tiering system for two-tier cloud storage using deep reinforcement learning. IEEE Trans. Parallel Distrib. Syst. **34**(2), 73–90 (2022). https://doi.org/10.1109/TPDS.2022.3224865
8. Macedo, R., Paulo, J.A., Pereira, J., Bessani, A.: A survey and classification of software-defined storage systems. ACM Comput. Surv. **53**(3), 1–38 (2020). https://doi.org/10.1145/3385896
9. Mansouri, Y., Erradi, A.: Cost optimization algorithms for hot and cool tiers cloud storage services. In: Proceedings of the 11th International Conference on Cloud Computing (CLOUD 2018), pp. 622–629. IEEE (2018). https://doi.org/10.1109/CLOUD.2018.00086

10. Mansouri, Y., Toosi, A.N., Buyya, R.: Cost optimization for dynamic replication and migration of data in cloud data centers. IEEE Trans. Cloud Comput. **7**(3), 705–718 (2017). https://doi.org/10.1109/TCC.2017.2659728
11. Mansouri, Y., Toosi, A.N., Buyya, R.: Data storage management in cloud environments: taxonomy, survey, and future directions. ACM Comput. Surv. **50**(6), 1–51 (2017). https://doi.org/10.1145/3136623
12. Muralidhar, S., et al.: F4: Facebook's warm BLOB storage system. In: Proceedings of the 11th USENIX Symposium on Operating Systems Design and Implementation, pp. 383–398. USENIX Association (2014)
13. Myerson, R.B.: Game Theory: Analysis of Conflict. Harvard University Press, Cambridge (1997)
14. Naldi, M., Mastroeni, L.: Cloud storage pricing: a comparison of current practices. In: Proceedings of the International Workshop on Hot Topics in Cloud Services (HotTopiCS 2013), pp. 27–34. ACM (2013). https://doi.org/10.1145/2462307.2462315
15. Nikolov, N., et al.: Conceptualization and scalable execution of big data workflows using domain-specific languages and software containers. Internet Things **16**, 100440 (2021). https://doi.org/10.1016/j.iot.2021.100440
16. Nuseibeh, H.: Adoption of cloud computing in organizations. In: Proceedings of the Americas Conference on Information Systems (AMCIS 2011). AISeL (2011)
17. Oh, K., Chandra, A., Weissman, J.: Wiera: towards flexible multi-tiered geo-distributed cloud storage instances. In: Proceedings of the 25th ACM International Symposium on High-Performance Parallel and Distributed Computing (HPDC 2016), pp. 165–176. ACM (2016). https://doi.org/10.1145/2907294.2907322
18. Qiu, X., Li, H., Wu, C., Li, Z., Lau, F.C.: Cost-minimizing dynamic migration of content distribution services into hybrid clouds. IEEE Trans. Parallel Distrib. Syst. **26**(12), 3330–3345 (2014). https://doi.org/10.1109/INFCOM.2012.6195655
19. Robinson, K.: Why companies are flocking to the cloud more than ever (2021). https://www.businessinsider.com/cloud-technology-trend-software-enterprise-2021-2. Accessed 20 Feb 2023
20. Roman, D., et al.: Big data pipelines on the computing continuum: tapping the dark data. Computer **55**(11), 74–84 (2022). https://doi.org/10.1109/MC.2022.3154148
21. Rydning, D.R.J.G.J., Reinsel, J., Gantz, J.: The digitization of the world from edge to core. Technical report, Framingham: International Data Corporation (2018)
22. Thompson, W.R.: On the likelihood that one unknown probability exceeds another in view of the evidence of two samples. Biometrika **25**(3–4), 285–294 (1933)
23. Tung, A.K.H.: Rule-based classification. In: Liu, L., Özsu, M.T. (eds.) Encyclopedia of Database Systems, pp. 2459–2462. Springer, Boston (2009). https://doi.org/10.1007/978-0-387-39940-9_559
24. Yang, C., Xu, Y., Nebert, D.: Redefining the possibility of digital Earth and geosciences with spatial cloud computing. Int. J. Digit. Earth **6**(4), 297–312 (2013). https://doi.org/10.1080/17538947.2013.769783
25. Zhang, Y., Ghosh, A., Aggarwal, V., Lan, T.: Tiered cloud storage via two-stage, latency-aware bidding. IEEE Trans. Netw. Serv. Manage. **16**(1), 176–191 (2018). https://doi.org/10.1109/TNSM.2018.2875475

Industry Projects Track

Towards a Decentralised Federated Learning Based Compute Continuum Framework

Mohamad Moussa[1,2]([⊠]), Philippe Glass[2], Nabil Abdennahder[1], Giovanna Di Marzo Serugendo[2], and Raphaël Couturier[3]

[1] HEPIA, University of Applied Sciences and Arts, Western Switzerland,
4 Rue de la Prairie, 1202 Geneva, Switzerland
`{mohamad.moussa,nabil.abdennadher}@hesge.ch`
[2] Computer Science Center, University of Geneva, Geneva, Switzerland
`{philippe.glass,giovanna.dimarzo}@unige.ch`
[3] Université de Franche-Comté, CNRS, institut FEMTO-ST, 90000 Belfort, France
`raphael.couturier@univ-fcomte.fr`

Abstract. The proliferation of sensing device technologies, and the growing demand for data intensive IoT applications calls for a seamless interconnection of IoT, edge and cloud resources in one computing system, to form a Compute Continuum, also referred to as edge-to-cloud.

This paper targets self-adaptive Machine Learning applications that rely on data coming from IoT sensors. These applications are often "context-aware", with high context sensitivity, different physical settings and complex usage patterns. Their intelligence, deployed on the edge, is updated on the fly.

We present two Compute Continuum strategies for the deployment of such applications: (1) a centralised approach, which involves training a model on a centralised server, and (2) a decentralised approach using Federated Learning. The former approach involves centralising data from multiple sources onto a single server, while the latter locally decentralises both the training process and the aggregation and communication tasks across edge devices. In both cases the inference model is deployed on edge devices close to the collected data. The decentralised architecture relies on a coordination platform favouring self-adaptation and decentralised Federated Learning. Results show that the decentralised Federated Learning approach offers networking performances and privacy-preserving advantages compared to non-private centralised models, with a slight trade-off in prediction accuracy. According to our simulations, the deployment cost of the decentralised architecture is much lower than that of deployment on the centralised architecture.

Keywords: Compute Continuum · Edge · Cloud · Federated Learning · Self-Adaptive IoT applications · Coordination model

1 Introduction

The unstoppable proliferation of sensing device technologies, and the growing demand for data-intensive applications in the edge and cloud, are driving the

© IFIP International Federation for Information Processing 2023
Published by Springer Nature Switzerland AG 2023
G. A. Papadopoulos et al. (Eds.): ESOCC 2023, LNCS 14183, pp. 219–230, 2023.
https://doi.org/10.1007/978-3-031-46235-1_14

next generation of computing systems architectures. In these architectures, "Services" that were initially deployed on the Cloud will migrate to the edge. The resulting paradigm involves combining IoT, edge and cloud resources in one computing system, to form a Compute Continuum (CC).

We define here CC as a current trend of developing, deploying, and running highly distributed, Machine Learning (ML) based self-adaptive, computing intense and data-sensitive IoT applications on a set of IT resources ranging from high density compute and storage to very lightweight embedded computers running on batteries or solar power.

To deploy such ML-based applications, there is a growing shift from a centralised IoT-Cloud architecture to a hierarchical IoT-Edge-Cloud architecture where the learning algorithms are executed in the cloud while the inference models (generated by the learning algorithms) are executed on the edge. Several research projects and industrial products are addressing hierarchical IoT-edge-cloud solutions where IoT sensors (*resp.* edge devices) are controlled and managed by the edge devices (*resp.* the cloud). In this context, the intelligence deployed on the edge devices is improved by the cloud, as detailed in Sect. 2. Nevertheless, the IoT-Edge-Cloud architecture cannot cope with decentralised applications where the learning cannot be centralised in the cloud. In fact, in many cases, the learning needs to be collaborative among edges. To the best of our knowledge, there is no tool that fulfils the two following characteristics:

- ability to provide end-to-end transaction resiliency of applications broken down in a set of micro-services deployed on IoT sensors, edge devices, Cloud and HPC infrastructures.
- ability to secure and timely handle the increasing and latency flow (east-west or peer-to-peer) of sensitive data and applications.

This paper proposes and compares two CC architectures, a centralised and a decentralised one. In the remainder of this article, we will refer to Edge-to-Edge (E2E), for the decentralised architecture; and Edge-To-Cloud (E2C) for the centralised solution.

The rest of the paper is structured as follows: Sect. 2 presents the state-of-the-art related to the hierarchical IoT-Edge-Cloud solutions (E2C) and Federated Learning (FL). Section 3 describes a decentralised FL-based CC framework where the edge devices collaborate in a peer-to-peer fashion to improve and adapt their intelligence (E2E). Section 4 deals with a self-adaptive smart grid energy application, currently being developed as part of two European projects SWARM [1] and LASAGNE [2]. Section 5 presents a simulation of the deployment costs of the smart grid energy application on four CC environments. Since the architecture of these four environments is E2C, we adjusted their economic model to suit the E2E architecture of the smart grid energy application. Finally, Sect. 6 concludes the paper.

2 Related Works

This section describes the state of the art related to the E2C solutions and the FL techniques, in particular decentralised FL.

2.1 E2C and Industrial Solutions

Generally speaking, a self-adaptive ML based application deployed on an E2C solution is composed of a set of cloud modules (such as database, learning algorithms, etc.) and edge modules supporting ML Models (MLMs) and optimised for a limited resource edge device. As detailed in Fig. 1 of our previous work [3], the scenario is the following: An artificial intelligence-based (AI) inference module is deployed on this edge device, which is responsible for making predictions on the input data. The AI inference module is endowed with a ML model (MLM). This MLM is built and trained in the Cloud.

The system enters a feedback loop enabling continuous intelligence adaptation. The edge device autonomously processes IoT sensors' data. Two cases may occur: the prediction is satisfying or not satisfying. The related sensing input which is failing inference is uploaded to the Cloud as "low-performance" data. This bad data is again labelled and fed for ML training to the AI learning module: a new MLM is generated which is then redeployed to the edge device.

Several research projects and industrial products are addressing CC needs as defined in this paper. AWS Amazon and Microsoft Azure offer proprietary solutions: GreenGrass [4] and IoT Edge Azure [5]. Google proposes a solution based on a dedicated hardware edge device [6]. Open-source solutions are also provided by Balena [7], SixSq [8] and EdgeXfoundry [9]. Research projects such as ACES [10] and ICOS [11] are proposing alternatives to build operating systems applied to CC.

2.2 Federated Learning vs Decentralised Federated Learning

In 2016, Google first proposed FL [12]. It introduces a novel approach where MLMs are trained collectively by multiple clients. These clients collaborate without sharing their individual training data; instead, they transmit the models learned from their local data to a central node. This stands for **centralised FL**, also simply called **FL**, where all machines send their data to a central server for model execution. FL comes in various types, depending on whether the model weights are combined at the central server or on individual edge devices. In the usual approach [13], each node gets the model weights from the main server. It works on the model, sends the changes back to the server, which then handles combining the updates from all nodes.

An alternative approach, called **decentralised FL** [14], also called **gossip learning** [15] operates in a fully decentralised manner. In this method, the local node itself handles both the aggregation and communication tasks. This strategy reduces the exchange of information among nodes and ensures that confidential local data remains secure from other nodes. During inter-node communication phase, each node exclusively shares the calculated weights of its learning model.

3   Towards a Decentralised Federated Learning Based Compute Continuum-Oriented Architecture

The research work presented in this paper focuses on the implementation of the E2C and E2E approaches in a CC framework. The first approach, as discussed in Sect. 2, is E2C setup, where data from edge devices is processed and analysed at both the edge and cloud levels.

This section describes the architecture and implementation of the second approach, an E2E architecture that leverages decentralised FL and a coordination platform. Here, decentralised learning takes place across the edge devices without any central entity. The coordination platform plays a crucial role in selecting the "peers" among neighbouring devices, supporting gossip learning, and providing a full CC-oriented architecture.

3.1   E2E Architecture - Decentralised Federated Learning

Our main contribution is a decentralised E2E architecture based on a FL algorithm and a coordination platform as depicted in Fig. 1. This approach fosters collaboration among edge devices, leveraging the power of FL. In this decentralised learning paradigm, edge devices work collectively to train models while preserving data privacy and minimising the need for data transmission to a central server. Figure 1 shows a network of edge devices where each edge device (or group of edge devices) trains its own MLM using only its local data while sharing model weights with its neighbours. The decentralised FL allows each edge device to leverage its local data to train a personalised model. In this setup, the edge devices share model weights with their neighbouring devices, facilitating collaborative learning and knowledge exchange. An underlying coordination platform provides communication, sharing and aggregation of data and learning models among the various edge devices. The coordination platform provides a collective adaptive approach to decentralised FL, as it naturally supports gossip learning, through a flexible choice of the data aggregation operator, and the spreading option (to which neighbouring edge devices and to which hopping distance). Section 3.2 discusses the strengths and weaknesses of the E2C and E2E approaches.

3.2   Limitations and Advantages

We examine the limitations and advantages between the centralised learning approach implemented via E2C architecture and the decentralised FL approach implemented through E2E architecture (Fig. 1). Table 1 summarizes the key differences between the two approaches, based on the following criteria:

- Privacy: E2C raises privacy concerns as data is transferred and processed in a centralised data center, while E2E prioritises privacy by performing local training at the edge devices, ensuring data remains on the devices without being shared with a central entity.

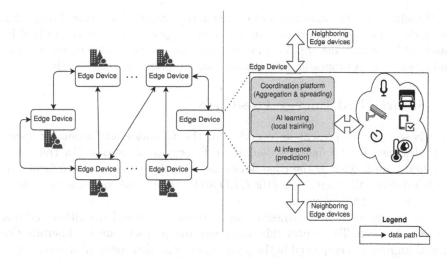

Fig. 1. Decentralised FL-based approach: edge collaborative intelligence

- Latency: E2E enables local training at the edge devices, eliminating the need for data transfer to a central server, resulting in efficient network usage.
- Scalability: E2E approach supports large-scale training as it can be distributed across multiple edge devices via FL.
- Genericity: This criterion relates to the model's ability to perform well on new edge devices. In FL, where training occurs locally, new edge devices joining the network may lack direct access to the latest version of the model. As a result, E2E approach doesn't provide inference models for these new devices, impacting their initial performance. Thus, a new edge device should anticipate bad performance while it gathers the data needed to build its model. In contrast, E2C models leverage the cloud's resources, allowing new edge devices to immediately access the latest model version.
- Hardware (HW) constraints: E2C reduces dependency on resource-constrained edge devices by offloading heavy computational tasks to the cloud, while E2E performs local training at the edge devices themselves, necessitating a certain level of performance from the edge device.

Table 1. E2C vs. E2E

Learning/Architecture	Aspects				
	Privacy	Latency	Scalability	Genericity	HW constraints
Centralised learning/E2C	×	×	×	✓	✓
Decentralised FL/E2E	✓	✓	✓	~	×

By addressing the limitations of traditional centralised learning through E2C methods and respecting privacy concerns, we propose a novel decentralised FL-based E2E setup. This approach involves communication between edge devices and emerges as a promising solution for handling sensitive data at the edge.

4   Smart Grid Energy Use-Case

In this section, we present an overview of the CC-oriented framework specifically designed for ML-based self-adaptive Energy applications. For the sake of simplicity, we'll refer to the edge device used in this context as the Grid Edge Device (GED). We then discuss the GED architecture and components, followed by our real-world deployment.

The energy market is witnessing an increasingly digital transition and market liberalisation. To support this transition and promote market liberalisation, digital frameworks employed in the power energy market must incorporate smart services and enable seamless deployment of ML-based self-adaptive energy applications. These applications operate on both the GED and the cloud. Some tasks play out on GEDs, while, other tasks take place in the cloud.

Energy applications cover here peak shaving services, aggregation of resources, negotiating energy transactions and/or flexibility between consumers and producers, etc. These applications mainly rely on a forecasting service provided by a dedicated digital platform, managed and operated by a CC middleware.

4.1   Grid Edge Device (GED) Architecture and Components

This section details the edge components of the smart grid energy application. Figure 2 zooms in on each GED, illustrating the edge components of the application. The GEDs are connected with Cloud via North/South (N/S) links. The Edge coordination protocol can operate in either a peer-to-peer (P2P) or a centralised fashion: in the former case, GEDs talk to each other via East/West (E/W) links (dashed double arrow) through the coordination platform, in the latter case, GEDs upload edge application data to the Cloud via extra N/S link (dashed upward arrow). Essentially, each GED is composed of various functional components that collectively enable diverse functionalities, enhancing system flexibility. These services are the essential building blocks of the intelligent framework:

- SmartGrid-Ready interface library: This service enables seamless communication, energy/load management, and appliance control within the GED. For instance, it supports dynamic charging management to reduce electricity peaks during electric car charging, aligning with the grid via the SmartGrid-Ready interface.
- Database (DB): The DB service employs SQLite as the current storage solution for the GED. It serves as a repository for device-related data, allowing efficient and reliable storage of critical information.

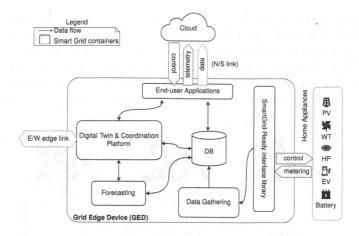

Fig. 2. GED - architecture and components

- Data Gathering, each GED collects consumption and production data from appliances and writes it into the local database. Data are collected at frequent intervals and can goes up to one measurement each 10 s.
- Forecasting service, which generates accurate load prediction for effective energy management in smart grids, currently exists only as a proof-of-concept. However, it is planned to be further implemented for our real-field deployment. This service is crucial as it significantly influences the reliability of power systems and their economic aspects. It involves the prediction of both consumption and production for improved energy management.
- Digital Twin and Coordination Platform, this service is able to use the actual data gathered from our living lab, and support contracts for energy exchange, peak shaving and decentralised FL.

These services form the core of the GED's Service-Oriented Architecture (SOA), enabling efficient and effective energy management within the intelligent framework. Collectively, these services within the GED's SOA form a robust and adaptable framework for intelligent and sustainable energy management. By providing the necessary infrastructure and services, the SOA empowers the GED to operate intelligently. Our CC framework relies on the NuvlaEdge [16].

The white blocks, as illustrated in Fig. 2, correspond to the basic services that form the foundation of our framework. Indeed, this deployment demonstrates our commitment to the CC approach. By aligning with this paradigm and leveraging the combined strengths of the GED-based E2C infrastructure and NuvlaEdge, we fully use the capabilities of the system.

4.2 Meyrin Deployment

We conducted a field study in "Meyrin", a municipality in the canton of Geneva (Switzerland), deploying GEDs in operational microgrid infrastructures, specifically at a school. We selected the CLEMAP device [17] as GED; and NuvlaEdge

[8] a cutting-edge edge computing software solution provided by SixSq, to configure the GED. The CLEMAP GED device, is a Raspberry Pi 3 Model with 1GB of RAM, that runs on a 32-bit ARMv7l architecture. This integration of GEDs and NuvlaEdge software establishes a resilient CC infrastructure, where GEDs collect and transmit data while NuvlaEdge orchestrates the necessary computing power and intelligent analytics for data processing and analysis at the edge.

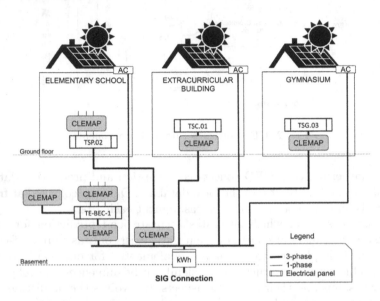

Fig. 3. Electrical diagram of the CLEMAP devices (GEDs) deployment

The Living Lab of "Les Vergers" [18] in Meyrin consists of three school buildings as illustrated in Fig. 3: Gymnastic room, After-school building, Primary school and an Underground space. The current deployment relies on an E2C infrastructure, but we are pursuing the development of an E2E alternative. The current installation is composed of seven CLEMAP (GEDs) across the three different buildings. These GEDs measure the power flows of various electrical appliances. Starting from May 2022, we have been collecting measurement data. Each GED collects power, voltage, and amperage measurements every 10 s. These measurements are regularly sent to a cloud server provided by Exoscale [19]. In addition to the GED data, the local utility provider, "Services Industriels de Genève (SIG)", contributes power measurements from its own supply and solar panels.

5   Experimental Work and Cost Comparison

The goal of this section is to evaluate the cost of deploying ML-based self-adaptive IoT application on E2C and E2E CC platforms. Currently, communications among edge devices are not supported by the CC platforms. They can, however, be programmed at the application level. Therefore, our approach will be to:

1. adapt the economic/business models of the E2C solutions to meet E2E architecture's requirements. For instance, consider adjusting pricing structures to accommodate the different resource usage patterns of E2E deployments.
2. simulate the execution of a given ML-based self-adaptive IoT application on a set of E2C platforms for a given number of edge devices over a given period of time.
3. use the same application to simulate its execution on the "E2E" versions of the selected E2C platforms by using the adapted economic/business models.

As discussed in our previous study [3], the E2C approach introduces costs associated with infrastructure provisioning, data storage, and computational resources, depending on the scale of the deployment, data volume, and retraining frequency. Retraining, driven by unsatisfactory predictions, can lead to increased cloud resource utilisation and subsequently higher expenses. In the case of E2E, this cost is reduced to zero because the learning takes place on the edge devices. Additionally, as detailed in [20], the proposed decentralised FL-based approach provides privacy-preserving benefits in comparison to non-private centralised models, albeit with a minor compromise in prediction accuracy.

Moreover, our comparative study of the deployment cost of self-adaptive applications assumes that CC solution providers will not be charging for exchanges between edge devices nor for running edge applications. The cost breakdown is structured into the following six services:

- **Edge management**, it refers to the expenses associated with managing and maintaining the edge computing infrastructure within an IoT system. The main cost includes:
  - Registration: registering an edge device within the management system, which may involve fixed costs such as specific telemetry metrics or licensing fees.
  - Yearly Subscription: the cost associated with an annual subscription
  - Connectivity: the cost per minute of connectivity, assuming that the edge device remains connected 24/7.
- **Messaging**. We take into account the costs related to communication between the edge and the cloud, which involve telemetry and application messages. Telemetry messages provide real-time data for analysis and monitoring, while application messages trigger cloud operations such as device status updates, statistic aggregation, and dashboard visualisation. We ensure accurate pricing calculations by converting message volume-based pricing if necessary. We consider that E2E communication are free of charge.
- **Data transfer**. Transferring data between the edge and the cloud, as well as between different cloud services, may have associated costs. We categorise these transfers into three types: Cloud-to-Edge, Edge-to-Cloud, and Intra-Cloud. Regarding Intra-Cloud transfers, we assume they occur within the same data center or closely connected centers.

- **Storage**. Storing each unit of space carries a cost, and performing read and write operations may also result in associated expenses.
- **Computing**. Using any application's cloud component for each hour will result in costs. Additionally, there are extra charges for a minimum amount of attached storage.
- **Helpdesk**. Technical support.

In order to conduct a comparative cost analysis between the E2C and E2E approaches, we have used the cost estimation model developed in [3] The cost estimation was performed using the application described in Sect. 4. In this simulation, we used four CC environments: Amazon AWS, Microsoft Azure, NuvlaEdge + Exoscale and Balena + Exoscale. Table 2 shows the parameters used for the analysis. The cost evaluations are based on the premise that each "solution" addresses all the messaging, data transfer, storage, and computation needs of the edge application. Among the four CC environments used in the experiment, AWS and Azure are the only ones offering fully-integrated solutions, while the remaining technology providers such as Balena and Nuvla require partnerships with other service provider. As aforementioned, we used NuvlaEdge and Exoscale for our E2C deployment; and our current E2E deployment exclusively relies on NuvlaEdge for edge management. Figure 4 provides a cost breakdown comparison between E2E and E2C for a deployment comprising $1K$ GEDs over a one-year period, considering various solution providers. In our deployment, messaging and edge management are the primary cost factors. The E2C approach for edge applications incorporates separate communication channels for application messages and infrastructure control messages. We categorize messages into two classes: application and telemetry, which includes monitoring and logging functionalities. These messages are efficiently handled by distinct services within the system. Application messages flow through the Communication Hub component, while telemetry messages are processed by a dedicated sub-component of the IoT Infrastructure Management, or alternatively, by the Communication Hub if the dedicated service is unavailable. With the E2E approach, messaging costs are significantly reduced, and in all cases, nearly eliminated altogether. Unlike the traditional cloud-based approach, where messaging infrastructure is necessary for application and telemetry messages, the E2E approach operates independently from the cloud. As a result, the E2E approach substantially reduces costs

Table 2. Cost model's parameters

Parameter	Description	Value
Event rate	MLM Trigger Rate	60
Raw data footprint	MLM Input Size	$\sim$0.1 MiB/sample
ML error rate	MLM Prediction Error	9%
ML training time	MLM Training Time (1 vCPU)	$\sim$4 h @ $1vCPU$
ML training rate	MLM Training Rate (Cloud)	$\sim$8 round/month

related to messaging, computing, storage, and data transfer. However, it's crucial to consider the limited resources of edge devices when implementing the E2E approach. This consideration becomes paramount as E2E involves local training and collaboration between edge devices, without relying on centralised cloud resources.

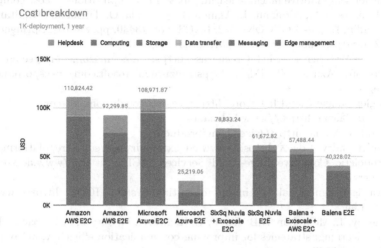

Fig. 4. Cost breakdown for 1K-deployment over 1 year: E2C vs E2E

6 Conclusion

This paper presents two CC-oriented architectures used to deploy ML based self-adaptive IoT applications: Edge-to-Cloud (E2C) and Edge-to-Edge (E2E) architecture. In the E2C architecture, the edge intelligence is controlled by the cloud, while in the E2E architecture, the intelligence is the result of a peer-to-peer decentralised collaborative/FL among the edge devices. The E2E approach is well suited to IoT applications where the learning cannot be done centrally and/or where data privacy is a major issue. We have experimented the two models in the concrete case of a smart grid energy application. We also simulated the deployment cost of the same application, using the two models, on four different CC environments. In the four cases, the deployment cost of the E2E architecture is much lower than that of the E2C architecture.

It's worth reminding here that the current available CC platforms do not support direct exchanges among edge devices (E2E architecture). These communications must be handled by the developer at the level of the IoT application. The framework presented in Sect. 4 aims to support this type of communication through the coordination platform. Finally, future work involves exploiting further the coordination platform for providing decentralised and gossip-based learning with higher accuracy results.

Acknowledgment. This paper is supported by the LASAGNE project funded by ERA-NET 108767, and the SWARM project funded by Eurostars E!115513.

References

1. SWARM project. https://lsds.hesge.ch/smart-and-widely
2. LASAGNE project. https://lsds.hesge.ch/digital-framework-for-smart-grid/
3. Poleggi, M.E., Abdennadher, N., Dupuis, R., Mendonça, F.: Edge-to-cloud solutions for self-adaptive machine learning-based IoT applications: a cost comparison. In: Bañares, J.Á., Altmann, J., Agmon Ben-Yehuda, O., Djemame, K., Stankovski, V., Tuffin, B. (eds.) GECON 2022. LNCS, vol. 13430, pp. 89–102. Springer, Cham (2022). https://doi.org/10.1007/978-3-031-29315-3_8
4. Amazon Web Services: IoT Greengrass. https://aws.amazon.com/greengrass/
5. Microsoft: Azure IoT Edge. https://azure.microsoft.com/en-us/products/iot-edge/
6. Google: Google Cloud IoT Core. https://cloud.google.com/iot-core
7. Balena: Balena. https://www.balena.io/
8. SiqSq SA: Nuvla. https://sixsq.com/products
9. EdgeXfoundry: EdgeX. https://www.edgexfoundry.org/software/platform/
10. Autopoietic Cognitive Edge-cloud Services, ACES. https://www.aces-edge.eu/partners/
11. Towards a functional continuum operating system, ICOS. https://www.icos-project.eu
12. Konečný, J., McMahan, H.B., Yu, F.X., Richtárik, P., Suresh, A.T., Bacon, D.: Federated learning: strategies for improving communication efficiency, arXiv preprint arXiv:1610.05492 (2016)
13. Savi, M., Olivadese, F.: Short-term energy consumption forecasting at the edge: a federated learning approach. IEEE Access **9**, 95949–95969 (2021)
14. Liu, W., Chen, L., Zhang, W.: Decentralized federated learning: balancing communication and computing costs. IEEE Trans. Signal Inf. Process. Netw. **8**, 131–143 (2022)
15. Hegedűs, I., Danner, G., Jelasity, M.: Gossip learning as a decentralized alternative to federated learning. In: Pereira, J., Ricci, L. (eds.) DAIS 2019. LNCS, vol. 11534, pp. 74–90. Springer, Cham (2019). https://doi.org/10.1007/978-3-030-22496-7_5
16. NuvlaEdge. https://sixsq.com/nuvlaedge
17. With CLEMAP into the energy future. https://en.clemap.ch
18. Les Vergers | Ecoquartier Meyrin Les Vergers. https://www.lesvergers-meyrin.ch/ecoquartier/les-vergers
19. A solid European cloud hosting alternative. https://www.exoscale.com/
20. Moussa, M., Abdennahder, N., Couturier, R., Di Marzo Serugendo, G.: Towards a scalable compute continuum platform applied to electrical energy forecasting (2023)

Detecting Model Changes in Organisational Processes: A Cloud-Based Approach

J. Fabra[1](✉), V. Gallego-Fontenla[2], J. C. Vidal[2], J. García de Quirós[1],
P. Álvarez[1], M. Lama[2], A. Bugarín[2], and A. Ramos-Soto[3]

[1] Computer Science and Systems Engineering Department,
Engineering Research Institute of Aragon (I3A), University of Zaragoza,
Zaragoza, Spain
{jfabra,jgarciaqg,alvaper}@unizar.es
[2] Research Center in Intelligent Technologies, University of Santiago de Compostela,
A Coruña, Spain
{victorjose.gallego,juan.vidal,manuel.lama,alberto.bugarin.diz}@usc.es
[3] Inverbis Analytics, Lugo, Spain
alejandro.ramos@inverbisanalytics.com

Abstract. Process mining techniques extract knowledge from event logs within organizations to understand and improve the behavior of their business processes. These techniques utilize a wide range of methods to automatically generate process models from event log data, simplify these models, calculate various indicators to optimize performance, and visualize and explain model behavior. However, these techniques often treat process models as static entities, despite the inherent dynamic nature of processes. Commercial platforms frequently lack the ability to detect and describe changes (also known as *concept drift*) in the models, which can impact the conclusions and results derived from process mining. This paper presents the INSIDE-TUTTO project, which has developed a concept drift detection algorithm for application in business organizations and transition to the commercial market through *Inverbis Analytics*. The original algorithm was not designed to operate in real-world scenarios with large volumes of data. By combining distributed architectures and the cloud computing paradigm, the algorithm was evolved into a commercial version deployed within Inverbis Analytics' *Azure*-based technological infrastructure.

Keywords: Process models · Concept drift · Cloud computing · Research results transfer · Microsoft Azure

1 Introduction

Process mining techniques have emerged as a powerful tool for understanding organizational behavior through knowledge extraction from information systems' event logs. These techniques aim to discover, monitor, and enhance real processes [3].

© IFIP International Federation for Information Processing 2023
Published by Springer Nature Switzerland AG 2023
G. A. Papadopoulos et al. (Eds.): ESOCC 2023, LNCS 14183, pp. 231–236, 2023.
https://doi.org/10.1007/978-3-031-46235-1_15

Several process mining techniques have been widely adopted in commercial platforms, including: (i) Process discovery, which seeks to automatically generate a process model capable of reproducing event log traces while accurately and concisely representing activity relationships. All commercial platforms utilize process discovery algorithms [8] because the analytics derived from these models form the foundation of process mining; (ii) Process model simplification, which modifies process models for improved comprehension, especially for unstructured processes that require high-completeness models. Although recent proposals integrate infrequent behavior into abstract activities [5], most platforms employ an incremental visualization strategy, adding observed behavior to the model based on its frequency; (iii) Process conformance checking, which describes and quantifies differences between the process model and the event log's observed behavior [4]. Commercial platforms use suboptimal strategies to align traces with the process model, which are sufficient to identify deviating trace types and the extent of the deviation; (iv) Visualization and description of process/model analytics (enrichment) offer textual descriptions that complement model visualization utilities and process analytics, aiding user navigation and focusing attention on process-relevant aspects [6]. Currently, no commercial platform incorporates components for generating textual descriptions.

These techniques often consider the process model as static, assuming a single model encapsulates all event log behavior. However, processes are inherently dynamic, especially unstructured ones where the model is a temporal combination of multiple process models. Identifying and describing when a process model no longer represents the observed behavior due to abrupt or gradual changes [7] is a crucial aspect of process analysis. Yet, no commercial platform includes techniques for detecting and describing changes (concept drift) in the models, limiting the conclusions and results obtained from other process mining techniques. Moreover, change detection algorithms are resource-intensive, relying on model extraction as new process executions (or traces) are generated. Therefore, adapting and deploying such algorithms in the cloud is a prerequisite for developing a commercial solution for detecting process model changes.

In this context, the INSIDE-TUTTO project is funded through the I+D+i-Proof of Concept call by the Ministry of Science and Innovation of the Government of Spain. It is also partially financed by the European Union within the NextGenerationEU program. The project is coordinated by the University of Santiago de Compostela and the University of Zaragoza and has a duration of 24 months. The primary objective of the project is to design a flexible and adaptive service infrastructure capable of detecting and describing changes in process models. This system will: (1) operate across multiple cloud providers, optimizing for performance and cost intelligently, and (2) integrate seamlessly into individual company technological frameworks, particularly concerning data repositories. Moreover, a service-oriented application will be developed to assist business analysts in understanding their processes.

A key aspect of the project is adapting an algorithm for the abrupt detection of changes in process models and deploying it in the cloud for operation in big data environments. This algorithm, as cited in [7], monitors process compliance metrics (namely fitness and accuracy) over time, enabling the detection of most changes without significantly increasing computation time. Thus, the algorithm's adaptation and deployment in the cloud, leveraging flexible resource allocation based on log size, are critical. This paper introduces the developed solution and its integration with InVerbis Analytics [1], a cloud-based process mining platform. This platform facilitates big data environment process analytics extraction, encompassing variant analysis, model discovery, pattern extraction, and conformance analysis. The integration of the change detection algorithm represents a strategic milestone for InVerbis Analytics, given that these analytics hinge on the process model.

The paper is structured as follows: Sect. 2 presents the cloud-based architecture supporting the concept drift algorithm's execution; Sect. 3 describes the architecture's deployment on Microsoft Azure; and Sect. 4 summarizes the paper's main achievements and discusses future work.

2 Distributed Architecture of the Algorithm

The concept drift algorithm presented in [7] was designed for sequential execution. Processing medium-sized logs to detect changes in corresponding models proved time-consuming. Experimental analysis concluded that while the algorithm effectively addressed the detection problem, it was not readily applicable to real production environments where logs are complex and voluminous. As such, the architecture of the original algorithm required redesign, integrating existing techniques, but leveraging parallel and cloud computing solutions.

An architecture, based on the *Master-Worker* pattern, has been designed to support the parallelization of the new drift detection algorithm version. Figure 1 depicts the primary components of this architecture. In this design, the log of execution traces for analysis is stored in a centralized database. The parallel processing of these traces is performed by a *master* and a set of *workers*. The master divides and distributes the workload among the workers, retrieves results, and manages drift detection. This requires the master to maintain a record of pending traces for analysis and the state of workers involved in distributed processing. The workers operate in a request-response manner: upon receiving a new request, they execute the drift detection algorithm for the specified set of traces and return the corresponding result (whether a change was detected or not) to the master.

The architecture accommodates the integration of two pools of workers. One is static, with a predetermined number of workers, configured prior to system execution (at the bottom of Fig. 1). The other is dynamic, adjusting the number of workers according to performance and system processing workload (left side of the figure). Additional workers can be deployed on-demand (or halted when not needed) to respond to unexpected situations, such as unwarranted failures and communication delays. This adaptability gives the architecture a dynamic nature, manageable at runtime by either the master or the system administrator.

Finally, several components are responsible for supporting the operation of the distributed pattern. The *Resource Registry* contains information about the location, configuration, and access credentials of the database and the workers. This information is dynamically utilized by the master to set up and start the execution of the processing infrastructure. The *Monitoring Service* records various metrics regarding workers' performance. The *Decision Advisor* continuously analyzes these metrics, providing recommendations for configuring on-demand workers.

3   Deployment and Delivery of the Distributed Algorithm

The architecture depicted in Fig. 1 has been deployed using Microsoft Azure [2], as illustrated in Fig. 2. Azure is Microsoft's suite of cloud computing services, providing a diverse range of solutions for businesses. This includes infrastructure as a service (IaaS), platform as a service (PaaS), and software as a service (SaaS), along with an extensive array of products for networking, storage, mobile, web applications, machine learning, AI, IoT, security, and more. Users can build, deploy, and manage applications across Microsoft's global data centers.

We have optimized the deployment processes, utilizing both Azure Virtual Private Cloud and Azure Compute services. These services facilitate easy scaling of resources based on problem requirements. This is particularly valuable in our

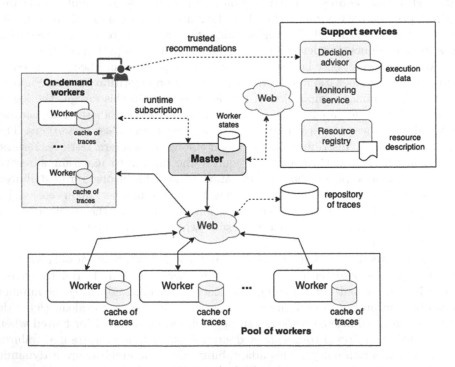

Fig. 1. Architecture

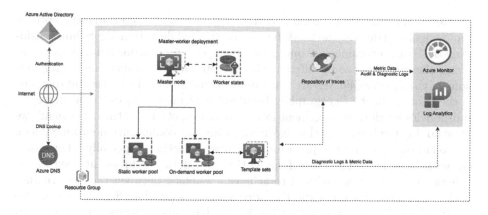

Fig. 2. Deployment of our approach on Azure

architecture where we might need to add more worker nodes to distribute the load. Moreover, Azure assures high availability, offering a robust infrastructure less prone to downtime.

Notably, the static and on-demand worker pools are separate resource groups, with the on-demand pool linked to a set of virtual image template services. The entire resource set is connected to Azure Monitor and Log Analytics services to collect and display diagnostic logs and metrics.

For the trace repository, we chose Azure Cosmos DB, a globally distributed, multi-model database service for managing data at scale. This decision was influenced by the fact that the data models of InVerbis Analytics are deployed on this data service, thus simplifying the integration of the distributed algorithm with the InVerbis technological infrastructure.

The entire deployment was conducted using basic services common to other cloud providers. Virtual machines encapsulate all the business logic through scripting and compiled code, which means this deployment could be easily replicated with other providers such as Amazon Web Services (AWS) or Google Cloud.

4   Preliminary Conclusions and Future Work

This paper presents the adaptation of a process model change detection algorithm (concept drift) to operate in big data environments. Specifically, it delineates the necessary adjustments made for its deployment on the Microsoft Azure platform using the same data model as InVerbis Analytics, a commercial process mining platform that integrates discovery, conformance, simplification, and process description algorithms. It is noteworthy that the change detection algorithm has been successfully tested on process logs in logistics, telecommunications, and industry, detecting changes in the model that have helped to understand and improve process behavior, as it facilitates model visualization.

Large-scale experimentation is currently underway to determine the optimal deployment and delivery methods for the distributed detection algorithm, considering business, economic, and operational perspectives. On one hand, we are analyzing the performance of different virtual computing instances and configurations of the *Master-Worker* architecture (optimal size of the static and dynamic worker pools, effect of geographic distribution of instances, different strategies and policies for data management in worker nodes, etc.). On the other hand, we are studying the impact of the algorithm's different configuration parameters on its execution time and the precision of change detection, especially when working with large logs. The cost of computing and data resources involved in the different executions is analyzed to achieve a balance between the performance of the contracted resources and the price customers pay for effective and precise results. The ultimate goal is that the knowledge gained during this experimentation allows InVerbis Analytics to configure a customized deployment for each particular customer.

As for future work, we propose to validate the change detection algorithm, and specifically, the cloud architecture, in environments with noise (unstructured processes), where there is a greater number of false positives (new traces that are not actual changes). We will also carry out tests in real big data environments to contrast the preliminary performance/cost results with those obtained from actual executions.

References

1. Inverbis Analytics. https://processmining.inverbisanalytics.com/
2. Microsoft Azure. https://azure.microsoft.com/
3. van der Aalst, W.M.P.: Process Mining - Data Science in Action. Springer, Berlin, Heidelberg (2016). https://doi.org/10.1007/978-3-662-49851-4
4. Carmona, J., van Dongen, B.F., Solti, A., Weidlich, M.: Conformance Checking - Relating Processes and Models. Springer, Berlin, Heidelberg (2018). https://doi.org/10.1007/978-3-319-99414-7
5. Chapela-Campa, D., Mucientes, M., Lama, M.: Understanding complex process models by abstracting infrequent behavior. Futur. Gener. Comput. Syst. **113**, 428–440 (2020). https://doi.org/10.1016/j.future.2020.07.030
6. Fontenla-Seco, Y., Lama, M., González-Salvado, V., Peña-Gil, C., Bugarín, A.J.: A framework for the automatic description of healthcare processes in natural language: application in an aortic stenosis integrated care process. J. Biomed. Inform. **128**, 104033 (2022). https://doi.org/10.1016/j.jbi.2022.104033
7. Gallego-Fontenla, V., Vidal, J.C., Lama, M.: A conformance checking-based approach for sudden drift detection in business processes. IEEE Trans. Serv. Comput. **16**(1), 13–26 (2023). https://doi.org/10.1109/TSC.2021.3120031
8. Kerremans, M., Iijima, K., Sachelarescu, A.R., Duffy, N., Sugden, D.: Magic quadrant for process mining tools

Short Papers

Short Papers

A Taxonomy for Workload Deployment Orchestration in the Edge-Cloud Continuum

Toon Albers[1]([✉])(ID), Mattia Fogli[2](ID), Edwin Harmsma[1], Elena Lazovik[1](ID), and Harrie Bastiaansen[1]

[1] TNO, Groningen, The Netherlands
{toon.albers,edwin.harmsma,elena.lazovik,harrie.bastiaansen}@tno.nl
[2] University of Ferrara, Ferrara, Italy
mattia.fogli@unife.it

Abstract. As compute resources continue to proliferate from static large-scale enterprise-grade cloud environments to various types of more dynamic and resource-constrained edge environments, the need increases to orchestrate the deployment of workloads of data and processing applications across the emerging edge-cloud continuum. For many use cases in various application domains and contexts, similar workload deployment orchestration challenges arise. We present a taxonomy for workload deployment orchestration in the edge-cloud continuum that captures the various views and perspectives on workload deployment orchestration. We evaluate and valorise the proposed taxonomy by means of three illustrative and representative types of use cases from different domains and present opportunities for future research.

Keywords: Cloud Orchestration · Deployment Orchestration · Edge Computing · Edge-Cloud Continuum · Federated Cloud · Taxonomy

1 Introduction

Current digitisation of societal sectors and infrastructures can be characterised by: (1) ubiquitous sensing, processing, storage, and communication capabilities and (2) the emergence of (distributed and federated) edge-cloud data storage and processing infrastructures. As such, orchestration of data sharing and processing workloads over dynamic federated cloud-edge infrastructures poses a recurring challenge in different operational contexts. Workload deployment orchestration (also referred to as 'App Deployment Orchestration') is the process that enables cloud and application providers to define how to select, deploy, monitor and configure (multi-container) packaged applications in the cloud at run-time. It encompasses the deployment, execution and maintenance phases [4,7]. A workload deployment orchestrator is responsible for resource limit control, scheduling, load balancing, health checking, fault tolerance management and autoscaling.

© IFIP International Federation for Information Processing 2023
Published by Springer Nature Switzerland AG 2023
G. A. Papadopoulos et al. (Eds.): ESOCC 2023, LNCS 14183, pp. 239–250, 2023.
https://doi.org/10.1007/978-3-031-46235-1_16

Exemplary for a broader context in which the importance of cloud technology and workload deployment orchestration are currently gaining major interest are the developments around the European Data and Cloud strategy [8]. Driven by the importance attributed to the emerging data economy with extra attention to data sovereignty and security, legal [9] and technical frameworks are being created for a converged data and cloud environment. Reference architectures (such as the IDSA[1], Gaia-X[2] and DSBA[3] initiatives) and the DSSC[4] are being developed, coordinated under the umbrella of the EU Directorate-General Connect (DG CONNECT). These initiatives show the importance of the emerging 'converged' data plan and cloud infrastructure.

A large diversity of perspectives and challenges on workload deployment orchestration exists for an edge-cloud continuum. Therefore, a taxonomy describing these perspectives can be of major benefit for (1) efficiency in identifying its challenges and complexities in a specific context and, as such, (2) supporting the effective design and development of a workload deployment orchestrator for that context, or (3) evaluating existing orchestrators for a specific use. In this paper we refer to the edge-cloud continuum, whilst increasingly individual 'devices' are taken into account, giving rise to a 'device-edge-cloud continuum'. Although well-recognised by the authors, within this paper it will be referred to as edge-cloud continuum without impacting the contents of the taxonomy.

This paper addresses the research topic to "*design a taxonomy for workload deployment orchestration in the edge-cloud continuum that describes the broad variety of challenges in emerging and converged data sharing and federated cloud infrastructures, and supports architects in exploring the design complexities and developing solutions for such orchestration*". This topic has been addressed by means of the *Experience Report* methodology [17]. Based on experience in various use cases and projects such as ENERSHARE[5] and ECiDA[6], we established the relevance for an overarching taxonomy describing the various aspects of workload deployment orchestration in different contexts. In combination with an exploration of related work on such a taxonomy, the need for an extended taxonomy applicable to the edge-cloud continuum was identified and elaborated.

This paper has the following structure: Sect. 2 introduces and describes the proposed taxonomy for workload deployment orchestration in the edge-cloud continuum. An overview of related taxonomies is provided in Sect. 3. The proposed taxonomy is evaluated and valorised by means of three representative types of use cases in Sect. 4, after which the future direction and the overarching conclusions are presented in Sect. 5 and Sect. 6, respectively.

---

[1] International Data Spaces Association (IDSA), https://internationaldataspaces.org.

[2] EU Gaia-X Initiative, https://www.gaia-x.eu.

[3] Data Space Business Alliance (DSBA), https://data-spaces-business-alliance.eu.

[4] Data Spaces Support Centre (DSSC), https://dssc.eu.

[5] See enershare.eu.

[6] See commit2data.nl/en/projects/ecida-evolutionary-changes-in-distributed-analysis.

2   Taxonomy

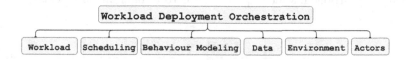

Fig. 1. Main concepts of the taxonomy

We have identified a set of six high-level concepts, shown in Fig. 1, constituting the general problem space of workload deployment orchestration in the edge-cloud continuum: Workload, Scheduling, Behaviour Modeling, Data, Environment and Actors. When further broken down into sub-categories[7], these concepts allow specific problem instances to be identified and characterised.

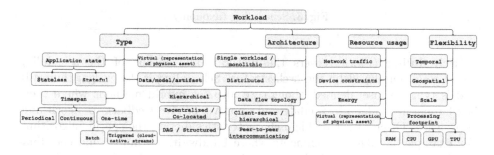

Fig. 2. Workload taxonomy

Workload (Fig. 2) covers the asset that is being orchestrated. These are typically applications, but could also entail data gathering or movement, or virtual representations of physical assets. Specific challenges arise for applications depending on if they are stateful (storing data persistently to operate successfully) or stateless. We can also distinguish jobs in relation with their timespan: those running once until completion, periodic jobs and permanently running jobs require different strategical workload mechanisms to apply. There is also a difference in who triggers the job, and does it handle batch or streaming data. In the latter case, secondary control mechanisms ensure that effects decided by the orchestrator, are subsequently applied to the streams connected to real-world assets. Workload composition, e.g. monolithic versus distributed, also poses distinct challenges. Furthermore, we can identify different topologies in both data-flow and infrastructure, ranging from peer-to-peer data flows between multiple

---

[7] A digital version of this taxonomy can be found at https://github.com/TNO/
deployment-orchestration-taxonomy-supplimentary-materials.

heterogeneous clusters, to hierarchical client-server communication. Workloads from applications often use resources - virtual or physical - and might have inherent characteristics that introduce flexibility in orchestration, for example when they can be postponed, scaled up, or moved to a different data centre.

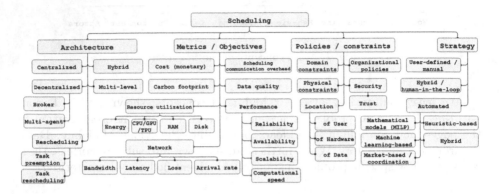

Fig. 3. Scheduling taxonomy

Scheduling (Fig. 3) covers the methods and means of the scheduling paradigm(s) employed by the orchestrator. Scheduling is done algorithmically and is typically user-defined, though we also see hybrid methods where there is a human-in-the-loop to validate and approve, or give feedback to algorithmic approaches. Often, other problem characteristics dictate the specific algorithm. For example, in edge environments where bandwidth is limited and coordination is expensive, a locally deployed machine learning model working on incoming data may be more suitable. The scheduler operates with input metrics that are observed, a set of policies and constraints, and typically optimizes for one or more objectives. Depending on the actor model, as well as environmental constraints, the scheduling solution can be centralised (with a broker or similar middleware between nodes for more control) or decentralised (with nodes as independent actors with their own behaviour).

Behaviour Modeling (Fig. 4) identifies the ways in which modeling approaches are used in deployment orchestration. Modeling can be applied to many types of challenges in deployment orchestration. Typical approaches include workload characterisation—where resource usage of workloads is monitored in order to construct a generalised model—and methods to achieve specific goals on consistency of running computations—for example, to use anomaly detection techniques as a method that aims to identify abnormal data or patterns, typically by comparing against previously established models. There are myriad methods to facilitate modeling, each with their strengths and weaknesses.

Data (Fig. 5) entails the different ways in which data is stored, accessed, used, monitored, and managed throughout deployment orchestration in the edge-cloud continuum. We consider specific challenges in the security domain, for

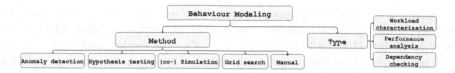

Fig. 4. Behaviour modeling taxonomy

example when managing secrets, when handling privacy-sensitive data, and in facilitating access to restricted data. Additionally, data location can be altered for various purposes, such as for data gravity, caching, migrations or backups.

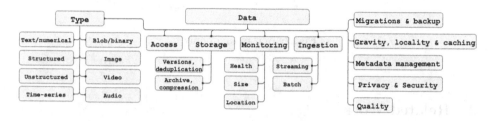

Fig. 5. Data taxonomy

Environment (Fig. 6) characterizes the computational context and topology of the IT infrastructure hosting the workloads. This context can be static and unchanging, or dynamic. In the latter case, orchestration solutions should be aware of this changing environment, incurring additional monitoring overhead. Orchestration solutions might exist in, and manage, virtualised environments, or bare-metal infrastructure. Likewise, the compute and networking resources available to them may vary drastically, and even be unavailable for extended periods of time.

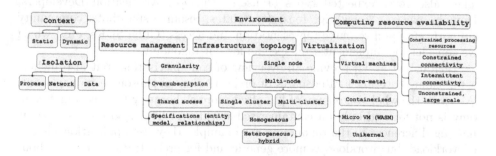

Fig. 6. Environment taxonomy

Actors (Fig. 7) maps the ways in which stakeholders might interact in a given deployment orchestration problem. These actors could be end users, application providers, or even infrastructure providers. The way in which they interact, for example standalone, collaboratively, competitively, or even maliciously towards each other, introduces additional constraints to the deployment orchestration problem, and will be reflected in the scheduling solution's structure. Scheduling is easiest with a single stakeholder, and requires extra organisational and technical interoperability solutions if multiple stakeholders are involved.

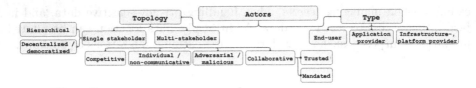

Fig. 7. Actors taxonomy

3   Related Work

Other taxonomies often focus on specific deployment orchestration aspects. We have made a matching between these taxonomies and the taxonomy proposed in this paper to ensure full coverage of their concepts, aside from having added new concepts not present in related work.

Nguyen et al. [15] provide a taxonomy of IoT deployment orchestration, although they focus more on analyzing scientific literature compared to what is out in the field. Their taxonomy also discusses implementation details such as DSL, programming model and inter-workload communication mechanism, which we purposefully avoid.

Weerasiri et al. [18] created a taxonomy for cloud resource orchestration. They briefly cover workload deployment orchestration but do not go into details. They also cover expected types of users (DevOps, Application Developers, Domain experts), knowledge reuse (templates, resource snapshots, community support, etc.) and resource representation and access (CLIs, SDKs, etc.) which we consider too implementation-specific for our taxonomy.

Bentaleb et al. [2] provide an overview of containerisation, but also include a taxonomy covering limited parts of orchestration and resource management. We cover the whole taxonomy of [2], often more elaborately because our taxonomy is not focused only on containerised workloads. This also results in some naming differences in the taxonomy. For example, they use application instead of workload, but workload is more generic and for orchestration we care about specific workloads and not the applications to which they belong. They do not elaborate the scheduling part of their taxonomy, instead delegating this task to tools such as Kubernetes, but for deployment orchestration we consider this an important aspect. Unlike [2], our taxonomy does not explicitly mention lifecycle management as we consider the whole orchestration to be based around it.

Mampage et al. [14] provide a taxonomy focusing on *serverless* workloads. However, many of the aspects of serverless workloads, such as workload management and QoS goals, are also applicable to (containerised) workloads in general. They also include 'billing model' in their taxonomy, which we consider to be part of the cloud provider perspective and therefore do not include.

Rodriguez and Buyya [16] provide an elaborate cluster orchestration taxonomy. Comparing these taxonomies, the workloads are defined in a similar manner but Rodriguez and Buyya expand upon *resource usage* in our taxonomy with *resource requests, limits* and *consumption estimation*. They also expand upon network and performance isolation, but we consider these an implementation detail of the provider platform. The taxonomy presented in this paper more elaborately describes workload type, flexibility and scheduling strategy. The topics of deployment modeling, data and actors are also not covered by them.

Finally Carrión [3] describes a taxonomy specifically catered to the Kubernetes orchestrator, and referencing scientific literature aiming to improve this orchestrator. They separate performance from scheduling and application, however we consider performance metrics to be part of the scheduling process. They also separate infrastructure and cluster, but for us the cluster is part of the environment in which a workload runs. The taxonomy is also limited, for example only few scheduling metrics are mentioned.

None of these taxonomies completely describe all aspects related to orchestration in converged data sharing and federated clouds and edges. The majority concentrate on workload concepts, some of them also elaborate the scheduling more deeply. There is no taxonomy that includes data or (multi) actor aspects, or makes the bridge to the modeling of the application and infrastructure behaviour. As a result, no complete taxonomy exists which covers all relevant aspects of the orchestration, and that is why we propose our taxonomy. Some taxonomies cover the same aspects using different terms, depending on their research question and perspective. The taxonomy presented in this paper is created from the perspective of running in the cloud-edge continuum, therefore it uses terms from that domain. Some aspects of our taxonomy are also elaborated further compared to other taxonomies for the same reason.

4   Use Cases

The applicability of the proposed taxonomy for workload deployment orchestration on federated and adaptive cloud infrastructures is demonstrated and assessed in this chapter by means of three types of use cases. As their scope varies strongly, they are considered to be illustrative and representative for a multitude of additional types of use cases for which the taxonomy can be used.

4.1   Local Access to and Processing of Sensitive Data

AI algorithms must be able to access data sources to be trained or deployed. However, the data cannot always simply be shared with an external organisation that provides the algorithm, e.g. when the amount of data to be transferred is too large or too sensitive to share (due to confidentiality, ethical, privacy or legal reasons). In such cases, the data must remain within the security domain of its provider and only controlled access to the data may be allowed for a (distributed) AI algorithm. This is also referred to as *"data visiting"*. Data visiting can be implemented by means of Privacy Enhancing Technologies (PETs), such as secure Multi-Party Computation (MPC) [6] and Federated Learning (FL) [5]. PETs can be applied to train or deploy algorithms on data that is either horizontally or vertically partitioned. In the former, the same type of data is provided by different organisations. In the latter, different types of data applying to the same "entity" are provided by different organisations.

For training over horizontally partitioned data, the use case of medical data distributed over various hospitals can be used. Data on a particular illness, but applying to different patients, is often spread over many hospitals. The dataset at a particular hospital could be too small to successfully train a model. Federated Learning allows a 'worker' to compute a version of the FL model on local data within the (security) domain of the hospital. Subsequently, the individually trained models are combined to compute an aggregate model. Repeating this process several times, the FL model is trained over the combined local datasets, without raw data having been shared.

For training over vertically partitioned data, we can use the use case of the emerging Smart Energy Systems. Due to an increase in renewable (distributed) energy sources, energy grids increasingly encounter congestion. Insight into the state of the energy grid is needed to improve the planning for congestion and mitigate the effects thereof. Data from diverse devices, owned by households and facilitated by third parties, can be used to get an insight into the state of the low-voltage (LV) grid. However, this is sensitive data as it reveals consumer behaviour patterns. Hence, data visiting could be used for LV grid state estimation. In this case, models should be provided access to local household data. The model weights are aggregated in the semi-global model of the FL framework to calculate the overarching grid state, allowing the physical LV system to be monitored and (re-)configured [5].

The taxonomy as proposed in this paper provides a good basis for identifying and defining the main deployment orchestration aspects for both the horizontally and vertically partitioned data. The usage of the taxonomy helped in this use case to identify the choice on scheduling mechanism, the KPIs for data management and requirements for the computational environment.

4.2   Varying Trust and Security Levels of Clouds

Data sharing and processing collaborations between organisations involving sensitive data require policies and agreements on the actual processing in cloud infrastructures that are owned and operated by external organisations. In this case, deployment of workloads on specific clouds will depend on whether their trust and security offerings comply with constraints as specified by the organisation that deploys the workload, and the applicable legislation.

Hence, the trust and security constraints introduce restrictions on the deployment on cloud and edge environments. Traditionally, legal agreements are made between the deploying organisation and the provider(s) of the cloud services in combination with an auditing approach on conformance with the agreements, rules, norms and standards. However, the more often that data collaboration occurs in which data(sets) are transferred between various cloud service providers, the more complex this (often manual) approach of contracting and auditing becomes. New efforts on automated compliance as for example in Gaia-X aim to solve the labor and overhead involved in this process [10]. Gaia-X introduces the concept of labelling the trust and security levels of clouds, adhering to the European values of data sovereignty. As such, cloud service providers are expected to emerge with differentiation in trust and security offerings. In such a diverse cloud landscape, the deployment orchestrator has to ensure that the workload distribution over various clouds stays within the trust and security constraints as prescribed by business rules and applicable legislation. Additionally, the strategic multi-cloud perspective takes varying trust and security levels into account in the workload deployment orchestration. Users contract multiple cloud service providers with the ability to move workloads between them, to become less dependent on a single cloud provider.

This use case relates to the Scheduling concept of the taxonomy, in which it specifically addresses the security and trust aspects under policies. From a trust and security perspective other concepts in the taxonomy can apply as well. For instance, data classification may require that all data processing is performed only by mandated parties. This relates to the Actors concept in the taxonomy. Similarly, requirements on the availability of (processing) services applies to the Environment concept in the taxonomy.

4.3   Non-reliable Availability of Cloud and Edge Infrastructures

The (availability of) individual cloud processing infrastructures can not always be relied upon. A first use case applies to the emerging 5G network infrastructures with integrated edge and cloud computing service offerings. Applications that rely on (live) access to processing capabilities at the edge of a telecommunication network or in an interconnected remote cloud, face differences in availability of the network. In this case mobile edge computing (MEC) and cloud locations might be available, but from the device in the field that requires the processing capabilities it is (temporarily) not accessible. A workload might need to be stopped, moved or placed into a different operating mode to ensure the least impact of the signal-loss to the end-user. This type of self-adaptivity or resilience of the processing infrastructure influences the deployment orchestration as it introduces variability within the orchestrated environment. In previous research the conclusion was drawn that slicing within the 5G network cannot ensure end-to-end low latency and availability guarantees alone [12], and edge and redundancy planning of the deployment orchestrator is an important open challenge to be addressed. Moreover, in the particular case of the mobile edge, specific viewpoints are needed on offloading strategies.

A second use case in this category applies to military mission contexts, in which federations of tactical clouds aim at filling the gap between recent advancements in sensing, processing, and storage capabilities for acquiring and processing data and the still disadvantaged tactical networks interconnecting such capabilities on the battlefield [1]. Workload deployment orchestration in such an environment will fundamentally differ from those operating in civilian enterprise clouds: they are not provided with abundant cloud processing resources, they may be on the move (in aircraft, drones or battlefield vehicles), may not have guaranteed power supplies, may have very limited and unreliable connectivity (in terms of bandwidth, latency and latency variation) and may not have trustworthy availability (due to military adversarial activity and resource mobility). Moreover, military mission partners must retain both autonomy and granular control over the policies that define what others can see and do on 'their' cloud environments. Various NATO Research Task Groups (RTGs) have explored the concept of a federation of tactical clouds in which mission partners mutually expose their cloud resources through well-defined Application Programming Interfaces (APIs) [1] and have quantified the performance of various common-of-the-shelve and open-source container orchestration distributions in military tactical networks [13]. This requires workload deployment orchestration across the edge-cloud continuum, for which the RTGs identified the following major challenges: (1) Some edge nodes provide specialised resources that might go offline quite frequently, although their workloads may be mission-critical. Typical examples are camera drones or free-floating ocean sensors; (2) Workloads with high priority may preempt resources previously allocated to other workloads, for which a one-shot ("fire-and-forget") deployment orchestration process is not acceptable; (3) Mission partners do not typically equally trust each other, and trust might change throughout the military operation. Hence, the deployment orchestrator must consider trust while scheduling workloads.

In these use cases multiple concepts from the taxonomy apply. Clearly, the (non-) reliability of cloud infrastructures relates to the Environment concept, and specifically to its availability branch. Moreover, the Actors concept applies from the perspective of the multi stakeholder environments in the context of these use cases. From Scheduling, the trust (and security) aspects are of major relevance.

5   Future Directions

Based on the taxonomy as defined in Sect. 2 and the results of the deployment thereof in the use cases as presented in Sect. 4, we have identified two connected directions for future work. First of all, the execution of the use cases has triggered several areas in which the taxonomy itself should be extended:

1. Strategic decentralisation, e.g. for autonomous swarming concepts to ensure overall resilience [11].
2. Availability of secure enclaves in multi-cluster environments enabling confidential computing scenarios.

3. Dynamic utilisation of available programmable (or configurable) hardware elements, e.g., FPGA boards.

The three aspects above were identified either during the study or in the evaluation process of the use cases. Though, in the analysis the three aspects were not sufficiently mature or complete to be included in the taxonomy presented.

As a second angle of future work, this analysis demands a new design of an open and modular software architecture that enables implementations of a generic, re-usable, modular deployment orchestrator, where the various concerns of the presented taxonomy can be implemented without creating a specific orchestrator for each individual use case as was done in this study. In such an architecture, openness is key to ensure that third parties can easily extend the orchestrator to address aspects of the taxonomy that are important to them.

6 Conclusions

The primary objective of this paper was to provide a taxonomy for deployment orchestration in a converged data sharing and federated cloud infrastructure, and assess its usability against a set of illustrative and representative use cases. A preliminary conclusion is that the proposed taxonomy for each of the use cases proved its added value in terms of (1) efficiency in defining the context and problem space in which an associated deployment orchestrator has to be developed, and (2) identifying the boundary condition and scope limitations in developing a generic deployment orchestrator being re-usable for multiple / various use cases. Future work includes further validation of this taxonomy from additional use cases and from development of a generic, modular and re-usable implementation based on the taxonomy.

Acknowledgments. This paper is the result of the joint effort of several research and innovation projects: the Dutch Centre-of-Excellence on Data Sharing and Cloud (CoE DSC, https://coe-dsc.nl/), the EU project Big Data for Energy (BD4NRG, https://www.bd4nrg.eu), and the NATO Research Task Group IST-193 'Edge Computing at the Tactical Edge'. We would like to thank the sponsors of these initiatives for providing us the opportunity to do this highly relevant and interesting research. Moreover, the authors would like to thank Mr. G. Pingen and Mrs. A. Kosek (both former TNO employees) for their valuable preliminary work forming the basis for this paper.

References

1. Bastiaansen, H., et al.: Federated control of distributed multi-partner cloud resources for adaptive C2 in disadvantaged networks (2020). https://doi.org/10.1109/MCOM.001.2000246
2. Bentaleb, O., Belloum, A.S.Z., Sebaa, A., El-Maouhab, A.: Containerization technologies: taxonomies, applications and challenges. J. Supercomput. **78**(1), 1144–1181 (2021). https://doi.org/10.1007/s11227-021-03914-1

3. Carrión, C.: Kubernetes scheduling: taxonomy, ongoing issues and challenges. ACM Comput. Surv. **55**(7), 1–37 (2022). https://doi.org/10.1145/3539606
4. Casalicchio, E., Iannucci, S.: The state-of-the-art in container technologies: application, orchestration and security. Concurr. Comput. Pract. Exp. **32**, e5668 (2020). https://doi.org/10.1002/cpe.5668
5. Causevic, S., Sharma, S., Ben Aziza, S., van der Veen, A., Lazovik, E.: LV grid state estimation using local flexible assets: a federated learning approach. In: 2023 International Conference and Exposition on Energy Distribution (CIRED), pp. 1–4 (2023)
6. D'Acquisto, G., Domingo-Ferrer, J., Kikiras, P., Torra, V., de Montjoye, Y., Bourka, A.: Privacy by design in big data: an overview of privacy enhancing technologies in the era of big data analytics. CoRR (2015). http://arxiv.org/abs/1512.06000
7. Casalicchio, E.: Container Orchestration: A Survey, pp. 221–2035. Springer, Cham (2019). https://doi.org/10.1007/978-3-319-92378-9_14
8. European Commission: A European strategy for data (2020). https://digital-strategy.ec.europa.eu/en/policies/strategy-data
9. European Commission: European Data Governance Act (2022). https://digital-strategy.ec.europa.eu/en/policies/data-governance-act
10. Gaia-X: Automated compliance - GAIA-X institute position paper (2022). https://gaia-x.eu/publication/automated-compliance/
11. Juan Ferrer, A.: Next Steps for Ad-hoc Edge Cloud and Swarm Computing Realization, pp. 189–195. Springer, Cham (2023). https://doi.org/10.1007/978-3-031-23344-9_12
12. Ksentini, A., Frangoudis, P.A.: Toward slicing-enabled multi-access edge computing in 5G. IEEE Network **34**(2), 99–105 (2020). https://doi.org/10.1109/MNET.001.1900261
13. Kudla, T., Fogli, M., Webb, S., Pingen, G., Suri, N., Bastiaansen, H.: Quantifying the performance of cloud-oriented container orchestrators on emulated tactical networks. IEEE Commun. Mag. **60**, 74–80 (2022). https://doi.org/10.1109/MCOM.003.00975
14. Mampage, A., Karunasekera, S., Buyya, R.: A holistic view on resource management in serverless computing environments: taxonomy and future directions. ACM Comput. Surv. **54**(11s), 1–36 (2022). https://doi.org/10.1145/3510412
15. Nguyen, P.H., et al.: A systematic mapping study of deployment and orchestration approaches for IoT. In: IoTBDS, pp. 69–82 (2019). https://doi.org/10.5220/0007675700690082
16. Rodriguez, M.A., Buyya, R.: Container-based cluster orchestration systems: a taxonomy and future directions. CoRR (2018). http://arxiv.org/abs/1807.06193
17. Tonella, P., Torchiano, M., Bois, B.D., Systa, T.: Empirical studies in reverse engineering: state of the art and future trends. Empir. Software Eng. **12**, 551–571 (2007). https://doi.org/10.1007/s10664-007-9037-5
18. Weerasiri, D., Barukh, M.C., Benatallah, B., Sheng, Q.Z., Ranjan, R.: A taxonomy and survey of cloud resource orchestration techniques. ACM Comput. Surv. **50**(2), 1–41 (2017). https://doi.org/10.1145/3054177

Intent-Based AI-Enhanced Service Orchestration for Application Deployment and Execution in the Cloud Continuum

Efthymios Chondrogiannis[1]([⊠]), Efstathios Karanastasis[1], Vassiliki Andronikou[1], Adrian Spătaru[2], Anastassios Nanos[3], Aristotelis Kretsis[4], and Panagiotis Kokkinos[4]

[1] Innovation Acts LTD, Kolokotroni. 6, 1101 Nicosia, Cyprus
`timchros@gmail.com`
[2] West University of Timisoara, Bd. Vasile Pârvan. 4, 300223 Timişoara, Romania
`adrian.spataru@e-uvt.ro`
[3] Nubificus LTD, 501 West One Peak 15 Cavendish Street, Sheffield, UK
`ananos@nubificus.co.uk`
[4] Institute of Communication and Computer Systems, Iroon. Polytech. 9, 15773 Athens, Greece
`{akretsis,kokkinop}@mail.ntua.gr`

Abstract. Given the complexity of contemporary applications, the varying goals and intents of their owners, and the availability of resources with fundamentally different characteristics and capabilities, the optimal deployment and execution of applications and their internal components is a rather challenging subject in the Cloud Continuum era. This includes the selection and the configuration of the resources to adequately cover the set technological and business requirements and constraints from the side of both application owners and resource providers. The aforementioned process is often and to a great extent, done manually and hence not optimally, with direct impact to the execution of an application and the usage or the available resources. In this work, we present the approach followed for the design and development of a Service Orchestrator equipped with AI techniques and the underlying multi-layered abstraction model enabling its functionality. These components were incorporated in a platform for infrastructure-agnostic deployment of data-intensive applications and tested in real-life scenarios.

Keywords: Intent-based Application Deployment and Execution · Machine Learning Techniques · Abstraction Models · Service Orchestration · Edge Computing · Cloud Continuum

1 Introduction

The complexity of contemporary applications that may come from different vertical sectors, the diversity of the hardware and environment-related requirements, and the varying goals and intents of the application owners make the deployment and execution of applications and their internal components a rather challenging topic in the Cloud Continuum (CC) era. Therefore, the selection and proper configuration of computing

© IFIP International Federation for Information Processing 2023
Published by Springer Nature Switzerland AG 2023
G. A. Papadopoulos et al. (Eds.): ESOCC 2023, LNCS 14183, pp. 251–262, 2023.
https://doi.org/10.1007/978-3-031-46235-1_17

resources with fundamentally different characteristics and capabilities to adequately cover the set technological and business requirements and constraints of applications is a very complicated endeavour, which is often tackled, to a great extent, in a manual manner, and hence not optimal. Beyond that, computing resource re-allocation, when the application owner needs it to be changed, is difficult.

The layered architecture followed in the SERRANO project [1] simplifies this process and makes intent-based service orchestration feasible. More precisely, the AI-enhanced Service Orchestrator (AISO), which is the main component in the upper layer of the SERRANO platform architecture, undertakes the translation of the application owner's intent to the appropriate resource requirements taking into account a large body of available knowledge that may directly or indirectly come from the end users, leaving the technical details regarding the proper selection and management of the available resources to the lower levels of the platform and in particular, the Resource Orchestrator (RO). The telemetry data produced by the resources are collected and managed by another component named Central Telemetry Handler (CTH).

In this work, particular focus is given to the AISO, which serves as a mediator between the technical and business needs of the application owner, expressed as application and service requirements, and the resource orchestration process. In order to cover its purposes, innovative algorithms and AI techniques were developed and integrated with the AISO so that it can satisfy the posed needs through the maximization of the benefits gained from the use of the available resources. The approach followed was applied for the deployment and execution of data- and compute-intensive applications with satisfying results.

2 Related Work and Background Knowledge

2.1 Intent-Based Service Orchestration

Intent-based description of application requirements enables users who wish to deploy and execute an application in the Cloud Continuum (CC) to formally express in the highest level of abstraction "what" should be done deployment- and execution-wise rather than the technical details of "how" it should be done. Hence it facilitates the CC orchestration components to automatically configure and use different resources so that the user intentions are satisfied hiding the technical details of this process.

Rafiq A., et al. [2] presented a system for Intent-based Networking (IBN) for 5G mobile networks. The system consists of three layers. The Application Layer is dominated by the Intent-based Management System (IMS) that enables operators to define the Quality of Service (QoS) in the form of contracts, which it accordingly translates to the appropriate configurations for the Management Layer depending on the platform selected (i.e., the TOSCA[1] file for M-CORD[2] and the appropriate JSON messages for

---

[1] OASIS TOSCA, https://www.oasis-open.org/committees/tosca/.

[2] O. N. Foundation, CORD platform, https://opennetworking.org/cord/.

ETSI-OSM[3]). The Physical Layer encompasses multiple Virtualized Networking Functions (VNF) that were developed using the OpenAirInterface (OAI)[4] Evolved Packet Core (EPC) and Simulator (SIM) components.

Intent-based Cloud Services for Security Applications (IBCS) [3] is a system that enables security service providers and security service consumers to setup appropriate security policies without any security expert being involved in this process. The security service consumer initially expresses the intent to use the desired security policy in an abstract way (i.e., high level security policy). The IBCS then translates the high-level security policy to a concrete low-level one, so that it can be accordingly used for detecting the appropriate Network Security Function (NSF) from those registered, based on the capabilities of each one of them. Finally, the IBCS creates an instance of the selected NSF by also delivering the translated security policy to the NSF that will be responsible for the particular policy enforcement.

Wu C., et al. [4] presented an Intent-based Cloud Management framework for bridging the gap between the cloud users that focus on the "service-level" requirements (e.g., number of requests per second) and the cloud providers that need to know the particular cloud resources being necessary to meet the performance requirements (e.g., number of vCPUs, size of vMemory). For this purpose, Logs about the performance are collected from the cloud environment and accordingly used for training regression models. The ML models are then used in order to find potential resource configurations (from the available/possible ones) so that the cloud user performance intent is satisfied.

The aforementioned systems/frameworks presume that the application has been already developed and can be deployed and executed in a computer environment on condition that the appropriate configuration takes place. In case that particular hardware accelerators such as GPUs and FPGAs should be used on demand by an application (or some parts of it) so that the user needs are covered, additional programming effort is often required [5]. Moreover, the automatic deployment and (re)configuration of the internal components of an application in the CC is a quite complicated process when no pre-defined Virtual Machine (VM) or container images are used.

The Aeolus model [6] enables users to describe several component characteristics as well as their interface at different states of the configuration and deployment process. Hence, it facilitates the synthesis of an application by specifying a desirable state and following a process/path to reach it. This problem is undecidable for the full Aeolus model, but there are fragments of the Aeolus model that make this problem decidable. Lascu T.A. et al. [7] presented an algorithm to solve the deployment problem when capacity constraints and conflicts are ignored. This algorithm initially computes the reachable states, which are then used for constructing an abstract plan with the type of components needed and finally the concrete one. Georgievski I. et al. [8] applied Hierarchical Task Network (HTN) planning to solve the problem of composing applications ready for deployment in the cloud infrastructure. Bravetti M. et al. [9] used a simpler model for the description of microservices according to which a microservice can be in two different states, i.e., created and bound/unbound. Based on this model, the automated deployment of microservices can be algorithmically treated.

---

[3] ETSI-hosted, Open Source MANO software stack, https://osm.etsi.org/.

[4] OpenAirInterface (OAI), https://openairinterface.org/.

2.2 Machine Learning and Data Mining Techniques

Machine Learning (ML) and Data Mining (DM) techniques enable software agents to learn from data, and model complex systems behaviour. These techniques are often organized into two broad categories, i.e., supervised and unsupervised (e.g., clustering methods), depending on their necessity for labelled data.

There are several supervised ML techniques including but not limited to Linear/Logistic Regression (i.e., special cases of Generalized Linear Models) and Gaussian Discrimination Analysis (GDA) Models (i.e., a particular type of Generative Learning Algorithms). Bayesian Networks [10] are probabilistic graph network that representing variables and the relations among them; with the simplest one of such networks being the Naïve Bayes Network. Decision Trees [11] are tree-like structures that can be used for detecting the category that data belongs to, after several decisions that are made at each node. Their performance can be significantly improved with the "combination" of several Decision Trees (aka Random Forest). Support Vector Machine (SVM) [12] is a ML technique that intends to develop a hyperplane that separates the data (i.e., maximize their distance from the hyperplane) based on the minimal classification risk. Hence, it is ideal for binary classification problems and, in combination with kernel methods, it can efficiently deal with those cases where the data are not linearly separated.

Clustering methods [13] intend to find patterns in highly dimensional data, with the most widely known methods being hierarchical clustering (i.e., a particular case of connectivity models) and K-means clustering (i.e., a particular case of centroid models). Density models such as DBSCAN [14], group the data points in such way that their outcome is dense and connected regions. Frequent Pattern Mining techniques intend to discover previously unknown patterns or association rules from the data. The FP-Growth algorithm [15] creates a compact representation of the transaction data recorded in a relational database in the form of a tree that facilitates detection of the frequent patterns (FPs), and it is much more resource-efficient than an Apriori algorithm [16]. The FPs detected can be then used for generating association rules.

Artificial Neural Networks (NNs) consist of several interconnected artificial neurons that utilize the information gained from the nodes of the previous layer for the classification of input data. They may contain one or more hidden layers (aka Deep NNs or Deep Learning (DL) networks) and they can efficiently deal with high-dimensional data and discover complex patterns or hidden correlations among them. Convolutional NNs (CNNs) [17] are a particular type of Deep Feed-Forward NNs. They typically have sparse interactions and hence the units existing in the deeper layers indirectly interact with most of the units residing in the previous layers. Recurrent NNs (RNNs) are a special type of NN that belong to the aforementioned category. They have been designed so that they have memory (i.e., their behaviour depends on their past experience). Particular types of RNNs are the Long Short-Term Memory (LSTM) and the Gated Recurrent Units (GRU).

The aforementioned techniques are of great importance for the design of the background mechanisms of the AISO so that it can benefit from the data being collected and extract useful patterns that can accordingly drive the orchestration process. It should be noted that the ML/DM techniques may also be an important component of the applications themselves and hence proper configuration and usage of the available resources is necessary so that the application can benefit from their capabilities and the set application-level requirements/goals/intents are satisfied.

3 Approach Followed

3.1 Overview

Successful deployment of applications and efficient usage of computer resources is a challenging task that depends on several parameters, including but not limited to the capabilities and available capacities of the set of Cloud Continuum (CC) resources that are linked at each given time with the platform (e.g., CPU power of edge devices), the particular needs of each application (e.g., data storage volume), the goals or intents of the users and the priority assigned to each one of them.

For the description of each application (i.e., provision of application-specific metadata), the *Application Model (AM)* has been developed with the intention to capture the overall goal of the application provider (i.e., intent) in an abstract infrastructure-independent manner as well as the particular application requirements and/or prerequisites that are necessary for the deployment and proper execution of the internal application components. The metadata provided via this model need to be then expressed in a more concrete way so that they can be used by the other components of the platform for the actual deployment and execution of the application services. For this purpose, the *Resource Model (RM)* was developed, which contains all those parameters being necessary for the deployment of the given application/services to the appropriate infrastructure by the Resource Orchestrator. The data collected from the deployment and execution of the application in the platform can be expressed using the elements of another model developed, namely the *Telemetry Data Model (TM)*.

For the automatic deployment of each application based on the given application requirements and user's intents, a framework was developed that is capable of dealing with the complicated relations among these models using AI techniques. The *AI-enhanced Service Orchestrator (AISO)* undertakes the first part of the orchestration process and cooperates with the *Resource Orchestrator (RO)* for the proper deployment of applications in the infrastructure. For this purpose, several Mapping Rules (MRs) have been specified and are employed by the AISO in order to translate the initial abstract parameters to an intermediate or lower level so that they can be finally used for the application deployment, execution and monitoring by the RO. Additional MRs have been defined so that that telemetry data captured by the *Central Telemetry Handler* (CTH) can be linked with the relevant AM entities, and hence the extent to which the initial user requirements have been satisfied can be measured.

3.2 Abstraction Models

Application Model (AM). The AM provides the terminology required for the formal description of a software application from a user's point of view, including the particular requirements that the application should satisfy as well as the users' goals and/or intents. The design of this model was driven by, but not limited to, applications being part of particular use cases that belong to the broad domains of Security, Finance and Manu-facturing. Also, the model (part of which is presented in Table 1) follows a structured format in multiple levels, which considerably aids the translation process. Regarding the model parameter values, in many cases the value is a (plain) number or an amount (a number followed by a unit of measurement, such as the storage volume). In some other cases, the value can be Boolean (e.g., whether GPU usage is preferable or not), or even a term (e.g., the data encryption algorithm to be used).

Table 1. Part of the Application Model.

Category	Sub-category	Parameters
Usage Demand	Number of Users	Total Number of Concurrent Users
Performance	Execution	Total Execution Time
	Hardware Acceleration	GPU / FPGA
Data Storage	Volume	Volume Size
	Secure Storage	Data Encryption Algorithm
		Erasure Coding Schema
	Location	Geographical Location
		Proximity to End User
Network	Network Capacity	Upload/Download Bandwidth
		Network Latency
	Message Encryption	Message Encryption Algorithm
Energy	Total Energy Consumption	
Cost	Overall Cost	

For the formal expression of the particular application requirements and user intent, a model-based approach was followed, according to which several constraints are specified based on the parameters included in the AM and the possible values of each one of them (i.e., the desired set or range of values that the value of the respective parameter should belong to). For each constraint specified by the end user, additional data can be given, such as the relevant importance of a constraint in comparison with the other ones specified. The users can also define whether these constraints apply to the whole application or some of their internal components, including the relation among them, taking into account the approach followed by the OpenWDL[5].

Apart from the aforementioned AM constraints, additional or different data may be required, including lower-level technical details about the application's internal compo-nents, the interactions among them and the endpoints of external services being used (e.g., database name, port, etc.), which can be directly consumed by the RO compo-nent for deployment or other purposes. This information (aka Deployment Description)

---

[5] OpenWDL, Open Workflow Description Language (WDL), https://openwdl.org/.

should be provided by the application owner and would contain parameters that cannot be inferred from the given constraints.

Resource Model (RM). The RM identifies both hardware attributes and definitions for interacting with the respective entity. Figure 1 presents the class diagram of a small part of the RM along with the attributes of the respective entities.

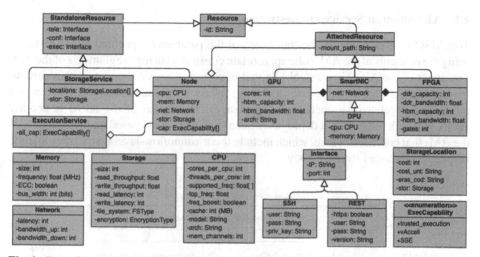

Fig. 1. Part of the Resource Model. The upper part of this figure is the class diagram whereas at the bottom of this figure exist the attributes of different entities.

Standalone resources are resources that have computational capabilities and can be accessed externally via some interface (e.g. SSH, REST) regarding the telemetry data collection (tele), resource configuration (conf) and execution (exec). Standalone resources encompass both hardware and software resources. The base hardware resource type is modelled using the concept of a Node. A Node can represent an Edge Device, a Virtual Machine, or even Bare Metal servers and it may have one or more *Attached Resources* such as GPUs, FPGAs, SmartNICs (smart network interface cards) or DPUs (data processing units). Software resources aggregate hardware resources and offer functional facilities on top. A Storage Service handles multiple Storage Locations, each having a cost, and a cost unit, and estimated storage amount, depending on where the data is stored (cloud, edge) and reliability requirements. Additionally, a Storage Location can provide data protection using erasure coding. An Execution Service aggregates hardware resources and may use different deployment models to execute applications on these nodes.

Telemetry Data Model (TM). The TM captures the infrastructure *runtime measurements* of the various components that comprise the platform. The data being collected are organized in five broad categories, i.e., compute, memory, disk, network and hardware info. The data of each one were further organized into sub-categories to adequately describe the state of the hardware and software components available for allocation and usage (e.g., CPU and filesystem statistics). The data gathered were also linked with a timestamp and stored in a time series database that provides querying capabilities for a specific time range.

4 Software Components and Background Mechanisms

4.1 AI-Enhanced Service Orchestration

The AISO is responsible for the translation of the parameters specified by the end user using the elements of the AM to the appropriate constraints using the elements of the RM. The input of the AISO is a JSON File that encompasses several constraints regarding the application and its execution (including user's intents and other application and infrastructure-related parameters of importance). The output of the AISO is another JSON File with the potential deployment scenarios (expressed based on the elements of the RM) that could take place, which include the medium/low-level restrictions that the respective resources should satisfy.

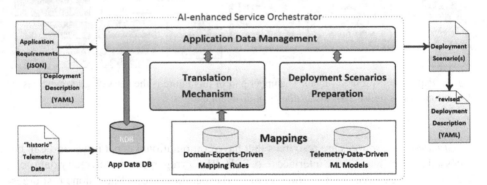

Fig. 2. The internal components of the AI-enhanced Service Orchestrator incl. Input/output.

The main component of the AISO (Fig. 2) is the Application Data Manager, which is responsible to handle the application metadata provided by the end user regarding the execution of an application as well as the Telemetry Data collected by the CTH. For this purpose, it internally uses two different components. The first component (Translation Mechanism) uses the MRs specified (analytically described in the following subsection) for making the appropriate decisions regarding the deployment scenarios that can take place and translating the application / component (aka microservice) parameters to the appropriate resource constraints. The second component (Deployment Scenarios Preparation) further processes the output of the previous component taking into account the internal components of each application and the interactions among them.

The RO then selects the appropriate deployment scenario, taking into account the restrictions provided and the available computer resources linked with the platform and accordingly "injects" the additional constraints in the deployment descriptor YAML file before its usage. When the deployment phase has been completed, the application is available to the respective users and hence several tests can take place. The data collected by the CTH regarding the execution of each application are expressed using the elements of the TM and stored in a time series database (i.e., Prometheus[6]) so that they can be further analysed (either online or offline) for improving the decisions made by the AISO during the translation process.

4.2 Background Mechanisms

Mapping Rules (MRs). The functionality provided by the AISO depends on the MRs specified that express the correspondence among the elements of the AM with the ones specified in the RM and TM. Each mapping rule has several parameters including but not limited to source and target elements along with the process that should be followed (aka transformation) for moving from one data representation to the other one. Apart from the aforementioned parameters, each MR includes additional data, such as the prerequisites that should be fulfilled so that this MR can be used, and metadata, such as the origin of the MR, its direction of usage (i.e., for "moving" from source to target elements), etc.

The MRs were specified either manually (in close collaboration with domain experts) or automatically (through the analysis of collected telemetry data), and can be organized in three broad categories. The first category contains the MRs among a subset of AM and RM parameters. For instance, when the aim is to avoid high network utilisation or to achieve low response latency, it is preferable to deploy an application to an edge device (or fog node) rather than to a cloud provider [18]. The second category covers the mapping of a subset of TM parameters with the corresponding ones in the AM. For example, the total execution time is highly relevant to the execution speed-up measured. The third category encompasses the MRs specified for capturing the complex relations among RM and TM parameters and it was mainly driven by the collected telemetry data and the utilization of ML techniques. In particular, several ML models were developed (using traditional ML techniques such as Linear/Logistic Regression) so that they could best predict the value of different TM parameters (e.g., energy consumption), based on a particular resource configuration.

Translation Mechanism. The AISO examines the data provided by the end user regarding the particular application requirements and user intent along with the source and target elements of each MR for detecting the ones that can be directly or indirectly applied to the given AM constraints. In case that all source elements of a MR are available (i.e., a constraint has been specified regarding the appropriate set or range of their values), a MR can be directly applied for the translation of the source parameters to the appropriate target parameters. For instance, when low data transfer latency is necessary, the system will propose the deployment of the application in an Edge Device (i.e., the one being close to the location where the data are being produced) rather than in a cloud provider. On the other hand, when all target elements are available, the AISO examines possible resource configurations so that the given AM requirements are satisfied. More precisely, for each possible configuration it uses the predefined ML models for detecting/predicting the expected value of a TM parameter and hence selecting the ones

---

[6] Prometheus, https://prometheus.io/.

the outcome of which is compatible with the given AM constraints, taking into account the MRs specified among the parameters of the TM and AM. For instance, when a particular task should be completed in a limited amount of time, the system uses the ML models for predicting the expected amount of time (or a relevant parameter that can be directly linked with this one, such as execution speed-up factor) for different type of resources and proposes the usage of those resources that should produce an outcome that is compliant with the initial requirement.

The MRs detected through the aforementioned process are accordingly applied one after the other, taking into account the priority assigned to the respective AM constraints. During this process, more than one deployment scenario (branches) can be produced, even for the same type of resources, when the same application constraints can be expressed in more than one ways to resource constraints. In case of a conflict (e.g., when there are contradictions in the generated constraints that arose from the application of different MRs) the user is informed.

5 Usage and Discussion

5.1 Example of Usage

The system developed and in particular the AISO has been used for the deployment of a compute- and data- intensive application in the manufacturing sector. The owner's intent for the application was instant response to events coming from sensors while keeping energy consumption as low as possible. The application was containerised and the Kubernetes[7] deployment descriptor YAML file was prepared in advance, so that it could be accordingly used for resource allocation purposes.

In this particular example, the AISO suggested the preferred usage of an Edge Device (rather than proposing, e.g., deployment to the cloud) as well as the device's GPU, since the expected energy consumption of this configurations was lower than the expected one when only using the device's CPU, according to the ML model(s) developed for this application. The RO accordingly used the generated resource constraints for revising the given deployment descriptor (e.g., node CPU/GPU cores requirement) which was then used for the actual deployment of the application. The data that were accordingly collected using the CTH indicated that the deployment that took place was aligned with the application owner's needs.

5.2 Discussion

In this work, particular focus was given to application deployment and especially the selection of the appropriate resources being necessary so that certain requirements are satisfied. For this purpose, the establishment of direct links among the parameters of the TM and AM was necessary, so that these relations can be accordingly exploited for identifying the appropriate resources being required each time. Alternatively or even additionally, the application owners can be included in this process, by providing their

---

[7] Kubernetes, https://kubernetes.io/.

feedback regarding the translation process that took place, in order to establish or improve the relations among requirements and resource suggestion. Regarding the ML models developed, traditional ML techniques were used for capturing the relation between the resource configuration and the relevant telemetry data. However, in some other cases, the correspondence among them may be more complicated and hence DL methods could better model the relations.

The allocation of the appropriate type and resource quantities for the deployment and execution of an application was done by means of a deployment descriptor. In this work, since Kubernetes was internally used for Resource Orchestration purposes, the technical details regarding the deployment of each application were expressed in a Kubernetes-specific YAML file using the Kubernetes YAML Generator[8]. An alternative GUI could be used for this purpose, such as the one offered by Alien4Cloud[9] (A4C). A4C is compatible with TOSCA [19] (i.e., a standard modelling specification language for describing applications that reside on a cloud computing platform) and supports the Kubernetes topology through the usage of a plugin.

6 Conclusion

Efficient usage of computer resources is a challenging task taking into account the diversity of applications in terms of their computation needs and the particular goals of their owners. For this purpose, three conceptual models were developed in order to organize and correlate the data that is used by the different software components responsible for undertaking the intent-driven application deployment and execution. The AISO that was developed facilitates the deployment and execution of each application taking into account the data provided by the owner and their impact to the particular resource requirements, through the usage of several ML-model-driven mapping rules. The valuable contribution of the AISO for the deployment and execution of applications in accordance with the set requirements and intent, including, but not limited to, usage of particular types of computing resources, response latency and energy consumption, was demonstrated via the example presented in this paper.

Acknowledgement. This work has been supported by the SERRANO EU project and partially funded by the EU's Horizon 2020 research and innovation programme under grant agreement 101017168. This paper expresses the opinions of the authors and not necessarily those of the European Commission. The European Commission is not liable for any use that may be made of the information contained in this paper.

References

1. Kretsis, A., et al.: SERRANO: transparent application deployment in a secure, accelerated and cognitive cloud continuum. In: Proceedings of the IEEE MeditCom Conference, pp. 55–60 (2021)

---

[8] Kubernetes YAML Generator, https://k8syaml.com/.

[9] Alien 4 Cloud, https://alien4cloud.github.io/index.html.

2. Rafiq, A., et al.: Intent-based end-to-end network service orchestration system for multi-platforms. Sustainability **12**(7), 2782 (2020)
3. Kim, J.T., et al.: IBCS: intent-based cloud services for security applications. IEEE Commun. Mag. **58**(4), 45–51 (2020)
4. Wu, C., et al.: Intent-driven cloud resource design framework to meet cloud performance requirements and its application to a cloud-sensor system. J. Cloud Comput. **10**(1), 1–22 (2021)
5. Che, S., et al: Accelerating compute-intensive applications with GPUs and FPGAs. In: Proceedings of the IEEE 2008 SASP Symposium, pp. 101–107 (2008)
6. Di Cosmo, R., et al.: Aeolus: a component model for the cloud. Inf. Comput. **239**, 100–121 (2014)
7. Lascu, T.A., Jacopo M., Gianluigi Z.: A planning tool supporting the deployment of cloud applications. In: Proceedings of the 2013 IEEE 25th ICTAI Conference, pp, 213–220 (2013)
8. Georgievski, I., et al.: Cloud ready applications composed via HTN planning. 2017. In: Proceedings of the IEEE 10th SOCA Conference, pp. 81–89 (2017)
9. Bravetti, M., et al.: Optimal and automated deployment for microservices. In Proceedings of the 22nd FASE Conference, pp. 351–368 (2019)
10. Ben-Gal, I.: Bayesian networks. In: Encyclopaedia of Statistics in Quality and Reliability, 1 (2008)
11. Ali, J., et al.: Random forests and decision trees. Int. J. Comput. Sci. Issues **9**(5), 272 (2012)
12. Noble, W.S.: What is a support vector machine? Nat. Biotechnol. **24**(12), 1565–1567 (2006)
13. Jain, A.K.: Data clustering: 50 years beyond K-means. Pattern Recogn. Lett. **31**(8), 651–666 (2010)
14. Schubert, E., et al.: DBSCAN revisited, revisited: why and how you should (still) use DBSCAN. ACM Trans. Database Syst. **42**(3), 1–21 (2017)
15. Han, J., Pei, J., Yin, Y.: Mining frequent patterns without candidate generation. ACM SIGMOD Rec. **29**(2), 1–12 (2000)
16. Agrawal, R., Srikant, R.: Fast algorithms for mining association rules. In Proceedings of the 20th VLDB Conference, pp. 487–499 (1994)
17. Gu, J., et al.: Recent advances in convolutional neural networks. Pattern Recogn. **77**, 354–377 (2018)
18. Cao, K., et al.: An overview on edge computing research. IEEE access **8**, 85714–85728 (2020)
19. Binz, T., Breitenbücher, U., Kopp, O., Leymann, F.: TOSCA: portable automated deployment and management of cloud applications. In: Bouguettaya, A., Sheng, Q.Z., Daniel, F. (eds.) Advanced Web Services, pp. 527–549. Springer, New York (2014). https://doi.org/10.1007/978-1-4614-7535-4_22

Optimizing the Cost-Performance Ratio of FaaS Deployments

Richard Patsch[(✉)] [iD] and Karl Michael Göschka [iD]

UAS Technikum Wien, Vienna, Austria
{richard.patsch,karl.goeschka}@technikum-wien.at

Abstract. Autoscaling serverless architectures utilizing Function as a Service (FaaS) is an established model. While there is virtually no limit to scalability in theory, in practice, a trade-off between price and performance determines the cost-efficient scalability of cloud deployments. Finding the correct specifications becomes even harder when the computational demands depend highly on the functions' inputs. Consequently, a single configuration is often not cost-efficient enough.

To solve this problem, our paper proposes a deployment model for multiple specifications to cover inputs with differing computational demands. By defining categories for the functions' inputs, requests can be routed to particular deployments to increase the overall cost-performance ratio. Applied filters to the functions' triggers alleviate the complexity of multiple deployments, and deployments can actively select inputs within their assigned category.

We evaluated our approach with multiple use cases and programming languages on Amazon Web Services (AWS) and Azure. Multiple deployments can generally be justified, if cost is higher for shorter duration. The efficiency of our approach depends on (i) the assignment of correct categories, (ii) the number of requests in each category, and (iii) the configuration granularity of the cloud service provider. While different languages do not influence the effectiveness of this approach, it is hindered by limited configuration possibilities on Azure. Thus, it is easier to find the best cost-performance ratio on AWS.

Keywords: function as a service · cloud computing · resource efficiency

1 Introduction

Function as a Service (FaaS) is a cloud computing service model which provides a containerized environment to execute stateless functions. Its utilization is often mentioned in combination with a serverless architecture. Serverless computing

This work has been supported by the Doctoral College Resilient Embedded Systems, which is run jointly by the TU Wien's Faculty of Informatics and the UAS Technikum Wien.

offers simple deployment models, fine-grained scaling opportunities with linear cost-to-resource pricing, concurrent invocations, and seamless integrations with other cloud computing services [11]. Use cases for serverless computing range from simple checks to see whether a website is down and working up to more complex use cases such as Deep Learning [8], Federated Learning [13], Distributed Machine Learning [16], Data Analytics [9], Compensation of Peak-Traffic [14], High Energy Physics Distributed Analysis [10], scientific computing [15] and many more.

Autonomously provisioning resources in the cloud to deal with peak workloads and deallocate them afterward reduces cost. Therefore, the concept of autoscaling gained immense popularity within the cloud computing continuum [12]. FaaS is autoscaling by design since resources are only allocated and provisioned if needed. The compatibility and effort to switch to FaaS also depend on how independent concurrently invocated functions work and whether they communicate with each other [7]. Offloading computations on a method level, like in FaaS, usually comes with increased overhead and complexity in terms of synchronization [17].

Today, Cloud Computing always involves a trade-off between price and performance of provisioned resources. Another consideration is how long the resources will be provisioned. Thus, also the point in time when the deployment or setup should be completed. In the grand scheme of things, ideally, a complex software application can allocate the resources it needs on its own to handle current workload caused by users of the system. This would then increase the dynamic of the already existing *PayPerUse* concept that Cloud Computing Providers offer. Depending on response time requirements, deployment of such resources may become a runtime decision. The first step on this journey is to gather the *optimal* specifications for the application or the partition of an application that is being outsourced to the cloud, and provision the most ideal resources for given specifications afterward. There is a plethora of offerings, ranging from provisioning whole virtual computers with different levels of flexibility and complexity to deploying modular pieces of code in FaaS. As computational requirements for different inputs may differ, having one single deployment for all inputs is potentially inefficient. To further improve the cost-performance ratio of a deployed FaaS function, this paper proposes differential routing to multiple deployments with different configurations.

In case of uncertainty about specifications, some researchers [14] will either adopt the maximum configuration to reduce the possibility of running into limitations in that regard or optimize it for certain use cases and inputs. However, this may needlessly increase the total cost, leading to wrong assumptions about the cost comparison between FaaS and Infrastructure as a Service (IaaS).

Finding the right specifications for the executing FaaS environment is crucial to the cost efficiency of the hosted function. Eismann et al. already attempted to do so by proposing Sizeless [4]. They used a multitarget regression model capable of predicting the execution time of a serverless function for all memory sizes based on monitoring data for a single memory size. Several tools exist to find the optimal specification for a given input exhaustively, but our concept deals with different optima for different inputs instead of looking for one optimal configuration across all possible inputs.

The key contribution of this paper is to fill this gap by proposing input-based specification selection in FaaS deployments. Having the same function running with multiple specifications can increase the overall cost efficiency and reduce the cost of the deployment. Sharing resources across cloned functions reduces the additional cost to a minimum. By delineating input ranges for the corresponding optimally dimensioned FaaS instances, the correct FaaS instance is assigned automatically and alleviates the burden of dealing with the selection of the right function.

Methodology: The chosen methodology for this research is Design Science Research. Through an iterative creation of artifacts, new knowledge is generated and written down [2] to acquire new insights on this subject.

The emulations were executed on AWS and Azure to cover different pricing models and to rate the efficiency of this approach under different circumstances. Since AWS and Google Cloud have a very similar pricing model, only AWS was chosen. After removing the top and bottom 2.5%, the average was used for all figures and comparisons. All data, implementations, measurements, and calculations used in this paper are publicly available on Github[1] for verification.

Overview: Section 2 will present the main contributions of this paper and describe the research questions. Section 3 covers related work, while Sect. 4 elaborates on the key ideas of the proposed approach. An exhaustive evaluation based on numerous proof-of-concept implementations and measurements is found in Sect. 5. Finally, Sect. 6 summarizes and concludes the findings incurred.

2   Contribution

This paper proposes a FaaS deployment design that deploys a function multiple times with different computational specifications. This approach aims to improve the cost-to-performance ratio by assigning different input categories to differently configured FaaS deployments. Although FaaS instances are limited in terms of configurations, it can still be profitable to have several configurations hosted, depending on the ratio of function invocations with inputs with low computational demands to those with high computational demands. To conceal the fact that multiple deployments exist, additional infrastructure and functionality of Cloud Service Providers (CSP) are used; i.e., the function itself chooses its input based on defined ranges or categories for respective deployment configurations. This is achieved either by applying filters to the functions or by leveraging

---

[1] https://github.com/richardpatsch/OptimizingCostPerformanceRatioOfFaasDeployments.

a workflow service that passes the state. We evaluate our contribution based on the following research questions (RQs):

- RQ1: Does it pay off to follow the proposed design?
- RQ2: Which scenarios favor the efficiency of this approach?
- RQ3: Are there significant differences between AWS and Azure when this model is applied?

3   Related Work

Son et al. propose Splice, an automatic framework for the cost- and performance-aware blending of IaaS and FaaS [14] to reduce Service Level Objective violations. To achieve this, Lambda functions based on annotations within the original source code and a compiler-driven approach are implemented. The configuration of deployed Lambda functions, however, is always set to maximum. While Splice also focuses on the cost-performance ratio, the resulting *aaS executables do not consider their input parameters for an even more efficient configuration. Elagmal et al. optimize costs through Function Fusion and Placement [6]. They proposed an algorithm to explore different solutions and reduce the price while remaining under a certain latency threshold, which also considers the state transition cost. The said cost is charged when the state has to be passed between multiple consecutive serverless functions. While they consider different configurations for each function before analyzing the potential efficiency of Function Fusioning, only one configuration is ultimately selected. Software-as-a-Service (SaaS) offerings such as Dashbird [3] allow one to define policies and scale an observed Lambda function up or down, depending on the set policy and the defined goal (execution time, memory usage, etc.).

A close competitor to FaaS is dynamic microservice allocation [1]. In contrast to monolithic applications, which are usually much harder to scale up or down, the deployment time and complexity of microservices are lower. The scaling can, therefore, occur at a higher granularity. FaaS, on the other hand, is even more fine-grained, since it deploys single functions instead of whole services. Although one service or a greater set of functions can be deployed into a single FaaS container, it contradicts the concept of a single modular piece of code, for which FaaS was originally designed. Furthermore, the increased level of scalability due to the offloading at the method level comes at the cost of potentially having to synchronize responses afterwards. Like the studies mentioned above, the dynamic allocation of microservices also does not consider different computational demands for different inputs. This way of improving the cost-performance ratio seems to be a novel approach.

4   Input Based Deployments

The main idea of this concept is to deploy multiple FaaS configurations for the same function, thus improving the overall cost-performance ratio. Naturally, the function itself is the fundamental part of this concept. How the resource requirements of a function scale with one input parameter, or with the combination of multiple input parameters, is key. This relation determines the categories and attributes based on which inputs are assigned to their corresponding FaaS deployments.

While the ability of a function and its libraries to fully leverage resources is crucial to its performance; it also has to be factored in how different CSP's assign computational resources to your deployment. Thus, the optimal solution largely depends on the choice of the CSP, but also on the main objective of a use case. The metrics to decide on the best configuration are duration and price billed. As long as a better configuration provides a better performance, every additional price can be justified. The same argument is valid when it comes to the price. In most cases, however, both duration and price are taken into account when making a decision. Finding the most suitable configuration for a function is a process that ideally every FaaS deployment goes through to improve performance and potentially reduce cost.

Uniqueness: The proposed concept goes one step further and assigns different inputs to different deployments. When the base configuration is high, further deployments for inputs with lower computational demands will not increase performance, but will reduce costs in exchange for additional run-time duration. This trade-off can be advantageous when a certain duration has to be met and when a lower configuration is sufficient for different inputs. This reduces cost while maintaining the same quality of service. When the base configuration is low, additional deployments with more capacity will only reduce cost if the initial determination of the base configuration has not been made judiciously. However, it will increase the performance for inputs with higher computational demands. The prerequisite of this endeavor is understanding the function deployed to correctly categorize inputs and access to the final metrics that lead to correct deployments. In this paper, it will be assumed that the categorization has already been performed. This concept only investigates the different categories to which the inputs of the functions were assigned before. The easiest to determine and probably most efficient use cases for this approach are when certain duration thresholds have to be met for all inputs and faster executions are not advantageous. In that case, the configuration for every category or classification can be selected by looking at the duration of different inputs.

As depicted in Fig. 1, this approach creates additional allocated resources and therefore potentially increases the effort of developers or users, since they have to choose between available deployments. To alleviate the complexity of dealing with multiple deployments, the deployment chooses its input by itself, by applying a filter that is aligned with the categorizations of input classes. However, this luxury comes at the cost of another provisioned resource. This may be a queue, an API gateway, or file storage.

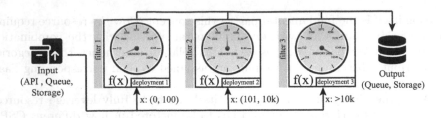

Fig. 1. Proposed Deployment Model

5 Evaluation

To evaluate the proposed concept, different use cases were tested and analyzed to find out whether multiple deployment configurations can be beneficial. Evaluations were done on AWS and Azure. All implementations and the resulting data sets are available on GitHub.

1. **Image Resizing:** to compare different programming languages
2. **Text2Speech:** investigate the effect on workflows with multiple functions
3. **Face Detection:** concept applied to simple use case/function

Examples from the list above have been evaluated on AWS and Azure. The main differences between their FaaS service are configuration granularity and dependency management. While dealing with dependencies is mainly a concern for deployment, the configuration also affects the containerized environment during the runtime, and, therefore, influences performance. On AWS 2 to 6 CPU cores are assigned, depending on how much memory is configured. Memory configurations range from 128 MB to 10240 MB, and all memory configurations within these limits are possible. The percentage of how much this core can be utilized scales between those *CPU steps*. On Azure only a few different machines can be selected, which are tied to different pricing plans and support 1–4 CPUs and between 3.5 and 14 GB of memory. Thus, all Azure-related figures below have significantly fewer measurement points on the x-Axis because the number of different configurations is very limited.

5.1 Image Resizing

To compare the effect of this concept on different programming languages, we implemented an image resizing function. It takes an image from the respective storage service and scales it to a width of 100 px. The languages used are C#, Ruby, Go, JavaScript, Java, and Python. Since Azure does not support Ruby and Go, these were only tested on AWS.

As seen in Fig. 2, there is no significant change in behavior throughout the possible configurations, and therefore this concept and it can be applied regardless of the language. Performance does differ in languages, but this is related not only to the language used, but also to the image library used for this implementation.

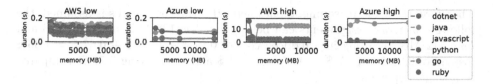

Fig. 2. Image Resizing in all available languages

5.2 Text to Speech

We also evaluated a text-to-speech workflow as it was analyzed in [5]. The workflow starts with a message in written form, and there are two functions running in parallel at the beginning. The first detects profanity within the message, while the other converts the message to audio. The audio is in mp3 format and is later converted to wav format. The parallel workflow ends here, and the inputs of the *Conversion* and *Profanity* function are merged as input for *Censor*, where found profanities are removed. The last step reduces the sample rate of the wav file to make the final file smaller. The assignment of categories is done on the basis of string length. In this implementation, the length of the string is passed in the initial JSON body. Without this additional parameter, an initial function would be necessary, which also passes the length of the text. The initial idea was to pass only the state (audio) through the functions in the workflow using *Amazon StepFunctions* and *Azure Logic Apps* but due to limitations of the state size that can be passed through, a storage service was used. To determine whether it makes sense to apply the proposed concept to this workflow, the following categories were assumed and evaluated: *short* string length 101, *medium*: string length 1059 and *long*: string length 2092.

AWS. Figures do not show the first few memory configurations, because the CPU's percental performance scaling makes the functions so slow, such that this configuration would not be used and figures become hard to read.

The function to convert mp3 to wav is investigated in Fig. 3b. While this function has increased performance with more memory assigned, the price increases as well. Therefore, when the duration of this performance does not matter and longer executions do not interfere with the amount of necessary concurrent executions, the lowest configuration can be selected. In most cases, however, a certain threshold has to be met. Assuming that the function should terminate successfully in 1 s and the inputs of the categories are distributed equally, having multiple deployments saves 8.6% cost. This is achieved by selecting 128 MB memory for category *short*, 512 MB memory for the category *mid* and 1024 MB memory for category *long*.

With multiple deployments, the cost would come to (in order of *low* + *mid* + *long*) 0.34 \$ + 0.83 \$ + 1.70 \$ = 2.87 \$ instead of 0.48 \$ + 0.96 \$ + 1.70 \$ = 3.14 \$ with all categories handled by the deployment with 1024 MB memory. The compression function is similar to the conversion function as shown in Fig. 3c.

Therefore, the same reasoning applies here. If a threshold of 1 s is assumed, the following memory assignments can be applied: *low* 128 MB, *mid*: 256 MB and *long* 512 MB, resulting in a reduced cost of 0.27 \$ + 0.43 \$ + 0.67 \$ = 1.36 \$ instead of 0.31 \$ + 0.47 \$ + 0.67 \$ = 1.44 \$ and thus saving 5.57 % compared to a single deployment.

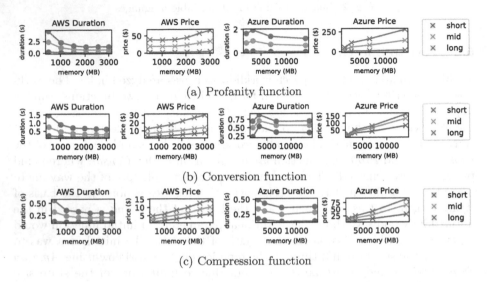

(a) Profanity function

(b) Conversion function

(c) Compression function

Fig. 3. Measurements of the text-to-speech functions on AWS and Azure

Azure. Looking at the Profanity function in Fig. 3a, with an assumed duration threshold of 1.5 s, the deployments for different categories could be split into Consumption for *short* and *mid*, and EP2 for *long*. This results in 0.58 \$ + 2.93 \$ + 16.19 \$ = 19.70 \$, instead of 5.54 \$ + 11.21 \$ + 16.19 \$ = 32.94 \$ and therefore in a cost reduction of 40.22%. Then again, this configuration split only makes sense when the saved 0.25 s are beneficial. This high potential of cost savings is due to the circumstance that Azure deployments are very limited, which explains the drastic price increase from one configuration to the next. The Azure part of Fig. 3b shows that it is not worth splitting the conversion function on Azure into multiple deployments with different configurations, because the cheapest deployment configuration is also the fastest. The compression function shows that there is no decrease in duration from EP2 to EP3, and the differences in duration are only slight.

5.3   Face Detection

The main idea is to upload an image to the respective file storage service of a CSP, which triggers a function. This function detects faces in uploaded images and blurs them out. The output of this function will be saved in the same file storage in another folder. The function has been tested with a low-, medium-, and high-resolution image to obtain their respective prices and run-time durations on different FaaS configurations. In most cases, not all possible configurations were tested because provided that memory was not sufficient and, therefore, execution with these settings was not possible. Having additional deployments with a better configuration to enable more demanding input could be another argument to justify this concept. To apply the concept of Sect. 4, a filter can be applied for the file upload trigger. Without further implementations, this filter is restricted to the filename or path. Thus, the file has to have a prefix or be in a specific folder to be processed by the right function/deployment. To obtain more information about the used image file, another function would be necessary to read and provide such details. This has been tested on AWS and Azure, used images (inputs and outputs), and implementations are also available on GitHub. The implemented versions used do not only scale with the resolution and file size of the image, and therefore the categories are *low resolution*: 40 KB, *medium resolution*: 2 MB, and *high resolution* 7 MB.

AWS. Figure 4a compares different category of images on AWS. As the axes are scaled to have the same range, it becomes evident that multiple implementations can be applied in this case. Assuming an arbitrary quality of service requirement of ten seconds for high-resolution images, almost any configuration can provide this for the low and medium categories. As a matter of fact, the reasoning can also be done in the other direction; when high-resolution images only account for a very low percentage of all requests or processed images, the optimum can be looked for in the other categories, and the configuration for the higher computational demand is only to cover these inputs as well, without having ridiculously high response times. From this point of view, performance is gained by applying this concept, although this comes at a higher price.

Azure. Figure 4b compares different image categories on Azure. Again, the small number of different configurations also limits the possible combinations across various categories to improve the cost-performance ratio. In this case, it can be beneficial to have multiple deployments for the same function on Microsoft Azure. Since Azure offers only four different configurations, the maximum number of categories is also four. If these four categories really would allocate only the appropriate amount of memory based on the observed resource consumption, this would allow many more categories, since then, multiple *same* configurations can be used for different inputs, and because of a deviating observed memory usage with its input, this would create another possible configuration for a category. Using the proposed approach of this paper, other categories get away with using *better* configurations for their respective computational demands.

6 Discussion

While the proposed concept is applicable in many situations, the veracity of
chosen configurations can only be determined by exhaustive evaluation. Finding the optimal FaaS configuration for every input *range* is not practical, and
therefore input classification must be performed to limit the number of different
deployments. The key challenge is to know what the major influences of a certain
input are on a function's runtime and memory usage. Based on that, classification can be done and several FaaS can be deployed for their respective inputs.
The implementation that utilizes multiple processes had the best performance
in proportion to the number of inputs, and therefore the best cost-performance
ratio.

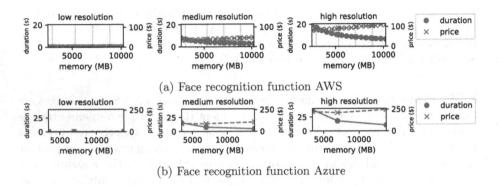

(a) Face recognition function AWS

(b) Face recognition function Azure

Fig. 4. Measurements for the face recognition function

6.1 Future Work

The presented work investigates the efficiency of input-based deployment configurations by assigning each input to a specific deployment. By now, the selection
is based on superficial attributes, such as the filename or the value of a number.
Determining which attributes or values of an input cause certain changes in a
function's computational requirements is outside this paper's scope but would
be conducive to its practicability and integration into modern CI/CD pipelines
to improve its workflow. This paper can be seen as a prequel to this endeavor
to ensure that this concept can be advantageous. Determining the correlation
between data types, semantic structures, and complexity of a function to approximate its computational demands in FaaS environments, respectively, to its CSP's
specific behavior, is the next step to a modern Software Engineering workflow
with assumptions and manual steps involved. Moreover, this paper conducted
only experiments with functions with only one input parameter. The impact of
several input parameters and the effect of their combination on computational
demand have not yet been researched.

6.2   Conclusion

This paper evaluated the efficiency of splitting workload in FaaS deployments based on its input to increase performance and decrease cost. Several implementations have been tested on AWS and Lambda to obtain data on different configuration and pricing models. To rate the applicability of our concept, we evaluated (1) image resizing, (2) text-to-speech and (3) face detection. Finally, all cases were measured by comparing multiple input categories to judge the proposed concept based on these implementations.

Given this paper's findings we reflect on our research question in Sect. 2:

- **RQ1: Does it pay off to follow the proposed design?**
- Yes, deploying multiple FaaS configurations for the same function can pay off. Use cases where only certain response times for all different categories are sufficient, are conducive to the applicability of this approach.

The key takeaway is that one has to be aware of how chosen FaaS configuration utilizes its resources and which resources are available. The proposed model can be profitable in several scenarios, always depending on the goal and relevant metrics. When a function is taken out of a *full-stack* application and is outsourced without further optimization, the efficiency cap depends on the CSP's resource scaling.

- **RQ2: Which scenarios favor the efficiency of this approach?**
- The efficiency of this approach depends on (1) how appropriate the categories are delineated, (2) the amount of requests in each category, (3) how fine-grained FaaS deployments can be configured and (4) how performance and price develop with better configurations.

The correct assignability of inputs to categories is key to routing every input to its most ideal deployment. Designing these categories requires a deep understanding of how the computational demands of a function grow with which input. This becomes even more complex when a function has multiple inputs. Moreover, the relationship between inputs that have low computational demands and inputs with high computational demands determines how high the gain in performance or cost savings really is. In the case of an efficient classification, however, and a reasonable amount of requests for given input classes, the achieved cost reduction covers additional expenses for further Cloud Computing infrastructure and man-hours for setup and maintenance.

- **RQ3: Are there significant differences between AWS and Azure when this model is applied?**
- As of now the main difference between the evaluated CSP's (AWS and Azure) are the more limited configuration capabilities on Azure and therefore the amount of categories is capped but also the most optimal configuration is harder to find, since there are less configurations available in total.

Fewer different configurations lower the probability of finding the most cost-efficient configuration for every single use case. Thus, some use cases have only one optimal configuration for both categories. This circumstance makes additional deployments superfluous. Azure reduced its configuration possibilities to a minimum with the reasoning of becoming more *serverless*. If more CSP's follow that example, this will hinder the efficiency of the proposed design. CPU power scales differently on AWS. Azure offers more memory in its most potent configuration, whereas Amazon offers up to six CPU cores instead of four.

The minimal amount of configurations also limits the relevant variables to compare different providers. To find the most suitable deployment, CPU demands, memory demands, duration threshold, and the approximated number of requests are necessary. Only pricing information must be available to make a decision. Even when computational demands are unknown, an exhaustive evaluation of different providers can rate the efficiency of possible categories.

References

1. Alencar, D., Both, C., Antunes, R., Oliveira, H., Cerqueira, E., Rosário, D.: Dynamic microservice allocation for virtual reality distribution with GoE support. IEEE Trans. Netw. Serv. Manag. **19**(1), 729–740 (2022)
2. vom Brocke, J., Hevner, A., Maedche, A.: Introduction to design science research. In: vom Brocke, J., Hevner, A., Maedche, A. (eds.) Design Science Research. Cases. PI, pp. 1–13. Springer, Cham (2020). https://doi.org/10.1007/978-3-030-46781-4_1
3. Dashbird: Performance monitoring for aws lambda. Web, March 2023. https://dashbird.io/blog/performance-monitoring-for-aws-lambda/
4. Eismann, S., Bui, L., Grohmann, J., Abad, C.L., Herbst, N.R., Kounev, S.: Sizeless: predicting the optimal size of serverless functions. In: Proceedings of the 22nd International Middleware Conference (2021)
5. Eismann, S., Grohmann, J., van Eyk, E., Herbst, N., Kounev, S.: Predicting the costs of serverless workflows. In: Proceedings of the ACM/SPEC International Conference on Performance Engineering, pp. 265–276. ICPE '20, Association for Computing Machinery, New York, NY, USA (2020)
6. Elgamal, T., Sandur, A., Nahrstedt, K., Agha, G.: Costless: optimizing cost of serverless computing through function fusion and placement. In: 2018 IEEE/ACM Symposium on Edge Computing (SEC), pp. 300–312 (2018)
7. Hellerstein, J.M., et al.: Serverless computing: one step forward, two steps back. ArXiv abs/1812.03651 (2019)
8. Ishakian, V., Muthusamy, V., Slominski, A.: Serving deep learning models in a serverless platform. In: 2018 IEEE International Conference on Cloud Engineering (IC2E), pp. 257–262 (2018)
9. Kim, Y., Lin, J.: Serverless data analytics with flint. In: 2018 IEEE 11th International Conference on Cloud Computing (CLOUD), pp. 451–455 (2018)
10. Kusnierz, J., et al.: A serverless engine for high energy physics distributed analysis. In: 2022 22nd IEEE International Symposium on Cluster, Cloud and Internet Computing (CCGrid). IEEE, May 2022
11. McGrath, G., Brenner, P.R.: Serverless computing: design, implementation, and performance. In: 2017 IEEE 37th International Conference on Distributed Computing Systems Workshops (ICDCSW), pp. 405–410 (2017)

12. Qu, C., Calheiros, R.N., Buyya, R.: Auto-scaling web applications in clouds: a taxonomy and survey. ACM Comput. Surv. **51**(4), 1 (2018)
13. Savazzi, S., Nicoli, M., Rampa, V.: Federated learning with cooperating devices: a consensus approach for massive IoT networks. IEEE Internet Things J. **7**(5), 4641–4654 (2020)
14. Son, M., et al.: Splice: an automated framework for cost-and performance-aware blending of cloud services. In: 2022 22nd IEEE International Symposium on Cluster, Cloud and Internet Computing (CCGrid), pp. 119–128 (2022)
15. Spillner, J., Mateos, C., Monge, D.A.: FaaSter, better, cheaper: the prospect of serverless scientific computing and HPC. In: Mocskos, E., Nesmachnow, S. (eds.) CARLA 2017. CCIS, vol. 796, pp. 154–168. Springer, Cham (2018). https://doi.org/10.1007/978-3-319-73353-1_11
16. Wang, H., Niu, D., Li, B.: Distributed machine learning with a serverless architecture. In: IEEE INFOCOM 2019 - IEEE Conference on Computer Communications, pp. 1288–1296 (2019)
17. Wang, J., Pan, J., Esposito, F., Calyam, P., Yang, Z., Mohapatra, P.: Edge cloud offloading algorithms: issues, methods, and perspectives. ACM Comput. Surv. **52**(1), 17–18 (2019)

The Microservice Dependency Matrix

Amr S. Abdelfattah[1] and Tomas Cerny[2](✉)

[1] Computer Science, Baylor University, One Bear Place, Waco, TX 97141, USA
amr_elsayed1@baylor.edu
[2] Systems and Industrial Engineering, University of Arizona, Tucson, AZ, USA
tcerny@arizona.edu

Abstract. Microservices have been recognized for over a decade. They reshaped system design enabling decentralization and independence of development teams working on particular microservices. While loosely coupled microservices are desired, it is inevitable for dependencies to arise. However, these dependencies often go unnoticed by development teams. As the system evolves, making changes to one microservice may trigger a ripple effect, necessitating adjustments in dependent microservices and increasing maintenance and operational efforts. Tracking different types of dependencies across microservices becomes crucial in anticipating the consequences of development team changes. This paper introduces the Endpoint Dependency Matrix (EDM) and Data Dependency Matrix (DDM) as tools to address this challenge. We present an automated approach for tracking these dependencies and demonstrate their extraction through a case study.

Keywords: Microservice Dependency · Static Analysis · Service Dependency · System Evolution · Automated Reasoning

1 Introduction

Microservice Architecture is widely used for complex systems that require selective scalability or the decomposition of complex organizational structures into smaller, independently managed units handled by separate development teams. As software systems evolve due to market demands, technological shifts, patches, or optimizations, new features are implemented, and bugs are fixed, potentially introducing new services and system dependencies [2]. Isolated modifications of individual services typically do not cause disruptions to others [8]. Nevertheless, as systems undergo evolution and dependencies naturally emerge within the architecture, posing challenges to the system's consistency and maintainability. Hence, it becomes crucial to proactively monitor and uphold the principles of low coupling and minimize dependencies within the architecture. In fact, consider a scenario where a critical bug is identified in a particular microservice. By accurately tracking the system dependencies, developers can confidently modify and debug the specific microservice without worrying about unintended consequences

© IFIP International Federation for Information Processing 2023
Published by Springer Nature Switzerland AG 2023
G. A. Papadopoulos et al. (Eds.): ESOCC 2023, LNCS 14183, pp. 276–288, 2023.
https://doi.org/10.1007/978-3-031-46235-1_19

or unintended disruptions to other interconnected services. This highlights the importance of actively managing and preserving a low-coupling architecture to ensure the long-term stability and scalability of microservice-based systems.

Recent studies highlight the lack of methods to prevent maintainability problems in microservices [1]. While existing metrics focus on direct dependencies introduced through endpoint calls between microservices, other aspects introduce dependencies too. For example, the presence of a common data model between microservices can lead to inconsistencies and coupling, where changes in one microservice may require modifications in others. This perspective provides another dimension to understanding the interconnectivity between microservices.

The main objective of this paper is to introduce and identify system dependencies at different perspectives, including direct endpoint calls and data dependencies, by analyzing the source code of microservices-based systems. We aim to offer a comprehensive understanding of service dependencies.

One of the key contributions of this paper is the development of an automated approach that extracts this dependency information directly from the codebase, ensuring that the obtained insights are up-to-date and free from outdated or stale information. The paper's contributions are summarized as follows:

- Describing automated approaches for constructing the Endpoint Dependency Matrix (EDM) and Data Dependency Matrix (DDM) of microservice-based systems.
- Implementing a prototype that applies the proposed approaches.
- Conducting a case study on a real public microservice project to generate the dependency matrices and discuss the results.

The paper is organized as follows. Section 2 presents the proposed method for constructing the dependency matrices. Section 3 presents the case study results for validation. Section 4 discusses the approach and potential threats to validity. Section 5 introduces related works. Finally, Sect. 6 concludes the paper.

2 The Proposed Dependency Methodology

The proposed method focuses on capturing the dependencies within microservice systems by considering both endpoints and data entities. Microservices systems utilize specialized frameworks to streamline the development of diverse capabilities. These frameworks often leverage object-oriented concepts and offer robust implementations. Through the utilization of static analysis techniques applied to the source code of the microservices, the necessary components are extracted to facilitate a comprehensive understanding of the system's dependencies.

To construct the EDM, the method identifies the direct endpoint calls within the source code, capturing the dependencies between microservices. The DDM is generated to represent the dependencies based on the shared data entities among microservices. By combining the information from EDM and DDM, a holistic depiction of the system's dependencies is achieved, providing insights into the flow of dependencies between both endpoints and data entities.

This approach serves as a valuable tool for practitioners to gain a comprehensive understanding of the intricate dependencies within microservice systems. By examining the system from both the endpoints and data perspectives, potential bottlenecks, inefficiencies, or critical dependencies can be identified, enabling better decision-making for system maintenance and evolution.

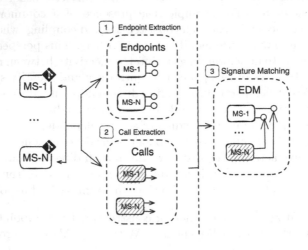

Fig. 1. Endpoint Dependency Matrix Generation Process.

2.1 Endpoint Dependency Matrix (EDM)

The dependency between endpoints reveals the interdependencies among different microservices, where one microservice's source code contains a request call to an endpoint of another microservice. Our process examines the distributed source codes of microservices to extract the defined HTTP endpoints and request calls. This process consists of three phases, as depicted in Fig. 1: Endpoint Extraction, Call Extraction, and Signature Matching.

In the **Endpoint Extraction** phase, we identify and extract the HTTP endpoints defined in the source code. Typically, endpoints are specified using framework-specific functions or annotations. This approach ensures consistency in metadata identification. During this phase, we collect various attributes for each endpoint, including the path, HTTP method, parameters, and return type.

The **Call Extraction** phase focuses on extracting the requests made from the source code. By identifying the corresponding client, we determine where these endpoints are called from other services. Through code analysis, we can gather metadata about every call in the system by identifying the appropriate function call formats specific to the known HTTP library. Therefore, we extract the path, HTTP method, parameters' values, and the expected return type.

The **Signature Matching** phase involves comparing endpoint method signatures with data and parameters exchanged during REST call interactions. This process finds the matches between endpoint and request calls in the distributed source code. The collected endpoint and call details are merged to establish associations between calls and their corresponding endpoint components. However, direct matching is complex due to the endpoint definition including parameter data types, while request calls involve parameter values or variables in the request's body or path. Our approach initially considers path and parameter count matching. Subsequently, regular expressions are employed to identify the optimal match for parameter types with values in the calls. A successful match signifies a communication path between microservices via the matched endpoint.

Consequently, we can generate an EDM that illustrates the number of request calls between each pair of microservices in the system, thereby displaying the communication dependencies.

2.2 Data Dependency Matrix (DDM)

Each microservice establishes a data-bounded context that defines the scope where its specific domain model applies. To identify data dependencies, this method employs static analysis techniques to extract bounded contexts from each microservice's source code. It then proceeds to determine the correspondence between data entities across the individual bounded contexts. The construction process for data dependencies consists of three phases, as illustrated in Fig. 2: Components Extraction, Entity Filtration, and Entity Matching.

In the **Components Extraction** phase, all local classes declared in the project are extracted. Once these classes are identified, the **Entity Filtration** phase follows, which selects both Data Transfer Objects (DTOs) and classes representing persistent data. It focuses solely on data-related entities, excluding other classes like those serving as REST controllers or internal services. These two phases leverage enterprise standards and frameworks' components, such as annotation descriptors, to differentiate between class types based on their semantic purpose.

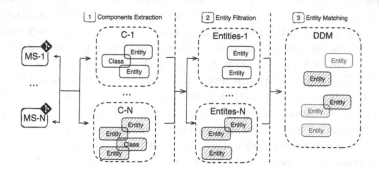

Fig. 2. Data Dependency Generation Process.

Finally, the **Entity Matching** phase examines all extracted entities across the microservices to generate a matching list between them. Different bounded contexts may have distinct intentions for the shared entities, resulting in potential variations in the fields they retain. This phase matches entities based on their names, considering if they are the same or similar. Additionally, it examines whether some of their fields share the same data type and possess similar or identical names. This process yields the DDM, which provides insight into the common data entities among microservices.

3   Case Study

To demonstrate the effectiveness of our method, we apply it to a real-world scenario. It showcases the capabilities of capturing and understanding the dependencies present in microservice systems. Additionally, we seek to provide valuable insights into the interconnectedness of endpoints and data dependencies, leading to a comprehensive understanding of the system's overall dependency landscape.

Our approach was implemented into a prototype, which we utilized to analyze a publicly available testbench. This allowed us to construct matrices depicting the dependencies of endpoints and data. The comprehension of system dependencies provided by these matrices serves as a valuable tool for facilitating seamless modifications and preserving the maintainability of the system. Moreover, these matrices play a crucial role in monitoring the evolution of dependencies throughout system changes. By generating and analyzing the dependency matrix, developers can track the impact of each commit on the system, observe how it affects system dependencies, and evaluate system coupling and stability. This enables informed decision-making and proactive management of dependencies, ultimately leading to a more robust and adaptable system architecture.

3.1   Prototype Implementation and Testbench

We developed a prototype[1] implementation of our proposed approach specifically designed for analyzing Java-based microservices projects utilizing the Spring Boot framework. The prototype utilizes Graal [5], the runtime system developed by Oracle Labs. The prototype takes a GitHub repository containing microservices-based projects as input. It downloads the repository and generates a list of directories for each microservice project.

For the **Endpoint Dependency Matrix**, the prototype scans the project files for JAX-RS annotations that define endpoints. By combining class-level and method-level annotations, it creates a comprehensive definition for each endpoint, including its path, HTTP method, parameters, and return type. The prototype also scans each microservice to identify the Spring Boot REST client (RestTemplate client) and detects HTTP calls between services. It then applies the signature matching technique to match the detected calls with the corresponding endpoints. The prototype generates a JSON structure that represents

---

[1] Prototype: https://github.com/cloudhubs/graal-prophet-utils

the dependencies between microservices and the matched calls. Each microservice name serves as a key in the structure, containing two list values: Dependencies and Dependant services. These lists provide detailed information about the involved endpoints associated with each microservice node.

Regarding the **Data Dependency Matrix**, the prototype extracts all local classes in the project using a source code analyzer. It filters this list down to classes serving as data entities using persistence annotations (JPA standard entity annotations such as @Entity and @Document). It also considers annotations from Lombok[2], a tool for automatically creating data entity objects (e.g., @Data), although these annotations do not explicitly indicate persistence. The prototype then examines the entities of different bounded contexts and their fields, applying the matching rules described above. To detect name similarity, the prototype employs the WS4J[3] project, which relies on the WordNet [4] dictionary. The prototype generates a JSON format, including entities and relationships for each microservice. It also presents a list of entities that provides a holistic context map of the system after eliminating duplicated matched entities.

Testbench: To demonstrate our case study, we utilized a public microservices testbench known as the train-ticket[4] testbench system. It comprises 47 microservices, with 42 of them based on the Java-based Spring Boot framework. The system adheres to enterprise conventions by employing distinct controllers, services, and repositories for layering the application. Inter-service communication between microservices in the system is facilitated through REST API calls.

3.2   Results

The prototype was executed on the testbench to construct the endpoint and data dependencies. To ensure the data extraction's completeness, the prototype outcomes were manually validated. The resulting dependencies were analyzed separately and subsequently combined to form a comprehensive dependency view of the system. The heatmap is used as the visualization approach for the dependencies. Due to space constraints, the discussion refers to the microservices IDs listed in Table 1. For more detailed results, please refer to the provided dataset[5].

Endpoint Dependency: The endpoint dependency matrix (EDM) is depicted in Fig. 3. The first column represents the microservices IDs containing request calls to the microservices listed in the first row. The values within each cell indicate the number of endpoint calls between each pair of microservices. Microservices containing no request calls to other microservices have been removed from the first column. This includes the following 16 microservices: $1, 4, 7, 9, 11, 13, 16 - 18, 20 - 22, 31, 32, 40$, and 42. Similarly, microservices that do not have any request calls made to them have been eliminated from the

---

[2] Lombok: https://projectlombok.org.

[3] WS4J: https://github.com/Sciss/ws4j.

[4] Train-ticket V1.0.0: https://github.com/FudanSELab/train-ticket/tree/v1.0.0.

[5] Dataset: https://zenodo.org/record/8106860.

first row, resulting in removing the following 16 microservices: $1, 19, 23, 24, 26 - 30, 32 - 35$, 39, 41, and 42.

The dependency matrix showcases dependencies between multiple microservices, primarily consisting of one or two endpoint calls. However, there are four dependencies with a degree of three: $25 \rightarrow 18$, $27 \rightarrow 7$, $29 \rightarrow 17$, and $39 \rightarrow 36$. Notably, these dependencies originate from different microservices. The highest degree of dependencies observed is four, which occurs in seven pairs of microservices: $23 \rightarrow 6$, $27 \rightarrow \{9, 16, 18, 22\}$, and $28 \rightarrow \{14, 15\}$. The microservice `ts-admin-basic-info-service` (ID 27) exhibits a fourth-degree dependency on four distinct microservices, while the microservice `ts-admin-order-service` (ID 28) relies on the microservices `ts-order-other-service` (ID 14) and `ts-order- service` (ID 15), each with four endpoint calls.

Examining the longest rows containing values in the matrix reveals microservices with the highest number of dependencies, indicating that they make requests to a significant number of other microservices. For instance, the `ts-rebook- service` (ID 24) exhibits dependencies on eight different microservices, while the longest row belongs to `ts-preserve-other-service` (ID 34) and `ts-preserve- service` (ID 35) with eleven dependencies. On the other hand, analyzing the longest column highlights the microservices with the most dependants, meaning they receive requests from a greater number of microservices. The matrix indicates that `ts-route-service` (ID 17) and `ts-train-service` (ID 22) have a length of seven dependent microservices. However, the longest column contains eight dependants, which are microservices with IDs 14, 15, and 18.

Table 1. List of train-ticket microservices and associated IDs

ID	Name	ID	Name	ID	Name
1	ts-common	15	ts-order-service	29	ts-admin-route-service
2	ts-travel-service	16	ts-price-service	30	ts-admin-travel-service
3	ts-travel2-service	17	ts-route-service	31	ts-consign-price-service
4	ts-assurance-service	18	ts-station-service	32	ts-delivery-service
5	ts-auth-service	19	ts-food-delivery-service	33	ts-execute-service
6	ts-user-service	20	ts-station-food-service	34	ts-preserve-other-service
7	ts-config-service	21	ts-train-food-service	35	ts-preserve-service
8	ts-consign-service	22	ts-train-service	36	ts-route-plan-service
9	ts-contacts-service	23	ts-admin-user-service	37	ts-seat-service
10	ts-food-service	24	ts-rebook-service	38	ts-security-service
11	ts-payment-service	25	ts-basic-service	39	ts-travel-plan-service
12	ts-inside-payment-service	26	ts-cancel-service	40	ts-verification-code-service
13	ts-notification-service	27	ts-admin-basic-info-service	41	ts-wait-order-service
14	ts-order-other-service	28	ts-admin-order-service	42	ts-gateway-service

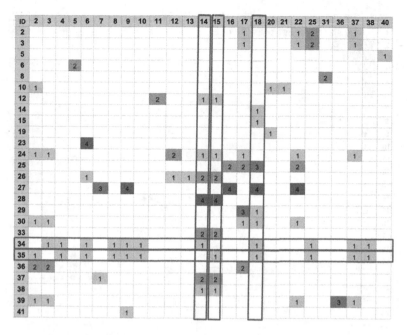

Fig. 3. Endpoint Dependency Matrix (EDM). The longest rows and columns are visually marked using a red rectangle. (Color figure online)

Table 2. Endpoints receiving more than three calls from other microservices.

ID	Endpoint Path	Method	#Calls	#μs
17	ts-route-service/api/v1/routeservice/routes	GET	8	7
18	ts-station-service/api/v1/stationservice/stations/id	GET	4	3
22	ts-train-service/api/v1/trainservice/trains/byName	GET	6	6
25	ts-basic-service/api/v1/basicservice/basic/travel	POST	6	4

Further analysis delves into whether the dependants of a microservice make requests to the same endpoint or if they are spread across multiple endpoints within the microservice. The table presented in Table 2 highlights the endpoints that receive multiple requests from other microservices, specifically focusing on endpoints with more than three requests. It is important to note that not every call originates from a distinct microservice as shown in column (#μs). Notably, the GET endpoint with the path `ts-route-service/api/v1/routeservice/route` receives eight calls from seven different microservices. This observation could indicate a potential functional bottleneck in the system, where multiple microservices rely on this endpoint to fulfill their respective use cases.

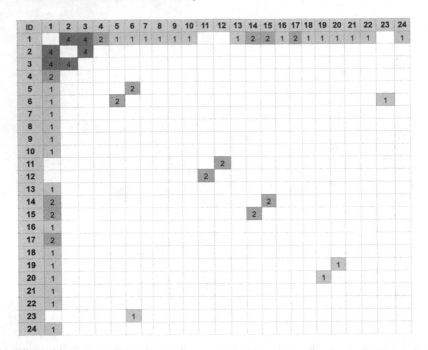

Fig. 4. Data Dependency Matrix (DDM). The longest rows and columns are visually marked using a red rectangle. (Color figure online)

Data Dependency: The data dependency matrix (DDM) in Fig. 4 represents the number of common data entities between microservice pairs. The rows and columns correspond to microservice IDs, while the cell values indicate the count of matched data entities. Unlike the endpoint dependency matrix (EDM), this matrix is symmetric and undirected, meaning the values remain the same regardless of whether one starts from the rows or columns. A total of 18 microservices (IDs 25–42) have been excluded from the rows and columns of the DDM because they do not share any common data entities with other microservices.

The matrix reveals that multiple microservices share one or two common data entities with other microservices. However, the maximum number of common entities between a pair of microservices is four, observed between ts-common (ID 1) and both ts-travel-service (ID 2) and ts-travel2-service (ID 3), and also between ts-travel-service (ID 2) and ts-travel2-service (ID 3).

Moreover, the longest row in terms of values belongs to ts-common (ID 1), indicating that this microservice shares the most common entities with other twenty microservices. However, the next longest row corresponds to ts-user-service (ID 6) with a length of only three, highlighting a significant disparity in data dependencies among the microservices, with a concentration of dependencies in a single microservice (ts-common). Upon further examination of the most common data entities across all microservices, we identified eight commonly shared entities: AdminTrip, Order, OrderAlterInfo,

StationFoodStore, Travel, Trip, TripAllDetail, and User. All these entities also exist in ts-common, but are shared only across three distinct microservices.

Comprehensive Service Dependency: By combining the EDM and the DDM, we generate a comprehensive perspective of the system's dependencies known as the Service Dependency Matrix (SDM), as shown in Fig. 5. The SDM represents microservice IDs as both columns and rows. The cell values in the SDM are decimal numbers, where the integer part corresponds to the endpoint dependency degree from the EDM, and the fractional part corresponds to the data dependency degree from the DDM.

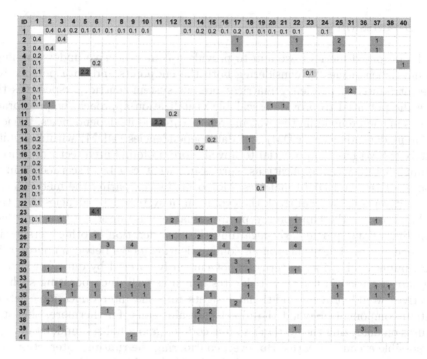

Fig. 5. Service Dependency Matrix (SDM).

To visually distinguish between different types of dependencies, the matrix utilizes different colors for endpoints-only dependencies, data-only dependencies, and dependencies involving both endpoints and data. The inclusion of data dependency in the fractional part of the SDM does not diminish its value compared to the endpoint dependencies. The construction of the decimal value is primarily related to the data formatting rather than the absolute significance of the cell value. For instance, consider the cell at position (row: 23, column: 6) in the SDM, which has a value of 4.1. This value indicates that ts-admin-user-service microservice (ID 23) has made four calls

to `ts-user-service` microservice (ID 6), and there is one common entity
(`UserDto`) shared between them.

Analyzing the SDM, it becomes apparent that the responsibility of hold-
ing common data entities among microservices is predominantly concentrated in
the `ts-common` microservice. This concentration results in distinct separations
between the dependencies of endpoints and data entities. However, some over-
laps can still be observed between the following four microservice pairs: $6 \rightarrow 5$,
$12 \rightarrow 11$, $19 \rightarrow 20$, and $23 \rightarrow 6$. These pairs demonstrate a strong dependency
within the system, as they depend on each other for both direct endpoint calls
and the presence of common data entities. These dependencies highlight their
interconnected nature and the importance of their mutual interaction.

4   Discussion

In the proposed method, we aim to provide a comprehensive understanding of
system dependencies by considering both the endpoints and data perspectives.
The introduced dependency matrices present system-centric perspectives that
have the potential to provide a scalable visualization approach, helping practitioners in comprehending the system architecture and its dependencies. Blending
endpoint dependencies (EDM) and data dependencies (DDM) within a unified
matrix (SDM) has the potential to unveil more profound architectural concerns
within microservices applications, surpassing what can be discerned from the
separate EDM and DDM matrices. Moreover, by comparing the metrics across
different versions, we can track the evolution of system dependencies over time.

While our method and prototype are valuable, it is important to acknowledge
their limitations, particularly regarding the consideration of other perspectives
of dependencies. The asynchronous communication model between microservices
(e.g., publish-subscribe pattern), is not currently covered by our approach and
they are not used in the train-ticket testbench as well. Incorporating such perspectives would provide additional insights into the interconnections between
system components beyond the direct endpoint calls. Furthermore, this study
focuses on analyzing the system's source code to gain a holistic understanding of
all possible execution paths. However, considering the runtime interactions captured in logs and traces could provide valuable insights into the actual number
of calls made to a particular microservice. This additional perspective could offer
an additional depiction of the dependencies between microservices and enhance
our understanding of the system's behavior.

Threats to Validity: The method does not address all potential microservice
dependencies, its purpose is to illustrate how dependency matrices can assist in
system analysis. Our prototype tool is tailored for the Java platform, potentially
restricting its relevance to other programming languages. However, it's important to emphasize that the focus was on introducing the methodology rather
than creating an exhaustive tool. In certain cases, the prototype tool might
encounter challenges in accurately matching method signatures, particularly in
situations where there are ambiguous method names. Additionally, the entity

matching process is currently restricted to basic similarities such as names and field matches, indicating that there are inherent limitations in approximation.

The case study analysis may be influenced by specific constructs present in the selected testbench, potentially limiting the prototype's generalizability across different systems. However, manual validation of the prototype's outcomes was performed to ensure the completeness of information extraction from the source code. Furthermore, the chosen testbench is employed in various research and is regarded as a well-established and representative microservice system.

5 Related Work

Numerous studies underscore the significance of managing dependencies in microservice architectures. According to Lewis and Fowler [8], loosely coupled microservices offer advantages in independent modifications but pose challenges as systems evolve. To analyze such dependencies, scholars have introduced various techniques. Apolinário et al. [1] focus on endpoint calls, Sangal et al. [11] employ static analysis for dependency models, and Eski and Buzluca [6] use evolutionary code coupling. Our approach uses static analysis to extract and integrate both endpoint and data dependencies for a comprehensive system view.

In the realm of heterogeneous dependencies in distributed systems, Fang et al. [7] devised specialized tools for compile-time dependency extraction through static analysis. They targeted entity dependencies within components and hardcoded API dependencies, using text comparison. In contrast, our method goes beyond text-based analysis, incorporating semantic similarities and fine-grained dependency capture through signature matching.

Effective visualization is crucial for comprehending system dependencies. Multiple studies [3,9,10] propose graph-based visualizations depicting microservice dependencies, focusing on communication patterns via endpoint calls. In contrast, our approach employs dependency matrices to visualize and analyze the system, offering a distinct view of microservices' dependencies.

6 Conclusion

System dependency analysis in microservices provides valuable insights for practitioners to comprehend the system. This paper integrates endpoint and data dependencies, offering a comprehensive understanding of system dependencies and facilitating informed decision-making in developing and evolving microservice-based systems. The analysis is addressed through static code analysis providing perspectives that enable reasoning about system maintainability and monitoring system dependency evolution across different versions. Our approach encompasses a detailed analysis of individual microservices, combining the results to a holistic dependency perspectives that can be visualized and interpreted. The focus was on generating the EDM and DDM from the source code and further combining them to create the SDM for a more comprehensive perspective. The proposed methodology was implemented in a prototype and validated through a case study, highlighting its efficacy in understanding system dependencies.

Future work will include asynchronous call dependencies, recognizing their importance. We also aim to expand the prototype for analyzing system polyglots.

Acknowledgement. This material is based upon work supported by the National Science Foundation under Grant No. 2245287.

References

1. Apolinário, D.R.F., de França, B.B.N.: A method for monitoring the coupling evolution of microservice-based architectures. J. Braz. Comput. Soc. **27**(1), 1–35 (2021). https://doi.org/10.1186/s13173-021-00120-y
2. Cerny, T., Abdelfattah, A.S., Bushong, V., Al Maruf, A., Taibi, D.: Microservice architecture reconstruction and visualization techniques: a review. In: 2022 IEEE International Conference on Service-Oriented System Engineering (SOSE), pp. 39–48. IEEE (2022)
3. Cerny, T., Abdelfattah, A.S., Bushong, V., Al Maruf, A., Taibi, D.: Microvision: static analysis-based approach to visualizing microservices in augmented reality. In: 2022 IEEE International Conference on Service-Oriented System Engineering (SOSE), pp. 49–58. IEEE (2022)
4. Christiane, F., Brown, K.: Wordnet and wordnets. In: Encyclopedia of Language and Linguistics, pp. 665–670. Oxford: Elsevier (2005)
5. Duboscq, G., Stadler, L., Würthinger, T., Simon, D., Wimmer, C., Mössenböck, H.: Graal IR: an extensible declarative intermediate representation. In: Proceedings of the Asia-Pacific Programming Languages and Compilers Workshop, pp. 1–9 (2013)
6. Eski, S., Buzluca, F.: An automatic extraction approach: transition to microservices architecture from monolithic application. In: Proceedings of the 19th International Conference on Agile Software Development: Companion, pp. 1–6 (2018)
7. Fang, H., Cai, Y., Kazman, R., Lefever, J.: Identifying anti-patterns in distributed systems with heterogeneous dependencies. In: 2023 IEEE 20th International Conference on Software Architecture Companion (ICSA-C), pp. 116–120 (2023)
8. Lewis, J., Fowler, M.: Microservice. https://www.martinfowler.com/articles/microservices.html. Accessed 13 Dec 2022
9. Oberhauser, R., Pogolski, C.: VR-EA: virtual reality visualization of enterprise architecture models with archimate and BPMN. In: Shishkov, B. (ed.) BMSD 2019. LNBIP, vol. 356, pp. 170–187. Springer, Cham (2019). https://doi.org/10.1007/978-3-030-24854-3_11
10. Rahman, M.I., Panichella, S., Taibi, D.: A curated dataset of microservices-based systems. In: SSSME-2019 (2019)
11. Sangal, N., Jordan, E., Sinha, V., Jackson, D.: Using dependency models to manage complex software architecture. In: 20th ACM SIGPLAN Conference on Object-Oriented Programming, Systems, Languages, and Applications, pp. 167–176 (2005)

Author Index

A

Abdelfattah, Amr S. 35, 276
Abdennahder, Nabil 219
Aknine, Samir 136
Albers, Toon 239
Al-Wosabi, Abdo 153
Álvarez, P. 231
Amoroso d'Aragona, Dario 19
Anagnostopoulos, Dimosthenis 188
Andronikou, Vassiliki 251

B

Bastiaansen, Harrie 239
Bickham, Ashley 35
Blume, Maximilian 119
Bugarín, A. 231
Bussler, Christoph 205

C

Cerny, Tomas 19, 35, 276
Chondrogiannis, Efthymios 251
Couturier, Raphaël 219
Cruz-Filipe, Luís 3

D

Dagenborg, Håvard 153, 170
de Quirós, J. García 231
Delzer, Ole 103
Di Marzo Serugendo, Giovanna 219
Diou, Christos 188

F

Fabra, J. 231
Fogli, Mattia 239

G

Gallego-Fontenla, V. 231
Glass, Philippe 219
Göschka, Karl Michael 263

H

Harmsma, Edwin 239
Hobeck, Richard 103
Hunter, Joshua 35

J

Janes, Andrea 19
Jawabreh, Ezdehar 55, 70

K

Karanastasis, Efstathios 251
Karwaczyński, Piotr 84
Khan, Akif Quddus 205
Khan, Mohsin 153
Kokkinos, Panagiotis 251
Korontanis, Ioannis 188
Kostopoulou, Sofia 3
Kretsis, Aristotelis 251
Kwiatkowski, Jan 84

L

Lama, M. 231
Lazovik, Elena 239
Ledwoń, Zbyszek 188
Lehman, Austin 35
Lenarduzzi, Valentina 19
Li, Xiaozhou 19
Lins, Sebastian 119

M

Makris, Antonios 188
Matskin, Mihhail 205
Montesi, Fabrizio 3
Moussa, Mohamad 219

N

Nanos, Anastassios 251
Nikolov, Nikolay 205

© IFIP International Federation for Information Processing 2023
Published by Springer Nature Switzerland AG 2023
G. A. Papadopoulos et al. (Eds.): ESOCC 2023, LNCS 14183, pp. 289–290, 2023.
https://doi.org/10.1007/978-3-031-46235-1

P
Pateraki, Maria   188
Patsch, Richard   263
Prodan, Radu   205
Protopsaltis, Antonis   188
Psomakelis, Evangelos   188

Q
Quenum, José G.   136

R
Ramos-Soto, A.   231
Roman, Dumitru   205

S
Salazar, Jorge Yero   35
Samir, Areeg   153, 170
Schulte, Stefan   103

Soylu, Ahmet   205
Spătaru, Adrian   251
Sunyaev, Ali   119

T
Taibi, Davide   19, 35
Taweel, Adel   55, 70
Theodoropoulos, Theodoros   188
Tserpes, Konstantinos   188

V
Vidal, J. C.   231
Vistrup, Jonas   3

W
Wasielewski, Mariusz   84
Weber, Ingo   103

Printed in the United States
by Baker & Taylor Publisher Services

Printed in the United States
by Baker & Taylor Publisher Services